Jung and St Paul

A STUDY OF THE DOCTRINE
OF JUSTIFICATION BY FAITH AND ITS
RELATION TO THE CONCEPT
OF INDIVIDUATION

by

DAVID COX

ASSOCIATION PRESS • NEW YORK

First published in England by
Longmans Green and Co., Ltd., London 1959

First United States of America Edition published by
Association Press, 291 Broadway, New York 7, N.Y., 1959

Library of Congress catalog card number: 59 6844

Printed in the United States of America

CONTENTS

ACKNOWLEDGEMENTS

We are indebted to Messrs. Routledge & Kegan Paul Ltd. for extracts from *Two Essays on Analytical Psychology*, *Psychology and Alchemy*, *The Practice of Psychotherapy*, *The Development of Personality*, *Psychological Types*, and *Answer to Job*, all by C. G. Jung, and *The Secret of the Golden Flower* by R. Wilhelm and C. G. Jung.

DEDICATION

To the memory of John Reginald Lumb, sometime Rector of Chislehurst, who of his kindness gave me the opportunity to prepare and write this book during the time that I was his Assistant Curate:
And to the people of Chislehurst who did not grudge the time spent by one of their clergy on work which was not directly concerned with the Parish.

PREFACE

IT has been obvious for many years that there are important relations and overlappings between modern psychotherapy and religion, and a certain amount of work has been done on the border line between the two, but if one considers what has been done in this field it is obvious that the greater part has been done by professional psychologists and psychotherapists. If I laid claim to any special qualification for entering this arena it would be that I am not a psychologist, and that I have no knowledge of practical psychotherapy: all that I know of the subject I know from reading books available to everyone. I say that this is a qualification because it means that I do not start with the assumption that psychology must have the last word, and I am not concerned to show, as so many writers appear to be, that Christianity is psychologically 'respectable': if psychotherapy and Christianity prove incompatible, I am quite ready to say 'so much the worse for psychotherapy!'

I do not think that psychotherapy and Christianity are incompatible, but I do think that much that is said by psychotherapists is incompatible with the true Christian faith, and that it is often those who claim to be most sympathetic to religion who say such things, because their sympathy too often takes the form of reducing religion to a would-be psychological system, whereas if psychotherapy and Christianity are to be related in such a way that both are treated with the respect that they deserve the limits of psychotherapy must be borne in mind from the start. The psychologist observes, catalogues and relates what goes on in the human mind, and in doing so he necessarily evolves ultimate categories of 'explanation', and when he has reduced particular 'psychic events' to such ultimate categories he has (psychologically) explained those events, and the danger is that the psychologist may think that the categories which are ultimate for his own science are ultimate in an absolute sense, so that there is one and only one way of explaining the material with which he deals: if this danger is avoided, however, it is possible to claim that theology deals with the same events (and more as well) but 'explains' them by reducing them to categories quite different from those used by the psychologist. In other words, to relate psychology and theology it is necessary to keep in mind the fact that 'ultimate explanations' are different in the two disciplines. One of the things which I have tried to do in this book is to show how the 'explanations' of theology and psychology differ, and how they may be related.

A mistake which is too often made is to think that one may take a psychological statement and relate it directly to a theological statement, and it is even possible for people to string together theological and psychological phrases and imagine that they have produced a meaningful sentence. In fact psychology and theology use two quite different languages, and no comparison can be made between statements in the different languages until one has been 'translated' into the other or both have been 'translated' into a third language. To give one example: the denotations of the word 'sin' and of 'manifestation of the unconscious' are in many ways (but not all) the same, and very often the theologian talking about 'sins' is referring to the same things as the psychotherapist talking about 'manifestations of the unconscious', but it would be quite absurd to suppose that the phrases were interchangeable, because by saying 'sins' we relate the events which we are talking about to a theological system, and by saying 'manifestations of the unconscious' we relate them to a psychological system. It follows from this that it is necessary to analyse the language, whether theological or psychological, in 'ordinary', everyday terms, and I have tried to show all the time what are the observable events with which the theologian and the psychologist are concerned.

To show, by a demonstration of the method, how I think theology and psychology should be related is one of the purposes which I have had in mind throughout this book, and in order to emphasize the necessity of keeping the two languages distinct the whole book is so arranged that one chapter is concerned with the understanding of theological assertions and the next with the understanding of psychological assertions, although, of course, it has been necessary to glance at parallels in the other language in every chapter. But although this purpose of comparing and contrasting the two languages runs through the book it is not the primary purpose of the book. The whole enquiry was suggested by reading in Jung's work: 'Unfortunately our Western mind, lacking all culture in this respect, has never yet devised a concept, nor even a name, for the *union of opposites through the middle path*, that most fundamental item of inward experience, which could respectably be set against the Chinese concept of Tao'[1]; for as I read I replied, in my own mind, 'We have the doctrine of Justification by Faith'. My first plan was simple: in order to show that Justification by Faith does refer to and involve the 'union of opposites through the middle path' I planned to give a detailed account of the doctrine, and set alongside that account the parallel psychological account of the 'union of opposites', and I pictured myself as a sort of show-man who would say no more than, 'Look at these two processes, and observe how alike they are.' This plan was, of course, too simple, and I found that the two processes were not only alike, but also, in many important respects, very different, so that I have had to examine and discuss both parallels and contrasts. But I also discovered another difficulty: in order to give a full account of Justification by Faith, I found that I had to make my own exegesis of the doctrine, because it is impossible to lay one's hand upon any one authoritative statement about what was in St Paul's mind; but having come to my own conclusions I realized that in doing so I had introduced into my account of the doctrine ideas which I had learnt from Jung's psychology. Since it was impossible to pretend to myself that I was approaching the theological doctrine with an open mind it seemed best honestly to accept the inevitability of the reflection of psychological ideas in my theological statement, and to show how those ideas influenced my views on Justification by Faith, and I have done this by placing the psychological chapters before the chapters dealing with parallel theological themes.

The psychological system with which I have been concerned is that of Jung, and this is not simply Jung's presentation of 'psychology', but a complex system with a character of its own. Strictly I should say 'in Analytical Psychology', and 'in the language of Analytical Psychology', 'Analytical Psychologists' and so on, but whenever it has seemed to me that no confusion will result I have simply said 'psychology', 'psychologists', etc., and it must be seen from the context when Jung's special psychology is opposed to psychology in general, and when the general term is used with reference to his particular system.

I have to acknowledge my great debt to Professor Ian Ramsey, which goes back to 1947 when he taught me what little I know about linguistic analysis, without which knowledge the present work would

[1] *Two Essays on Analytical Psychology*, § 327.

have been impossible. But he also, of his great kindness, read the whole of the first draft of this book, and his kind but searching criticisms were invaluable. Moreover I have learnt from him certain ideas about how we should use the word 'God' in theology, and although explicit reference is only made to these ideas in one or two places they have a pervasive influence over the whole enquiry. On the other hand, Ian Ramsey is in no way responsible for the views put forward here, and I do not know that he would acknowledge even his general ideas in the form that I have made them my own. I should also thank Dr Gilbert Russell for taking the trouble to read the psychological chapters, and for giving me confidence that I have not wholly misinterpreted Jung's writings: and many others, foremost among whom is my wife, have listened to or read bits and pieces, and, by their comments or silences, contributed to the final result.

Finally, I owe a great debt to the readers and editorial staff of my publishers for much helpful criticism, and patient searching out of obscurities; and to Kenneth Anderson for help with the proofs.

CHATHAM

February 1956

NOTES

1. It has naturally been impossible to avoid technical terms, and both in Analytical Psychology and Christian theology many of these terms are ordinary words used in a special way. Had I always used inverted commas to mark such words the book would have been unreadable; I have, therefore, tried to put in inverted commas every word used in a special sense when I have first used it (usually throughout the first paragraph in which it appears) and from then on to use it without inverted commas.

2. 'Individuation' is used in a special sense by Jung, and I have marked this by using a capital 'I' for the noun and for its derivatives. Having done this it seemed best to use capitals not only for 'Justification by Faith' but also for 'Justification' and derivatives.

LIST OF ABBREVIATIONS USED IN TEXT

(*see also Bibliography, p. 350*)

Alchemy	Jung, *Psychology and Alchemy**
Allport	G. W. Allport, *The Individual and his Religion*
Aristotle	Aristotle, *Nicomachean Ethics*
Ascent	St John of the Cross, *Ascent of Mount Carmel*
Berg	Charles Berg, *Deep Analysis*
Bicknell	E. J. Bicknell, *A Theological Introduction to the Thirty-nine Articles*
Bultmann	Rudolph Bultmann, *Theology of the New Testament*
Confessions	The *Confessions* of St Augustine
Descent	Charles Williams, *The Descent of the Dove*
Development	Jung, *The Development of Personality**
Dodd	C. H. Dodd, *The Epistle of Paul to the Romans*
Essays	Jung, *Two Essays on Analytical Psychology**
Farmer	H. H. Farmer, *The World and God*
Harton	F. P. Harton, *The Elements of the Spiritual Life*
Horney	Karen Horney, *Our Inner Conflicts*
J	Lampe, G. W. H. (ed.), *The Doctrine of Justification by Faith* (The symbol *J* is followed, in the text, by the name of the specific author)
James	William James, *The Varieties of Religious Experience*
Job	Jung, *Answer to Job* (in *Psychology and Religion**)
Kant	Kant, *Critique of Pure Reason*
Knox	R. A. Knox, *Enthusiasm*
Labyrinth	S. H. Hooke (ed.), *The Labyrinth*
Law	William Law, *Selected Mystical Writings*
Lotze	R. H. Lotze, *Outlines of the Philosophy of Religion*
Mackintosh	H. R. Mackintosh, *The Christian Experience of Forgiveness*

* These books have been published in the Collected Edition of Jung's works, and the references are to the numbered paragraphs of that edition.

*'Every scribe who hath been made a disciple to the
kingdom of heaven is like unto a householder, which
bringeth forth out of his treasure things new and old.'*

INTRODUCTION

IF it is true that human nature cannot be changed, then there can
be little hope left for the world. Human nature as we know it is
marked by greed, selfishness, sheer stupidity, and inexcusable
fallibility, and whatever else may be changed it seems that the world
is doomed unless human nature can be changed. Whatever forms of
government (national or international) the Sociologists may evolve
and the Politicians effect, whatever devices the Scientists may invent,
the running of the government and the control of the devices must be
left in the hands of men and women, and faults or inadequacies in
human nature can bring all to ruin—for there are mistakes which can
now be made which there will be no time to repair before they take
effect in disaster. It is not that all men are equally proud, selfish, or
foolish, nor that most men have not some virtue to offset their vices,
but that the best suffer from some failings, and that, on balance, there
is little likelihood that only the best will be chosen to fill places of the
greatest responsibility. Hope, if there is any hope, depends upon the
possibility that men and women may be changed in the depths of their
being, and it behoves those who have not yet given up hope to give
careful attention to any -ism or -ology which is concerned with the
possibility of such a change, and with the ways in which it may be
brought about.

The problem is so urgent that some people from the West have
looked for an answer from the East. Zen Buddhism and Taoism, for
examples, have been offered us as panaceas for our ills, and at least
one shop in London has a wide enough display of books giving
Eastern answers to Western problems to convince anyone who doubts
whether such answers are being offered. It is possible, of course, that
it is only from the East that an answer can come, but we have our own
systems in the West which are directly concerned with the change
and development of individual character, and surely we should
examine our own answers with care and sympathy before we accept
large assertions about the 'spiritual bankruptcy' of our civilization.

1—J.S.P.

The two Western systems which have most to say about the possibility of changing human nature are Christianity on the one hand and psychotherapy on the other, and it is with these that this study is concerned. Each deserves a consideration as objective and unprejudiced as it can possibly be given.

Strictly speaking neither Christianity nor psychotherapy is a 'system' at all. Each is a ramified organism of ideas, sometimes only loosely connected, sometimes even contradictory, and each is divided into different and conflicting forms. A complete survey of all Christian and all psychotherapeutic answers to the problem of changing human nature is impossible in a single book, and it is necessary to select a particular form of each for our study. The form of psychotherapeutic theory which will be considered is that of C. G. Jung, as he sets it before us in his books: the form of Christianity is less easily defined. The difficulty of stating precisely what form of Christianity is to be studied comes from two things. The first is that the aspects of Christianity connected with the possibility of changing human nature have not been brought together in any one sect or denomination, but are found scattered among all the different forms which Christianity takes, so that it would be very difficult simply to speak of the Roman, the Anglican, the Methodist or any other view on this matter. The second is that the author is a member of the Church of England, and it is the intention of that Church to leave all but the central beliefs to the interpretation of her individual members: as a result, one aim of the chapters concerned with the teaching of Christianity will be to set out an interpretation which does not conflict with the teaching of the Church of England, which takes into account the thought of modern theologians of whatever denomination, which does justice to traditional formulae, and which is in accordance with the New Testament.

We shall be engaged in a study and comparison of the claims made by a form of Christianity on the one hand, and a form of psychotherapeutic theory on the other about the possibility of changing human nature, and it is right that we should state clearly where our own bias lies, and also give some hint of the conclusions to which we shall come. Our bias lies, ultimately, on the side of Christianity, but this does not mean that we claim that Christianity is always right, and psychotherapy always wrong: what it means is that we believe that in the last analysis Christianity can do what psychotherapy aims to do, and do it better. On the other hand, just as Jung points out that a man who has faith in the power of his Church to heal him will be better helped by that Church than by an analyst (*Practice*, 218), so we must point out that a man who has faith in psychological analysis and not in Christianity may be helped by psychotherapy, and will not be helped by religion.

Some will find the attitude to psychotherapy taken here, and implicit in the last paragraph, an unusual one. It comes from reading what Jung himself writes, rather than from experience of psychological analysis, which means that it is based upon the larger *claims* which Jung makes, rather than upon the actual successes achieved in practice. In many of his writings Jung speaks of a way of living, and of means to achieve it, which is more satisfying and satisfactory than that of the 'average' or 'normal' man, whereas, in practice, modern psychotherapy is an offshoot of medicine, and for many more or less obvious reasons the majority of those analysed are suffering from specific mental disorder. Jung, however, clearly believes that his principles have far wider application, and that properly understood they can help the 'normal' man to develop in the most satisfactory way possible to him. In our study we shall not be very concerned with psychotherapy as a technique for curing specific mental disease, but with principles for living derived from psychotherapy. On the other hand, it must follow from the parallels between Christianity and Analytical Psychology which we hope to establish that Christian principles properly applied and firmly believed have more direct application to mental disease than is commonly supposed.

Our concern is with the normal, not the abnormal, and the reader who expects to be regaled with psychological case-histories, or marvellous incidents from the lives of the Saints will be disappointed. In order to show that Analytical Psychology has something to teach us 'normal' people it is little use recounting the success of analysts in curing the gross misfits, the mentally deranged, and the 'problem children': when the application of psychological principles to 'normal' people has been established, then case-histories of less 'normal' people become important, in that they bring out our own problems by presenting them to us in an exaggerated form, but in a preliminary study like this they would be out of place. Similarly, few even among convinced Christians begin with any serious wish to be 'Saints' as sainthood is commonly understood, and it is only *after* it has been shown that the underlying foundation of sainthood is something desirable for every man that special features in the lives of 'the Saints' are important, to high-light aspects of the common ideal. Yet this neglect of special cases does not mean that we do not wish to 'get down to cases'; what it means is that the 'cases' with which we are concerned are the ordinary, trivial incidents of everyday life—plans and purposes, decisions which have to be made, successes and mis-happenings—and we shall try to show that the technical languages of theology and psychology are ultimately concerned with such things as these.

At this point it may well be asked: 'Even if it is true that Jung's psychology involves principles for living, is there any reason to suppose that those principles are concerned with a way of life anything like the way of life urged upon us by Christianity?' whether the question is asked by those who are not prepared to hear the case for psychology if they believe that it conflicts with Christianity, or by those who would reject Christianity if they felt that it was psychologically unsound. By indicating how one must set about trying to answer this question it is possible to introduce the method which will be used in the following chapters in order to compare Christianity and psychotherapy. In order to compare the two ideals the first thing that must be done is to consider what Christians, on the one hand, and Jung, on the other, say about the sort of life which they think is the best. When we do this, we find that the ideal is described in two wholly different sets of terms: Christians speak of 'salvation', 'eternal life', 'Christlikeness', 'obedience to God' and so on; Jung speaks of 'Individuation', 'Integration', 'accepting the unconscious', 'the appearance of a "new centre"' and things like that. No attempt to compare directly ideals set before us in such different languages can possibly result in anything but confusion, and nothing but harm is done by those who unthinkingly compare psychological and religious formulae as though they belonged to a single language. It is not merely that the terms used are different, they belong to two different systems of thought and language, and each set of terms must be understood in relation to the thought-and-language system to which it belongs. In order to compare the two ideals we have to consider what is said about each within its own language system, and we cannot compare them until we have somehow related each to a 'neutral' language—the language, that is, of ordinary speech, in which we ordinarily talk about the common matters of daily life. This means that the two ideals cannot be compared until the systems to which they belong have both been examined as a whole, and the analyses of the languages are an important part of the present study. There is no short cut, and the answer to the question 'Is Jung's ideal in any way like that of Christianity?' depends upon the results of the discussion before us. The answer to which we come can be *stated* here, but it cannot be defended until the thought-systems of Christianity and Analytical Psychology have been analysed in some detail.

Both the language of psychology and that of theology will be analysed, but the analysis will not be carried out in the same way for both. Whereas the analysis of Jung's language is carried out as a whole in the second chapter the analysis of theological language is done piecemeal, as occasion arises. This is not due to Christian bias, since the intention is to present the two systems as impartially and objectively as possible, and it is therefore as well to give the reasons why the two languages are treated differently. There are three:

(i) We are not concerned with Analytical Psychology as it is practised and written about by many psychotherapists, but with the expression of it in the books of one man—Jung himself. This means that within rather wide limits (wide because Jung is not always exact and consistent) there is a uniformity in the use of terms in the psychological language which is lacking in theology. A strict analysis of theological terms in general, like that which is given of Jung's, is impossible because there is a minimum of consistency in their use.

(ii) Secondly, we believe that psychological language is very much more a 'special' language than theological language. The reasons for this are not particularly important, but they include the fact that theology developed its special terms in Latin and Greek and not English, and the very much longer period of time during which there has been continual interchange between the language of theology and our ordinary talk. On the whole, although theology has its own special words and phrases they are *used* very much as words and phrases are used in ordinary speech, but psychological terms have very special meanings of their own, and when the same term is used both in psychology and ordinary speech it often has two quite different meanings. Moreover, many psychological terms which appear to be used in the way that we use a common name in ordinary speech are found, on analysis, to be concepts which do not name any 'things' at all. For these reasons it is imperative to analyse psychological terms at the start, in order to avoid confusion, whereas the same necessity does not arise in regard to theological terms.

(iii) Thirdly, it happens that the way in which we have come to understand much of the theological language arises from insights which have been gained through psychology, and this fact would be obscured if we were to analyse theological terms before giving an account of those insights. In order to make this clear we have not introduced our interpretations of theological formulae until after we have explained the psychological ideas from which they are derived, and this accounts for the rather piecemeal analysis of theological language.

The method which we use makes it impossible to offer reasons for our answer to the question whether Jung's ideal is like that of Christians until we have completed our study, since that answer is based upon material (acceptable interpretations of theological and psychological assertions) which will only become available in the course of the work. All that can be done is to say here, without making any attempt to defend what we say, that we believe that the goals for living *in this world* set before us by Christians, on the one hand, and Jung, on the other hand, are so alike that they might almost be one and the same. Stripped of special terms (in either language) the goal which both present might be described: that men and women should live full lives in which all their capabilities find full expression, that in doing so they should feel that they fit smoothly into their physical and social environment,[1] that each should make a full contribution to the good of the whole, that they should be free from frustrations arising from their own inadequacy and that the life of each should be guided by someone or something which they feel to transcend their own individual being. Whether such an ideal is one which appeals to men and women, whether if it does it is one which men and women could possibly believe, and whether either Christianity or Analytical Psychology can provide us with techniques which will bring it about

---

[1] I have some reason to think that Jung has tended to move away from the idea that the individuated man is necessarily a *direct* benefit to the community, but in 1942 he said, 'Individuation means precisely the better and more complete fulfilment of the collective qualities of the human being, since adequate consideration of the peculiarity of the individual is more conducive to better social achievement than when the peculiarity is neglected or suppressed' (*Essays*, 267). It needs to be added that the Christian is not *ipso facto* a good citizen of *every* society. The value for society of one who has achieved the goal depends much upon the society in question.

are further questions, but we believe that we can show that this is, broadly speaking, the ideal set before us by two great Western systems concerned with changing the character of men and women.

This central idea that Jung and Christians claim to set before us a way which leads from an unsatisfactory way of living to one which will satisfy us raises an important language difficulty. We shall have occasion to refer both to the unsatisfactory state in which men and women find themselves and also (though less often) to the goal to which they are directed, without wishing to commit ourselves to the religious or psychological account of either, and in order to do this we need 'neutral' terms, which do not belong to either system: but ordinary language has already been ransacked by psychology and religion, and all the suitable terms have already been 'borrowed' by one or the other, and become technical terms. To choose a rather less suitable term and give it a special meaning of our own would mean that we were creating yet another jargon, and this is something which we are particularly anxious to avoid. What we have done is to borrow from the vocabulary of theology, and the reason for doing this rather than borrow from psychology is that the theological words do seem to be used in a sense closer to that in which they are used in ordinary speech (even when given a technical meaning) than the psychological words. In order to refer to the unsatisfactory state from which we all start we shall use the term 'natural man'. In theology this is a complicated technical term, but it seems a very satisfactory phrase by which to refer to 'man as he finds himself', with special emphasis on the idea that he has not yet been 'got at'—either by religion or psychology. Used in this way 'natural man' is not intended to *describe* what man is like, but to leave open the question whether the descriptions given in theological and psychological terms agree with or contradict each other. In the same way, if we require a 'neutral' term for the goal or ideal we shall use the word 'salvation', not in the technical Christian sense, but with the thought of being 'saved' from whatever it is that natural man needs to be saved from, and by whatever means. The term is not intended to foreclose the question what 'salvation' involves, but to leave open the choice between the salvation offered by Christianity, and that offered by Jung, if it should prove, in the end, that the two are not alike. There is a real difficulty in using technical terms in this way, but it should not cause serious trouble to the sympathetic reader.

Our conviction that there is an essential similarity between the two goals gives rise to another and more complicated problem. In Jung's terms it is tempting to say that a man who is 'Individuated' is a man who has reached the goal; in Christian terms it is equally tempting to say the same thing of one who is acknowledged to be 'a Saint'. If our conviction were correct it seems, at first sight, that we should have to say that every 'Individuated' person was a Saint, and that every Saint' was Individuated, and such a claim would be impossible. Psychologically considered it is not true that all (or even most) Saints were 'Individuated', and from a Christian point of view it is unlikely that many (or even any) of those said to be Individuated would be regarded as Saints. This preliminary objection, which seems to throw serious doubt on our claim that the goals are alike, needs to be answered, and there are three complementary answers which can be given:

(1) The judgements 'this man is a Saint', 'this man is Individuated' are human judgements, and therefore liable to be mistaken. If anyone is convinced that the goals of Christianity and Analytical Psychology are *identical* he would always be able to say that if a man could not be described as Individuated the judgement that he was a Saint would be mistaken, and that if a man could not be described as a Saint then the judgement that he was Individuated was mistaken.

(ii) In fact it is very doubtful whether the premise that a Saint on the one hand, or an Individuated man on the other is one who has reached the goal *in this world* is correct. Strictly speaking when a man is canonized (declared to be 'a Saint') by the Church the claim is not made that his earthly life was *perfect*: all that is claimed is that during this life his eyes were so fixed upon God that now, having died, he is 'with God in heaven'.[1] Similarly, as we shall point out in the last chapter, there is an important sense in which it is not true that a man who is said to be 'Individuated' is one who has reached the goal which Jung sets before us. There is some ambiguity in Jung's use of the word, and in the sense in which it is possible to say that this or that person is 'Individuated' it seems to mean that that person is on the right road, and has negotiated an important and difficult stretch of that road, rather than that he has arrived at his journey's end. As we shall see, it is as though every achievement of Individuation results in a

---

[1] This phrase clearly needs analysis, but it falls outside the scope of this study, as is explained below. All that matters here is that it is clearly not synonymous with 'perfect in this world'.

new problem, and a new need for a further achievement of a 'higher' Individuation. Although we may, and must, speak of the goals which are set before us it is very doubtful whether we can ever point to any-one who has achieved either the one or the other, and since, as we shall make clear, the *ways* to salvation offered are very different in the two systems little can be proved by comparing one who has 'nearly arrived' along one of the ways with one who has 'nearly arrived' along the other. Even if the goal is the same we should have, as it were, two roads approaching the same place from different directions, so that one who had nearly reached the goal along one road might still be in a very different place from one who had nearly reached it along the other. That is, even if Christian perfection in this life is identical with psychotherapeutic perfect health it might still be that the not-yet-perfect Christian had developed one set of characteristics which are necessary to perfection, whereas the man not yet perfected psycho-logically speaking had failed to develop these, but had achieved others (equally necessary) lacked by the Christian—as, at a lower level, one man might have a high regard for and practice of truth but fail in tolerance, while another might be full of charity and tolerance and lack any feeling for truth.

(iii) Thirdly, the difficulty is only acute for those who insist that the goals of psychotherapy and Christianity are strictly identical, whereas all we shall argue is that they are very much alike. When this much has been said there are many possible relations between them, for example although alike they might be mutually exclusive, so that by choosing one we give up the chance of the other; or one goal might be no more than a point on the route leading to the other: whatever the further relation, so long as one does not argue for strict identity, there is no reason why the goals should not be similar, even though there were marked differences between those who had achieved one and those who had achieved the other.

Any one of these answers would be sufficient as a reply to the criticism that not all Saints are Individuated, and all those Individuated are not Saints. All three have been given because this whole study is in the nature of a preliminary investigation, and although we have no doubt that the goals of religion and psychotherapy are very much alike we would not want to commit ourselves as to what further relation exists between them. As a matter of personal opinion we should favour the second answer, but whatever relation between the goals seems most likely to the reader, one of the three answers will provide a reply to the criticism.

In comparing the goals of religion and psychotherapy it has been necessary to qualify what was said of the former by the phrase 'in this world', or 'in this life'. Some Christians may feel that this damns the whole enquiry from the start, because they will say that Christianity is not concerned with this world, but with the next. If this is supposed to mean that God is not concerned with what we do in and with His created universe, or that He did not intend to make the world 'very good' for us as well as for Him, or that the servant of God is to win happiness in heaven at the price of misery on earth, then the complaint may be ignored. Those who think any of these things stand outside the main stream of Christian thought. If, however, it means that we must be willing to sacrifice any earthly good for the sake of obedience to God and the joys of heaven, then the complaint must be taken very seriously: what we may say in reply is:

(i) As we outlined the goal on p. 6 we did not include any claim that one who reached it would gain any of the particular goods which he seeks. A goal of the kind described is compatible with the sacrifice of pleasures and good things which we desire. On the other side, Christians have always claimed that 'obedience to God' brings a deeper and truer happiness in this life than any other way of living, and even though it is meant to lead to something greater and better after death, it must have direct relevance to life on earth.

(ii) More expressly, there is a strong Christian line of thought, stemming mainly from the Gospel according to St John, but also from one element in St Paul's teaching, which has received considerable attention in recent times, according to which Jesus came to bring salvation 'here and now'; that is, in this world. According to this line of thought it is pointed out that 'eternal life' is to be thought of as a present possibility, a new *quality* of life, a way of living in this world, rather than something to be had after death: or, alternatively, that we are already living in the 'new aeon', the 'age' or world 'period' inaugurated by Jesus, in which all those who have accepted Jesus as their Saviour are included. Such thinking, which is orthodox Christian thinking, emphasizes the value of Christianity for life in this world.

(iii) It is fortunate that this should be so, because from a practical point of view one would hardly know how to commend Christianity

to the Modern World if it were not. There is so much doubt and uncertainty today that most people are ready to jump the life to come if
they can be offered a worthwhile way of living for the present, and if
Christianity was unable to do this, but was committed to a world-
renouncing view of life, then it would have no message at all for the
majority of our contemporaries.

In so far as we seek to commend Christianity by showing that it
has at least as much to offer as psychotherapy, we are forced to select
one aspect of the Christian goal: all that belongs to the 'next world',
all hope of 'being with Christ' after death, all belief in the Second
Coming of Our Lord and a General Resurrection, must be set to one
side. The limits of our study must be set by the system which covers
the smaller area, because we can only compare the two systems on
ground common to both. If we can show the value of Christianity
within the limits set by the concern of psychotherapists with human
behaviour in this life, then that value can hardly be significantly
lessened because there are Christian insights and dogmas not directly
concerned with this life. Its overall value may be increased by those
insights and dogmas, or they may (if they should be false) add nothing
to it, but they cannot seriously detract from it. Nor should it be
thought that our only concern is to press the claims of Christianity:
we are also concerned to show that modern psychotherapy is to be
taken seriously as something more than a technique for curing special
mental diseases. We wish to show that Jung is concerned with the
same problems as those with which the Church has been struggling
since its beginning, that his solutions are complementary rather than
contradictory to Christian solutions, and, above all, that a comparison
between his techniques and those implicit in Christianity enables us
to understand Christian teaching in relation to the problems and
thought-forms of the Modern World. We believe that cross-fertiliza-
tion between Christianity and Analytical Psychology can result in
tasty and refreshing fruit.

The limits set by the nature of our discussion also exclude any
detailed consideration of the truth of Christian beliefs. In particular
there can be no serious discussion of the existence of God as an
objective person, because that question would force us to step beyond
the limits of psychology. It is true that Jung steps beyond those limits
in *Synchronicity*, and that we have been forced to make some
reference to the problem in chapter 10, but the relevance of psychology

to this matter remains doubtful and uncertain. Subject to what is said on pp. 295-7, it seems reasonable to claim:

(i) If God exists as a 'person' external to and other than mankind, then His activity is only the direct concern of psychology when He acts on or through human minds. Let us suppose that God does exist in this way, and that He 'puts a thought' in my mind. Psychologists must naturally take account of this thought, but all that they will be able to say about its *origin* is that it is alien to all the other contents of my mind, and that its occurrence cannot be explained by anything previously in my mind.

(ii) By means of the concept of 'unconscious mental processes' (which is analysed at length in chapter 2) psychologists are able to relate strange and apparently alien thoughts in our minds to thoughts and events in our forgotten past, and we can then speak of those strange thoughts as effects of the past events. So far as the psychologist succeeds in establishing such a relation the thought with which he is concerned ceases to be alien, however strange it may still seem to us, and if he can explain all that goes on in our minds in this way we could not claim that anything was 'put into' them by the direct action of God (not that this would disprove His objective existence).

(iii) Jung claims that certain things which come into our mind cannot be explained as effects of events in our past history, and in the last analysis he is unable to *explain* their origin at all. In order to discuss them he is forced, as we shall see below, to use concepts which are *essentially* indefinable when they are considered as naming things or events. In this way he is able to bring all that goes on in the mind within the field of his psychology (as he has every right to do), but at the expense of an inability to point to the origin of much that happens.

(iv) Whereas the Christian may see the activity of a personal, transcendent God in mental occurrences of which the origin is obscure and indefinable, the pantheist will see the workings of impersonal deity in nature, and some psychologists (again, quite rightly) will seek to lay open their origin in known and understood events, thereby gradually whittling away everything alien. But whatever may be found out in the future, the present problem of living is what attitude should we take to the seemingly strange and alien things in our minds, and in so far as Christians refer them to a personal, objective God they are indicating an answer to this question, just as Jung indicates an answer to the same question when he introduces indefinable concepts. When we compare the two systems in connection with alien thoughts if we are to remain within the limits of psychology what we have to compare are the answers given to the question 'What attitude are we to take to the alien in our own minds?' To ask, further, about the ultimate source of these things is to go beyond psychology—whether the question takes us into anthropology, history, biology, physics or theology (any of which is possible).

(v) We should add that we do not believe that the Christian belief in an objective, personal God can be profitably discussed in terms of the relations between such a God and individual minds alone: if the belief has meaning (and we believe that it has) it is concerned with all the special sciences at once, and it is closely associated with the fact that each one of them reveals different aspects of a world which is essentially one.

We have tried to answer some of the criticisms which are likely to be made of our treatment of our subject, and it may be well to underline three points. First, we have spoken of Christianity and Analytical Psychology as 'systems', but each is at once too wide and too vague to be strictly regarded as 'a system'. They might be better described as 'ways of thinking about life', but this description is also inadequate, because it fails to do justice to the organic unity which each possesses. 'System' is unsatisfactory, but it seems less unsatisfactory than the alternatives. Secondly, there are some who will be irritated by the theoretical nature of the discussion, and who would prefer specific instances of the achievements of religion and psychotherapy. The discussion must be theoretical, because it is concerned with the claims made by the two systems, not with the successes they may or may not have achieved. Thirdly, Christians are naturally concerned with the truth or falsehood of their beliefs about God, but they will find nothing here to confirm or to disprove these beliefs. Psychology is concerned with the psychic effect of a belief, not with its truth or falsehood, and this is a limitation which must be accepted if religion is to be compared with psychotherapy.

It remains to make a last comment upon the way in which the enquiry is presented. This is not an attempt to lay down dogmas, nor to formulate a new system, and the conclusions to which the discussion leads are the least important part of the book. The aim is to show how religion and psychotherapy may be compared and contrasted, without either being subordinated to the other. The best way to show this is to do the work in public, as it were, and the reader is continually asked to examine the process whereby the conclusions have been reached, rather than the conclusions themselves. He is asked to step into the workshop of the mind and to watch what is going on. This method of presenting the discussion involves a real danger of losing the reader among the trees, and in order to prevent this as much as possible brief summaries of the argument are included at each stage.

I

JUSTIFICATION BY FAITH AND INDIVIDUATION

IT has been explained in the introduction that it is not enough to compare Christian with psychological formulae, and that those formulae must first be understood in relation to the 'system' in which they belong. Nevertheless the comparison of the two systems is given point and clarity when it is carried out in relation to a definite feature common to both systems. The feature common to both which is the centre of this discussion is, broadly speaking, the claim (which each makes) that human living can be effectively improved, and in each system this claim is focused upon a special idea. In Christianity the focus of the claim to influence human living is known as the 'Doctrine of Justification by Faith'; in Analytical Psychology it is the concept called 'Individuation'. In this chapter these two will be discussed and compared in general terms, and something more will be said of the method by which the two systems are compared.

'Justification by Faith' is the name of a Christian doctrine, and this doctrine has frequently played an important part in the history of the Church. The ideas which go to make it up took shape in the mind of St Paul in the first years of the Christian Church; it contributed to the Augustinian synthesis, which enabled the Church to stand when the secular power of Rome fell; it was a battle-cry of the Reformation; and F. J. Taylor in *The Doctrine of Justification by Faith* speaks of 'The cardinal importance attached to this doctrine of justification in the formative period of Anglican theology' (*J—Taylor*, 11). It seems somehow that it is a doctrine specially appropriate to times of transition when an old order is giving place to something else, and when theology must renew itself if it is to play its full part in the new age. If so, then it is no accident that it is receiving attention in this century, for we live in a time of rapid change, and the future is dark and uncertain. That the doctrine is important, and important for this age is certain, but, remarkably enough, there is considerable uncertainty about how the doctrine should be understood, and it is difficult to find even two

theological writers who are in complete agreement in their interpretation of it.

The name 'Justification by Faith' fastens our attention upon an
event in the lives of those who become Christians, which they refer
to as 'Justification', or 'Being Justified', and in so far as the doctrine
has been given specific forms in one and another Christian sect the
special character of each form has been related to the way in which
this event is understood to occur. But even though Justification may
be the most important element in the process of becoming a Christian
and living a Christian life, it is only one element in a larger whole,
and much of the controversy which surrounds the doctrine is the result
of the failure to consider the event Justification in relation to the whole
of which it is a part. 'Justification' as the name of an event is something which happens once, and which either has happened or has not
happened to a man, so that a man is either Justified or not and never
in process of being Justified : but the doctrine called 'Justification by
Faith' has to take into account the whole process in which Justification
is embedded, and this means that both a *process* (becoming a Christian
and living a Christian life) and an *event* will come under discussion,
and 'Justification by Faith' may refer to either. In a very similar way
'Individuation' can be used to refer both to a process which involves
all that leads up to Individuation, and also to the climax or goal of
that process.

The strict Lutheran can say that psychology is irrelevant to a study
of Justification by Faith, because he begins by assuming that Justification does not affect a man's character or his habits. Anders Nygren, for
example, is insistent that St Paul's terms must not be understood in
any psychological sense; and he says, to give one instance, that the
'righteousness of God' which comes upon Christians 'is not an
inner quality of man's, but an objective power' (*Nygren*, 146).
Theologians who reject the formalist Lutheran view, however, must
be prepared to allow psychologists to meddle with the doctrine. This
does not mean that psychology can explain away the doctrine, or
show that its origin has been misunderstood, but only that psychologists must be allowed to speak about it. Any view of the doctrine
which is more than formal implies that it refers to an observable change
which takes place in the mind or life of a man who accepts Jesus as
Lord, and such a change is as much material for psychology as it is
for theology. There is much that the doctrine says in connection with

what happens when a man is Justified which is not the direct concern of the psychologist, but the human experience itself falls within the field proper to psychology, and if the theologian claims that something has happened 'within' a man, then he cannot deny the psychologist's right to speak about what he says has taken place.

It might be objected that either the psychologist will say nothing new, or else he will offer a rival 'explanation' of what has happened. It is impossible to stop a psychologist from offering such an explanation, but it is wrong to assume that any explanation which he offers must be a 'rival' to the theological account. What the psychologist should be expected to do is to 'explain' the events of which the theologian speaks by relating them to other events which the theologian would be likely to regard as irrelevant, and so to provide a further point of view from which to consider what takes place. Psychology is properly concerned with the observed facts of human living, and it is not in a position to explain them by referring them to ultimate causes: the job of the psychologist is to bring the observed events into ordered relationship with each other, and, by revealing such relationships, improve our understanding of the events related; and whether psychic events are self-explanatory, or entirely dependent upon physical events, or in some way under the guidance of God are not questions which the psychologist, as such, is in a special position to answer.

This view of the proper limits of psychology is not special pleading on the part of a theologian. It can be found in the writings of psychologists. Writing on mysticism Silberer remarks: 'As for the metaphysical import of the mystical doctrine, I might maintain that the psychoanalytic unmasking of the compelling powers cannot prejudice its value. . . . I must emphatically declare that if psychoanalysis makes it conceivable that we men, impelled by this and that "titanic" primal power, are necessitated to hit upon this or that idea, then even if it is made clear what causes us to light upon it, still nothing is as yet settled as to the value for knowledge of the thing discovered' (*Silberer*, 371, 2). Jung says of a certain Chinese concept: 'It is certainly not within the competence of the psychologist to establish the metaphysical truth or falsity of this idea; he must be content to determine wherever possible what is psychically effective' (*Secret*, 107). G. W. Allport writes: 'I make no assumptions and no denials regarding the claims of revealed religion. Writing as a scientist, I am not entitled to do either' (*Allport*, ix). In other words, there may be causes beyond the observed psychic events but those causes do not fall within the psychologist's field, and the psychologist who claims to pronounce upon the existence of such causes, whether in a positive or negative sense, cannot do so with the authority which he has in his own proper field.

A system of psychology will help the understanding of Justification by Faith if the 'psychic events' to which the doctrine refers can be fitted into that system, which would mean that within the system those events were related to other 'psychic events'. Jung's system, which he calls 'Analytical Psychology', is appropriate to the study of Justification by Faith for two reasons, and the first is that Jung has always claimed to be an 'empirical psychologist'. This claim is justified, although it might not seem to be to a casual reader of his works. He means that he does not offer ultimate explanations, and it will be found that, although he uses many abstract concepts, and although he speaks as though they referred to concrete entities, he actually uses these concepts to order and relate observable events. Jung's psychological terms can all be analysed in terms of things that can be seen going on in human life, although the analysis is often very difficult, and he says repeatedly that if his abstract terms do name 'things' he has no idea what those 'things' could be (cf., e.g., *Religion*, 64; *Secret*, 118; *Essays*, 405; *Practice*, 537). If the experience of Justification should prove to be like other events of which Jung speaks, he would be the first to insist that this would not 'explain' the experience, if 'explain' is taken to mean 'give a complete account of the cause'. All that would have been done would be that this experience was brought into relation with other aspects of human life.

The second reason why Analytical Psychology is appropriate to the study of Justification by Faith is that it includes the concept 'Individuation' which brings together experiences which have apparent similarities to the experience of Justification. When it is used in this way 'Individuation' should be spelt with a capital 'I' because it is not so much a description as a name, for the word 'individuation' is used by Jung with a special sense, which is not its ordinary meaning, and the capital indicates that it is to be taken in the sense in which he explains it. Individuation is the name of a concept which relates together certain events which Jung has watched taking place in some of his patients, and he believes that these experiences are instances of something which has taken place again and again in human history. That these events are something like Justification is shown by the fact that Jung cites the experience of St Paul in illustration of the goal to which he points (*Secret*, 133), and there is no difficulty in seeing how this system of psychology can be applied to a study of Justification by Faith: the actual application may be difficult, but the principle is straightforward. The system must be studied in order to discover the characteristic (observable) features of instances of Individuation, and, when it is found that these features are also implied by St Paul's doctrine, the way in which they are related in the psychological system can be used to throw light on the meaning of the doctrine. Such a method is cumbersome and from a theological point of view it is only justified by the confused state of the doctrine today.

For different reasons it is impossible to give a brief formulation which can stand without qualification either of Justification by Faith or of Individuation. There is so much difference of opinion about the former that any statement of it needs elaborate defence, and Jung's language is so technical that any statement of the latter needs elaborate interpretation. The interpretation of Individuation, and the defence of a formulation of Justification by Faith will be found in the next two chapters, but subject to correction and explanation in those chapters it may be said:

(1) A man is Justified when, being penitent, he has faith in Jesus as his saviour. To be Justified is to be 'in Christ' or to 'have the Spirit'.

(2) A man is Individuated when, being aware of unconscious forces, he allows them full expression. To be Individuated is to be ruled by 'the Self'.

In this chapter something is to be said about what sort of statements these are, and about some of the difficulties to be met in trying to relate them to each other.

Justification by Faith and Individuation are both accounts of something which was seen to take place before the account was elaborated. They are not, like 'blue prints', anticipations of something not yet visible. In his epistles St Paul does not say 'you need to be justified' or 'you ought to be justified', but, writing to Christians, he says 'you are justified'. In speaking of Justification by Faith he is referring to events which have already taken place, and which he expects his readers to know have taken place; and he assumes that both he and his readers have had experiences which are instances of 'being Justified'; and he uses his own experience to illustrate the thing which has happened to them all. The doctrine was thus originally an interpretative account of something which had happened, and not the assertion that something might happen, or ought to happen. Jung came to the concept of Individuation in much the same way, his account of Individuation was not originally an aim which he set before himself or his patients, but an interpretative account of something which he saw happen: he noticed a certain kind of experience taking place (with individual variations), and he provided Individuation as a general term applicable to all instances of this kind. 'Here and there' he says, for example, 'it happened in my practice that a patient grew beyond the dark possibilities within himself, and the observation of the fact was an experience of foremost importance to me' (Secret, 88, 89); and again: 'I must therefore expressly emphasize that my method of treatment does not consist in causing my patients to indulge in strange fantasies for the purpose of changing their personality, and other nonsense of that kind. I merely put it on record that there are certain cases where such a development occurs, not because I force anyone to it, but because it springs from inner necessity' (Essays, 369). First the observation of many similar things, then the general name, and, with the name, a fuller account—the pattern is the same whether we are speaking of St Paul or Jung.

Although Justification by Faith and Individuation were originally accounts of something seen to take place, they quickly became something more. In giving their accounts St Paul and Jung both imply that they think that it was a good thing that what they speak of did happen, and that it would be a good thing if a similar thing should happen to other people. St Paul does not say this. In his epistles to Christians there was no need for him to urge them towards Justification because he regarded them as men who were already Justified, but in 'placarding' Christ crucified before the eyes of those who were not Christians he implicitly recommended Justification by Faith. The purpose of such 'placarding' was to bring men to Christ, and to make them Christians, and, for St Paul, that meant to bring to them the experience of Justification. So Justification by Faith is not only the name of something that has happened, it is also the name of an essential step on the road to salvation (or else salvation itself), and it is the best thing that could happen to anyone who is not Justified already. Jung is less universalistic. The 'development' of which he speaks must 'spring from inner necessity', and he does not say that this can happen to everyone. Yet he makes it clear that he thinks that when it does happen it is to the great advantage of the individual concerned, and, through that individual, to mankind in general. There is no doubt that in practice when he sees 'inner necessity' at work he co-operates with it to the best of his ability, and since he gives great attention to Individuation in his books we may say that he also 'placards' his beliefs, and much of his 'placarding' looks very much as though it is designed to bring 'inner necessity' to the notice of many who might not otherwise be aware of it, and so bring to them the experience of Individuation. The importance which St Paul attaches to Justification by Faith, and Jung to Individuation shows that neither is content to record that something sometimes happens—they both want the thing of which they speak to happen more often.

Justification by Faith and Individuation are both 'ways'. Justification by Faith is put forward as a way which it would be best for everyone to travel, Individuation as a way which it is a very good thing for some people to travel. Even so, neither is anything like an A.A. route. Regarded as ways they share a curious feature, because each is presented as a way which a man cannot find and follow by his own conscious and deliberate effort. 'God justifies', says St Paul, and He does not justify a man because of anything that the man does, but because 'Jesus died for the ungodly'. It is the man who does not seek his own way who is guided by God along the way of Justification by Faith. Of the way of faith St John of the Cross says: 'Wherefore, upon this road, to enter upon the road is to leave the road; or, to express it better, it is to pass on to the goal and to leave one's own way, and to enter upon that which has no way, which is God' (*Ascent*, 76), and although he is not explicitly referring to the doctrine of Justification by Faith, it would be hard to find a better summary of this aspect of it. Jung is equally insistent that the way which he recommends men to take cannot be planned ahead, and he says: 'The step to higher consciousness leads away from all shelter and safety. The person must give himself to the new way completely, for it is only by means of his integrity that he can go further' (*Secret*, 93), and he also invokes God: 'I do nothing; there is nothing I can do except wait, with a certain trust in God, until, out of a conflict borne with patience and courage, there emerges the solution destined—although I cannot foresee it—for that particular person' (*Alchemy*, 37). Justification by Faith and Individuation are both ways, and they are both ways which cannot be mapped until they have been trodden.

St Paul and Jung both speak of a way, and they both claim that it is good for men to travel on the way of which they speak. This means that both imply that there is something which men lack, and which they could have. Although the accounts which they give are very different, there are at least three questions which can be asked of either of their ways:

(1) What is the state from which it leads?
(2) How can a man prepare himself to travel on it?
(3) What does it mean to be travelling on it?

These questions will be answered for both ways in later chapters. The significance of the questions is that they show how it is possible for theology and psychology to overlap. Each of these questions is as relevant to the theological account as it is to the psychological account, and this is sufficient indication that there is common ground. The answers given to these questions by a theologian speaking of Justification by Faith will be quite different from the answers given by a psychologist speaking of Individuation, and this is inevitable, but it does not mean that the theologian and the psychologist must be speaking about different events. It may only mean that they are speaking of similar events from different points of view. If this is so it can only be shown by a careful examination of the two ways, and such an examination should be begun with a clear understanding of the difficulties involved.

The first difficulty is concerned with the understanding of St Paul's doctrine. It is due to the fact that St Paul was not faced with the questions which confront a modern theologian. Today we want to know what being 'Justified' is like, whether there is anything which a man can do in order to be Justified, and, if so, what it is. St Paul assumed that his readers were Justified, and passed on to the question 'being Justified, how ought a man to behave?' so that although he referred to the thing that had happened in various ways, and by various names, he did not spend time analysing it, and his 'doctrine' has to be gathered from the hints contained in the names which he gave the event, and in the way in which he spoke of it. To understand the doctrine is to interpret phrases like 'you are free from sin', and 'you have put on Christ'; and, as the wealth of interpretations shows, such phrases leave a wide field for controversy. Because of this the modern theologian cannot say 'this is the doctrine of Justification by Faith', and to try to understand the doctrine now is to thread one's way through a maze of rival interpretations. Either one must accept some one traditional view of the doctrine, and be content with that, or one must grasp at any clue which may be offered from outside theology. It looks very much as though Individuation may provide such a clue.

The second difficulty is concerned with Individuation, and it is quite different. Jung has devoted much time to the questions 'what is Individuation?' and 'what can a man do to become individuated?'; and whereas St Paul has given us very little material to help with the corresponding questions about Justification Jung provides more than enough. He has written so much himself that the question of choosing between rival interpreters does not arise. If he has not been able to make his meaning clear it is not likely that anyone else will have done better. The difficulty in understanding Jung is that he uses a language which is not that of ordinary speech, and which, as a technical language, is comparatively new. He does not simply use 'psychological language', he uses his own psychological language, and he cannot be understood unless this language is understood, and it seems to be unnecessarily difficult. In Analytical Psychology terms like 'the Unconscious', 'the psyche', 'psychic reality', 'psychic effect', 'complex', 'individuation', 'the self', have slightly different meanings from those which they have when used in any other context, and even common categories like 'causality' are affected: Jung's epistemological background is strictly Kantian, and this has to be constantly remembered, because it influences all the analogies from our experience of physical things which he uses to illustrate what he says about the 'psyche': he has said that in psychology you must not make a statement unless you are ready to add its opposite: he has prefaced a whole book with the comment that what he says is, in principle, no different from what primitive man says when he speaks of his god as a snake: he defines his terms, but he is not always consistent in his use of them, remarking, for example, 'I am no terminological rigorist —call the existing symbols "wholeness", "self", "consciousness", "higher ego", or what you will, it makes little difference' (*Practice*, 537): finally, his works cover a period of some fifty years, and neither his thought nor his terminology has remained static during that time. All these things make the task of understanding Individuation a matter of some complexity.

The third difficulty is that of relating two accounts which are expressed in different technical languages. One account is theological and the other is psychological, and both theology and psychology use special terms in special ways. The nature of these languages needs some discussion. Theological language has been in use for centuries, and much of it has passed into common use, and this can cause confusion because it can hide the fact that this language is really a special language, with a special purpose. It is tempting to think that if the terms used can be defined there is no great difference between theological language and ordinary language, but this is not true, because to use theological language is to have a specific purpose, and that purpose is to relate observable events to God, and to His activity. Theological language is apt to this purpose because it includes terms and categories which refer to God, to His activity, and to our attitude to God: 'Sin', for example, refers to a relation between a man's behaviour and 'the will of God', and it cannot be properly used (in theology) without that reference. So much is generally true of any 'theological' language, with whatever religion it may be connected. The language of Christian theology determines a way of relating events to God and the language itself selects, or points to, certain events in history, and the use of the language brings those events of which we happen to be speaking into relation with the events selected. To say 'this is the activity of God' is to say, at least, 'this is like those events recorded in the Bible, and described there as God's activity': to say that a mystic 'saw Jesus' is to imply that his experience was like that of those who knew Jesus during His earthly life: 'righteous' relates human behaviour to the longing of Israel for redemption, expressed in the Old Testament, and to the character of Jesus Christ as revealed in the New Testament: and so on. To use theological language to talk about something is to bring it into relation with those things which are central for Christianity.

Theological language determines points of reference. To use it is to give supreme importance to the history of Israel and to the life of Jesus Christ. Some special languages not only determine points of reference but are also limited to certain kinds of things or aspects of

things, so that for example you cannot discuss the beauty of a picture
in the language of Physics. Theological language is not a language of
this sort, but it can be used to talk about every kind of event, and the
ideal of theology is to bring everything that goes on in the world into
relation with its central events. Yet in doing this it does tend to select
aspects of the events of which it speaks, and it may pass over relations
between events which another special language might emphasize. If
two events are each brought into relation with the life of Jesus, then
the task of theology could be complete with respect to them, even
though a direct relation between them were passed over. 'Drunken-
ness is sin', and 'the mystic knows God', for instance, are theological
statements; but 'some people when they were drunk have had
experiences like those of some mystics' is not, although it may be a
statement of which the theologian ought to take note. Again, two acts
may be alike to the theologian because they both reveal a Christ-like
character, although from any other point of view they may be entirely
different from each other. Theological language selects that aspect of
events which brings them into relation with the Biblical accounts,
and in doing this it moves away from a bare description of the events
involved. This is apparent in St Paul's account of being Justified: he
is not concerned with the experienced character of what has happened
to Christians, but with the relation of what has happened, and of its
effects, to Christ, who lived, died and rose from the dead.

If Analytical Psychology could be regarded as nothing more than
a way of giving a description of human experiences there would be
no difficulty in relating it to theology, and some psychologies do aim
at doing this. It seems to be the intention, for instance, of both
William James and Gilbert Ryle, using very different methods from
one another. Other psychologies use languages which determine points
of reference, very much in the way that theological language does, and
different systems of psychology may have different languages, determining different points of reference. The systems grounded in analytical
experience have languages which relate events to the 'analytical
situation', that is to the clinical experience of the psychologist, and
when Jung 'explains' something he relates it to his clinical experience.
In 'The psychology of the Transference' (*Practice*, part 3), for example,
he claims to be using alchemical literature as a clue to the understanding of his own experiences, but it would be just as correct to
say that he elucidates that literature by appealing to his experience.

There is a two-way effect: when Jung has understood the alchemists, then their writings do, no doubt, illuminate his clinical experience, but he 'understands' them first by relating them to that experience, and by detecting parallels between their writings and what he sees going on. The language of Analytical Psychology is as much a means of relating the events under discussion to certain 'key' events as is theological language, but the 'key' events to which it points are different from those to which theological language points. A psychological account also moves away from the bare description of events, and it moves in a different direction, as it were, from that in which a theological account moves.

Psychological language has not, in principal, the universal application of theological language. There are events about which it is impossible to talk in psychological language, and to decide to use psychological language is to commit oneself to a discussion of 'psychic events'. Human behaviour, thought of as an expression of the human 'psyche', can be discussed in such language, but events such as the eruption of a volcano cannot. For example, since 'archetype' is a strictly psychological term, it is very doubtful whether Jung is justified in saying 'the archetype fulfils itself not only psychically in the individual, but objectively outside the individual' (*Job*, 648), because it is doubtful whether any meaning can be given to the statement: on the other hand, the preceding remark, 'non-psychic parallel phenomena can occur which also represent the archetype', is significant, so long as 'represent' is understood in a weak sense, and not regarded as implying some sort of casuality. The ideal of psychology is to bring within one system of relationships all events which we regard as 'manifestations of mind', and it is partly 'accident' that Analytical Psychology should do this by relating them to clinical experience: in other words the central points of reference could be changed without doing violence to the language. In theology, on the other hand, such a change would make the language no longer 'Christian'.

That it is a means of relating observable psychic events is the clue to the understanding of Jung's language. It explains why he can talk about things like 'unconscious elements', and still say that he does not know what such a thing is, nor whether it is anything at all. There is nothing particularly unusual in talking in this way, and the physicist, for instance, does it a great deal. The physicist has no difficulty in talking about an 'electron' as though it were a small thing, but if he is asked what an electron 'really' is, he can give no clear answer. The attempts to define 'electrons' in terms of probability values show well enough that the physicist does not know what an 'electron' is, nor whether it is anything at all. Again, we can relate many electrical phenomena by talking about 'a flow of current from positive to negative', but we do not expect to be able to find the 'current', or to find anything 'flowing' in this way. We know a lot about what electricity does, but we have no idea what it is. Moreover, we can go on talking about currents from positive to negative, even though we know that it is better to talk about electrons, going from negative to positive, and this is only a better way of talking (that is, a better 'theory') because it enables us to relate together more electrical phenomena than we can by talking in the other way; it is not that we can see the electrons but not the 'current'. We do not look for 'electricity' but for its effects, and we do not look for 'electrons' but for their effects. So we are not to look for the 'unconscious' as we might look for the liver. The strange terms of Analytical Psychology are concepts designed to relate observable psychic events, and not the names of invisible things. To say that a man is 'unconsciously afraid', for instance, is to say that although he sometimes behaves like a man who admits that he is afraid, and although his dreams and fantasies are like those of someone who is afraid, he does not admit that he is afraid even to himself when he is being honest with himself; that is, he does not 'feel afraid'. 'Unconscious fear' is a concept which relates certain features of the man's behaviour which are observable to himself and to others and other features which are observable only to himself; it is not the name of an 'invisible' attitude of mind. The psychological terms bring to our notice relationships between psychic events which we should be likely to overlook without them, but they would be useless if statements which include them could not be analysed in terms of observable psychic events.

The first thing to be done is to interpret Jung's language. This makes it possible to see what is going on in an instance of Individuation. We shall find that we have an account of certain observable events, which form a pattern of life and thought. When we have this pattern before us, we have to ask whether it is the sort of pattern which could be the observable basis of St Paul's account of Justification by Faith. We shall find that in many respects Individuation does look like the sort of thing about which St Paul might have said the things which he said of Justification. We shall also find that in other respects it does not look like this at all. Yet even those aspects of Individuation which are not, as such, aspects of Justification by Faith will help in the understanding of the doctrine.

The clear parallels are these. First, both St Paul and Jung find that the mark of the 'natural man' is that he seeks to follow his own conscious devices and desires. Secondly, both demand that a man should cease to rely upon his own will. Thirdly, both claim that when a man does cease to rely on his own will, in the way they suggest, something important happens to him. Finally, both agree that as a result of all this a man comes to a way of living in which he seems to be directed by a 'centre' which is not what he calls 'I'. On the other hand the contrasts are these. First, St Paul requires that a man should condemn his own will, but Jung insists that he must hold fast to his conscious values. Secondly, Jung insists that the 'unconscious' should be allowed to 'express itself', and this means that a man's will must not be opposed to the tendencies which he regards as 'evil', whereas St Paul insists that he must maintain his condemnation of such things. Thirdly, St Paul looks to Christ to bring about a change in a man, but Jung looks to the man's own 'integrity'. Finally, for St Paul, Christ is the 'new centre', and the character of Christ is already known; for Jung the 'new centre' is 'the Self', and its character is never known. Although these contrasts appear to be due to the presence of ideas diametrically opposed to each other in the two systems this is not so, and a careful study of the systems shows that the two sets of ideas are related in unexpected but illuminating ways.

The next two chapters introduce the two ways with which this essay is concerned. Chapter 2 is divided into two parts: in the first part Individuation is described in Jung's own language, and in the second part that language is analysed. This preliminary study of Jung's way brings out certain features which are relevant to the doctrine of Justification by Faith, and in chapter 3 it is shown how they can help to elucidate what St Paul and others have said about Justification. The third chapter is thus a general survey of the Christian way.

In chapters 2 and 3, Individuation and Justification by Faith are considered as wholes: in the following eight chapters each way is taken step by step. These eight chapters are in four pairs: the first chapter of each pair is a discussion of some feature of Individuation, and the second a discussion of a parallel feature of Justification by Faith, and the arrangement of these chapters is as follows:

A. *The state from which St Paul and Jung seek to 'save' men*
    Chapter 4. Jung's account of 'natural man' as being in a state of antagonism between consciousness and the unconscious.
    Chapter 5. St Paul's account of 'natural man' as being in bondage to sin.

B. *What man can do for himself*
    Chapter 6. An account of the theory of a Jungian analysis, showing how it leads a man to 'accept the unconscious'.
    Chapter 7. An account of penitence, showing in what way it is like 'accepting the unconscious'.

C. *Faith*
    Chapter 8. A discussion of the theory of 'projection' and of its bearing on faith.
    Chapter 9. A rebuttal of criticisms of Christian faith which might be based upon Jung's psychology.

D. *The Goal*
    Chapter 10. An account of Jung's concept of the Self, considered as that which 'unites the opposites' and as itself a 'union of opposites'.
    Chapter 11. An enquiry into the nature and function of Christ, showing that He too 'unites the opposites' and is Himself a 'union of opposites'.

After this detailed comparison of the two ways, some conclusions are brought together in chapter 12.

2

INDIVIDUATION

1. *The Individuation Process*

THE account of Jung's way in this section is given in Jung's own terms. After the account has been given the language is analysed in the second section of the chapter. This is the natural order. All languages except those of pure mathematics and mathematical logic are in use before definitions and syntactical rules are laid down, and definitions and rules are discovered by examining the way in which a language is used. Nevertheless, to avoid confusion, it may be said at once that although words like 'the unconscious' are used in the first section as though they were the names of 'things', it will be shown in the second section that there are no things which they name, and that they refer to concepts. This should be kept in mind throughout section 1. The account in this section is intended to be a summary of what Jung says himself, but a certain amount of explanation is inevitable, and when one 'explains' it is always possible that one will also misinterpret.

Jung opens an account of Individuation with these words: 'There is a destination, a possible goal, beyond the alternative stages dealt with in [the] last chapter.[1] That is the way of individuation. Individuation means becoming a single, homogeneous being, and, in so far as "individuality" embraces our innermost, last, and incomparable uniqueness, it also implies becoming one's own self. We could therefore translate individuation as "coming to self-hood" or "self-realization"' (*Essays*, 266). Since the account is psychological it is concerned with what is going on 'inside' a man, and that means it is about his 'psyche'. In order to understand what is meant by 'becoming one's own self' it is necessary to know what the psyche is like before this happens, because if the process results in a 'homogeneous' being, then there must be a sense in which the psyche is not 'homogeneous' before the process begins.

The psychologist's account of the psyche is built up from his

---

[1] Square brackets in quotations indicate minor modifications in wording or my intrusive comment.

experience of his patients and of himself, from his general observation of other people and, particularly in the case of Jung, from a wide study of more or less esoteric literature. Although we shall speak as though Jung's account were the correct description of the psyche, it is only the way in which he organizes the results of his observations. Freud's account, for example, is different, but the two accounts are not like two different descriptions of what can be seen in a room, one right and the other wrong. The two accounts are like two different physical theories, such as the 'current' and 'electron' theories of electricity. The Jungian may say that Jung's account has wider application and greater heuristic and therapeutic power than Freud's, but not that Jung's account is true, and Freud's false. Jung himself says of the theories of Freud and Adler: 'Since both theories are in a large measure correct—that is to say, since they both appear to explain their material—it follows that a neurosis must have two opposite aspects, one of which is grasped by the Freudian, the other by the Adlerian theory' (*Essays*, 57), and of his own contribution he remarks: 'The fundamental distinction which experience has forced upon me merely claims the value of a further point of view' (ibid., 218). His claim may not be acceptable to everyone, but it is important to see just what it is that he does claim. He does not claim that his theory is 'true' and the others 'false', but that his theory has wider application than either of the others. That is, he admits that the other theories do bring many facts into an ordered system, but claims that he provides a wider system which will include all the facts related by either of the others, and more besides.

'The fundamental distinction which experience has forced upon me' is the distinction between the 'personal unconscious' and the 'collective unconscious'. The idea of the psyche as being divided into two parts, one conscious and the other unconscious, is common to many systems of psychology and has even passed into common speech, and for much psychotherapy this is the most important distinction which can be made. But both Freud and Jung have found it necessary to introduce further distinctions into their account of the psyche; Freud has coined terms such as 'subconscious' and 'id', Jung such terms as 'collective unconscious' and 'archetypes'. In relation to Jung's system as a whole, and to Individuation in particular, the simple division into conscious and unconscious is relatively unimportant, and according to Jung, the 'great gulf' in the psyche lies within the unconscious (cf. *Essays*, 103, 235)[1], and separates the personal unconscious from the collective unconscious. Thus Jung divides the psyche into three parts, consciousness, the personal unconscious and the collective unconscious. According to Jung's theory the personal unconscious is usually 'contaminated' with the collective unconscious (*Essays*, 236; *Alchemy*, 31, 38), and his technique is designed to dissociate the one from the other, by bringing the personal unconscious into close relation with consciousness and, ultimately, by making its 'contents' conscious: the collective unconscious, according to Jung, must always remain other than consciousness (*Essays*, 240, 241, *et al.*). Thus from the point of view of the individual there is, at first, no distinction between personal and collective unconscious; then (in the course of analysis) a man becomes aware of the need to assimilate the personal unconscious; and, finally, if a man does assimilate the personal unconscious, his consciousness is confronted by the collective unconscious. In the final stage of Individuation these 'opposites', consciousness and the collective unconscious, are united.

The account of the psyche of a man who has not yet started on the way of Individuation is not simply a description of what may be known about him by direct observation, whether the observer is himself or someone else, because much of it is inferred from what has happened to other people who have advanced to later stages of the process. As will be shown below the same is true of the state of being 'in bondage to sin', because the true nature of that state is only known by those who have seen what happens when a man is Justified. Inference of this kind is legitimate and common, even though it fails of absolute certainty. A watchmaker may have a sufficient idea of the mechanism of a particular watch without examining it, because he has examined other watches like it; he may be able to diagnose what is wrong with a watch at a glance, because he has repaired other watches which have gone wrong in the same way: we infer stomach, heart and liver in everyone, although not everyone has been examined by the surgeon: symptoms of organic diseases make diagnosis possible because other people have had the same symptoms, and the organic defect has been

---

[1] The statement in this chapter is a general statement of Jung's views, gathered from hints, cross-references from one book to another, and from a general understanding (or misunderstanding!) of the drift of his thought, as well as from specific passages. This means that the majority of the references in this section are offered by way of illustration and example, and not as the basis of our argument. More detailed references are given in later chapters when special points are considered in more detail.

seen. In every instance the inference is legitimate, though the weight which is given to it varies from one instance to another. In Analytical Psychology what is said of consciousness is known by direct observation in the present, just as the symptoms of disease are known; what is said of the personal unconscious is a diagnosis which interprets what is known by direct observation in the light of what commonly takes place in the early stages of an analysis; what is said of the collective unconscious is a 'deeper' diagnosis which is made possible by an experience of advanced stages of analysis. Each of these three parts of the psyche requires a brief discussion.

Consciousness

In ordinary speech there is no need to talk about 'conscious psychic elements', or 'elements of consciousness'. 'Consciousness', in ordinary speech, refers to a state or quality of the whole man. As a state it is opposed to sleep or anaesthesia, as a quality it distinguishes man from plants. All psychic elements or events which we know and can talk about are elements or events of which we are conscious. In psychology, however, 'consciousness' is used in such a way that it enables us to distinguish between different classes of psychic elements, and when it is used in this way not all those elements which we know can be said to be 'elements of consciousness'. Unfortunately psychologists use 'consciousness' in a loose sense, as well as in a strict sense, and it is difficult to see how this could be avoided. It would be absurd, for example, to say we were not conscious of the content of a remembered dream or of a daydream, because we know it and it is therefore 'in consciousness'; yet, in the strict sense, it does not 'belong to consciousness'. The distinction to which this idea of 'belonging to consciousness' refers is one which is known well enough apart from psychology. In ordinary speech we distinguish between the things which we deliberately think or do, and the thoughts and actions which seem to 'happen to us', although no one else is responsible for them. We may say, 'it suddenly came into my head', 'I don't know how I came to do that', 'it slipped out when I wasn't thinking', 'I was carried away', and many other similar things, and when people talk like this we have no difficulty in understanding them. In the strict psychological sense of 'consciousness' the things which 'happen to us' are not 'part of consciousness', but 'manifestations of the unconscious'.

3—F C D

Consciousness includes what we may call 'psychic states' on the one hand, and 'psychic events' on the other. The psychic states form our character at any given time, and the psychic events are the thoughts, decisions and actions which express our character. Yet this distinction can hardly be said to be between different kinds of psychic elements. Hatred, for example, may be a state or an event. Hatred of cruelty might be a characteristic attitude, whereas the hatred of a particular act of cruelty would be an event arising from that attitude. The hatred of a person would be an event if it arose at a particular moment and quickly passed, but it would be a state if it were an enduring characteristic. Consciousness can be thought of as a system of psychic states, and psychic events are parts of consciousness if they arise out of, or express elements of, that system. There are systems of academic psychology whose function is to analyse this picture which is implied by much of our ordinary speech, and from the point of view of such a system it might well be necessary to reduce psychic states to psychic events: 'hatred of cruelty', for instance, might be analysed in terms of statements about the way in which a man reacts, or is likely to react to acts of cruelty, or to such questions as 'do you hate cruelty?' Analytical Psychology is not a psychological system of this sort, and Jung accepts the picture of consciousness implicit in common speech and models his picture of the unconscious on it. As in consciousness, so in the unconscious there are psychic states, and as the psychic states which form the conscious character give rise to psychic events, so do the psychic states in the unconscious: a psychic event to which an unconscious 'psychic state' gives rise may be unconscious, or it may be conscious. The events in consciousness which arise from unconscious psychic states are the things which seem to 'happen' to us.

The distinction between psychic states and psychic events has been used to try to clarify the picture of consciousness implicit in ordinary speech. It is not a distinction which will concern us further. The picture is that of a character, or characteristic attitude, relatively permanent, which is formed of a number of psychic elements closely related to each other. A consistent character is one in which these elements are so related that they co-operate with each other, and reinforce each other. That is, one in which less important desires and tendencies are subordinated to greater purposes, or what are regarded by the individual as greater purposes. An inconsistent or vacillating character is one in which the elements are not well integrated, and thought and action are sometimes determined by one, sometimes by another opposing element. The elements which are combined to form the 'core' of consciousness are those which a man acknowledges as elements of his character, whether those elements are bound together into a well-integrated system or whether they remain more or less isolated from one another. The thoughts, decisions and actions which arise from these elements are expressions of that character.

In ordinary speech the word 'I' is closely connected with the idea of a 'core' of consciousness, made up of interrelated psychic elements. But 'I' is commonly used in at least three senses, which are not usually carefully distinguished in ordinary conversation. First, 'I' is used to refer to the subject of all that a man thinks or does, when he himself is talking: although it is clear that I do not consciously plan a dream, or even arrange that I shall have a dream, I still say 'I dreamed such and such'. Secondly, there is a 'stronger' sense of 'I' in which it is used by a man to refer to the combination of elements which forms his character. The phrases 'I did that, but I did not mean to', or 'I don't know how I came to think in that way' are almost impossible to analyse unless a distinction is made between these two senses of 'I'. We should like to be able to say 'that happened to me, but I didn't do it', or 'that thought came to me, but I didn't think it', but the first, dominating use of 'I' prevents us from doing so. St Paul confronted this difficulty, and at one point boldly used 'I' in the more restricted sense, when he said 'But if what I would not, that I do, it is no more I that do it, but sin which dwelleth in me': the shift from one use of 'I' to another is unmistakable. The third use of 'I' is a way of confining it to the subject of those thoughts and acts which we regard as expressing our true character, and yet escaping the difficulties which beset the second use. 'I' may be used in such a way that it seems to refer to an invisible 'centre' of consciousness. In so far as the elements which form a man's character are well integrated they combine with one another and act as a single entity, and when this happens it is as though they were directed from a central 'control-point'. If we make a decision we may be able to see by introspection that many aspects of our character played their part and contributed to the making of that particular decision and none other, but if we do not analyse the decision in this way we think of it as 'our' decision, and as the result of an act of will, so that a decision which arises from the co-operation of many elements seems to have been made by a further element

'standing apart' from the others. In ordinary speech 'I' often refers
to the idea of such a 'controlling element', as when we say 'I weighed
the pros and cons', or 'I had to decide between competing tendencies
within me'. There is really little distinction between this third use of
'I' and the second use, according to which 'I' refers to our 'true
character': according to one use 'I' refers to character when it is
thought of as being made up of several elements, according to the
other it refers to those elements which make up their character when
they are thought of as acting together in unity.

'The ego' is used in psychology in the same way as 'I' is used in
the second two senses in ordinary speech. 'The ego' is not used in the
first sense of 'I', because when we speak of a man from outside 'I' is
not the natural way of referring to what he does, and when a man says
'I' the observer can simply say 'he', or 'the man': 'the ego' always
refers to the 'core' of consciousness, whether it is thought of as a
system of psychic elements, or as a 'controlling point'. It must be
realized, however, that the observer cannot detect any actual controlling
element any more than the individual concerned, and what is in
question is a way of picturing consciousness, so that the ego is sometimes pictured as an arrangement of many elements, and sometimes as
a centre. Jung occasionally speaks of the ego considered as a system of
elements as the 'ego-complex', and he frequently uses 'ego-
consciousness' as a synonym for 'consciousness', not, as we might
be misled into thinking, as equivalent to 'self-consciousness'. For
example, Jung defines 'consciousness' as follows: 'By consciousness
I understand the relatedness of psychic contents to the ego in so far as
they are sensed as such by the ego. In so far as relations are not sensed
as such by the ego, they are unconscious. Consciousness is the function
or activity which maintains the relation of psychic contents with the
ego. Consciousness is not identical with *psyche*, since, in my view,
psyche represents the totality of all the psychic contents, and these are
not necessarily all bound up directly with the ego, i.e. related to it in such
a way that they take on the quality of consciousness. There exist a great
many psychic complexes and these are not all, necessarily, connected
with the ego' (*Types*, 535, 536). In this definition, and elsewhere in
the same book, Jung speaks of the ego as though it were a single,
central element, but in the definition of *ego* he says: 'By ego, I understand a complex of representations which constitutes the centrum of
my field of consciousness and appears to possess a very high degree of

continuity and identity. Hence I also speak of an *ego-complex*. The ego-complex is as much a content as it is a condition of consciousness' (ibid., 540).

Consciousness is thus to be thought of as a close-knit group of psychic elements which determines those thoughts and actions which we acknowledge as expressions of our 'true character', and to which other elements are related, or may be related from time to time. The 'ego' refers to this group of elements, with special emphasis on their tendency to function in harmony as an integrated whole. Although 'the ego' is used in many ways in which the individual concerned would use 'I' it is not used, as 'I' is, to refer to the subject of all a man's thoughts and acts, for if a man acts in a way contrary to his conscious decision we must say 'the ego made the decision, but the man acted in a contrary way'.

Unconscious Elements

The unconscious is modelled[1] on the picture of consciousness which is implied by ordinary speech. 'Unconscious psychic elements' are thought of as being like conscious elements, and it is assumed that we know what a conscious element is. We take it that when a man says 'I am afraid' he is asserting the presence of a psychic element called 'fear', and that he knows this element by introspection. This is the assumption of ordinary speech. In ordinary talk we distinguish between the fear and the expression of that fear in appropriate speech and action; if a man says, 'I was afraid', we may reply 'Well, you didn't show it in any way', and we know well enough what is meant. This kind of talk implies a psychic element which is known in itself, although its effects are not observed: an unconscious psychic element, on the other hand, is one which is not observed in itself, although its effects are known. To give a crude example, we could infer the existence of an unconscious element called 'fear' if a man showed every symptom which we associate with fear but was unable to 'find' the element 'fear' by the most careful and honest introspection: that is, if he were honestly unable to say 'I am afraid'. If a psychic element is conscious it is expressed in many ways, and an important expression of it is the verbal statement that it exists: if the element is unconscious

---

[1] This means more than that we form a picture of the unconscious: the unconscious is what it is pictured to be, and the underlying model controls the way in which the word is used.

it is not expressed by the verbal assertion of its existence, even in a man's private and most frank thoughts, but it will tend to express itself in all the other ways in which it would be expressed if it were conscious. This tendency, however, will rarely produce a straightforward expression of the unconscious element (as in the crude example above) because it has to compete with the conscious elements by which the man's life is directed, and its natural expression is liable to be frustrated by them.

An unconscious element is a psychic element which exerts an influence upon a man's life, but which is 'detached' from consciousness. The idea of an element wholly unrelated to consciousness is the extension of something which we experience in ordinary life. We do know psychic elements which are relatively 'detached' from consciousness, although they are sufficiently related to it to be 'in consciousness'. We have tendencies to behave 'out of character', thoughts which we regard as absurd or evil, and ideals which we acknowledge as good but reject for ourselves for one reason or another, and we dream, both asleep and awake: many of these things seem so unimportant, or irrelevant to our situation, that we pay little attention to them: they are then said to have little 'psychic energy'. Sometimes, however, some of them cannot be easily overlooked and seem to 'press' upon us, clamouring for attention. When this happens such things are said to have much 'psychic energy'. When things do press upon us in this way they cause strain and tension. So long as the evil tendency or the too difficult ideal remains in consciousness it is a threat to the synthesis of elements which is the core of consciousness. The elements which press upon us can only be integrated with the elements which form this core if the whole conscious synthesis is reorganized, just as a scientist may not be able to incorporate a new fact in his system without reconstructing his basic theory. So long as we know such elements and feel their force we are drawn in two opposing ways: it seems that we must either be 'true to our character' and neglect the opposing element, or else allow the opposing element to have its way and act contrary to our character, and if we will do neither of these things the conscious synthesis must be broken up and re-formed in such a way that the opposing element can be integrated in it. Thus St Paul opposed the threat of Christianity until the synthesis built in his mind by Judaism was overthrown, and when this happened the old elements were re-united in a new way, and the 'stone' which he

had rejected before became the corner-stone of the new synthesis.
The road of death and rebirth to a fuller life is only possible if a man
can endure the tension which arises when the conscious synthesis is
opposed by other elements. If he cannot endure this tension there are
ways in which he may escape from it, and one way is to 'devalue'
the opposing elements, which means to dissociate them from consciousness as much as possible. To say that such elements may
become unconscious is to say that this dissociation can be carried to
the extreme point at which the man is no longer aware of them at all

A psychic element can be devalued in several ways. It is devalued,
for instance, when it is not taken into account when we make conscious
plans and decisions. When we neglect elements in this way we usually
provide ourselves with reasons for doing so : we may, for example,
regard them as trivial, irrelevant, or evil, and to do any of these things
is to devalue them. If, however, we find that an element has so much
psychic energy that we cannot neglect it by taking one of these
attitudes to it we can 'repress' it. *How* we repress a psychic element
nobody knows, but what happens is that the element which is repressed
ceases to be 'in consciousness', and we cease to have any knowledge
of its existence. Repression is a phenomenon which is known apart
from psychology, and all that modern psychotherapy has done is to
show that it occurs more frequently than we should expect. It is
repression when a man honestly forgets a promise which it would be
awkward to keep, a statement which he wishes he had not made, or
an incident which it pains him to remember, and it does happen that
things like this are honestly forgotten, even though we are suspicious
when other people say that they have forgotten them. The 'discovery'
of psychology is that although we may devalue or repress a psychic
element it continues to influence our life and thought, and to say
that a psychic element is unconscious is to say that it exerts an influence
on our life even though we do not know that it exists.

To speak of a psychic element as being unconscious is to speak of
the way in which it influences our life, and what is said of unconscious
elements in this connection is true of elements which have been
devalued. A fully conscious element contributes to the conscious
determination of thought and action, but an unconscious or devalued
element does not. In other words, the names of conscious elements
appear in the account which we give when we are asked, 'Why did
you think, say, or do that?' whereas the names of unconscious or

devalued elements do not, except when we deplore what we have done and admit that we were 'overcome' by an evil tendency, or when we cannot find an explanation: when we cannot find an explanation we sometimes guess at an unconscious element, beginning our answer, 'I suppose it must have been because . . .'. Unconscious and devalued elements do contribute to the determination of thought and action, but we are not usually aware of their influence. We discover their influence by attending to those thoughts and acts which we have difficulty in explaining. Elements of this kind give rise to slips of the tongue, remarks which we are surprised to hear ourselves making, behaviour which hinders our conscious purpose, thoughts which come into our heads for no apparent reason, dreams, and waking fantasies. All those things which 'happen to us' from within, and those things which we cannot explain from our knowledge of ourselves are due to the influence of unconscious and devalued elements. These things may be referred to as the 'odd' things in our lives, and odd things of this kind are regarded as expressions or manifestations of the elements which give rise to them.

The Personal Unconscious

The personal unconscious is made up of psychic elements which have been conscious, but are no longer conscious, and of some elements which have 'just failed' to become conscious. The elements which have been conscious have either 'fallen out' or been 'thrown out' of consciousness (*Essays*, 204). Jung speaks of subliminal sense-impressions and forgotten memories of all kinds as being in the personal unconscious, but such things do not 'belong' to the unconscious if they are available for use at the appropriate times, and knowledge 'put aside' for use when it is needed belongs to consciousness. For instance I know that an Archdeacon should be addressed as 'Venerable', and this knowledge is available to me if I need it (to address a letter, to answer the question, 'How should an Archdeacon be addressed?', or to use it as an illustration as I am doing here), so that although I rarely think about this piece of knowledge it is not 'unconscious'. The elements which have 'just failed' to become conscious are ideas and tendencies which have been, as it were, 'on the edge' of our mind, but which we have preferred not to acknowledge. The elements which are 'typical' of the personal unconscious are those which have been 'thrown out' of consciousness; that is, repressed.

The repression of psychic elements has two unfortunate results. When elements are repressed they exert a malign influence on conscious life, and, at the same time, the fact that they are lost to consciousness means that consciousness is 'impaired'. The repressed elements have, as it were, been locked in a cupboard, and the key thrown away: we have looked at them, and decided that we do not want to have anything more to do with them. But a psychic element cannot be so hidden that it is as if it no longer existed, because although we may not acknowledge its existence in any way its psychic energy has not been taken from it, and this means that it continues to influence conscious life and thought. The theme of many ghost stories expresses very accurately what happens when psychic elements are repressed. Often, in the stories, the more securely the evil influence is hidden the more its power is felt and the more pervasive is its influence, and the evil force frequently reaches its fullest strength only when its source seems to be securely barred away. So with unconscious elements, those which are most hidden from consciousness have the greatest malign influence upon life. This is the first unfortunate result of repression, but the second is just as important.

An important feature of Jung's thought is the idea that consciousness is impaired by the loss of those elements which are repressed and he says that the elements which form the personal unconscious 'ought' to be conscious (*Essays*, 218). He does not deny that it is possible for a man to get through life with a consciousness impaired by repression, but he would say that such a man was one-sided, and that his life was not so complete as it might have been. He might also say, in some instances, that this was 'really' best for the man concerned (*Essays*, 257), because the search for a fuller life might lead him to great danger, but he makes it clear that he believes that the 'best people' continue to develop psychically throughout their life (*Essays*, 291), and it is with the ideal of such continued development in mind that we are to think of repression as impairing consciousness. Continued psychic development means that new psychic elements are continually discovered and integrated into the conscious synthesis, and repression brings this process to a stop. Jung implies that it is not a matter of arbitrary choice whether one or another psychic element shall be included in the conscious synthesis, and that the actual structure of consciousness at any given time determines what element can be added next, so that the elements which 'press upon' us are just those elements which are suitable for inclusion in consciousness, and if consciousness is to develop, these and no others must be integrated with it (*Essays*, 76, 93). If such an element is 'seen' and rejected ('thrown out of consciousness'), or not allowed to 'appear' at all ('just fails to become conscious'), then it is repressed, and becomes a part of the personal unconscious. Since the appropriate element has been refused there is now nothing which can aid in the development of consciousness. If a man will not accept those psychic elements which would lead to a widening of consciousness there is no other road of development open to him, and his character and attitude hardens into a set form. It is a fact that there are many people who seem quite unable to receive any new ideas, and if Jung's theory is right such people have repressed psychic elements.

The personal unconscious is made up of those psychic elements which have a close 'compensatory' relation to consciousness, and which we refuse to acknowledge. It is the 'other side' of our character, and the loss of this other side makes our conscious character one-sided and unadaptable. The personal unconscious, if it could be made conscious, and if the elements which form it could be integrated with the conscious elements, would provide a valuable addition to consciousness, but so long as those elements are repressed the influence which they exert is unfortunate and undesirable.

The Collective Unconscious

The elements of the personal unconscious are closely related to consciousness. They are compensatory, and they are the psychic elements which are necessary for the further development of consciousness. Many of them have been conscious. They 'ought' to belong to consciousness, and they can be integrated with the conscious elements. To integrate them with the conscious elements is to 'bring them under the control of the ego', although the ego (regarded as a complex) is likely to be modified in the process. Jung claims it as his discovery that these 'personal elements' are not the only unconscious psychic elements. There are, he says, other elements in the unconscious which cannot be integrated with conscious elements in the same way (*Essays*, 237)[1], and he calls these other elements 'elements of the collective unconscious'.

---

[1] For expansion and defence of this statement see below, pp. 44, 5 : 195-7.

Personal elements in the unconscious press upon consciousness and influence conscious life because they are related to conscious elements. Since they are unconscious they also become related to elements of the collective unconscious. Complexes (that is, syntheses of psychic elements) are formed in the unconscious, and an unconscious complex may include both personal and collective elements. Jung speaks of personal elements being 'contaminated' by collective elements, but in so far as he uses 'contaminated' to suggest that there is something wrong he is simply referring to the fact that the elements are mixed together; he does not mean that 'good' personal elements have been 'infected' by 'bad' collective elements. It would probably be better to say that personal elements are 'complicated' with collective elements.[1] However we express it the implication is that the influence of personal elements on thoughts and acts is reinforced and modified by that of collective elements, and in this way the collective unconscious has influence upon consciousness through the personal unconscious so long as the latter has not been integrated with consciousness, that is so long as it exists.

If we try to form a picture of the psyche there are two slightly different models which we can use. They are both suggested by analogies drawn from historical situations. If we think of the psyche as made up of three parts, then we can use the analogy of three political states—two Great Powers and a 'buffer state' between them. We could suppose that the buffer state had historical connections with one of the Powers, and that a natural frontier ran between the buffer state and the other Power. So long as the buffer state was estranged from the first power the second could establish a foothold in it and try to exert pressure on the other through it. If the first Power were to assimilate the buffer state it would be important for it to get rid of the representatives of the second Power established in it, and when the process of assimilation was complete the two Powers would face each other across a common frontier. If, on the other hand, we are thinking of unconsciousness as a mode of the existence of psychic elements, and do not wish to think of two different modes of unconscious existence we can model the psyche according to another analogy. We could think of a city surrounded by a wilderness, and we could suppose

[1] In another context Jung equates 'contaminated by' and 'identified with' (*Essays*, 144).

that warlike tribes lived in the wilderness. We could then imagine that groups of men were exiled from the city and cast into the wilderness. These groups remain near the city, but mingle with the tribesmen and intermarry with them. Then we must suppose there is a change of heart among the rulers of the city, and they wish to recall the exiles although they do not want tribesmen within the city. The exiles have to be dissociated from the tribesmen and if this is done and they return then only tribesmen remain outside the city. Although the pictures of the psyche constructed in accordance with these analogies are different their implications for practical purposes are the same: the process of integrating the personal unconscious involves dissociating personal elements from collective elements, and it results in a state in which consciousness is in direct relation to the collective unconscious.

It is clear that the elements of the collective unconscious ought not, in Jung's view, to be treated in the same way as those of the personal unconscious. This will be explained in greater detail in Chapter 6, but it should be mentioned here that this is not always clear to the casual reader because Jung uses the same word ('assimilation') whether he is speaking of the way in which the personal unconscious should be dealt with or of that in which the collective unconscious should be dealt with. The need of a different approach is brought out by the structure of the essay (in *Essays*) 'Relations between the Ego and the Unconscious', which is divided into two parts: the first part deals with the assimilation of the personal unconscious by incorporation in consciousness, and concludes with an explanation of the failure of the same method when it is applied to the collective unconscious; the second part deals with the assimilation of the collective unconscious by the creation of a balance between it and consciousness. The same distinction between the methods applied to personal and collective elements is implicit in the assertion which Jung makes again and again, that the ego must not presume to try to control collective elements, whereas it should and must take charge of personal elements. It may be that so long as they are unconscious all psychic elements have the same status, or exist according to the same mode, but personal and collective elements must be distinguished when we consider what can, or ought to happen to them. The collective elements have not been conscious in the past, and they cannot become conscious in the same way as personal elements can, that is, they cannot[1] come under the control of the ego. The ego is known as the centre of consciousness, and it is the potential centre of the enlarged consciousness which includes both consciousness and the personal unconscious, but it is not, and cannot become, the centre of the whole psyche: it can be said of personal elements that they 'ought' to belong to consciousness, but this cannot be said of collective elements. When psychic development reaches the point at which consciousness is unequivocally faced with the collective unconscious the danger arises that the ego should try to exercise authority over the collective unconscious, treating collective elements as though they were related to it in the same way as conscious psychic elements are. If the ego does this the conscious personality is liable to be engulfed or overthrown by the unconscious. Individuation is the road along which a man must pass if he is to avoid these dangers.

Individuation

Individuation (or its equivalent)[2] brings homogeneity to the psyche. The psyche of the 'natural man' is not homogeneous because it is split into three 'parts' and because these 'parts' of the psyche do not work in harmony with one another. The personal unconscious screens the collective unconscious from consciousness, so that we are not able to take account of collective elements, and the personal elements themselves are ignored. When unconscious elements are not taken into account they interfere with and distort conscious thought and action. The fault lies in the attitude of consciousness, and the mistaken attitude is the determination to maintain the present synthesis at all costs. So long as a man takes this attitude real co-operation between conscious and unconscious elements is impossible. Analytical technique aims at changing the attitude of consciousness. If the attitude is changed it is

---

[1] But this should not be taken to mean that there are certain known and fixed psychic elements which are *always* part of the collective unconscious: it is the 'collective unconscious' which the ego can never control, and 'collective elements' are those elements which belong to it at any given time.

[2] Jung applies his terms to processes which are not so much psychological as religious, so that there is a sense in which such processes are equivalent to the psychological processes described in the same terms: on the other hand the psychotherapist's patient has no other description for what he is doing than that provided by psychology, whereas a man following some other discipline describes what he is doing in the terms proper to that discipline, and this means that the two things are only 'equivalent' in a modified sense. In a similar way it might be said by a Hindu, for example, that those who thought they worshipped Allah, or Yahweh, or some other God were really honouring a form of Vishnu, although those of whom he was speaking would not agree.

possible for the personal unconscious to be accepted and for its elements to be integrated with the conscious elements into a new and wider synthesis, but the assimilation of the personal unconscious confronts the individual with the further problem presented by the collective unconscious. Homogeneity is not reached until the whole psyche functions as a unity, but whereas personal elements can be made conscious and integrated one by one collective elements cannot, so that consciousness has to come to terms with the collective unconscious as a whole.

Since Individuation is the process of coming to terms with the unconscious it involves assimilating the personal unconscious first; but since this can be done without Individuation taking place it is not strictly part of the process of Individuation. The essential part of that process begins when consciousness is faced with the collective unconscious. So long as it is a question of integrating into consciousness those unconscious contents which 'ought' to be conscious, and which 'ought' to be directed by the ego, there is no reason why the ego should not direct the process; but when this part of the process is complete the ego is no longer competent to take charge. The ego is entirely 'on the side' of consciousness, and what is needed to direct the last part of the process is something which somehow partakes of both the conscious and unconscious parts of the psyche. This something takes the form of what Jung calls a 'living symbol'.

That which guides the process in the last stage cannot be a defined concept or a conscious construction of any sort, for if it were it would belong wholly to consciousness: at the same time it must be something of which we can be consciously aware or it would be wholly unconscious. A 'symbol' satisfies both requirements because it is the nature of a symbol to be present to consciousness, and to have a 'felt significance' without being conceptually understood. A 'symbol' in this sense is an imaginative image which is formed from representations taken from consciousness, and in which these representations are so arranged that they symbolize the nature of unconscious elements. A 'living symbol' is one which is not arbitrarily constructed by conscious thought, but which arises naturally from the encounter between consciousness and the unconscious: that is, it is an image which 'happens to us', and which appears, as it were of its own accord, in dreams or waking visions or fantasy. In *Psychological Types*, under the definition of 'symbol', Jung gives an account of the process by which the symbol enables the two parts of the psyche to be united, and in this account he assigns an important part to the ego. The ego, he says, makes the process possible by dissociating itself from both of the 'opposites' which are united in the symbol, and he implies that it becomes in some way united with the symbol itself. This is a rather different account of the role of the ego from that which he gives in later works, but even in this account it can be seen that he regards the symbol rather than the ego as the effective guide of the process (*Types*, 606–610).

So long as the 'uniting symbol' is thought of as what it is in itself (that is as no more than an imaginative image), it is necessary to suppose that the ego has a determining role: but if we think of the symbol as revealing the existence of that which it symbolizes, this unknown something can be regarded as the guide of the process and the ego can be given a less important place. In the account in *Psychological Types* Jung treats the ego as equivalent to the individual's true individuality and he treats 'the steadfastness of the ego' and 'the fixity of the individuality' as interchangeable terms, but this is not altogether compatible with the idea that the ego cannot be the centre of the whole psyche—and this idea is dominant in all Jung's later work. When the contribution of the ego is regarded as less important it is the uniting symbol which is regarded as the bearer of the true individuality of the individual, and it is this true individuality of which it is the symbol. Jung refers both to this true individuality and to the symbol as the 'Self'.[1]

In the process of Individuation the symbol is manifest to consciousness and it appears to control the whole process, so that during the process it is not possible to distinguish between the symbol and that of which it is a symbol. When the process is complete the Self is in control of the man, and so it is not the symbol, but the whole man. The 'Self', as the whole man, has the same ambiguity as 'the ego', and as the 'I' of ordinary speech: it is both the centre round which the elements of the psyche are constellated, and the whole psyche considered as a united and organized whole. The process of Individuation is the process by which the psyche is changed from an aggregate of psychic complexes (of which consciousness is one), into an organized whole with an individual character of its own: that is, it is the process by which the psyche becomes the Self. When this process is complete

---

[1] Jung is content with a small 's', but his concept of 'the self' is so central, and the term itself is so technical that I have given it a capital throughout.

the Self is the organized psyche, but is as though it were a centre which controls the whole, and within the whole the ego takes a subordinate place. Consciousness, still constellated about the ego, becomes a part of something greater, and this greater whole includes the collective unconscious as well. Neither consciousness nor the collective unconscious has assimilated the other, but both are subordinated to the whole. The collective unconscious does not become conscious, for at the most we are 'aware' of the collective elements--we do not *know* them, and we are never more than obscurely aware even of the Self.

The Self, which manifests itself in the symbol, appears to be a guide directing the process of individuation, but it is not to be thought of as coming into being for this purpose. Although the psyche lacks homogeneity at first each individual psyche still has a 'potential' unity. That is to say that there is one arrangement in which the elements of a particular psyche can be harmoniously synthetized, and the purpose of Individuation is to bring them into just this arrangement. In this sense the Self may be said to 'exist' from the beginning (cf. *Practice*, 378). It can then be spoken of as a pre-existent guide which leads men to itself, and it can be said that in order to do this it takes to itself a form (the symbol) through which it reveals itself to men. These aspects of the Self, which are reminiscent of certain Christian concepts, are further mentioned in chapter 10.

2. *The Concept of Unconscious Elements*

The purpose of this section is to lay down the principles according to which Jung's language will be analysed in later chapters when occasion arises. It includes a general discussion of the nature of unconscious elements in which it is explained what is meant by saying that they are 'conceptual constructs' and not 'things'; an examination of the idea of the 'interference' of unconscious elements with conscious life; an analysis of 'impairment of consciousness' by the loss of psychic elements to the unconscious; a further account of the distinction between 'personal' and 'collective' elements; and, finally, a restatement of Individuation in the light of the analysis carried out.

General Analysis

Although Jung talks about unconscious elements as though they were 'things', they are a very curious kind of 'thing'. They are, in principle as well as in fact, both unobservable and indefinable: Jung says: 'The great question now is: in what do these unconscious processes consist? And how are they constituted? Naturally, so long as they are unconscious, nothing can be said about them. But sometimes they manifest themselves, partly through symptoms, partly through actions, opinions, affects, fantasies, and dreams' (*Essays*, 272), and 'of what [they] consist we have no idea,' 'we may assume that they are of a psychic nature comparable to that of conscious contents, yet there is no certainty about this' (*Religion*, 67). We do not 'find' unconscious elements, but he says 'we are forced to assume' their existence, and 'We can observe only their effects' (ibid., loc cit.). In view of these assertions it demands a superhuman feat of imagination to think of them as 'things' but the difficulties disappear when it is realized that they are not 'things' but concepts.

When the statement that 'we can observe only their effects' is taken seriously the conceptual nature of unconscious elements becomes apparent. This statement has to be taken absolutely. It is not like the statement 'we can observe only the effects of a diseased liver unless we operate (when we can see the liver and its diseased state)', or 'we can observe only the effects of subterranean disturbances (volcanoes erupting, or our seismographical instruments being affected) because no one could survive the heat at the disturbances' source': unconscious elements cannot be observed because they are not the sort of thing which is observable, not because we are not able to take the steps necessary for observing them. This means that nothing that is said about unconscious elements can have any significance unless it can be understood as a statement about actual or possible observable events called 'effects of unconscious elements'. In other words, anyone who talks about unconscious elements is talking about observable 'effects', and not about unobservable psychic elements. The names of unconscious elements are not names of things, but convenient words for talking about a wide variety of acts and thoughts.

To speak of observable events as 'effects' of unconscious elements suggests the analogy of the subterranean disturbances and their effects (such as eruptions, earthquakes, and movements in scientific instruments), and this analogy is misleading. Another analogy, which is less misleading although still inadequate, is that of the way in which we refer to the stars by talking about constellations. Nobody thinks that when he talks about 'Orion' he is talking about anything but the stars which form the constellation Orion, and in a very similar way 'effects of such and such an unconscious element' can be regarded as the name of a 'constellation' of observable events. The analogy helps to show how this way of talking can be useful, because movements of the stars can be referred to very much more conveniently by using the names of constellations than they could be if the individual visual spatial relations between the stars had to be listed in every description of the sky; but, at the same time, the analogy is inadequate, because the relations to which the names of constellations refer are simple, static, visual and spatial relations and nothing else, whereas the concept of unconscious elements refers to a wide variety of complex relations between events in the present and in the past, and to probable patterns of thought and behaviour in the future.

'To construct the concept of an unconscious element' means the same thing as 'to postulate an unconscious element as the source of certain observable events'. The psychologist does this when he is confronted by events which cannot be explained in the way in which we usually explain human behaviour; that is, when he is confronted by the 'odd things' mentioned in section 1. If a usually brave man unexpectedly runs away when he sees a mouse and says, 'I am ashamed to admit it, but I am afraid of mice', then his fear of mice is an 'odd thing': if the same man suddenly turns and runs as though he were afraid, and can give no explanation to himself or to anyone else that is also an 'odd thing'. The fear of mice is psychical and the unexplained running away is physical, and either might be part of the material from which an unconscious element was constructed. As a first approximation the formula for the construction of unconscious elements might be given 'when some one behaves as we should expect him to do if a certain psychic element were present in his mind and when this element is not present, then we may speak of that person's behaviour as the effect of an unconscious element, and we give that element the same name as the conscious element which we expect to find but do not find'. This formula is correct as far as it goes, but it is too restricted, as can be seen from the following example.

Suppose that a man were consciously afraid of dogs but that his fear of dogs was 'under control': that is, he would admit if taxed that he was afraid of dogs, or (if he would not admit it to others) he would admit it to himself, and he would experience a hesitancy or nervousness when he met large dogs and would attribute this hesitancy or nervousness to the presence of dogs. This is what is meant by saying that 'the conscious element "fear of dogs" is present in the man'.

If this man were to have to pass a house where a large and aggressive dog were kept, he might take care to assure himself that the dog was chained up; he might playfully pet a small dog and say jokingly, 'I like to keep on good terms with dogs', though neither he nor his hearers would take the remark seriously; he might be fond of a picture of a large dog, and say, 'I like looking at that picture, I'm not afraid of that dog'. We could explain the behaviour described by saying that the man was afraid of dogs, and that the various things that he did were effects of his fear of dogs. According to the formula above we could construct an unconscious element 'unconscious fear of dogs' if the man did examine the house carefully, looking particularly at the chain of the dog, if he did consistently pet little dogs, if he did have affection for the picture and yet denied (to himself, as well as to others) that he was afraid of dogs, and if he was nervous in the presence of dogs but did not connect his nervousness with dogs. Yet such a pattern of behaviour would not merely be 'odd' in the sense in which the term has been applied, it would also be distinctly unusual except in certain pathological cases. The formula which limits the use of un-conscious elements to cases such as this would restrict the use of the concept too severely. Unconscious elements are more often con-structed from events which look like the *distorted* effects of a conscious element.

The behaviour patterns from which the concept 'unconscious fear of dogs' was constructed might be something like this: not being consciously afraid of dogs the man would have no reason to inspect the chain of the dog in the house which he had to pass, but he might avoid passing it—for example he might decide to cross the road, honestly saying to himself 'there is more sun on the other side' or 'there are fewer people on that side', or he might find that he had a letter to post and so make a detour in order to pass a pillar-box, as a result of which he did not have to pass the house; he might show a special affection for little dogs, not even lightly thinking of propitiating the species; he might, perhaps, go out of his way to meet large dogs (in psychological language 'compensating for his unconscious fear'); he might be fascinated by the picture of the dog, but give as his reasons for liking it the excellence of the technique, or the quality of the colour. If in addition to these patterns of overt behaviour the man had dreams in which he was driving a team of great dogs, or being rescued by a St Bernard, or in danger of being eaten by wolves, then the psychologist would have good reason to 'postulate' the existence of unconscious fear of dogs. This example shows what sort of distortion is to be expected, the man who behaves in this way is like a man who is afraid of dogs but is trying to hide the fact from other people. The difference is that the man in the example is not aware of being afraid of dogs and so he looks like a man successfully hiding his fear from himself.

It may be noticed that if we speak for a moment of unconscious elements as though they were things we could say that a man may be more successful at hiding an unconscious element from himself than from other people. Suppose a man is preparing to catch a train in order to keep an appointment and that he fusses intolerably over his preparations, saying how important it is to keep the appointment and to put up a good appearance when he does. He fusses so much, and creates so many delays that he misses the train, and fails to keep the appointment at all. He may well give the appearance of a man who does not really want to keep his appointment, and this may be the opinion of those who watch him; but it is not his own opinion, and he is sincerely and deeply distressed by his failure. In instances like this the observer is convinced that he knows the reason for the man's behaviour, but the reason which the observer assumes is not one which the man himself will or can acknowledge—even to himself.

The construction of the concept of an unconscious element is very like the construction of the concept of a constellation: it depends upon the observation of certain 'visible' features of a number of events. It can be said that there are 'odd things' which happen to us, and that it is possible to group some of them according to their resemblance to the known effects of conscious psychic elements. This establishes the existence of the concept of unconscious elements, but it does not show that it has any value. The concept only has value if the resemblance of a number of isolated items of behaviour to the effects of the same psychic element is in fact associated with other relations between those items, or with relations between them and some other observable events: the therapeutic psychologist makes an implicit claim that it is, and the justification of his claim is to be found, if it is to be found anywhere, in his therapeutic practice. No attempt is made here to argue that the claim is justified, although it is an assumption which lies behind the whole discussion: the justification of this claim is an empirical question, which can only be answered by a full evaluation of the work of analysts, and here we are only concerned to see what it is that the claim involves. If the concept of unconscious elements has the significance which psychotherapists claim that it has, then it brings to our notice at least four types of relations between observable events. Two of these types of relations are relations between 'odd' things from which unconscious elements are constructed; one relates those 'odd' things to observable events in the past; the fourth relates them to possible occurrences in the future.

The first relation between 'odd' things which is implicit in the concept of unconscious elements is that of compresence. That is to say, the presence of a sufficient number of 'odd' things which look like the effects of a (non-existent) conscious element is said to imply the presence of further 'odd' things which look like the effects of the same conscious element. In the language of psychology, if an unconscious psychic element manifests itself in, say, a man's dreams, then it will also manifest itself in his waking life in some way or another. This is both a linguistic and a heuristic principle. It is linguistic in that if a psychologist postulates the existence of an unconscious element and is then unable to find further manifestations of that element he has given the wrong name to the 'odd' things from which he constructed the unconscious element—he would say that he had made a diagnostic error: it is heuristic in that when he has postulated an unconscious element the psychologist looks for further manifestations of it. If the relation of the compresence is not in fact associated with that of 'looking like the effects of the same conscious element', then therapeutic psychology will eventually break down completely, because this principle would fail. Therapeutic psychology is still too young a discipline for there to be any certainty as to whether this is likely to happen or not. Jung gives a very simple and spectacular instance which illustrates the principle of compresence. On the evidence of a single dream, and of a short conversation with an acquaintance he told him he 'was [unconsciously] seeking his death in the mountains'. The other man laughed at the idea, but 'six months later, on the descent from a very dangerous peak, he literally stepped off into space' and was killed (*Development*, 120-2). When the psychologist constructs an unconscious element he is stating his expectation that a careful examination of the life of the man concerned, both in the present and in the future, will reveal 'odd' things having the same characteristic (i.e. which look like the effects of the same psychic element) as those from which the element was constructed.

The second relation between 'odd' things which is implicit in the concept of unconscious elements is that of interdependence. To think of many 'odd' things as dependent upon the same unconscious element is to imply that a modification of some of them reveals a modification in the unconscious element and therefore of all. Omitting the reference to the unconscious element we can say that if some of the 'odd' things which look like the effects of the same psychic element are modified, then we shall observe parallel or compensatory modifications of the other odd things which have the same characteristic. Jung applies this principle again and again: for example, he consistently expects modifications in dreams and fantasies to be accompanied by modifications in actual living, and modifications in living to be accompanied by modifications in dreams and fantasies (cf. the dream series discussed in *Alchemy*). The same principle may also be used to suggest that if a certain group of the 'effects' of an unconscious element is prevented from taking place, then its 'effects' in other ways will be intensified: thus, for example, if the man who was unconsciously afraid of dogs were to be prevented from petting small dogs, he might become more disturbed in the presence of large dogs; if the symptoms of a compulsion neurosis are forcibly stopped then other symptoms may occur, or the patient may become yet more emotionally and mentally deranged than before.

The third relation between odd things which is implicit in the concept of an unconscious element is that of having a common cause. That is, if a number of odd things are said to be the effects of the same unconscious element then they are thought to originate in the same past event or events. To say that the odd things are caused by the unconscious element is a way of speaking proper to psychology, but when he says this the psychologist proposes a further step. Having postulated the existence of an unconscious element, the psychologist hopes to discover what brought the element into existence, and if he can do this it makes no difference whether what he finds is said to be the cause of the unconscious element, or the cause of odd things which are grouped as effects of that element. In the same way, for example, we may say of certain acts of a man 'he did those things because he is selfish, and he is selfish because his mother always gave way to him as a child', and his mother giving way to him is both the cause of his selfishness and the cause of the acts which we are attempting to explain. If we think of the series 'spoiling – selfishness – acts to be explained' as a chain with three links lying on the ground, then the corresponding chain 'bitten by a dog as a child—unconscious fear of dogs—fascination by a picture of a dog' may be thought of as a similar chain, of which the centre link is buried under the ground. To think in this way is to think psychologically, but if we are talking *about* psychological language, then the unconscious element must be thought of as like a construction line which we introduce to solve a geometrical problem: the postulation of the unconscious element suggests to the psychologist what sort of event he should look for in the past as a cause of the odd things from which he constructed that element, but when that event has been found no mention of the unconscious element need occur in his explanation of the odd things. It is enough to say, for example, 'the fascination that the picture has for the man is caused by the fact that he was bitten by a dog when he was a child'. If the concept of unconscious elements has value from this point of view, then the resemblance of a number of odd things to the effects of the same psychic element is an indication that they have a common source in the past: whether or not this is so is a highly intricate empirical question which it may take centuries to answer.

The fourth relationship implicit in the concept of unconscious elements refers to probable events in the future. By postulating the existence of an unconscious element the analyst decides how he will treat his patients, and this means that he thinks that the visible relation of being like the effects of the same psychic element connects odd things with the presence or absence of certain conscious elements in a man's mind. It means this because the analyst believes, in effect, that by talking to his patient in such a way that he changes the ideas in his mind he can cause the odd things to stop happening. The 'manifestations' of unconscious fear in the life of the man whom we have considered before for example would be expected to stop if he became consciously afraid of dogs. He might continue to behave in much the same way, but if he did he would know why he was behaving in that way, and he would have conscious control over his behaviour: for instance, he would no longer have an unreasonable estimate of the artistic excellence of the picture of the dog, but would know that he liked it because the dog could not hurt him. All therapeutic practice depends upon some variant of this principle, that if odd things are rightly described (in psychological language) as the effects of a certain unconscious element, then they will cease to occur, or cease to be odd, if the man becomes aware of the conscious element of the same name in his mind.

Unconscious elements are concepts, constructed out of observable odd things occurring in a man's life. Odd things are properly described, in psychological language, as 'effects of the same unconscious element' if they have a visible likeness to the effects of the same (conscious) psychic element. If psychotherapists are right in their opinions the concept of unconscious elements is useful because odd things which share the characteristic 'being like the effects of such and such psychic element' are also related to each other in other ways (compresence and interaction), have a common relation to observable events in the past, are related to the conscious state of a man's mind, and are likely to cease to occur if the man becomes consciously aware of the psychic element whose effects they resemble. It is impossible to say with certainty whether psychotherapists are right, but the very existence of psychotherapeutic techniques suggests that they are not entirely mistaken.

So far it has been tacitly supposed that conscious psychic elements are 'things' of some sort, which are directly known to introspection. Jung appears to make this assumption: when he is talking psychologic-ally he naturally speaks of both conscious and unconscious elements as though they were things, but sometimes he discusses his language and when he does this he queries the status of unconscious elements and admits that they are conceptual constructions but he does not raise the parallel question about conscious elements. The distinction which he makes is explicit when he says of unconscious elements, 'We may assume that they are of a psychic nature comparable to that of conscious contents, yet there is no certainty about this' (*Religion*, 67), for in saying this he takes the nature of conscious psychic elements as a standard. It is clear from the analysis above that if conscious elements are 'things' Jung is mistaken; and that unconscious elements are not in the least comparable to conscious elements, because they are not things but concepts. What Jung calls an assumption (that unconscious elements are like conscious elements) would have to be understood as a linguistic rule of his science that the names of unconscious elements are to have the same grammar as the names of conscious elements have in ordinary talk. It is not clear however that conscious elements are 'things' any more than unconscious elements, and to complete the general analysis of unconscious elements it is necessary to consider what is the distinction between conscious and unconscious elements if conscious elements are not regarded as things.

If conscious psychic elements are things then an experience such as 'being afraid of this dog now' involves a transient psychic element called 'fear'. This psychic element is transient because it only exists for the duration of the experience in question. A man who is at this moment afraid of this dog Hercules may not be a man who is 'afraid of dogs', or even a man who is always or usually afraid of Hercules: Hercules may be behaving in an unusually frightening way. This supposed 'thing' called 'fear' is further thought to be observable by the man in introspection. Yet if the man gives an account (either at the time or, more probably, afterwards) of what he observes introspectively he will not describe any. 'thing' called 'fear'. He will describe the 'effects of fear'—a desire to run away, an inability to move, a trembling, shuddering or shrinking away from Hercules, the idea of being bitten or mauled by Hercules, and a general feeling of great disturbance. When effects of this kind occur we say 'I am afraid', and we may explain such effects by saying 'fear made me want to run away', 'fear made me tremble', and the like, but we might as easily say, 'the sight of the dog made me want to run away, tremble, and so on' and it looks very much as though we do not use the word 'fear' to denote any additional observable 'thing', but to mark the fact that wanting to run away, trembling, funny feeling in the stomach, and thought of being bitten are related, contemporary effects of the presence of Hercules.

Similarly, if 'being afraid of dogs' is a 'thing' it is to be thought of as an enduring psychic element, since we say that a man who is afraid of dogs is afraid of dogs all the time, whether dogs are about or not. Yet introspection does not enable us to observe 'things' called 'fear of dogs', 'hatred of John Smith' and so on, but only their effects —trying to keep out of the way of dogs, contemplating images of John Smith boiling in oil with pleasure, for examples. If a man is afraid of dogs he is likely to show signs of fear when he meets dogs, to connect the idea of such effects of fear with the idea of dogs, and (if he is honest) to answer 'yes' to the question 'are you afraid of dogs?'. In other words, 'fear of dogs' does not name a psychic 'thing' but refers to observable events which are likely to occur, in certain circumstances, in the future. It seems extremely likely that conscious elements are, after all, very much the same sort of concepts as unconscious elements have been shown to be. Nevertheless there is certainly some difference which is marked by the use of the word 'unconscious' and it is important to discover what that difference is.

There are two related ways in which conscious and unconscious elements may be distinguished. The more precise distinction can be made very clearly by an examination of the following passage from *The Concept of Mind* by Gilbert Ryle: 'The way in which a person discovers his own long-term motives is the same as the way in which he discovers those of others. The quantity and quality of the information accessible to him differs in the two enquiries, but its items are in general of the same sort. He has, it is true, a fund of recollections of his own past deeds, thoughts, fancies and feelings; and he can perform the experiments of fancying himself confronted by tasks and opportunities which have not actually occurred. He can thus base his appreciations of his own lasting inclinations on data which he lacks for his appreciations of the inclinations of others. On the other side, his appreciations of his own inclinations are unlikely to be unbiased and he is not in a favourable position to compare his own actions and reactions with those of others. In general we think that an impartial and discerning spectator is a better judge of a person's prevailing motives, as well as of his habits, abilities and weaknesses, than is that person himself, a view which is directly contrary to the theory which holds that an agent possesses a Privileged Access to the so-called springs of his own actions and is, because of that access, able and bound to discover, without inference or research, from what motives he tends to act and from what motive he acted on a particular occasion' (*Ryle*, 90, 91). This passage begs an important question.

We have already instanced a man who makes fussy and prolonged preparations for an interview, and who, as a result, misses his train and fails to keep his appointment. Suppose the impartial and discerning spectator who has watched the whole affair judges that the man's every action was directed towards not keeping the interview, and that as a result he concludes that the man's motive was not to keep the interview. The spectator says, 'you did not want to keep the interview'; the man replies, 'Nonsense, I was trying as hard as I could to make all the necessary preparations and to catch my train', and we have to ask what sort of argument this is: the answer is that it is an argument about fact, not about words. The spectator (we suppose that he is not a therapeutic psychologist) is making a statement about the man's motives which he thinks (he is neither a behaviourist nor a follower of Ryle, but an ordinary person) the man knows more about than he does: we might analyse his assertion, 'Although you say that you wanted to keep the appointment, if you were honest with me you would admit that this is not true: on the other hand, if at the moment you really do think that you wanted to keep it, that is because you have not considered the information accessible to you. If you will pause for a moment you will find that you shrink from the idea of keeping the appointment, that you feel a lightness of heart that you missed the train, and if you admit this to yourself you may find good reason why you should not have kept the appointment.' In other words, the impartial spectator does not claim that his information is conclusive, but that it suggests either that the man is lying, or that he has failed to consider all the relevant information accessible to him, and not accessible to the spectator. If the spectator is convinced that the man is being honest with him and with himself, and that all the information specially available to the man leads to the conclusion that he did want to keep the appointment, then he must say, 'Well, I'm sorry, and I was wrong: but you must admit that it looked as though you were trying to miss that train'—and if the man is also discerning he will reply, 'Yes, I see that it did'.

This example illustrates a situation which Ryle passes by. Suppose, *per impossibile*, the impartial and discerning spectator has knowledge of all the available information relevant to the situation, his own observation of the agent, and the man's recollections and fantasies. What is he to say if the inferences from the two sets of items are different? Even if Ryle is right, and the items are in general of the same sort, there is no *a priori* reason why the two sets should lead to the same conclusion. The evidence from therapeutic psychology conclusively shows that they often do not, and simple observation of ourselves and others should lead to the same conclusion. If the items of information accessible to the individual concerned really do not agree with the inference of the impartial spectator that spectator is not in a position to impute motives to him. If a man's recollections, fancies and feelings do not justify the inference that he is 'afraid of dogs', for example, no amount of information about his behaviour can do so: in our ordinary talk even if a man's overt behaviour seemed to warrant it we should

not say 'he is afraid of dogs' if his private information did not: we
should say 'he acts as though he were afraid of dogs'. In other words,
although Ryle is no doubt right in rejecting a privileged access to the
'springs of our own actions', the privileged access which he admits
that we have to our 'memories, thoughts and fancies' is more important
than he allows. In ordinary talk this privileged access is determinative
for our use of the concept of conscious psychic elements.

When the observer's inference from the overt acts of a man does
not coincide with the man's inference from the information which he
has about his ideas and fancies the concept of an unconscious psychic
element enables us to do justice to both points of view. To the observer
there may be no difference between the information from which he
infers the presence of an unconscious psychic element and the information from which he infers that a man is telling lies or is mistaken. The
choice between the two inferences depends upon what further
information he is able to get. If he gets what he thinks is an honest and
full account of the man's memories and fancyings and has to agree that
nothing in this account would normally justify the man in inferring
the presence of the motive which the observer suspects, then he will
speak of an unconscious psychic element, and he will use the concept
to relate items of information which would remain unconnected in his
mind without it: if, on the other hand, the man seems to prevaricate
he will conclude that he is lying. He will, as we have seen, be particularly satisfied if the concept which he forms of an unconscious
element enables him to relate the man's present behaviour to an event
or events in the past which the man considers irrelevant or has forgotten.

Despite psychologists and logicians the idea that conscious psychic
elements are not 'things' is not easily acceptable. The reason for this
is that we naturally, without thought, relate together the 'effects' of
a psychic element. 'Fear' seems to be a 'thing' because the dry feeling
in the throat, the running away, the sinking feeling in the stomach,
and the imaginings of this or that unpleasant experience are in some
way associated together in our minds, so that they seem to us to be
parts of a whole. From his abstracting point of view the logician
cannot do justice to the sense that these things 'belong together', and
it always seems (wrongly enough) that when he denies that 'fear' is
a 'thing' he is trying to break the bond which unites them. If this felt
'belonging together' of the effects of a psychic element is ignored,

then there is little difference between the concept of conscious and unconscious elements, because when he speaks of unconscious elements what the therapeutic psychologist does is to bring together events which we do not ordinarily regard as closely related to each other. In the case of the man unconsciously afraid of dogs, for example, the tendency to cross the road and the excessive valuation of the picture do not look like closely related events, but when the psychologist has related them and shown why he thinks they should be related, then we can see that there may be some value in regarding them as related. If the man had been consciously afraid of dogs, then the crossing the road (to keep away from the house with the dog) and the fascination of the picture ('that dog won't hurt me') would have been related by the idea of 'fear of dogs' in his mind: since he is not consciously afraid of dogs the idea 'fear of dogs' is not applied to him in his own mind, and it is not, in ordinary talk, used to relate the two events, but the idea of 'fear of dogs' is applied to the man in the psychologist's mind, and the psychologist uses it to relate the events, and he marks the difference between the two ways of relating the events through this same idea (in the man's own mind, on the one hand, and in the observer's mind on the other) by calling the man's fear of dogs 'unconscious'. If the man then accepts the psychologist's account he will have the idea of fear of dogs in his own mind, but he will think the idea and not feel it, as he would if he were consciously afraid of dogs.

The second and less precise distinction between conscious and unconscious elements follows from what has just been said. Not only do we naturally regard some events as being grouped into a bundle, we also regard the 'bundles' of events as grouped into a larger bundle which we call 'my life'. We think of this bundle as being a system having an organization which we are able to understand more or less adequately, and in order to speak about this bundle of events as an organization we speak about impressions, psychic elements and the effects of psychic elements. When we have referred our acts and thoughts to the appropriate psychic elements as effects of those elements, and have explained (if we can) the origin of the psychic elements (e.g. 'he is selfish, because his mother spoilt him as a child'), then we feel that we have shown the place of those acts and psychic elements in the organized bundle called 'my life'. The odd things from which unconscious elements are constructed are things which do not fit into this organized system and they may fail to fit for one of two reasons: they may not fit first because we do not 'feel' that they belong anywhere, as we do not 'feel' that dreams or slips of the tongue 'belong', or secondly, because although we do place them, they do not look 'right' in that place to the impartial spectator—as the fascination of the picture may seem to the spectator inexplicable when it is said to be the result of artistic evaluation. The concept of unconscious elements is used to supply a relation between events which we do not know how to relate to the rest of our life and to correct relations which we infer when they seem inadequate to the observer. It must be added that the observer may be the agent himself: the man who missed his train may say, 'Well, I certainly thought that I was trying to catch that train, but it is clear enough that it was nobody's fault but my own that I missed it.'

The conclusion is that there are two kinds of human behaviour. There are thoughts and acts which we simply and naturally 'place' in the framework of our life, and there are thoughts and acts which do not seem to belong. From the first set we construct the concept of conscious psychic elements, and we do this without any effort of thought by the natural use of our language. From the second set the psychotherapist constructs his unconscious psychic elements with considerable intellectual effort. By means of the psychic elements constructed from the first set we give an account of man's character, and broadly speaking (because we rely to a great extent upon what the man says in estimating his character) the account which the man himself gives is not very different from that of observers. By means of the psychic elements constructed from the second set we give an account of something which looks like a man's character, but the account is not an account of what we ordinarily mean when we speak of 'character', and so we need to call it an account of his 'unconscious character'. Thus, using 'attitude' to mean 'a readiness of the psyche to act or react in a certain direction', Jung says: 'It is useful, however, to distinguish between conscious and unconscious, since the presence of two attitudes is extremely frequent, the one conscious and the other unconscious' (*Types*, 527). In other words a man's behaviour is not always consistent, and some of the inconsistencies cannot be fitted into the framework of the rest of his behaviour by the ordinary use of our ordinary language. If we need to take note of them we must use the concept of unconscious elements to do so.

'Interference' and 'Impairment'

Little more needs to be said to explain what is meant by saying that unconscious elements interfere with conscious life. To begin with this is a tautology, because the odd things from which unconscious elements are constructed are 'interferences' in a man's life. The man who uses the excuse of posting a letter for going a long way round to avoid the dog is prevented in his primary intention of going the shortest way: the overvaluation of the picture is a perversion of his aesthetic judgement; missing the train interferes with the conscious purpose of keeping the appointment. Odd things may also be things that do not happen, rather than things which occur: it may be 'odd' that a man fails to do what he sets out to do; that he cannot remember a name; or that he has no interest in a subject which he expected to enthrall him. Unconscious elements are said to 'interfere' with conscious life because they are designed to enable us to talk about the things which do interfere with it; nevertheless there is something more than tautology and linguistic convenience involved.

The concept of unconscious elements does not only help the psychotherapist to talk about the odd things which interfere with a man's conscious life, it also helps him to do something about them. An unconscious element is as much the 'source' of the odd things which it relates together as 'selfishness', for example, as the source of a man's selfish behaviour. When we say that a man is 'selfish' we are not only speaking about the way he behaves and is likely to behave, we are also speaking about the sort of man that he is, and suggesting that if we could teach him not to be selfish his behaviour would improve. When the psychologist speaks of unconscious elements he is not only speaking about the odd things which happen to a man, he is also saying that the man is the sort of man in whose life such odd things are likely to happen, and that this kind of odd thing is likely to happen to that man because he is that man with his particular character. Just as we might try to change a selfish man by talking him out of his selfishness, so the psychotherapist tries to change a man by talking him out of his unconscious fear, hatred, or whatever it may be. The 'talking technique' is different, but the principle is the same, and the failures of analysts may be no different, in essence, from the failure of any one of us to persuade someone out of his selfishness. Analytical technique does not provide a more perfect method than our ordinary persuasion of others; what it provides is a method for dealing with the odd things with which we do not know how to deal without it.

The idea that conscious life is 'impaired' by the loss of psychic elements to the unconscious is more complex, and more open to criticism. The present question is not, is it a true idea? but, what does it involve? The claim involved is that when there is in a man an unconscious element he would be somehow 'better off' if that element were conscious, or, in other words, that the unconscious element 'ought' to be conscious. To understand what this means it is necessary to consider what it means to say that an unconscious element becomes conscious, and what are the marks of being 'better off' in this connection.

An unconscious element does not rise to the surface like a submarine appearing above the water. There is no 'thing' that we can watch moving from unconsciousness to consciousness, nor even a 'thing' appearing bit by bit in consciousness. The process of 'talking an unconscious element into consciousness' is the reverse of talking a man out of his selfishness. The selfish man who is persuaded out of his selfishness ceases to be selfish, but when an unconscious fear of dogs is talked into consciousness a man who was not afraid of dogs becomes a man who is afraid of dogs. At the same time the things which were called 'effects of his unconscious fear' cease to be odd and are seen to be related (through his idea of fear of dogs, as applied to himself) to the rest of his life. Suppose that John Smith is said to be unconsciously afraid of heights. This is said, we will suppose, because he frequently indulges in foolhardy behaviour, climbing into difficult places where he is in grave danger of his life. He is inclined to boast of his fearlessness, and is liable to get himself 'dared' to attempt climbing feats of one sort or another. The psychological account of this behaviour is that although he is afraid of heights he considers that it is a thing to be ashamed of and so will not admit it even to himself, and that in order to make it clear to himself and to others that he is not afraid of heights he 'overcompensates' by making dangerous excursions. If John Smith is now convinced that there is nothing to be ashamed of in being afraid of heights (so long as that fear is kept under control), and also that there really is something to be afraid of in that a fall from a height may be dangerous, then his fear of heights may become conscious. That is, he will now contemplate difficult climbs and high places with a new attitude, and he may shrink from attempting the climbs he indulged in before. The excessively daring behaviour may cease, but though he will be afraid when climbing and take more precautions there is no reason why he should not be able to overcome his (now conscious) fear, and climb just as well as he did before should occasion arise. To say that an unconscious element becomes conscious is to say that a new attitude, a new idea, a new emotion, or a new susceptibility comes into a man's mind: it is as much the creation of a conscious element as the coming into consciousness of an unconscious element.

When an unconscious element is made conscious in a man's mind then that man is said to be 'better off' than he was before. In one sense, however, he is not better but worse off: he is confronted with a problem which was not present to him before, and this may be a source of distress to him. So long as his fear of heights was unconscious John Smith did not have to overcome any shrinking when he was faced with the necessity of climbing, but after his fear had become conscious he did. A person who is unconsciously selfish supposes that his selfish behaviour is directed by reason, custom or concern for others, and it seems to him mere accident that such behaviour works to his own advantage. He may even fail to notice that his behaviour does work to his advantage or think contemptuously of the advantage which it brings. Such a person may be very irritating to live with but he has no moral problem, and if a person of this sort becomes conscious of his selfishness, then he is confronted with a serious moral problem, and has to take his self-regarding tendencies into account when deciding upon a course of action. In the sense of making his life easier for a man it is not true that he is 'better off' when unconscious elements become conscious.

Jung claims that we are better off when unconscious elements become conscious, in that consciousness is then able to develop and grow (cf. *Alchemy*, 60, 74). When consciousness is seriously impaired by the loss of elements to the unconscious, then it becomes stuck in a groove or moves round in a circle. A man ceases to have any sense of 'going somewhere', and his life becomes uninteresting and monotonous. Most of us find that there are periods in our life when no new ideas come to us, when everything that we read seems dull and uninteresting, when our hobbies and pastimes cease to keep our attention, when each day seems like the last, and when our minds repeat the old ideas which we have held for years. This is the mood

of Ecclesiastes, and it is a mood which comes to most people at one
time or another. When this mood becomes a settled frame of mind
and continues from year to year, then, according to Jung, important
psychic elements which 'ought' to be conscious have become hidden
in the unconscious, and he tells us that a settled mood of this sort is
only too common in the modern West. A man stuck in a mood of this
sort, however, is not necessarily moody or depressed, he may be full
of energy within the confined sphere of his interests. Consciousness is
impaired in this way whenever there is no advance, and this fate may
fall upon anyone: the philosopher whose system becomes fixed and
final, the scientist who cannot accept the possibility of any new experiment upsetting his theory, the business man who cannot vary the
routine of his private life, and the labourer who becomes nothing
more than an automaton have all got 'stuck', and their life has ceased
to move forward. This getting stuck, according to Jung, is due to the
unconsciousness of psychic elements.

There is no need to argue the point that development of conscious
life requires the acceptance of new ideas, new attitudes to life, or of
acquiring new susceptibilities, or new understandings of people and
things, but the idea that it is the unconsciousness of psychic elements
which impairs consciousness implies more than this. It implies that at
any given time there are certain definite ideas, attitudes, susceptibilities
or understandings which a man must accept if his conscious life is to
develop. In teaching children, this principle is generally admitted, and
it is widely realized that you cannot teach a child something too far in
advance of his present standard: the ground must be prepared before
he can accept certain facts or ideas, and the attempt to put into his
mind ideas for which he is not prepared is doomed to failure, even if
he is able to learn the answers parrot fashion. The extension of this is
that anyone at any time is only prepared for receiving certain definite
psychic elements, and that these elements and not others must find a
place in his mind before he can develop. In childhood and youth there
may be a wide choice, and it may not matter which out of many ideas,
attitudes and so on are received first, but as man gets older the choice
narrows. The psychic elements which are unconscious are those
elements which he needs in his conscious mind if his consciousness is
to develop, and if he cannot or will not accept them he cannot receive
others instead, just as a train cannot go from London to Birmingham
without travelling over the line between them.

If the idea that consciousness is impaired by the unconsciousness of certain psychic elements is true, then it refers to an empirical fact. The observable events which tend to verify it can be stated although it may be impossible so to control an experiment as to provide anything like proof. Suppose that a man is 'stuck' in the way described, and suppose that an unconscious element is constructed out of a large number of 'odd' things which occur in his life. If the idea of impairment is true we should expect to find two things: first, we should find that all the man's attempts to find new interests, or to develop his mind failed: secondly, we should find that if he could be persuaded to accept as his own the motive which the analyst attributes to him by constructing an unconscious element his life would begin to develop once more. In other words the psychotherapist's construction of an unconscious psychic element from odd things indicates what conscious idea, attitude, emotion, susceptibility or other psychic element would, if it were in the man's mind, enable his consciousness to continue to grow.

This analysis of 'impairment' will be better understood if the psychological 'explanation' of what has taken place is now given without analysis. At a certain stage in a man's development a psychic element has either been in his mind, or has been about to come into his mind. For some reason the man has rejected this element, or refused to admit it. This element has then become unconscious, but it continues to influence his life. At some later period he reaches a stage of conscious development when no other element than this can be admitted to his mind; this repressed element constitutes a 'block', and until it is accepted nothing more can be accepted. Since the man has already rejected this element he vainly looks everywhere else to find something which will interest him, or give him new ideas. The work of the analyst is to bring this necessary element to consciousness, and if he does so the man ceases to be 'stuck' and his conscious life is able to develop. In the process of further development such a man is likely to find himself confronted with real moral and theoretical problems which did not beset him while he was 'stuck'. Analysts tell us that this is the kind of thing which they find occurring in their practice.

'Personal' and 'Collective' Unconscious Elements

The analysis which has just been made of the concept of unconscious elements applies to the use of this concept in psychotherapy generally.

In relation to Jung's psychology it is an adequate analysis of what he calls personal unconscious elements, or elements of the personal unconscious, but it is inadequate to his idea of elements of the collective unconscious.

Jung says that collective elements have never been conscious, or on the verge of becoming conscious (cf. *Essays*, 118, 204); that is, they have never been attitudes of the man concerned, nor ideas in his head: nor has he ever been at a point in his development when such attitudes or ideas were necessary to the further development of his consciousness. Collective elements are not elements which 'ought' to be conscious; that is, it would not aid the development of the man's mind if the ideas and attitudes connected with them became part of his mental equipment. Jung insists that the introduction of these ideas and attitudes into consciousness would have a bad effect, and not a good one (*Essays*, 161, *et seq.*). It must, however, be understood that in saying this we are considering a single point in time, since an idea for which a man is not prepared at a certain time may later be just the idea which he must accept if his consciousness is to develop. Collective elements have not become unconscious in the course of an individual's life: that is, the fact that they are unconscious does not depend upon a conscious, personal opinion or attitude of the individual, in the way that John Smith's fear of heights may be unconscious because he thinks it cowardly to be afraid of heights. Collective elements are simply 'there', and by saying that they are 'there' Jung means that they are 'psychically effective'; and to say that they are 'psychically effective' is to say that there are observable events which actually occur from which collective elements are constructed. The main part of an analysis of the idea of collective elements involves the distinction between the things from which personal elements are constructed, on the one hand, and those from which collective elements are constructed on the other.

Collective unconscious elements are constructed from things which are, we might say, 'odd in the second degree'. In the way 'odd' is being used most human behaviour was odd in the early stages of human mental development, when human acts were thought of as individual acts each needing a separate 'explanation', and when the explanation sought was usually one which would relate the act to be explained to some agent beyond the human being involved. The development of consciousness involved the tendency to 'explain' more and more human acts by reference to the human agent and his 'character', and this tendency is expressed in the development of language. The names and concepts of conscious psychic elements enable us to relate the greater part of what a man does into a single system, and to 'explain' much of it as the result of his past history. As has been pointed out, these concepts and the idea of 'character' do not provide a full account (even in principle) of all that goes on in a man's life, and odd things which happen to a man remain unexplained. Psychotherapy looks like a further development of thought and language which will enable us to 'explain' the odd things left out of our ordinary explanations, and, as can be seen, the concept of unconscious elements is gradually entering into ordinary talk. This concept, coupled with the idea of an unconscious 'character' or 'attitude', is used to express the interrelations between odd things, and, ultimately, to relate them to the rest of a man's life (just as the concept of conscious elements and the allied idea of character is used to relate things which we do not think of as odd), and how far it is adequate to this purpose is a matter of experience. Jung, however, claims that the common psychotherapeutic use of the concept of unconscious elements does not, and cannot, enable all odd things to be explained, but that to bring them all into one system of thought further concepts are required. The further concepts which he offers us are elements of the collective unconscious.

In *Two Essays on Analytical Psychology* Jung gives the account of a particular case in illustration of the need for postulating collective unconscious elements. A young woman patient had reached an advanced stage in analytical treatment. She had been suffering from an unconscious element which originated in an emotional entanglement with her father, and by means of a 'transference' she had been able to acknowledge the attitudes involved. In effect she had taken up towards the analyst the inappropriate attitude which she had previously taken to her father, and also, in the new situation, had been able to criticize that attitude with her conscious mind: nevertheless, despite her conscious criticism of the (now more or less conscious) attitude, she remained emotionally bound to the analyst. Following hints in her dreams Jung tentatively suggested (both to himself and to her) that the continuing emotional bond might be derived not mainly from her old entanglement with her father, but rather from an even more fundamental idea which did not appear to originate in her past life at all: 'Was the urge of the unconscious perhaps only apparently reaching out towards the person,' Jung writes, 'but in a deeper sense towards a god? Could the longing for a god be a *passion* welling up from our darkest, instinctual nature, a passion unswayed by any outside influences, deeper and stronger perhaps than the love for a human person?' (*Essays*, 214). This illustration is offered as an indication of method and whether Jung's theory in this case was right does not matter. It shows how the question of constructing collective elements does not arise until everything that can be done with 'ordinary' unconscious elements (i.e. in Jung's terms 'personal unconscious elements') has been done. It also shows how the question as to the adequacy of personal elements to 'explain' is closely related to the practical efficacy of the 'explanation' constructed by means of them. Both these points are brought together in Jung's insistence that the problem of coming to terms with the collective unconscious does not arise until the personal unconscious has been integrated in consciousness.

The analogy between the use of the idea of unconscious elements and the way in which we use the idea of conscious psychic elements in ordinary talk is very close. Suppose that we are intimately concerned with someone whose behaviour is selfish: we 'explain' this behaviour to ourselves by assuming that he is a selfish man, and as we talk to him we suppose that the conscious psychic element 'selfishness' is adequate for giving an account of the behaviour in question and our talk is aimed at changing the man's attitude: but if we fail in our aim we may do well to question our assumptions. We may then find that although the man is being perfectly honest with us he does not admit that he is selfish: he does things which we call 'selfish', and which admittedly accrue to his own advantage, but he insists that he does not do them because he puts his own interest first. He can offer alternative explanations of all these things which he does, and his explanations clearly satisfy him although they seem wholly inadequate to us. In other words he cannot properly be called 'selfish' although he does behave selfishly, and we have discovered this largely because of our practical failure to talk him out of his selfishness. In a similar way, when the analyst finds that talk based upon the assumption that a certain unconscious psychic element is 'present' does not have the desired effect, as Jung found in the case cited above, he does well to question his assumption. In regard to the apparently selfish man it may be that we can find other explanations of his behaviour in terms of conscious psychic elements: we may find he is 'thoughtless', or that he is 'devoted to an ideal', for example, but if we cannot find an adequate explanation in terms of conscious elements, then his behaviour is odd, and it is material from which a psychologist might construct unconscious elements. Similarly, if the Jungian analyst cannot find adequate explanations of a man's behaviour in terms of personal unconscious elements that behaviour is 'odd in the second degree', and material from which he may construct elements of the collective unconscious.

Suppose that we use the concept of 'unconscious selfishness' to explain behaviour which we could not explain in terms of conscious elements. When we assume such an explanation we are in a similar position to that in which we assumed that the man was selfish. Using analytical technique we attempt to talk him out of his unconscious selfishness (that is, we attempt to make him consciously selfish, so that he can come to terms with his selfishness): we shall not only try to make him see that his behaviour looks selfish, even though it is not true that he is selfish; we shall also try to link up this behaviour with his dreams, his past life and other aspects of his thought and action. We may find that much of his behaviour is due to the fact that he was spoilt as a child, or that he was jealous of his father. We will suppose that up to a point we make progress with this line of talk but that we then get stuck: we find that there are other elements contributing to his selfish behaviour beside the items from his childhood that we have discovered. It turns out, say, that he regards himself as a very special person quite unlike the ordinary run of men, to whom the usual rules do not apply. This way of thinking about himself may be unconscious, but in the course of analysis it is seen to be implicit in a great part of his behaviour. Now if this special regard for himself appears to have no origin in the events of his childhood, and if we are unable to relate it to the rest of his life by means of the concept of personal unconscious elements, then this attitude and the acts and thoughts connected with it are odd things even from the point of view of the psychotherapist, and they are material for the construction of collective unconscious elements. This shows what is meant when it is said that personal elements are 'contaminated' by collective elements. There are not, originally, two sets of odd things, one of odd things and the other of 'very odd' things: there is one set of 'odd' things which, we find out in the course of time, can only be partially explained by the concept of personal elements. In very much the same way the conscious elements in the mind of the man who fussed till he missed his train (for instance the desire to keep his appointment and to put up a good appearance) might be said to have been 'contaminated' by an unconscious element—the desire not to keep the appointment. The man's behaviour was not obviously divided into 'ordinary' and 'odd', and it was only when we attempted to give an account of it in terms of conscious elements that we found that our account in those terms was not adequate.

As a final illustration, that of the demagogue brings out the force of 'collective' as applied to these 'second level' concepts of unconscious elements. The demagogue is a man who claims special value for himself or for his ideas, and this is still true when the 'special value' which he claims is that he is representative of the ordinary man, because he then regards himself as The Representative Ordinary Man. It may be that the source of his overvaluation of himself lies in his own past history but it is more likely that the personal unconscious elements involved are seriously 'contaminated' by collective elements—and if the man is a *successful* demagogue this is almost certain, because nothing in his own past history can explain the significant fact that the multitude accept him at his own overvaluation of himself and tend to build an even more grandiose picture of him than he does. The claim that the man makes for himself seems to correspond to a need in the mass of men to whom he speaks, and Jung's claim that we need a special set of concepts to deal with the behaviour of such men is partly based upon the need of concepts which will enable us to take account of the relation between the claim of the man and its acceptance by the crowd. Collective unconscious elements not only enable us to relate odd things of the second degree occurring in the life of one individual, they are concepts which can also be used to relate odd things in the life of one man to odd things in the lives of others.

In regard to individuals, collective unconscious elements can only be safely postulated when the explanatory and therapeutic power of the concept of personal elements has been exhausted, which means that the concept of collective elements is useful at a relatively late stage in a normal analysis. Nevertheless, it is possible for theoretical purposes, as the experience of the need to postulate them widens, to distinguish among odd things some which are likely to require an explanation in terms of collective elements. In practice it may be unwise to introduce collective elements as topics of conversation at an early stage of an analysis, but it may be well to notice those things in relation to which they may be useful. Manifestations of collective elements (the phrase is, of course, equivalent to 'odd things from which collective elements are constructed') for instance are often marked by the attitude which a man takes to them. They may for example be regarded as specially significant or 'numinous', and most of us have dreams at one time or another which strike us in this sort of way: they may take the form of 'larger than life' behaviour; unwonted dogmatism at inappropriate moments; excessive emotion which is apparently unreasonable; or sudden and absolute submission to an idea: but perhaps the most noticeable feature of them is their transpersonal character, that is, their wide distribution.

It can be said as a general principle that a dream-form, or an attitude, or an idea, or any other aspect of human behaviour which is both odd and widely distributed is likely to require the concept of collective elements to bring it within a system when it appears in the life of an individual. Since the distribution of such things varies in extent this means that there is a sense in which there are 'degrees' of collectivity of unconscious elements. Jung notices these 'degrees' (*Essays*, 235) but so far as I am aware they do not play a very important part in his thought. These 'degrees' arise because behaviour of a particular kind may be distributed over the members of a family, a social class, a nation, an age (e.g. the 'Enlightenment'), a civilization, or over the whole world. The assumption is that the behaviour patterns involved occur in the life of a man because he is born at a particular time, in a particular place. They may be related to his immediate environment, to his general social environment, to the natural environment common to all men, or simply to the fact that he is a man: in this way the concept of elements of the collective unconscious not only enables us to bring system to the odd things of the second degree which occur in the life of an individual, it also offers the possibility of relating such things when they occur in the lives of different individuals. This is not merely a matter of language, although it is involved in the definition of collective elements, because there are two quite different ways of deciding from what things collective elements are to be constructed; on the one hand they are things which do not 'fit' when we try to explain the whole of a man's behaviour in terms of conscious elements and in terms of elements of the personal unconscious, and on the other hand they are things which occur, in the lives of others as well, so that if it is true that the odd things of the second degree in the life of one man are closely paralleled in the lives of others it is an empirical fact. At the same time it might become a tautology if it were made a rule that nothing should be regarded as odd in the second degree (i.e. as material for the construction of collective elements) unless it were widely distributed in the lives of many individuals, and since this is, at any rate, an heuristic principle, it is not at all easy to decide whether it is, in practice, treated as a linguistic rule or not.

Since there are two ways of constructing collective unconscious elements, and so of constructing the 'collective unconscious' which is the aggregate of those elements, it is natural enough that there should be two ways of picturing the collective unconscious. Jung offers us two models of it, and the relation of his models to the two ways in which collective elements may be constructed is clear. The first model is based upon an analogy[1] with the physical body (cf. *Essays*, 235) and it is related to the construction of collective elements from the odd things in the life of an individual which are known to be odd because they cannot be related to his personal history: the second model is based upon analogy with a mountain range, and it is related to the construction of collective elements from those odd things which are found to be similar in the lives of different individuals.

According to the first model the collective unconscious is to be thought of as a basic psychic structure the same in all men, in the same way that the basic physical structure of the human body is the same in all men. When this model is in our minds, then to say that the collective unconscious is the 'same' in different individuals is to say that although each man 'has' a separate collective unconscious these separate psychic structures are very much alike, and have similar effects in the lives of the men to whom they 'belong'. In other words there are some things which happen in a man's life which are to be thought of as happening because he is a man in a particular environment and not because this or that event has occurred during his life. In so far as the things which are to be thought of in this way are instinctive actions, or processes of rational thought this is not a very remarkable conclusion, but Jung's concept of the collective unconscious

---

[1] More than analogy is involved since Jung suggests that the similarity of the unconscious in different people is related to the similarity of the neuro-physical structure.

has a very much wider application. He claims that collective elements may be constructed from (as he would say, 'manifest themselves in') dreams, ideas, desires, unusual forms of speech and action, and many other things which seem to be peculiar to the individual concerned: so that while his concept of the collective unconscious is an extension of an idea which everyone accepts—that is, the idea that there is such a thing as 'typical' human behaviour—it also involves the claim that 'typical' human behaviour is represented by far more aspects of our thought and action than we usually suppose. Further, just as instinctive action is usually regarded as due to a man's physical make-up, so Jung is ready to believe that the structure of the human body may be the ultimate source of all those things which he calls 'manifestations of the collective unconscious'.

The second model implies a different sense of 'same' when it is said that the collective unconscious is the 'same' in all men. It implies the sameness of identity. When 'same' is used in this sense the collective unconscious is thought of as being like a mountain mass from which individual peaks rise up, and according to this model the peaks represent the differing 'personal unconsciousnesses' and consciousnesses of individuals all rooted in a single psychic substructure. This means that we are to think of one collective unconscious manifesting itself in the lives of many individuals, and this is connected with the use of the concept of elements of the collective unconscious to relate things which happen in one man's life to things which happen in the lives of other men. The model suggests that we cannot expect to understand the thoughts and actions of an individual considered in isolation from others, and Jung has been true to the principle involved in that he has carried his researches into all parts of the world, and over centuries of human history.

It is difficult not to ask which of these models is correct, but the question is mistaken. Jung himself uses both. It might be possible to say that in general the first model is 'right' when we are talking about the psychology of a single individual, and the second is 'right' when we are talking about the psychology of Man, but even to say this would be to draw too sharp a distinction. The pictures suggested by these models are correct just in so far as they help us to use psychological terms correctly, but in talking psychology we are not talking about unobservable things called 'the collective unconscious', or 'unconscious elements', but about the observable thoughts and actions of men. Either picture is 'wrong' when it is taken to be a representation of something which is somehow 'there' in a man.

General Summary

This analysis has been long and somewhat complex, but the principal conclusions can be stated simply enough:

1. Psychology is concerned with the observable thoughts and actions of men and women. The language of psychotherapy is a way of talking about thought and action, and it has developed out of the language which we ordinarily use to talk about such things.

2. In ordinary talk we relate a man's thoughts and actions to each other and to his personal history by the use of the concept of conscious psychic elements. This concept is sufficient for most ordinary purposes, but it is not adequate when we want to talk about the things which have been called 'odd'. Among odd things are dreams, ideas which 'come out of the blue', and actions which are 'out of character'.

3. The psychotherapist is concerned to talk about the odd things which do not 'fit' into the system of our ordinary talk. He is able to bring them into a system by means of the concept of personal unconscious psychic elements. Jung claims that while it is possible to relate many of these odd things to the rest of a man's life and to his past history by means of the concept of personal elements, this concept is still inadequate for talking about all that a man thinks and does: that is, he claims that there are among the odd things some which fail to 'fit' when the ordinary system in terms of conscious elements is extended by the inclusion of the concept of personal unconscious elements.

4. Jung believes that the concept of collective unconscious elements makes it possible to put in order the odd things which fail to fit into the extended system. This concept does not (like that of conscious elements, and that of personal unconscious elements) relate a man's thought and action to his own history, but to the nature of man and to the history of the human race. It can, therefore, relate odd things in one man's life to the thoughts and actions of other men.

Restatement of Individuation

It is not possible to give a full account of Individuation in any other terms than those which Jung uses. Although his terms can be analysed their significance lies as much in their use as in their definition, and we understand them in so far as we can use them, not merely when we know how they are constructed. Nevertheless a brief account of Individuation may be given in the light of the analysis carried out in this chapter.

1. The assertion of the existence of the personal unconscious involves the claims that the 'natural man' (that is the man who will benefit from analysis) is one who has become content with his present conscious character and attitude, and who is not ready to receive new ideas; and that he can only develop further if he becomes aware of and makes his own certain definite ideas and attitudes of mind, and that although he may have passing thoughts and fantasies connected with such ideas he refuses to give them his attention. This assertion is, at the same time, the claim that his dreams and the other odd things which 'happen' to him look very like the effects which those ideas which could advance his development would have if he consciously held them as his own.

2. The first condition of Individuation (i.e. 'integrating the personal unconscious') is that a man should give his attention to the ideas which he has failed to think about. The first aim of analysis (that is, the first aim of the analyst's talk) is to bring the required ideas and attitudes to the man's mind, and to persuade him to think about them. If this aim is achieved it 'broadens' the man's conscious attitude but, however successful the analyst may be, odd things which cannot be related to the patient's (broadened) conscious character and attitude still occur. This is what is implied when it is said that the collective unconscious exists.

3. The second stage of analysis is concerned to bring the man to a state in which he is prepared to take the odd things which happen seriously, even though he may not be able to understand them. That is, he is to be brought into a state in which he 'accepts the collective unconscious'. The mark of this state is that he no longer rejects actions which he tends to make, or thoughts which come into his mind, just because they do not seem to fit with his conscious attitude, or because he cannot see their purpose.

4. The goal is for a man to be his full self. The assumption behind Jung's concept of the Self is that we are very much more than we know ourselves to be, and that our response to the situations in which we find ourselves is not necessarily mistaken because we do not understand it. When a man has reached this goal he may act, and affirm the

act as his own, and yet not be able to explain why he has acted as he has—although he may well discover the value of his act when it is done and its effects become clear. In so far as he uses 'I' to refer to himself as he knows himself, a man who has reached the goal will hesitate to say that such acts are the results of the decisions of what he calls 'I' since they seem to be due to something which is greater than his conscious self.

In later chapters Individuation is to be 'taken to pieces'; that is, the stages of the process are to be examined one by one. The preliminary account of the whole in this chapter is meant to ensure that we have some idea of what it is that we are taking to pieces before we begin. Since we shall also be examining piecemeal the concept of Justification by Faith, it is necessary to have a general idea of what that is as well, so for the present we put psychology on one side and turn, in the next chapter, to theology. These two chapters then stand at the beginning of the more detailed comparison between the two concepts as complete (although very condensed) accounts of the two topics with which we shall be concerned throughout the remainder of the enquiry.

*

3

JUSTIFICATION BY FAITH

JUSTIFICATION by Faith is a doctrine about the Christian way of salvation. Like Individuation the doctrine of Justification by Faith involves an account of the 'natural man' before he starts on the way, a statement of the conditions which must be fulfilled before a man can travel on the way, and descriptions of the goal of the way: the state of 'natural man' is called 'being in bondage to sin', the condition which must be fulfilled is called 'penitence' (although it is often mistakenly supposed that it is faith), and the goal is variously described as 'being in Christ', 'Christ being in us', and 'having the Spirit of Christ'. These phrases are used by St Paul, and to interpret theological language is to explain such phrases as these in terms of things which we know to go on in human life. Most of us can attach little meaning to this sort of talk, but if we are to think about the Christian answer to man's problems we have got to relate expressions of this kind to man's living, and there is some hope that psychology may help us to do so. But as well as interpreting these and similar phrases we have also to take account of the considerable difference of opinion among theologians about the relation between faith and Justification, the meaning of 'Justification', and the nature of the goal, and the discussion of these questions will be carried out in conjunction with the attempt to understand the language used.

Jung's psychology is of value for this enquiry because Jung asserts (in connection with Individuation) two things which are also involved in St Paul's account of Justification by Faith, and these two things often seem to be difficulties in the way of a proper understanding of what St Paul says. St Paul's view is that Justification depends wholly upon God and not at all upon what man does, and also that when a man is Justified something does really happen to him; and both these assertions are liable to be attenuated in a discussion of Justification by Faith. The fact that Jung in a separate field also believes that an important event happens to men through the activity of something other than their conscious selves should encourage those who believe that such ideas are of central importance for theology: for Jung claims that Individuation depends upon the action of the Self, and cannot be achieved by 'conscious willing', and he also says that when a man is Individuated his life is changed.

St Paul's view may be attenuated in various ways: for example, when faith is regarded as a condition of Justification, and is also treated as a human activity, then the initiative, which St Paul leaves wholly with God, passes to man. The tendency to think in this way about faith and Justification is a very natural one, particularly as it ministers to human pride, by suggesting that there is something which man can do to save himself. It should be enough that this is not St Paul's opinion, but anything which can be adduced in support of St Paul's view is welcome, and the parallel in Jung's psychology should not be dismissed as irrelevant. Jung claims that what St Paul says is in full accord with his experience as an analyst: on those occasions when a man does advance to 'higher consciousness' or a 'fuller life', he tells us, the advance is not the direct result of his own conscious efforts. Jung, it is true, places the initiative with what he calls 'the Self', but he also says that the Self cannot be distinguished from the 'image of God' within us. There is sufficient correspondence between the two views to give some indication that in seeking to place all the initiative in Justifying a man upon God one is not only following St Paul, but also doing justice to the facts of human experience.

Again, when it is said that Justification results in nothing but a change of status, from bondage to liberty, from death to life, and from law to grace, in other words, when it is said that we cannot expect to observe any marks of being Justified in our own lives, then Justification is not thought of as an actual human experience: or when, on the other hand, we are told that what the grace of God does is to save us from the sense of guilt, and so enable us, ourselves, to refashion our lives; then it is no longer thought of as something which happens to a man but as something which man does. If such opinions are correct, then St Paul's great phrases which describe the state of the Justified sinner amount to no more than exhortation to take up a new attitude to what goes on in our lives, and although St Paul certainly does exhort those who are Justified to do this, on the face of it, he means something more when he says that 'Christ dwelleth in you'. The difficulty is to translate phrases like 'Christ in you' into accounts of actual human experiences, and once again Jung's psychology may be of help to the theologian, because it is clear that Jung wishes to speak of an experience very like that to which St Paul refers, and that he is not able to describe it in any more illuminating terms. When a man is Individuated, Jung says, it is as though the Self and not the ego takes control of his life, and he insists that such a state is one which defies description. Like St Paul, Jung claims to be speaking of an experience which is eminently desirable, and which is also one which cannot be easily described to those who do not themselves know what it is, and this should reinforce the impression that is given by St Paul that he is referring to something which a man can observe happening in his own life.

In examining the views on Justification by Faith put forward by some theologians the two principles referred to above will be used as touchstones. In the first place, no view of Justification by Faith will be considered adequate if it treats human activity (of mind or body) as the means whereby a man is Justified; secondly, a merely formal account of what Justification is will not be regarded as sufficient.

'Justification by Faith' is, in many ways, a misleading name: because it begins to describe that to which it refers it can easily be supposed that it is an adequate description of it, whereas, as a description, it is altogether inadequate. Every word gives rise to difficulties. It is not clear what 'Justification' is, nor in what sense we are to understand 'faith', nor what is the precise relation meant by 'by'; St Paul uses 'through faith' and 'by faith' indifferently, and the eleventh article of the Church of England has 'per' in the Latin and 'by' in the English. We can begin, however, with the assertions that whatever it may be Justification is not something which men achieve, and that whatever the relation between faith and Justification faith is not the source and cause of Justification. St Paul never writes that faith Justifies, and the whole drift of his argument is based upon the assumption that it is God, and only God, who Justifies men. God Justifies, and He Justifies by or through Jesus Christ, His death and resurrection. However we are to understand 'by faith' all efficacy and initiative must be left with God.

Whatever is meant by Justification it is clear that the Justification of an individual man, John Smith, is the result of the activity of God at the time that man is Justified: God Himself Justifies, and God's action is individual and personal to John Smith. Yet this individual act of God, and all similar acts in respect of other individuals are related by St Paul to the activity of God in Jesus Christ, which took place once and for all. St Paul's thought returns again and again to the death and resurrection of Christ, and it can be argued from what he says that these two events alone are the source of the Justification of men. On the other hand, although St Paul refers exclusively to these two events, they cannot be isolated from the rest of the life of Jesus and that life must be treated as a whole, as the activity of God within human history. At the most it is possible to say that the death and resurrection of Jesus are the central events, and that they alone show the meaning and purpose of the Incarnation in its fullness; and so long as they are given this importance it is not necessary to be bound by St Paul's failure to speak of any other aspects of Jesus' life. It is through Jesus Christ that Justification is made possible for men, and it is through his birth, life, death, resurrection, and ascension into heaven, and we cannot say that any part of his life has no significance for the Justification and salvation of men. What is clearly shown by St Paul's emphasis, however, is that it is to what Jesus did that we must turn, rather than to what He taught: we are Justified, if we are Justified, by God's activity in Jesus, and not merely by listening to the precepts and parables of Jesus.

It is, perhaps, too strong to say, without any qualification, that Justification is the result of what God did in Jesus, since it would then be impossible to make any distinction between those who are Justified and those who are not. What was done is the same for all men, yet some men receive the benefits of it, and some do not. What may be said is that Justification is only made possible by what God did in Jesus. We say that it is because Jesus was born, died, rose again, and ascended into heaven that God Justifies men, in the sense that if these things had not taken place no man would be Justified. The events of the life of Jesus, which took place once, at a given time in the history of the world, continue to have their effects in the world: the influence of those events spreads out over all men. If it is asked how that influence is mediated from Palestine in the first century A.D. to all places and all times, then it is possible to collect from St Paul the answer; by the Church, by the preaching of the Gospel, and by Baptism. There is room for discussion whether all three are equally necessary, and about their relations to each other, but two comments may be made. The first is that the idea that Baptism is effective for spreading the influence of the life of Jesus to men and women cannot be dismissed as 'magical' or 'materialistic', in contrast to a more 'spiritual' mediation through the preaching of the Word, for not only does preaching equally depend upon material media but the Incarnation, if it teaches anything, teaches that God does in fact choose that His work should be done by means of material things. The second is that to say that God uses certain means is not to limit the grace of God. It may be that God does confine himself to certain clear and definite channels, but it is not for us to say that he cannot go beyond them. To say that this or that means is 'necessary' is not to bind God, but to bind man: that is, it is to insist that so far as we are able, and in so far as it depends upon us to choose, we are to make use of the channels which God has provided, and that if God sometimes, or often, uses other channels that is no reason for us to neglect those which He has taught us to use.

With the picture of the effects of God's act in Jesus mediated to individuals through the Christian Church in mind the question which has to be asked is, 'Is it in accordance with what St Paul says to regard a man's faith as the occasional cause of his Justification?' That is, is Justification to be thought of as something which is made possible by Jesus, but which must be made actual by human faith? To think in this way would be to reject the premise that all initiative must be left to God, but it is so common for men to think in this way that the question cannot be passed by without discussion. It will be shown why it is that St Paul's meaning is easily misinterpreted in this way, and what difficulties are involved in the attempt to treat faith as an occasional cause, and still leave the initiative to God: an interpretation of what St Paul says which overcomes these difficulties will then be suggested.

It is easy to suppose that in his Epistles, and especially in the Epistle to the Romans, St Paul is 'preaching faith'; to suppose, that is, that he can be presented as saying 'have faith, that you may be Justified'. Yet whatever may have been his practice on the mission field, it is certain that in his Epistles he is not preaching faith. St Paul is writing to those who already have faith, that is, to those who, having heard the Gospel and believing in Christ Jesus, are already Justified. St Paul does preach in his Epistles, but what he preaches is the way of life which is to be expected from those who are already Justified by faith. In many Epistles he is directly concerned with the practical details of that way of life; in others, and especially in Romans, he is much more concerned with what that life is, but he is never directly concerned with entering into such a life, because those to whom he writes have already entered it. St Paul's pattern of thought in this connection may be represented thus:

Justification (through faith in Christ)→ a new way of life;

but in trying to understand the doctrine of Justification by Faith one is liable to have in mind the pattern:

The Gospel + faith = Justification.

Whereas the first pattern leaves the relation between Justification and faith undefined, the second commits one to the idea that faith is a cause or a condition of Justification.

The temptation to modify St Paul's pattern in the way just shown arises largely from St Paul's own comparison between the way of faith and the way of law, or of works. St Paul deliberately sets righteousness through the works of the law beside his own conception of Justification through Faith, and although his purpose is, explicitly, to point to the contrast between the two, the juxtaposition naturally suggests a parallel as well. The pattern of righteousness through the works of the law is:

The Law + works = righteousness:

that is, first the law is declared to men, then they do what is demanded by the law, and so they come to righteousness. It is natural, but mistaken, to suppose that the contrast between the two ways implies that they involve similar patterns, so that it could be said: first the Gospel is preached to men, then men have faith in Jesus, and so they come to Justification. In other words it is natural to understand St Paul's contrast to mean that although the terms must be changed the relationship between the new terms is the same as that between the old. St Paul's contrast, however, goes very much deeper than this. If St Paul had chosen the way of law and works as a helpful analogy for the understanding of Justification by Faith, then the parallels between the two would be important, but the fact is that the comparison between the two ways was forced upon him by his personal situation. St Paul's own upbringing, and the fact that Christianity arose within Judaism, both made it inevitable that he should examine the relation between the Christian way and that of the Jews, and he makes the comparison between the way of law and the way of Justification in order to bring out the contrast between the two ways, and not to show parallels between them. He does not only wish to replace the terms 'law', 'works', and 'righteousness', but also to show that the Christian way involves a wholly different approach to the question of man's salvation.

The pattern 'The Gospel + faith = Justification' is not adequate to the thought of St Paul, but it lies behind many accounts which have been given of Justification by Faith. It has now to be shown that the difficulties which arise when this pattern is taken as a starting-point reinforce the opinion that it is the wrong pattern. The following analogy is a pictorial representation of this pattern of thought. Justification may be compared to the flowing of water from the taps in men's houses: the initial act of God, which makes Justification possible, may be represented by the source of the water supply, which provides the pressure and power necessary to bring the water into the houses: the means whereby Justification spreads out from the initial act over all men would then be represented by the system of pipes, carrying the water from the source of supply: and the 'acceptance' of Justification (i.e. faith) by the turning on of the tap. The water will not flow in the individual house unless two conditions are fulfilled: there must be pressure in the pipes, and the tap must be turned on. So, it is said, the conditions which must be fulfilled before a man is Justified are (i) that God must have acted in order to make Justification possible, and (ii) that a man must have faith.

This picture covers a great deal of the ground. The source of the Justification of many individuals is one act (or series of acts forming a single whole—the life of Jesus), and this one act makes Justification possible. The influence of this act is carried from one place and time over all the world, and so to individual men, and men must accept its influence when that influence reaches them. God's act is necessary, and it is the cause of Justification, just as the water pressure is both necessary and the true cause of the flow of water from the taps. Man's acceptance is necessary, and, at the same time, it is not the cause of Justification, just as it is necessary that the tap should be turned on, although this is not the cause of the water flowing. According to this analogy faith is a necessary condition of Justification, and this is a very general view. For examples—

Faith is 'to make room for the divine initiative' (*Dodd*, 15).

'In response to faith . . . God Himself intervenes' (*Dodd*, 73).

'The condition of salvation which is necessary on the side of man is thus, according to St. Paul, "faith"' (*Scott*, 102).

'The ground of the justifying act is God's redemptive work, and the conditioning cause is faith . . .' (*Taylor*, 48).

'So it is in virtue of this turning to Christ, this personal relation to Him begun by our act of surrender that we are justified or accounted righteous' (*Bicknell*, 259).

The last quotation shows clearly the difficulty which is implied in all forms of this view, that, temporally at least, and in relation to the individual, it is something which man does which begins his Justification · this is also shown by the first quotation, since it is said that by our preceding act we make room for the divine 'initiative', although in an important sense this must mean that the initiative has passed to us.

To treat faith as the necessary condition of Justification is, in principle, to treat it as though it were the same sort of thing as a 'work' and this attitude to faith is implicit directly it is supposed that the pattern of the Christian way is the same as that of the way of works. If the pattern is left unchanged, then faith in the new way plays the part of works in the old, and as God is presented under the old dispensation as demanding the works of the law from men before he will treat them as righteous, so, if the pattern remains unchanged, He must be presented under the new dispensation as demanding faith before He will Justify them. Yet once the law has been understood primarily in an ethical sense, it is not clear that faith is an activity different in kind from the works demanded by the law. It is usual to assume, in discussions of this kind, that the 'works of the law' are external, outward things done by men, and to contrast with such works St Paul's demand for the inward quality of faith, but by the time of St Paul any respectable view of the law already laid emphasis on its inward demands and included 'states of mind' in the works of the law. Thus if God does demand faith in the same way that the Jew supposed that he demanded works it is not possible to say that the demand for faith is a different kind of demand; at most the difference would be that under the old order of law many things were demanded, under the new order only one, faith, is required. It is true that by insisting on faith as the condition and not the source of Justification it is possible to give the impression that faith is demanded in a different sense from that in which works are demanded by the law, but it is difficult to maintain that this is so, because in the end it must be said that if works make a man righteous, this is because God has 'decreed' that it shall be so: that is, it must be said that God so fashioned mankind that those who do the works of the law, and no others, are righteous, and this is not different, in principle, from saying that God decreed that those who have faith, and no others, shall be Justified. So from every point of view the distinction between works and faith vanishes if the pattern of the new way is supposed to be the same as that of the old, and this distinction lies at the very heart of St Paul's account of Justification by Faith.

The difficulties inherent in the idea that faith is the condition of Justification, and the danger that faith will be regarded as no different from a 'work', have, of course, been seen, and attempts of various kinds have been made to escape them. The traditional way of over-coming these difficulties is the doctrine of 'prevenient grace', and it is probable that this doctrine is still implicitly accepted by most theologians, although it is not often put forward explicitly; but there is something odd about this doctrine, and it is doubtful whether it can be satisfactorily maintained. This doctrine frankly accepts the view that faith is the necessary condition of Justification (which is certainly the simplest view of the relation between faith and Justifi-cation) and, at the same time, attempts to ensure that all initiative is left to God, and the way in which this is done is by saying that although faith is necessary, to have faith is something which man cannot do without the previous help of God. Man must have faith before he can be Justified, but he can only have faith by the prevenient grace of God. This theory fits neatly enough into the analogy of the water supply: turning on the tap is a necessary condition which must be fulfilled before water will run from it, but if the tap has got stuck, so that a man cannot turn it, he is not able to fulfil this condition. Prevenient grace is like the man from the water company who comes to release the tap which is stuck in a man's house.

The doctrine of prevenient grace means that an addition must be made to the representation of Justification by Faith which lies behind the theories which are under discussion. The modified representation is:

Prevenient Grace
$$\downarrow$$
The Gospel + faith = Justification;

that is, by prevenient grace God gives man faith in the Gospel which is preached to him, and his faith in the Gospel brings about his

Justification. This can hardly be said to accord with St Paul. According to St Paul God speaks to the deplorable state of man, in which he can do nothing of himself, through the Gospel: the drastic action of the death and resurrection of God incarnate was taken by God because it was the only way in which man could be saved. The doctrine of prevenient grace, on the other hand, teaches that without this action, or, at least, apart from the Gospel, God can do something for man, in that He can give him the precious gift of faith. If God can do so much apart from the death of Jesus why should he not also give man freely of all His grace in the same way? Or it may be said, if prevenient grace is necessary before a man can receive the Gospel, then the Gospel is not enough, and the Passion of Our Lord does not make available to men all the gifts of grace and all the means of salvation, for something else is required before man can accept what has been done for him. Again, if the Gospel cannot be accepted without faith, by what means does a man accept the prevenient grace which will give him faith? The doctrine of prevenient grace complicates the simple view that faith is the condition of Justification, and yet it does not solve any of the difficulties raised by that view.

Since the attempt to treat faith as the condition of Justification leads to difficulties, and since St Paul's own account does not commit us to this view, there is good reason to think that it must be mistaken. In seeking an alternative approach another analogy may be suggested, and one lies to hand. The water supply of cities is a very man-made and formalized mechanism by which to represent the ways of God, but the thought of the flow of water brings to mind the natural flow of streams and rivers, and this too can suggest a view of the relation between Justification and faith. The river has a source, and from the heights of its source it gains the force by which it flows across the plains to the sea, passing the individual towns in the lowlands. To reach the towns the river needs channels and water-courses; without them the waters are dispersed, the force wasted and the river ceases to be a river. Yet in the natural state of a river there is no prior condition which must be fulfilled before it can flow, the channels are not there before the river flows, and they would not be cut were it not for the force of the river, derived from the source in the hills. The waters, descending to the plain, cut their own channels. Such an analogy would suggest that the influence of the one act of God in Christ, flowing out over men, produces in men the 'channels' of faith which enable it to have power in the lives of men. Anderson Scott approaches some such view as this when he says 'Paul evidently looked to the proclamation of the "word of the Lord", the message about Christ, the Gospel, as able in itself and by itself to evoke faith' (*Scott*, 99).

Despite the passage just quoted Anderson Scott's account is not a great improvement on the doctrine of prevenient grace. He still considers that the Gospel and faith combine to bring about Justification, and he still pictures a second act of God which gives faith, only he believes that this second act is also related to the Gospel. The special act of God in giving prevenient grace is replaced by 'the proclamation of the Gospel'. In effect, according to this view, the Gospel has two distinct results: on the one hand it evokes faith, and, on the other, through the faith which it has evoked it brings about Justification, and on page 86 Anderson Scott was quoted as saying that faith is the necessary condition of salvation. In contrast Anders Nygren, on a limb of the Lutheran tradition, categorically denies that faith is a condition of Justification at all, and his view is admirably represented by the analogy of the river: 'For him [Paul]', he says, 'faith is not a subjective quality which must be present in man if the gospel is to be able to show its power. It is truer to say that [a man's] faith is evidence that the gospel *has* exercised its power on him' (*Nygren*, 71) and, again, 'When one hears the gospel and is conquered by it, that is faith. Faith is not prior to the gospel and independent of it. It arises only through one's meeting with the gospel' (ibid., 78).

If the choice lies between a theory like that of Nygren and the doctrine of prevenient grace everything seems to be in favour of such a theory. This theory covers the objection that faith is liable to be thought of as a human work, since, like the doctrine of prevenient grace, it insists that faith is wrought in man by God, but, unlike that doctrine, it does not require the idea of some other, special act apart from the Gospel. It is true that such a theory still leaves open the question why it is that the Gospel evokes faith in some men and not in others, but the same difficulty applies to prevenient grace, for it may be asked why God gives that grace to some and not to others. In fact, anyone who attempts to follow the thought of St Paul must expect to find that this question remains unanswered, for it was a question of which St Paul himself was aware, and one to which he was unable to offer any satisfying solution. The only objection to this theory is that it destroys the basis of all those other theories which assume that faith is the necessary, antecedent condition of Justification, but this is only an objection for those who are committed to such a view, and reasons have been given for thinking that it was not the view of St Paul.

The view that faith and Justification are parallel effects of the work of Jesus, as the influence of what He did spreads over men, is in full accord with what St Paul says and with the way in which he writes. It explains why looking back on the lives of those who have been Justified he almost invariably couples Justification and faith, and why he does not preach faith, but the Gospel. It makes Justification wholly and utterly the work of God, which is what St Paul supposed it to be, as is shown, for example, by 'For whom he foreknew, he also fore-ordained to be conformed to the image of his Son, that he might be the first-born among many brethren: and whom he fore-ordained, them he also called: and whom he called, them he also justified: and whom he justified, them he also glorified': there is never, in St Paul, the least hint that God waits upon man; the work is God's, and it comes upon men in power. It is altogether in keeping with the thought of St Paul that faith should be regarded not as a condition of Justification, but as a mark of the fact that a man is Justified. This is further suggested in the passage in Romans where St Paul faces the question why Israel has not believed, for if faith were a necessary condition of Justification, then the answer to the question would lie to hand, and St Paul could say that the Jews did not accept the Gospel because they lacked faith; but, on the contrary, St Paul says that 'Faith cometh by hearing', and goes on to explain the failure of the Jews by something more positive than lack of faith: the Jews rejected the Gospel because they were 'a disobedient and gainsaying people'. What St Paul says, and what the view of faith as an effect of the Gospel parallel with Justification implies, is that faith and Justification mutually imply one another. If a man has faith, then he is Justified, and no man who is Justified has not faith; if a man is Justified, then he has faith, and no man has faith who is not Justified. It might be said, in modern terms, that faith is one important element in the experience of the man who is Justified, and that it is the element of that experience which is open to self-consciousness, and so patient of definition.

Faith and Justification, it has been suggested, are parallel effects of the act of God in Jesus Christ which are related by the fact that each implies the other, but nothing has yet been said about what 'faith' means. In most accounts the question 'what is faith?' is complicated by the view that has been rejected that faith is the condition, or occasional cause, of Justification. Those who hold this view are in a dilemma. Since it implies some sort of causal relation between faith and Justification it seems to require that faith should be adequate to its effect, and from this point of view the tendency is to think of faith as an important activity of man. On the other hand, in order to leave the initiative with God, faith, considered as man's contribution to his own Justification, must be minimized, and from this point of view there is a tendency to regard faith as being a mere acceptance of what God has done, and hardly an activity of man at all. Thus the conflicting tendencies to stress the importance of faith on the one hand and to regard it as the absence of activity on the other are both found in the writings of theologians, and they are sometimes found together in one book.

If the pattern 'The Gospel + Faith = Justification' is retained, and if at the same time it is insisted that Justification depends wholly upon God, then it must be shown that man's contribution (faith) is infinitesimal in comparison with that of God. The simplest way of showing this is by regarding faith as man's acceptance of what God does. That is, to say that God does all that needs to be done, and that man's part is not to do anything at all, but simply to accept. Analogies can be had in plenty. If a man walks up to me in the street and holds out a five pound note, and I take it, it can be argued that I have done nothing, and that all the 'doing' was on the side of the man who gave me the money. If a man is drowning in the sea, and a lifebelt is thrown from a passing ship, so that it lies touching his hand, and he reaches out to take it, then it would hardly be said that he had saved himself: that the drowning man should grasp the lifebelt was a necessary condition of his being saved, but his 'salvation' depended entirely upon the man in the ship who threw the lifebelt to him. Along such lines as these the idea that faith is a condition of Justification can be made to conform with St Paul's insistence that man does nothing and God everything, by a determined effort to show that 'faith' is really nothing more than man's bare acceptance of what God has done, and the following passages from Dodd illustrate the tendency to minimize faith by treating it as man's mere acceptance of what God has done: faith, Dodd says, 'is to cease from all assertion of the self, even by way of effort after righteousness' (*Dodd*, 15): it is 'an abandonment of the self to God' (ibid., 73): and 'Faith, as Paul understood it, amounts to the negation of all that is merely subjective: it is the opposite of any assertion of the human personality, whether in thought or feeling or will; it is to "stand still and see the salvation of God"' (ibid., 140). There is no doubt whatever that all these statements are extremely important assertions about the Christian life, but it is most unlikely that they correctly represent St Paul's view of faith. Dodd, in fact, is characterizing penitence, and calling it 'Faith', but the things which he says are the sort of thing which must be said about faith if it is to be regarded as the condition of Justification, and if, at the same time, man's contribution is to be regarded as infinitesimal. Dodd is unusual in pressing the idea that faith is mere acceptance to this extent, and he does not do it consistently.

'Faith', after all, does *prima facie* refer to a human attitude. To self-consciousness it is not just 'nothing', but some sort of definite attitude of mind. But once it is agreed that faith is 'something', then it becomes a very real condition which is demanded of a man before God can justify him, and once faith is accepted as a real condition, it seems that it must be a condition worthy to be compared with that of which it is a condition. Vincent Taylor comes near to the view that faith is mere acceptance when he says 'We are justified when the soul breathes its deep Amen to all that God has accomplished on its behalf' (*Taylor*, 48), but having defined a sense of faith, he continues 'A faith of this kind cannot be a means to something fictitious; it is too rich and virile' (ibid., 55); and if faith is so 'rich and virile' it can hardly be regarded as an infinitesimal contribution. Even Dodd who, as has been shown, does treat faith as mere acceptance, also writes 'It is quite clear that for Paul faith is fundamentally a trustful attitude towards God' (*Dodd*, 166), and this is surely something more than to 'cease from all assertion of self'.

Another form of the tension between the tendencies to minimize faith, on the one hand, and to stress its importance on the other, arises in connection with the nature of the attitude of mind which is involved in faith. The least that can be said is that this attitude is one of intellectual assent, but the majority of theologians (including those who would say that faith is 'mere acceptance') seem to feel that intellectual assent is not enough to be the condition of Justification. It has already been pointed out that this consideration ceases to be important if faith is not regarded as the condition of Justification, and when attempts to show that faith means more than intellectual assent have been discussed, it will be argued that, properly understood, 'intellectual assent' is the best account of faith which is available.

The scholastic teaching about the nature of faith was that the faith which makes Justification possible is 'faith informed by love'. This opinion was taken directly from St Augustine, and it was based, by him, upon the verse in Galatians 'For in Christ Jesus neither circumcision availeth anything, nor uncircumcision; but faith working through love' (R.V. margin 'wrought by love'). From this text St Augustine argues 'even Paul himself did not refer to just any kind of faith, whereby a man believes in God, but to that saving and wholly evangelic faith whose works proceed from love' (*De Fide et Opera*, par. 21; quoted *Scott*, 106). After giving this passage Anderson Scott goes on to make clear his own interpretation of it: 'The faith that saves', he says, 'is something which along with other characteristics has this which is of vital import, namely, that it attaches one moral personality to another, in the bond which is called love.' This gloss, however, is hardly a restatement of St Augustine's view, but rather an alternative to it: all that the two views have in common is that both add something to the notion of faith as it is commonly understood. Faith is belief, it is said, but something else as well: Anderson Scott's account of what that something else is goes beyond the conception of 'informed by love', and needs to be treated separately.

There are two ways in which 'faith informed by love' may be understood. Luther understood this conception of faith as one which made a further demand on man, going beyond the bare requirements of faith: that is, as a denial that man is saved by faith alone. Understood in this way the demand for 'faith informed by love' is a demand for love as well as faith. Luther is certainly right in rejecting 'faith informed by love' in this sense, as contrary to St Paul's clear implication that it is faith which is the complement of Justification, but the phrase may be understood in another sense. 'Faith informed by love' may be thought to describe a special sort of faith, which is not really faith, but a hybrid something formed of both faith and love: something which has the marks of both. This, however, is too drastic to be based upon a single text, and the text in Galatians can be understood very well in other ways. St Paul is not speaking about 'faith' in the abstract, but about the Christian life, and he is not even speaking about the beginning of that life. St Paul is speaking to those who, like himself, are

'in Christ Jesus' and for whom Justification lies in the past, and he is
looking forward to the future. In the preceding verse he has written
'We through the Spirit by faith wait for the hope of righteousness', that
is, by faith the Galatians have been Justified, and now the new life is
open before them, and, St Paul continues, one of the marks of that
new life is faith, and another is love. This is the sort of thing that
St Paul often says; the Christian, being Justified, has already begun
in faith, and now he is to continue, both in faith and love. There is
no reason to think that in this text St Paul is saying anything else than
this, and the text is evidence that he regarded faith and love as distinct
rather than anything else.

Much the same is to be said of Anderson Scott's elaboration of St
Augustine's view. He 'defines' the 'faith that saves' as having, among
other characteristics, this 'that it attaches one moral personality to
another in love': he says, again, 'the faith that saves always involves a
union of will and life between the believer and the Saviour' (*Scott*,
107, 106). That some such unity with Christ follows faith might well
be argued, but Anderson Scott clearly believes that he is showing how
'saving faith' differs in itself from other kinds of faith, and not that he is
simply speaking of its results. But in relation to Justification by Faith it
is impossible that faith should be defined by what it does, for even if
faith were the condition of Justification it would be God and not the
man's faith who brought about the union between Christ and the
faithful man. In effect what Anderson Scott has done is to define
Justification, and then say 'saving faith is a faith which leads to
Justification', and on the view (which he accepts) that faith is the
condition of Justification, this is a tautology. If, however, he were
somehow offering a new kind of faith, then he would be making it
too grand altogether, because the need of the sinner is precisely this,
that he should come close to Christ and God, and this is the great
'free gift' that God offers him. If faith is the condition on which that
gift is offered, then it can hardly itself include the gift as well.

More tempting, and very popular, is the idea suggested by an earlier
quotation from Dodd that faith is 'a trustful attitude towards God'.
Bicknell offers an extreme example of this view: faith, he says, 'involves
the looking towards God in Christ, the trustful acceptance of His free
pardon and the desire to live in fellowship with Him. . . . It demands
a venture of the will, the readiness to throw in our lot with Christ . . .'
(*Bicknell*, 259). So also, Vincent Taylor says 'The righteous mind

needed is one which is illuminated and determined by utter trust in Christ in the totality of His person and work, as Prophet, Priest, and King' (*Taylor*, 60). On the view that faith is a prerequisite of Justification this is to ask that we should run before we can walk; for if we can indeed commit ourselves in such a way before we are Justified, and if such committal is the condition, and not the fruit of Justification, then nothing is left for God to do in Justifying us. If such a deliberate and complete committal is something which men do, then man does all, and God nothing; on the other hand, if it is said that this committal is only possible by the grace of God, this is the doctrine of prevenient grace, with all its difficulties. Not only this, but if such a thorough-going self-giving is really required of man before he can come to Christ, then St Paul's assurance that we are free from the bondage of the law ceases to be much comfort: it would be no worse to be confronted with the whole law than with this demand of complete surrender. We hope that such surrender may, at last, be the fruit of Justification, but if it is the condition of Justification man has very little hope in the world.

These attempts to elaborate a sense of 'faith' which will make it a more 'worthy' complement of Justification than is 'intellectual belief' raise more difficulties than they solve. It seems likely that they arise partly from the fact that 'faith' is often used in the New Testament in the sense of putting one's trust in a person, and partly from the feeling that if faith is no more than intellectual belief it is a poor thing to rank as one of the three great 'theological virtues'. It will be argued here that although the faith which goes with Justification certainly involves trusting a person, it does not follow that it also necessarily involves trusting oneself to someone, and that since 'intellectual belief' may include belief in the truth of value judgements, as well as of statements of fact, it is not the 'poor thing' which it is sometimes said to be.

If a man trusts himself to someone else, by giving him a power of attorney over his affairs, or explicitly following his advice, for example, his action is evidence that he does trust that person. If a man has occasion to trust himself to another person, and does not do so, that is an indication that he probably does not trust him. But if one has no occasion to trust oneself to a certain person and so does not do so, this is not evidence that one does not trust him. In other words trusting oneself to someone implies trust in that person, but trust in someone does not always imply that one trusts oneself to him, since it may only mean that one would trust oneself to him if one had occasion to do so. The Christian trusts himself to Christ because he trusts Christ, and because he believes that every man has occasion to trust himself to Christ, since every man needs the help that only Christ can give him. The failure of a man to trust himself to Christ may be an indication either that he does not trust Christ or that he is not convinced of his need to trust himself to Him. Trusting Christ and trusting oneself to Him are not the same thing, and it is the experience of many Christians that although they trust Christ they do not always find it easy to trust themselves to Him. Also, although a man either trusts Christ or does not, he may trust himself to Christ in a greater or less degree. With this distinction between 'trusting' and 'trusting oneself to' in mind the question to be asked is in which sense is faith the mark of the Justified sinner?

It will usually be the case that the man who is Justified has 'faith' both in the sense of trusting Christ, and also in the sense of trusting himself to Christ, and his 'faith' will be called greater or less according to whether he trusts himself to Christ in a greater or less degree; and the greater the extent to which a man trusts himself to Christ, the more fully he will lead the Christian life. St Paul, however, never treats 'good living' as a mark of being Justified: he says the man who is Justified ought to live a 'good' life, but he is clearly prepared to admit that such a man does not always do so. St Paul exhorts the Justified Christian to conform his life to the will of God, but he does not consider that the grossest sins show that a man is not Justified, and for him such sins are only made more heinous and damnable because the man is 'in Christ'. Thus for St Paul the extent to which a man trusts himself to Christ is irrelevant to the question whether or not he is Justified, and this means that the faith which is an inevitable con-comitant of Justification cannot be 'faith' in the sense of trusting oneself to Christ, because such faith admits of degrees; being Justified, and so trusting Christ, the Christian can, if he will, trust himself more and more to Christ, and grow in 'faith', and in this sense of faith the Christian life ought to be a continual growth in it; but St Paul says that every man who is Justified has faith already, and this 'faith' must be faith in the sense of trusting Christ. Trusting Christ is a matter of 'intellectual belief', but it is a belief concerned more with value judgements than with questions of fact.

To trust in someone is to believe certain things about him, in effect it is to believe that he is trustworthy. Faith in this sense is not merely the belief that Christ is God, that He lived and died at a certain time, that He rose from the dead, and that He lives for evermore: nor is it merely the belief that the death and resurrection of Jesus Christ were great acts of God for the redemption of the world; faith in Christ is all this, but it is more as well. If this were all, then the objections of those who say that faith must be more than mere intellectual belief would have force, because faith would be a matter of believing certain statements of fact. In the sense of trusting Christ (without necessarily trusting oneself to Christ), however, faith is intellectual belief in judgements about the value and importance of Christ now. Faith is belief that Christ has supreme value and significance for the individual here and now, and that if one does trust oneself to Him one has power to live a true life, and to gain a happiness that cannot be gained in any other way. This is 'intellectual belief', but it cannot be dismissed as 'mere intellectual belief'.

Two parts of the enquiry into Justification by Faith have now been carried out. The relation between faith and Justification has been examined, and also the meaning of 'faith'. The conclusions so far reached are:

1. 'Justification by Faith' is a misleading name for the doctrine, and it should not be taken as an account of what happens. Justification by Faith may be analysed into two parts, one called 'Justification', and the other 'faith', but these are abstractions from a whole; they are not successive events, but two aspects of one event. Faith is not the condition of Justification, but a mark of the fact that a man has been Justified.

2. Faith, as the mark of the fact that a man has been justified, is not the committal of oneself to Christ, but the 'intellectual belief' that Christ has supreme value, and that committing oneself to Him is the very best thing that one can do: yet whether or not a man does commit himself to Christ may be a very good indication whether or not he has faith in this sense. Faith, in this sense, is the condition which must be fulfilled before a man can, or will, trust himself to Christ, and to say that a man 'grows in faith' means that he more and more expresses his faith by relying upon Christ.

Two questions remain for discussion. The first is whether there is a condition which must be fulfilled before a man is Justified, and the second is what is the nature of Justification.

It is certain that there is a condition of some sort which must be fulfilled before a man is Justified, because not everyone who is baptized accepts the teaching of the Church, and not everyone who hears the Gospel seeks baptism. Christ's work of redemption is effective for all, and redemption is offered to all to whom the Gospel is preached, yet some who hear the Gospel are not Justified. To say that there is a conditio 1 of Justification is to say that there is some reason why some men are Justified and others are not, and at first sight it seems that the condition is either one that a man must fulfil, or else that it is that God should choose to Justify a particular man (and not others). Instead of this 'either, or', however, St Paul says that both these things are true.

In chapters 9 and 11 of the Epistle to the Romans, St Paul answers the question why it is that the Jews have not accepted Christ. He says that it is as though ('what if' is his own phrase) God chose that there should be 'vessels of wrath' as well as 'vessels of mercy', and that, if this is so, man has no grounds for complaint, because the creature may not challenge the ways of his Creator. In these chapters St Paul is setting the problem in the context of God's supreme government of the world, and examining it 'sub specie aeternitatis', and from this point of view no other answer is possible. At the same time this is not St Paul's only point of view, and in chapters 1 and 10 he is also concerned with man's refusal of God, and although in these chapters St Paul discusses man's refusal of God in general terms, what he says is equally applicable to the particular instance of man's refusal of Christ. In chapter 1 he says that the Gentiles 'refused to have God in their knowledge', and in chapter 10 he says that the Jews were a 'disobedient and gainsaying people'; in other words, whatever the truth may be 'sub specie aeternitatis', from the human point of view God's grace fails because men refuse it. If men hear the Gospel and are not Justified, it is because they will not accept what God offers them, and the condition which must be fulfilled before a man is Justified is that he should be ready to accept God's gift, and this means that he must be penitent.

There are three related reasons why a man may refuse the gift which God offers, and they are the same as those which may make a man refuse any offer of help. A man may refuse an offer of help because he thinks that he is in no need, because he thinks that he can help himself, or because he thinks that the help which is offered is inadequate; the last of these reasons, however, is relative. A drowning man clutches at a straw, but a man who is only a little tired of swimming will refuse straws as inadequate—in other words, if a man is aware of a great need he will not reject any offer of help as inadequate until he has, at least, given it a trial. If a man refuses God's offer of help it is either because he is not aware of the extent of his need, or because he believes that he knows a better way of coping with his need. Thus St Paul says that the Gentiles 'professed themselves to be wise', and that the Jews 'sought to establish their own righteousness', which is to say that the refusal of God's gift by Jews and Gentiles alike was due to the fact that each had confidence in themselves, and in a way which they knew apart from the Gospel. The condition that must be fulfilled before a man is Justified is that he must have no confidence in himself, or in any way of salvation other than that which is in Christ Jesus, and this is for a man to be penitent.

Dodd is quite right when he says that the condition of Justification is 'acknowledging our complete insufficiency for any of the high ends of life', and that a man should 'cease from all assertion of self, even by way of effort after righteousness', and he is also right when he says that this 'makes room for the divine initiative' (*Dodd*, 15), but it is wrong to call this 'faith', because it is not faith but penitence. As Luther says, 'here it is vital that our own righteousness and wisdom be brought to nought and rooted out of our hearts' (quoted *Nygren*, 15, 16), and until this has been done a man cannot accept the grace that God offers him. Since Justification is offered as the answer to man's need it will only be accepted by those who recognize that need: it follows inevitably that in order to be Justified a man must first acknowledge that he has not yet 'arrived'; that is, that there is a better and happier way of life which is not yet his, but which could be his, and he must then acknowledge that his own efforts to live such a life are intrinsically inadequate, and that if he relies upon himself he has no hope of achieving his aim: finally he must reject all ways of wisdom or righteousness offered by men, in order to be able to accept the new way offered by God. A man who acknowledges his need and his inadequacy, and who rejects all human roads is a man who is penitent, and a man must be penitent if he is going to accept God's gift: this is not a theological dogma, but a logical consequence of what Justification is believed to be. Penitence is the condition of Justification, and although a man may be brought to penitence by the Gospel, there are other means to the same end.

The Gospel may bring a man to penitence, but this power which it has must be distinguished from its power to bring men to Justification. The Gospel shares the power to bring penitence with other things, but it does not share the power to bring Justification with anything. In so far as the life of Jesus is effective to bring men to penitence it is merely exemplary, and from this point of view the function of the Gospel is to set before us an ideal, with which we may contrast our own life. The Gospel may be more effective in this respect than other things, but in principle this function is no different from that of any ideal. The decalogue, the life of Buddha or the maxims of Marcus Aurelius may, like the Gospel, cause a man to be discontented with his own way of life, and so bring him to penitence, and there are many ways in which God leads men to such a state of discontent. Although in Christian societies it is the Gospel which most often brings penitence about it is not in this way that it is unique; the Gospel is unique because although man's need may be shown to him in other ways, it is only through the Gospel that God answers his need, and it is only in accepting what God offers in the Gospel that a man is Justified.

The condition of Justification is penitence, which means to have no confidence in oneself: in other words, in order to be Justified a man must give up what he believes to be his wisdom and his righteousness. The condition of Individuation is that a man must acknowledge the place and importance of his 'unconscious'; that is, that he must give serious attention to the odd things in his life, even if he regards them as evil. At first sight these two conditions seem to be wholly different, but they have an important feature in common. To be penitent is to realize that what one believes to be right is valueless, in that by following one's own way one will not come to salvation: to take the 'unconscious' seriously is to realize that what one thinks is evil may have value, and this also means that one realizes that it is not enough to rely upon one's own judgement of what is right. Thus the condition of Justification and the condition of Individuation both involve a changed attitude to the distinction between right and wrong, good and evil. This parallel is further examined in later chapters. Also, in both systems, the change of attitude is regarded as all that a man can do by his own efforts: if a man has done this, then according to St Paul he must leave it to God to Justify him, and according to Jung he must leave it to the Self to take charge.

St Paul's teaching about Justification by Faith has given rise to many views and opinions about the relation between faith and Justification, and about the nature of faith. The meaning of 'Justification' is equally open to question. To a great extent the difficulties which arise in connection with Justification are the result of asking the wrong questions, but since these questions are raised by the language which St Paul uses it is inevitable that they should be asked. The word which reaches us in English as 'to justify' is more accurately translated 'to declare righteous', and what St Paul says is that we are 'declared righteous by faith', and that this 'declaring righteous' is God's act, rooted in His activity in Jesus Christ. St Paul uses the word for 'declare righteous' repeatedly and consistently, and also, in a few passages, he says that faith is 'reckoned for righteousness'. In the face of this language it is natural that attention should be concentrated on the relation between Justification and righteousness, rather than on the actual nature of Justification. So the controversy ranges between the extreme position, on the one side, of those who emphasize that the Justified Christian is only accounted righteous, and is not in any sense really righteous; and that, on the other side, of those who insist that God cannot account a man righteous unless he is really righteous. The result is that attention is taken from the question 'What is Justification?' and concentrated on the question 'In what way can the man who is Justified be "reckoned as righteous"?' or, in other words, 'in what sense is Justification as good as righteousness?' It is as though, confronted with a new invention, men were to haggle over its value before asking what it was for. Something, St Paul says, has happened to men, and, he adds, in effect, this something which has happened is as good as 'becoming righteous'; theologians then assume that 'being as good as righteousness' is a full account of what has happened, and argue this way and that about what the phrase means. It is no wonder that they become involved in difficulties. The proper thing is to ask first what it is that has happened, and then to ask in what sense this particular thing can be reckoned for righteousness. To begin with the relationship between an unknown something and righteousness is to begin in mid-air, but because this is the usual place to begin it is the place from which an examination of theories about Justification must begin, and the best that can be done is to bear in mind that this is unfortunate.

The formalist Lutheran teaching on Justification is the direct, logical consequence of the mistaken approach which is practically universal, for if all that can be said about Justification is that it is a 'declaration of righteousness', or 'imputed righteousness', or 'as good as righteousness', then it is hardly possible to reach anything more than a formal view of it. Approaching from this point of view it is inevitable, if one wishes to be logical, that one should stress the legal and formal aspect of the terms which St Paul uses, and such logic gives rise to the Lutheran position. First, faith is accepted as meaning 'intellectual belief', and then Justification is understood in the most formal way possible so that intellectual belief on the part of man leads to a formal declaration on the part of God. Thus the *Formula Concordiae* of 1580 explains that 'Christ's obedience is imputed to us for righteousness, and that this righteousness, offered to us through the Gospel and in the sacraments by the Holy Spirit, is applied and apprehended by faith' (quoted *Taylor*, 57). It is a further consequence of this formal approach that, strictly speaking, the Lutherans are indifferent to any effects which Justification may have upon the life of the individual, for if it is a sufficient definition of 'Justification' to say that it is 'as good as righteousness', then there can be no place for any form of actual righteousness. To suppose, even, that Justification leads to righteousness, is to imply that righteousness is really more desirable than Justification; that is, that Justification is not, after all, as good as righteousness. So Nygren, for example, is at pains to deny that Justification leads to righteousness in any sense: 'Can one not say', he begins, 'that Christ gives him the power to keep the law, so that he can really stand before God as righteous in this way?' and he dismisses the suggestion 'to speak in such a way . . . is nothing less than again to bring in the law, by a back door, as a way of salvation' (*Nygren*, 303).

Despite the logic it is hard to feel that the Lutheran opinion is altogether adequate to St Paul's thought, and it is fairly safe to say that no one outside the Lutheran tradition thinks that it is. Vincent Taylor, for instance, argues strongly against such a view: 'Since it is not a commodity, but a personal state, righteousness cannot be transferred from the account of one person to another' (*Taylor*, 57). So long as one sticks to logic it is easy to dismiss this criticism, since it misses the point that Justification is not, and is specifically not, righteousness, and that to suppose that it is is to reject the concept of Justification as it is presented by St Paul. Nevertheless, this insistence is important, because it expresses the inevitable reaction against the purely formal view of the Lutherans, in that it is the insistence that Justification must really be something and not just a name. In this respect it is a well-founded criticism, but it is mistaken in so far as Vincent Taylor demands that the thing which has happened must be thought of as, in some sense, bringing righteousness. Once it has been admitted that there is a valid sense of righteousness in which the Justified sinner may be said to be righteous, then there seems little reason for not accepting the post-Tridentine position of the Roman Church. If one attributes any sort of righteousness to the Justified sinner (as such), if Justification is not only 'as good as' righteousness, but in some way righteousness itself, then it is difficult to see why Justification should not involve a full righteousness. The formula of Trent provides the opposite extreme to the position of Luther, and this is not surprising since it was designed explicitly to exclude Lutheranism: 'Justification', it is decreed, 'is not the remission of sins alone, but also the sanctification and renewal of the inward man by the voluntary reception of the grace and gifts, by which man from being unjust becomes just' (vi, 7). This is to regard 'Justification' as an inclusive term, covering the whole of the Christian life, not only in its inception, but in its whole sequence and development.[1] It is, in fact, to use 'Justification' as Anderson Scott uses 'salvation', of which he says 'The conception of Salvation provides both a centre and a framework for all the religious

---

[1] As with all theological formulae that have been extant for any length of time the formula of Trent has been variously interpreted by theologians. It is understood here according to what Newman calls the 'high-Roman view', which he states succinctly, 'We are justified directly and solely *upon* our holiness and works wrought in us *through* Christ's merits *by* the Spirit', and he adds, 'It is no point of faith with the Roman Catholics to take the view which I have called Roman' (Newman, 348) An alternative view which Newman says is allowed in the Roman Church is that 'the presence of the Holy Ghost Himself, who is in the righteous, [is] the formal cause of their inherent righteousness', and he points out that this is to make a distinction 'between the divinely imparted principle of righteousness, even after it has been imparted, and the actual righteousness or renewed state of our minds' (ibid, 350, 351). Understood in this second way the Tridentine formula expresses precisely the conclusion to which we come in the text, and the only criticism which we would make is that it involves a revaluation of the word 'just', which is usually taken to mean the possession of an inherent righteousness of our own. The formula of Trent is acceptable if 'just' is taken to mean nothing else but 'one who is justified', but to understand the word in this way seems likely to lead to a confusion which we have tried to avoid. It may be added that in English it might be possible to make a useful distinction between 'just' (to mean being justified) and 'righteous', but that Latin, in which the Roman doctrine is formulated, lacks the advantage of having these two words— the natural translation of 'justitia' is 'righteousness', and the natural reading of the formula leads to the 'high-Roman view'.

and ethical ideas which have real importance in Christianity as St Paul understood it' (*Scott*, vii). Unfortunately, this cannot be dismissed as a mere quarrel about words, because Justification by Faith occupies so central and important a position in St Paul's thought, and in Christianity generally, that it must be taken that anyone who professes to define 'Justification' is offering a definition of that word as used by St Paul, and no one can be allowed to suggest that it would be better to use the word in some other sense.

As a definition of the word used by St Paul (which was not, of course, 'to justify' but δικαιοῦν) the formula of Trent must be dismissed, as it is by the consensus of non-Roman Catholic opinion, as a misuse of words. Justification as defined by Trent is not the meaning of the Greek word, which cannot mean 'to make righteous'. The word does not imply that the man to whom it refers is not righteous, but, on the other hand, it does not suggest that he is, because it does not refer to a man's actual state at all: it simply means that, whether he is righteous or not, a man is declared righteous (cf. *Sanday*, 30). The decree of Trent is mistaken on linguistic grounds, and it is also false to what St Paul says about Justification, because nothing could be clearer than that for St Paul the Christian is already Justified, even though he may be far from any actual righteousness. The formula of Trent implies that Justification is not complete until a man has come 'from being unjust to being just', but for St Paul it is something which has already happened to men who are not just, and for him it does not wait upon the 'sanctification and renewal of the inward man'. On the one hand St Paul makes it clear that those to whom he is writing have been Justified, because this is the basis of all his arguments, and it is because they are Justified that he tells them that they need no help from the Jewish Law, and it is because they are Justified that they can hope for the glory which shall be revealed. On the other hand, he tells the same people (and for the same reason) that they must make real ethical effort, and strive towards the goal of a full life according to the spirit of God. In other words, St Paul declares that men are Justified when they are still far from the goal, whereas the Tridentine formula claims that men are not Justified until the goal is reached.

Vincent Taylor, who, as it has been noticed, demands something which can be called 'righteousness' as the mark of Justification, does not find the formula of Trent satisfactory. He admits that full righteousness cannot be required before a man is said to be justified, and he suggests that the Justified sinner has something that he calls a 'germ' of righteousness. In this way he tries to hold to his own opinion that God cannot declare a man righteous if that man is not righteous in any way, and also to do justice to St Paul's assurance that this is precisely what God does do. Vincent Taylor suggests that these two views can be reconciled by supposing that this 'germ' of righteousness is really righteousness, and yet not fully righteousness: 'The believer', he says, 'is pronounced righteous because, in virtue of his faith resting upon the work of Christ, he really is righteous in mind and in purpose, although not yet in achievement' (*Taylor*, 58, 9). This, he says, is in full agreement with the opinion which he quotes from Dodd, 'He is righteous, in a fresh sense of the word; in a sense in which righteousness is no longer, so to say, quantitative, but qualitative' (ibid., 59), and he also insists that the Justified man must be righteous in 'a reputable sense of the term' (ibid., 57). Thus Vincent Taylor's aim is to offer a sense of 'righteousness' such that it is possible to say that the Justified sinner is 'righteous' (in that sense) without saying that he is fully righteous, and, at the same time, to be able to say that if a man is righteous (in this sense) God's decree that he is righteous (in the proper sense) is not a legal fiction but a valid statement of fact. It is by no means clear that he succeeds in this aim, nor whether anybody could succeed in it, but the aim itself is misconceived. To say that Justification is 'as good as righteousness', which represents St Paul's view, is to deny that it is righteousness—even 'righteousness of mind and purpose'.

By offering a 'fresh sense' of righteousness, Vincent Taylor attempts to retain the customary attitude to righteousness, while changing its connotation. If the 'germ' of righteousness is something which really does merit the approval which we think of as due to righteousness, then all sense of 'imputing' or 'accounting' righteousness to the Justified sinner has disappeared, God's judgement that he is righteous is the proper and rational judgement upon him, and there is no mystery left. Vincent Taylor's view offers further difficulties as well. If it were correct, then Justification would no longer be a 'free gift' spreading out from Christ, but a new attitude of mind on the part of man, involving a change from unrighteousness to 'righteousness of mind and purpose', and in order to retain the idea of God's initiative it must then be said that such an attitude cannot be achieved without the 'free gift' of grace through Jesus Christ. Thus Vincent Taylor says, 'the righteousness springs from faith as it is related to its object; the object gives to it its character as the condition of righteousness' (ibid., 58), and 'man's relationship of trusting surrender is not only to God, but to God in the activity of His redeeming work . . . God who in Christ does for us what we cannot do for ourselves and thus creates in us a righteous mind for which we can claim no credit' (ibid., 60). But the first of these passages is misleading: to do justice to St Paul it ought to mean that the 'object' of faith is active and effective to bring men to Justification—as when a coach is coupled to an engine, the 'object' of the act of coupling provides the motive power which makes the coach move—yet all that is said, and all that can be accepted without further argument, is that faith is only effective if it has the right object. In other words the righteousness springs from faith, not the object, only faith is not effective unless the object is right, and this places the initiative on man and not God. The second passage shows how little Vincent Taylor's view differs from that of Trent. There is a direct parallel between 'creating in us a righteous mind' and 'the sanctification and renewal of the inward man', and again, between 'God who does for us what we cannot do' and 'the voluntary reception of grace and gifts'; and the only important difference is that Vincent Taylor is content with less than the fathers of Trent. Trent requires a righteousness both of purpose and achievement (through God), Vincent Taylor asks only for righteousness of purpose. In the end to hold the 'germ' theory is not to demand a different sort of righteousness, but to accept something less which is accounted equal to something more, and instead of having the best of both sides it has the worst. It suffers from all the difficulties involved in supposing that Justification means to 'make righteous' and also from the difficulties involved in thinking that God is content with a token instead of the real thing.

The 'germ' theory appears to be little more than an unsatisfactory watering down of the Roman Catholic position. It attempts to overcome the fault of that position—that it makes Justification mean 'righteousness'—but in doing so it makes Justification mean less than righteousness, and does not allow full force to 'accounted' in the phrase 'accounted righteous'. Nygren offers a modification of the Lutheran position by which he attempts to overcome the disadvantage of that position that Justification is thought of as a purely formal judgement on the part of God which has no apparent effects upon the individual who is Justified; and the result makes very strange reading. On the one hand, Nygren is at pains to insist that Justification is very real, and that it is something which has happened to man, and not merely a formal decree, and from this point of view no words are too strong for him to describe the new state of 'being Justified', but, on the other hand, he emphasizes that this state is not in any sense a change of character, and that the Justified sinner does not possess anything which could be remotely described as 'righteousness'. The result is similar to the effect produced by a man who boasts about what he could do, and what he says that he has done, but whose performances never come up to his promises. Nygren makes it clear that he considers that when men are justified something has happened to them, and that this something is real and important, but he insists, at the same time, that what has happened is not a change of character but a change of status: 'for him [i.e. St Paul]', he says, 'justification is not something which occurs within the soul' (*Nygren*, 18); '[a man's] righteousness is an objective relationship, proffered to us by Christ into which we are received by faith in Him' (ibid., 75); and, 'To live in Christ means—(1) to be free from the wrath of God (chap. 5); (2) to be free from sin (chap. 6); (3) to be free from the law (chap. 7); (4) to be free from death (chap. 8)' (ibid., 32: the references are, of course, to the Epistle to the Romans). This emphasis upon a new status, rather than upon a change of character, is a very important one, but what is to be noticed is that Nygren's account of the new status is predominantly negative. St Paul's phrase 'being in Christ' is an altogether positive idea, but according to Nygren what it means can be set out by a series of negatives: it is not Christ, but wrath, sin, law and death which fill the picture, and the new state into which the Justified sinner is brought is not a new relationship to God so much as a new relationship to the inimical forces by which a man is surrounded in the world. This negative emphasis runs through Nygren's whole commentary, but although it is undoubtedly true that the Justified sinner has a new status, his new status is conceived of by St Paul as something positive, and involving first of all a new relationship to God Himself.

Dodd also regards Justification as a change of status, and unlike Nygren he makes it clear that the change of status, as he conceives it, involves a change in man's relationship with God. Unfortunately, in the last analysis, the view which Dodd sets forward takes the edge off St Paul's determination to give all responsibility for a man's salvation to God. In the end, the change of status which Dodd speaks of is a change of attitude on the part of man. It is true that he begins by saying that 'God has removed the barrier of guilt', but when he has said this he explains that what effects Justification is not that God has done this, but that a man comes to believe that He has (*Dodd*, 58). It is a man's belief which is really effective, and Dodd insists that what men require, and what Justification gives them, is freedom from that 'sense of sin' which 'daunts our courage, saps our confidence, and frustrates our effort' (ibid., 145). Once again, the new status is defined in negative terms, and this time in those psychological terms which Nygren repeatedly rejects. Dodd also speaks more positively as well, but his more positive approach is still marred by the fact that he approaches the problem from the side of man: looking forward from Justification he says: 'If we now think of the "sinful body" as a self organized out of bad and disharmonious sentiments, "to crush the sinful body" will be to disintegrate these bad sentiments, and so destroy the self as built out of them, in preparation for the organization of a new self about the centre supplied by Christ to the believer' (ibid., 91). This is excellent in many ways, but the part ascribed to Christ is too 'static'; He is simply 'there', waiting for the man who is Justified to rearrange his own character round him.

All the opinions which have been briefly reviewed have something to teach about the nature of Justification. It is by taking from each the positive truth which it is intended to defend that it is possible to come to a clearer understanding of what St Paul himself is saying. The demand for righteousness, and for a germ of righteousness, in the Tridentine formula on the one hand and in the view of Vincent Taylor on the other, is the demand that Justification should be regarded as something which can be 'seen' happening in a man's life, and this demand is made against all theories which treat Justification as a formal decree on the part of God which has no visible effects. The insistence that Justification is a change of status and not a change in the character of a man, on the other hand, is the insistence that what has happened is not a psychological shift of attitude upon the part of man, and it is made against all mere 'exemplary' theories of atonement, which suggest that all Jesus did was to reveal new aspects of God, which men could not know before. Finally, the theory suggested by Dodd draws attention to the fact that the change of status involves a new relationship to God Himself.

It has been said above that Dodd comes too near to regarding the new relationship established between a man and God as primarily consisting in a new attitude on the part of the man, and apart from the expression 'by faith' there is nothing in St Paul from which this can be argued. The Pauline teaching is too dynamic to fit such a view, and St Paul thinks of the Gospel which he preaches as an actual power of God, let loose in the world. St Paul clearly believes that when a man is Justified God's power has come into the world, and entered into the man, and that it works powerfully in him for his salvation. St Paul speaks of this new power, living and working within a man as 'Christ', or 'the Spirit of Christ' or 'the Spirit of God', or, simply, as 'the Spirit' and this last is sometimes a source of misunderstanding because it is easy to assimilate St Paul's use of 'the Spirit' to our own sense of the 'spirit' as a human attribute. St Paul rarely uses 'spirit' in the sense of the spirit of a man, and for him 'The Spirit' is the power of God which has come within a man, and it is the presence of this power which is the mark of Justification. The Christian life is new not because something in a man's character has been changed but because something has been introduced into his life which was not there before: the Christian 'has the Spirit', and he is 'in Christ', and it is this which marks him out as different from the Jews or Gentiles among whom he lives. It is not that a man must reorganize himself, but that Christ is in the man, and active in him, and that Christ will reform him if He is allowed to do so. If the Justified man does nothing to interfere with the work of the Spirit in him, then the Spirit (which is, 'the Spirit of Christ') will take charge of him, and Himself bring about the new organization within the man.

It is in connection with the idea of the Spirit as a power within a man that the psychology of Jung may be more illuminating than many commentators on St Paul. The theologian is often tempted to interpret St Paul's language in terms of common human experience. From this point of view, formal accounts of Justification amount to saying 'Justification as such is not a new kind of life, but a new way of describing and thinking about the life which men normally live'; and the identification of Justification with righteousness amounts to saying 'you know what it means to grow in righteousness, and when a man finds that he is able to do that, then he is to be said to be

"Justified"'. St Paul's account, on the other hand, implies that Justification is a new experience which can only be known to those who have it, but it seems to be too often thought (usually implicitly rather than explicitly) that St Paul could not have meant this, because that sort of thing does not happen: on the basis of Jung's psychology it can be replied that it does. Sometimes, Jung tells us, men have an experience which is such that it seems to them that a new power takes charge of their lives, and this means that St Paul's account may be taken at its face value, as referring to a kind of experience which is not known to all men, but which is known to some, not all of whom are Christians. This is not to say that being Justified and being Individuated are the same thing, but only that they share features in common.

The new status which St Paul claims for every Christian (that is, for every Justified sinner) consists in this, that God, who was before 'over there', outside the man, and making demands on him which he could not fulfil, has Himself entered within the man, to take charge of him, and to direct and govern his life. Something very real has happened, but what has happened is not, at least not at first, a change in the man's character: it is not a change but an addition. Justification might be compared to the moment of dropping a lump of sugar into a cup of tea. When the sugar has just been put in something has been done, but the tea has not yet been changed. The tea around the lump of sugar remains as it was before, and unless the cup is stirred it will not taste sweet. At the same time, the 'status' of the cup of tea has been changed, and it is now a cup for offering to those who take sugar, and not to those who do not. The Doctrine of Justification by Faith teaches that through Christ the day to which Jeremiah looked forward has come, but come with a difference. Jeremiah hoped for the day when God would 'write a new law on our hearts', but now that the day has come we are told that what is written in our hearts is not a law, but a person, and the person whom we shall find there is God Himself, the Creator and Preserver of the world. It is no wonder that Justification by Faith holds a central place in the thought of St Paul and in Christianity, for nothing could be more wonderful. When a man is Justified, then God is within him, and God is active and powerful in his life. What can be said in comparison with this? There can be no rules for the life of the Justified sinner, for to live that life is to let Christ who has come within us live in and through us: 'I live', said St Paul, 'yet no longer I, but Christ liveth in me', and again, 'It is

God that worketh in you, both to will and to do'. This is to be Justified, and when this is understood the question 'how can Justification, which is not righteousness, be accounted righteousness?' ceases to be a difficult one: Justification is not righteousness in any sense, 'reputable' or otherwise, but there is no need to ask whether it is 'as good as' righteousness, because it is so clearly better than righteousness. Righteousness has, as it were, been by-passed, and a man who is Justified no longer seeks to stand as righteous before God in order to enter into a right relation with the Holy One, because he has already become the temple of the Holy Spirit and there can be no more right, or closer relationship with God than that.

Justification by Faith is the account of a new way of life, and the gateway of that new way. The state of the man who enters the way is marked by faith, on the one side, and Justification on the other. Faith is the attitude to God of the man who is Justified, being Justified is the relation to God of the man who has faith. What such a way of life is like may only be known by those who live it, but something may be said about what may be expected to occur in the lives of those who are Justified, and three aspects of the life of the Justified sinner can be briefly mentioned:

1. A man may be Justified without ceasing to sin, and this is invariably what does in fact happen. This is implicit in the fact that St Paul exhorts his readers to mend their ways and renew their minds, and it is generally agreed by commentators. For instances: 'Whenever we believe in Christ, and trust ourselves to Him, He works upon our life with all the power which belongs to His actual redemptive activity, however little we may have apprehended its true character. As soon as we believe in Christ, that activity, whether it is recognized by us or not, is operative in our Christian experience, in spite of the fact that its power may be restricted by our intellectual prejudices and preoccupations' (*Taylor*, 224). 'The idea that the natural man lacks the capacity to fulfill the law, but that by the aid of the Spirit the Christian receives the ability to achieve it, is completely foreign to Paul's thought' (*Nygren*, 434; and to the same effect *passim*). 'The fact is, of course, that Paul saw clearly that although the principle of Life, the higher spiritual nature, was implanted in the believer on Christ, the lower nature was not destroyed. He remained ἐν σαρκί even though he was ἐν Χριστῷ' (*Scott*, 148). 'The present condition, then, of the Christian in this world is one of much suffering and weakness, with a

painful sense of incompleteness, tempered by a sure and certain hope'
(*Dodd*, 135). 'The Christian is in a state of tension between two
actualities. Fundamentally he is delivered from sin, redeemed, reconciled and sinless; as a matter of fact he is at war with sin, which is still
threatening, aggressive and dangerous' (*Sin*, 83). The explanation is
that Justification is the coming of the Spirit into the life of a man, and
not the taking up of his life into the Spirit. It can be said that the
mystery of the dual nature of Jesus is repeated in the Christian, only in
a more severe form. We believe that the human nature of Jesus was
perfect and sinless, but if He was truly tempted, then there must be a
sense in which, in His humanity, He might have rejected the guidance
of the Word of God; yet because He did not reject that guidance the
conflict within Him did not involve any setting of His (human) will
against the divine will. But the human nature of the Justified sinner is
not perfect, but sinful, and it refuses, time and again, to accept the
guidance of the Spirit, so that the life of the Justified man does involve
actual conflict between the Spirit and the 'flesh'. At the same time,
because the Spirit is within him, the life of the Christian is one of hope,
because he knows that the power of God is already at work within
him, and he looks forward to the day when God shall be all in all.

2. Because he 'has the Spirit' the Christian mortifies the flesh.
Since, for St Paul, 'the flesh' includes all the impulses of 'natural
man', whether they be 'low' (e.g. sensuality), or 'high' (e.g. pride),
this means more than asceticism as it is usually understood. All that is
human must be put aside that nothing of 'I' may impede the Spirit,
and true mortification is possible for the man who is Justified, and not
for anyone else, because in him the putting aside of all that is human
does not leave a 'vacuum', since the Spirit is present to direct him when
he forswears the direction of his own life. Thus the Christian life is
lived in faith, because it is only possible fully to mortify the flesh if
one can put one's trust in something else. To mortify the flesh is to
put one's faith in the Spirit of God.

3. The striving of the Christian is not directed towards any future
end. The only true end for man is fellowship with God, and God has
already given His fellowship to the man into whose life He has entered.
The Christian seeks to live 'in the Spirit' in response to the outpouring
of God's love upon him in the gift of the Spirit, and not for anything
that he may get out of it. When he mortifies the flesh the Christian is
simply making use of God's gift, because God has given it to Him, and

this is the meaning of the phrase 'become what you are'. The Christian loves God because God first loved him, and so, lastly and before all else, the Christian life is lived in love.

The account of Justification by Faith can be summarized:

1. Justification by Faith is made possible by what God has done in Christ: it is offered to all men, and given freely to those who accept it.

2. The condition which must be fulfilled before a man can be Justified by God is not, as is often thought, faith, but the readiness to accept what God offers. This is properly called 'penitence', because such readiness implies that a man acknowledges that he has failed to reach his goal, and that he is unable to reach it by his own efforts.

3. Justification by Faith is the name of the thing that God does when a man accepts His gift. On the one side it involves an attitude of faith in Jesus and in God's power to redeem him through Jesus on the part of the man, and, on the other, the presence of God Himself as a new centre of authority within the man.

4. From one point of view the Christian life is the mortification of those elements of a man's personality which seek to take charge of his life, from another it is the gradual or rapid 'taking over' of the man by Christ who has already entered his life. The beginning of the Christian life is the coming of Christ, or the Spirit, and the end is that God alone should be in full and undisputed control of every moment and every movement.

The similarities between Justification by Faith and Individuation are these:

1. Both 'diagnose' the disease from which all men suffer.

2. Both prescribe for the disease that they diagnose: that is, both suggest what should be done by those who would be cured.

3. Both show that the 'cure' which they prescribe is only ameliorative in itself. The action which a man takes does not, by itself, improve his state, but it makes a cure by someone or something else possible.

4. Both result in a new state, which is described by referring to a 'new controlling centre' within a man.

The differences are:

1. The 'diagnoses' and the 'prescriptions' are different, and *prima facie* this does not seem to be only because the terms are theological on the one hand, and psychological on the other.

2. The 'new centre' is called 'Christ', or 'the Spirit' by St Paul, and 'the Self' by Jung, and this again is more than a difference of terms: for one thing, the nature of Christ is known before He takes charge of a man's life, whereas that of 'the Self' is not.

3. Individuation is not said to have happened until and unless 'the Self' is sensed as effectively 'in control', but a man may be Justified although the Spirit has not taken full charge of his life. This means that there is nothing which corresponds closely to 'faith' in the life of the man who is Individuated, although a man needs faith of a sort in order to become Individuated.

These similarities and differences determine the plan of the remaining chapters. The 'diagnosis' of natural man according to Jung is compared and contrasted with that according to St Paul in the two following chapters, and the two prescriptions are discussed in chapters 6 and 7. The nature of faith is considered from the point of view of psychology in chapter 8, and from that of theology in chapter 9. In chapters 10 and 11 the new states which crown the two processes are examined in turn.

4

THE OPPOSITES

(Man's need according to Jung)

JUNG claims that Individuation is an answer to a human need. Individuation is, in effect, a 'Way of Salvation', and in that he offers a way of salvation Jung implies that there is something from which a man needs to be saved. The detailed study of Individuation must begin with an account of the need which it is said to answer, that is of the state from which a man is 'saved' by Individuation. The name of this state is 'antagonism between consciousness and the unconscious', and there are two broad questions about it which will be discussed. The first question is 'In what does this state consist?' or, in other words, 'What are the marks of this state?' The second is 'What are the relations between this state from which a man is saved by Individuation, and the state called "bondage to sin" from which a man is saved by Justification by Faith?' Before beginning the discussion of the first question, which occupies the greater part of this chapter, some general comments can be made on the second question. The natural order of the two questions will be reversed so that from the beginning something can be shown of the importance for the theologian of the psychological account.

Since it will be claimed that there is a close relation between being in a state of 'antagonism between consciousness and the unconscious' on the one hand, and being 'in bondage to sin' on the other, it must be shown that the people whom Jung describes as being in the first state are the same as those whom the Christian describes as being in the second. There is very little room for doubt about this, for it is not that Christianity offers Justification by Faith to some men who are said to be 'in bondage to sin', whereas Jung offers Individuation to others who are said to be in a state of 'antagonism between consciousness and the unconscious': Justification by Faith and Individuation are both offered to all men. The Christian doctrine is that all men who have not received the grace of Christ are 'in bondage to sin', and Jung implies that all who have not experienced Individuation (in some form)[1] are in a state of 'antagonism between consciousness and the unconscious'. Jung implies this when he says, for example, that this antagonism is a 'hard dilemma in which nature has placed us' (*Practice*, 470), and when he remarks that 'The resistance of the conscious mind to the unconscious and the depreciation of the latter were historical necessities in the development of the human psyche' (*Alchemy*, 60), because that which is brought about by 'nature', and that which is a necessity, must also be universal. The application of Jung's description to those whom the Christian says are 'in bondage to sin' is also shown by the fact that Jung would agree that a religious system may be as able to save a man from the state of antagonism between consciousness and the unconscious as a psychological analysis and by the fact that he even claims that it should. Jung's complaint is that religion too often fails: 'As a doctor', he says, 'it is my task to help the patient to cope with life. . . . I would be only too delighted to leave this anything but easy task to the theologian, were it not that it is just from the theologian that many of my patients come' (*Alchemy*, 32, 33).

Those who are in bondage to sin (according to the theologian) are also in a state of antagonism between consciousness and the unconscious (according to Jung), but it does not necessarily follow that Jung and Christian theologians are both describing the same state. What can be said is that both are describing a state of men in general, and not a peculiar state which some men happen to be in. Bondage to sin and antagonism between consciousness and the unconscious are both descriptions of the natural man, and there are three possible kinds of relation between them. The two descriptions may be related in any of the following ways:

1. They may describe wholly different aspects of the state of natural man: that is, the only important relation between them may be that they do refer to the same individuals.

Examples of this kind of relation between descriptive accounts are:

(*a*) A 'physical' map on the one hand, and a 'political' map of the same area on the other.

(*b*) An account of the physiological characteristics of a tribe on

---

[1] See note on p. 45.

the one hand, and an account of the social customs of the same tribe on the other.

2. They may describe different, but closely related aspects of the state of natural man.

Examples:

(*a*) A physical map of a mountainous country, in which the population is thick in the valleys and in which it becomes more sparse on the higher ground, and a map of the distribution of population in that country.

(*b*) A physiological account of a man, and an account of his athletic ability.

3. They may describe the same aspects of the state of natural man, but describe them in different terms.

Examples:

(*a*) The account of a countryside in terms of hills and valleys, and a contour map of the same countryside.

(*b*) The description of a circle as the locus of a point equidistant from a given point, and as the graph of the equation $x^2 + y^2 = r^2$.

There are many similarities between the theological and psychological accounts as will be shown below, and it is safe to assume that the relation between them is at least as close as relations of the second kind. Owing to the great difference between the terms used in the two accounts it is remarkably difficult to judge whether the relation between them is of the third kind or not: my own opinion is that it is in many ways closer than most relations of the second kind, and yet not a relation of the third kind. Three formal similarities between the two accounts will now be considered, before the more detailed examination of the psychological account is begun.

First Similarity

The theological and the psychological accounts both go beyond the observed events. They are both given as explanations of why certain events occur, and not merely as assertions that those events do occur. Once the denotation of 'sin' is known the statement 'all have sinned' is merely descriptive, since it simply asserts that in the life of every man events of the kind called 'sins' have occurred; on the other hand, 'men are in bondage to sin' does not merely mean that men sin, it means 'men sin, and they sin because they are in bondage to sin': that is, it refers to the state of natural man rather than to what he does. In the same way, when the denotation of 'odd things' is known then 'odd things interfere with conscious purposes' is a description of certain events in a man's life, but 'antagonism between consciousness and the unconscious' refers to the state of natural man which causes those events to occur. *Prima facie* both accounts are 'diagnostic' in that they do not merely assert the presence of certain symptoms but purport to indicate the fundamental disorder which gives rise to them as well.

This resemblance—that both are 'diagnostic'—between the two accounts does not disappear when the psychological terms are analysed, because once the question of analysis is raised the theological terms require analysis as well. It is true that the state of antagonism between conscious and unconscious cannot be seen, as a diseased liver *can* be seen, and it is true that 'the unconscious 'must be analysed in terms of observable events, but it is equally true that bondage to sin cannot be seen and that if the phrase has any meaning it must be analysed in terms of observable events too, and analysis of the two accounts shows that they both relate the events which they 'explain' (that is, the 'symptoms' for which they account) to a man's conscious attitude. 'Bondage to sin' relates sins to an attitude of disobedience towards God, and 'antagonism between consciousness and the unconscious' relates odd things to an overvaluation of consciousness. Both accounts relate the 'symptoms' to observable aspects of conscious life which are regarded as the heart of the 'disease' and so as the ultimate cause of the symptoms. Whether or not the accounts are analysed the function of both is the same.

The similarity of function between the two accounts enables us to see why it is difficult to be sure what is the exact relation between them. One relates sins to an attitude of disobedience towards God, the other relates odd things to overvaluation of consciousness, and whether we compare sins with odd things, or the disobedience with the overvaluation we find the same difficulty that the terms in each pair do not refer to the same things, and yet they do not refer to things which are wholly different. Sins and odd things are not the same because, for example, the conscious intention with which an odd thing interferes may be an intention to sin, or a sin in itself; but on the other hand, there is considerable overlapping between sins and odd things. In particular, no one would acknowledge that he was in bondage to sin and seek to be freed from that bondage unless some sins were also odd things, for to say that no odd things occur in a man's life is to say that he never fails in his conscious purpose, and if a man never failed in his conscious purpose although he might well sin, he would only do so because he wanted to sin, and if he only did what he wanted to do he would not be aware of his need for salvation. In other words, sins and odd things are overlapping classes, so that all sins are not odd things, and all odd things are not sins, but some sins are odd things. In a similar way disobedience to God may be very different from over-valuation of consciousness—it may, for example, involve a refusal to use the ability which God has given a man, or a slothful drifting with the crowd—yet direct and conscious disobedience is more likely to be rooted in the assertion of the absolute validity of a man's own judgement than in anything else, and such an assertion is a form of overvaluation of consciousness, so that the relation between the dis-obedience and the overvaluation is very like that between sins and odd things and, in general, the things to which one set of terms refers are neither the same as those to which the other set refers nor are they entirely different, and it is this which makes it difficult to judge the relation between the theological and psychological accounts.

Second Similarity

Bondage to sin and antagonism between consciousness and the unconscious are both states in which a man 'finds himself' and not states which he 'gets into'. This is implicit in calling them states of the natural man, which means that a man is in either state because he is a man, born at a particular time in human history, and not because he has behaved in a certain way. For example, actual sins which a man commits may increase his state of bondage, but he commits sins in the first place because he is already in bondage to sin, and, in this respect, it may be noticed that Jung's account of natural man is more like that of traditional Christianity than is the account of some modern theologians. St Paul teaches that all men 'born of Adam' are born in bondage to sin, and Jung claims the structure of a man's psyche is originally determined by what may be called the 'psychic state' of the civilization and social groups to which he belongs.

Individuation, as the name suggests, is a process whereby a man comes to express his true individuality. The original state of a man is one in which he is more 'collective' than individual. Jung, in an early essay, says that even those psychic elements which form the ego of the 'natural man', and which appear to give him a personality of his own, prove to be 'collective' and not individual. 'The persona', he writes, 'is the grouping of conscious and unconscious components that are opposed to the non-ego and constitute the ego. A general comparison of the personal elements belonging to different individuals shows the great resemblance between these components, which may even amount to identity, and largely cancels out the *individual* nature of the personal components and of the persona at the same time' (*Essays*, 505), and in a later version of the same essay he calls a chapter 'The Persona as a segment of the Collective Psyche'. In all Jung's writings it is everywhere implicit that the structure of a man's psyche is as much the result of the state of contemporary life and thought as it is of his own history. To give one example, he says 'the more powerful and independent consciousness becomes, and with it the conscious will, the more is the unconscious forced into the background' (*Secret*, 85), and when he says this he is speaking of a society, and not of individuals, since he goes on to refer to 'members of such a society': it is only in the individual members of a society that consciousness can become more powerful and independent, but Jung can speak of such an event as a feature of a society as a whole because he claims that it occurs in its members because they are its members, and not primarily as a result of their personal individual acts.

In the early stages of his development, Jung says, a man is almost entirely 'collective': 'General concepts of right, the State, religion, science, etc., current among civilized men' are 'Collective', and 'feelings' and 'whole functions' (e.g. thinking, or sensation) may also be collective (*Types*, 530, in definition 'collective'); that is to say they may be derived from the circumstances of a man's birth and upbringing at a particular time and place. On the other hand 'The collective psyche comprises *les parties inférieures* of the psychic functions, that is to say, the deep-rooted, well-nigh automatic, hereditary elements that are ubiquitously present' (*Essays*, 235). In other words the 'natural man' accepts a whole range of ideas and values, and rejects conflicting aspects of human nature without any exercise of deliberate thought or choice. Because everyone is born a man, in a particular age of a civilization, of a certain nationality, within a social group, of two parents, he judges certain things to be true, good, right, beautiful, or, generally, valuable;

and he judges others to be false, evil, wrong, ugly and undesirable; and within the psyche of the individual there is an antagonism between groups of psychic elements which is the result of heredity, or environment, or both, and this antagonism influences his acts and his history.

Antagonism between consciousness and the unconscious is universal, but it may take many different forms. Any psychic element may be either conscious or unconscious, and the antagonism between consciousness and the unconscious will appear very different when psychic elements are differently distributed between the two. For example, an element generally conscious in the West may be generally unconscious in the East, or an individual born into a minority group which rejects the ideas of the majority may accept values which are rejected by his civilization as a whole. Similarly bondage to sin is universal, but in different ages and in different parts of the world different sins may be common. The form which they take may vary, but antagonism between consciousness and the unconscious and bondage to sin are not only both universal, but both are also implicit in being human, and this is a striking similarity between them.

Third Similarity

Christian theologians and Jung both find that the account which they give can best be presented in connection with a myth. When Jung's account is examined below it will be shown that his myth shares important features with Christian myths of the Creation and the Fall. Jung's myth is the account which he gives of the development of consciousness out of the unconscious. This account is 'scientific' in that it is given in the language of psychology, and in that it is unexceptionable as a psychological account: it may not be true but it is to be judged as a psychological account, and not to be rejected on the grounds that it is something different from what it purports to be. On the other hand it is myth because in giving an account in his psychological language Jung necessarily hypostasizes 'unconscious elements' which he admits are unknowable. To describe his account as 'myth', moreover, is not to reject it or to devalue it, as the following quotations, with which I am in agreement, show: 'A myth', writes Alan Watts, 'is a complex of images or a story, whether factual or fanciful, taken to represent the deepest truths of life, or simply regarded as specially significant for no clearly realized reason' (*Watts*, 63), and according to Jung, 'Myth is the primordial language natural to these psychic processes, and no intellectual formulation comes anywhere near the richness and expressiveness of mythical imagery' (*Alchemy*, 28).

Since the psychological and theological accounts of the 'natural man' are both accounts of the same, universal human situation the fact that there are marked similarities between them is good reason for thinking that the two accounts will illuminate each other. In the rest of this chapter Jung's account of the antagonism between consciousness and the unconscious is discussed, and in the following chapter it will be shown that a similar dichotomy is involved in the idea of being in bondage to sin. It is convenient to discuss Jung's account of 'natural man' under four heads:

(1) The Myth, which explains in general terms how antagonism between consciousness and the unconscious arises.
(2) The way in which the individual aggravates the antagonism in his own life.
(3) The symptoms of the state of antagonism.
(4) The conscious attitude which perpetuates this state.

1. *The Myth*

Jung's account of the development of human consciousness can be summarized as follows:

(*a*) Everything psychic is originally unconscious. In the original unconscious everything is balanced and neutralized by its opposite.

(*b*) In order to become conscious psychic elements need to be divided from their opposites: when this happens the opposites of the elements which become conscious remain unconscious, but because they too are divided from their opposites (the conscious elements) they are no longer neutralized, but active in the unconscious.

(*c*) The elements which have become conscious are developed, and a synthesis of these elements is formed. This process takes time, and during its course further elements may be divided from their opposites and become conscious.

(*d*) A stage is reached in which no further development of elements already conscious is possible, and no more elements are divided from their opposites. At this stage in the process further development can only take place if the unconscious opposites of the synthetized conscious elements also become conscious. If this should occur, and these opposites are combined with the conscious synthesis drastic modification of that synthesis would have to take place. In this sense the opposites are a standing threat to any given conscious synthesis.

(e) If the 'opposites' are allowed to become conscious further development takes place through the modification of the conscious synthesis, so that they may be included in a fuller synthesis of psychic elements. This results in a state of the kind described under (d), as it were at a higher level. A new and fuller synthesis in consciousness is opposed by new elements divided from their opposites and still unconscious, because not only does each element have an opposite but the synthesis of two opposites itself has an opposite.

(f) The coming into consciousness of opposites, the synthesis of these opposites with the elements already conscious, and the coming of further opposites from the unconscious is repeated indefinitely, and at the end of each cycle consciousness is wider and more developed.

It is certainly true that the kind of development outlined by the myth does take place. It can be seen in great historical movements of thought, and in the development of social systems, and also in individual lives. Illustrations are liable to be extremely complicated, but the story of the man with an appointment to keep can be expanded to give a relatively simple illustration. We may suppose that when the appointment was first suggested the man was uncertain whether to make it or not, although no clear reasons for or against doing so occurred to him. In this state the motives for making and not making the appointment were both unconscious. If the man then became aware of reasons on both sides the 'opposites' would have become conscious together, and so long as they remained balanced the man would not come to a decision. Making the appointment and preparing to keep it meant a 'division of the opposites'—the reasons for not keeping it were ignored, and the reasons for keeping it synthetized to form the man's conscious purpose. We have already seen how in such a situation the ignored unconscious elements might prevent him from fulfilling his conscious purpose, but the development could have proceeded in a different way. In order to make his decision the man had to give preference to the reasons for making the appointment, but he need not have ignored the reasons against doing so. Having put aside the reasons against, so that he could 'develop' the reasons for—i.e. so that he could formulate his purpose—he might have acknowledged the reasons which he had put aside, and modified his purpose accordingly. The modification might take several forms, depending upon the nature of the reasons against making the appointment. The man might agree to an appointment, but choose a different time and place from that suggested; he might attach conditions to agreeing to the appointment at all; or he might simply make a private reservation to the effect that the appointment might be a mistake, or that he did not really expect anything to come of it. So long as the reasons against making the appointment were acknowledged and allowed some sort of adequate expression they would be conscious, and because they would be able to influence the conscious attitude they would not cause odd things to happen.

This illustration indicates the two possible ways in which the process of development may continue when the stage described under (d) is reached. If the opposites are ignored, then they tend to overthrow the conscious synthesis, as the unconscious desire not to keep his appointment prevented the man from doing so. If the opposites are accepted they modify the conscious synthesis, and become a part of it. In the first case the conscious synthesis is treated as absolute, and no modification is permitted: in the second it is admitted to be relative, and the unconscious opposites are accepted and allowed to influence it. However the process continues the final result is much the same. If the opposites are refused they remain unconscious, but they are in active opposition to consciousness and they eventually overthrow the conscious synthesis. When the conscious synthesis is overthrown a state is reached in which the elements of the synthesis and their opposites are all conscious, and further development involves the synthesis of them all. If the conscious synthesis is not deliberately modified in order to make way for the unconscious opposites it is catastrophically overthrown. Jung indicates at least two periods in the history of the West when a synthesis had been destroyed, or was being destroyed, and human consciousness was chaotic as a result. In connection with the period of the Roman Empire he speaks of 'that inner laceration of the later classical epoch which found its outward expression in an unexampled, chaotic confusion of hearts and minds...' (*Types*, 99), and in 1916 he wrote 'And at the present time, too, we are once more experiencing this uprising of the unconscious destructive forces of the collective psyche. The result has been mass-murder on an unparalleled scale. This is precisely what the unconscious was after' (*Essays*, 150; reaffirmed in a note in the edition of 1943). Whether the conscious synthesis is treated as relative or absolute the ultimate result is the same, but if it is admitted to be relative development is peaceable, if it is regarded as absolute development is catastrophic. So also, it is said in Christian theology that if we will not accept God's love we stand under His wrath.

The process of development as described by the myth necessarily involves *opposition* between consciousness and the unconscious, but *antagonism* between them only arises when the conscious synthesis is treated as absolute. Antagonism is the result of this attitude of regarding a particular synthesis as absolute, and development can take place without this attitude arising: 'it is merely', says Jung, 'the one-sided over-valuation [of consciousness] that has to be checked by a certain relativization of values' (*Practice*, 502). The myth explains why there should be division of the opposites, but not why consciousness should be overvalued so that antagonism between the opposites develops. Within the terms of the myth it can be seen that opposition must occur, because the division of the opposites is necessary if their neutralizing effect upon each other is to be overcome, but it cannot be seen, within the terms of the myth, why overvaluation of consciousness should occur. It is true that with our knowledge of human nature we can understand that any conscious synthesis, reached after an exacting process of development, is likely to be treated as final and absolute, but this is to leave the myth on one side and simply to consider human nature as we know it to be. Opposition is implicit in the concept of the original unconscious seeking to articulate itself in consciousness, but antagonism is not. This is the basis of one of the parallels between Jung's myth and the Christian stories of the Creation and the Fall which we have now to notice.

The parallel between the psychological and the theological myths centre round the ideas of (*a*) The Creator, (*b*) the activity of creation, (*c*) The Fall.

(*a*) It is in keeping with Jung's thought and with his talk of 'the opposites' that the original unconscious of his myth should recall both God and chaos: the 'prime mover' and the 'matter' moved. On the one hand we read '. . . all consciousness rests on unconscious premises, in other words on a sort of unknown *prima materia*; and of this the alchemists said everything that we could possibly say about the unconscious' (*Alchemy*, 516): on the other hand, the unconscious is not mere passive 'material', for, 'like the sea itself, the unconscious yields an endless and self-replenishing abundance of living creatures [sc. psychic elements], a wealth beyond our fathoming' (*Practice*, 366). In saying that the original unconscious is both the source of the activity and life in creation (God), and also the stuff from which creation is formed (chaos), however, it is to be remembered that 'creation' is to be understood to mean 'psychic creation'. Unlike other creation stories the psychological myth is not offered as an account of the origin of the physical universe, but as an account of the development of psychic activity.

(*b*) The story in Genesis recounts the successive acts of creation, but it does not offer any explanation of why God should perform those acts. If this question is raised the least unsatisfactory answer which a Christian can give is that it is the nature of God to create. Jung's myth elaborates the processes of the division of opposites and the synthesis of elements by which the unconscious articulates itself in consciousness, and the only reason that can be given why this should happen is that it is the nature of the unconscious to articulate itself in this way. 'The unconscious', Jung says, 'wants to flow into consciousness in order to reach the light' (*Job*, 740). In one myth creation results from the will of God, in the other from the 'desire' of the unconscious.

Since Jung's myth has obvious affinities with the gnostic myths of the early Christian centuries it might be supposed that it would offer closer parallels to those myths than to that of orthodox Christianity. In the gnostic myths the act of creation is usually regarded as itself a 'fall', or the result of a 'fall', but although Jung often does speak as though he held a similar idea the whole drift of his thought is against it, and properly understood his myth is more like the Christian than the gnostic myths in this respect. It is true that Jung remarks that 'The Creator, who found every other day of his work "good", failed to give good marks to what happened on Monday . . . on that day was the final separation of the upper from the lower waters by the interposed "plate" of the firmament. It is clear that this unavoidable dualism refused, then as later, to fit smoothly into the concept of monotheism. . . . This split, as we know from history, had to be patched up again and again through the centuries, concealed and denied' (*Job*, 619), but although there are other passages in the same sense they conflict with the general tenor of his writings. Apart from such passages there is never any hint in his writings that the development of consciousness is a bad thing, or that we should want to put the clock back. The articulation of the unconscious in consciousness is 'right' and the division of the opposites is necessary if this articulation is to take place. More important, the division of the opposites does not by itself bring about antagonism between them, and it is the antagonism and not the division which is 'wrong'. On Jung's own showing the activity of the unconscious may be valuable and compensatory, and not evil and antagonistic at all: 'I regard the activity of the unconscious', he says, 'as a compensation to the onesidedness of the general attitude produced by the function of consciousness. . . . The activity of the conscious is *selective*. Selection demands *direction*. But direction requires the *exclusion of everything irrelevant*. On occasion, therefore, a certain onesidedness of the conscious orientation is inevitable. . . . Compensation by the unconscious is, as a rule, not so much a contrast as a levelling up or supplementing of the conscious orientation' (*Types*, 532, 3, in definition 'compensation'). 'Creation' and the division of the opposites involved in it are in themselves good, just as God saw the world, with man already made, as 'very good'.

(c) In the place from which the last quotation was taken Jung also wrote, 'The more onesided the conscious attitude, the more antithetic are the contents arising from the unconscious, so that we may speak of a real opposition between the conscious and the unconscious; in which case, compensation appears in the form of a contrasting function. Such a case is extreme.' In this passage he puts forward two ideas: first, that antagonism (i.e. 'real opposition') is due to an unnecessarily onesided attitude of consciousness; second, that this is an 'extreme' attitude and, by implication, a rare one. In his later works he repeats the first of these ideas again and again, as, for example, when he says 'We know that the mask of the unconscious is not rigid—it reflects the face we turn towards it. Hostility lends it a threatening aspect, friendliness softens its features' (*Alchemy*, 29), but the second is implicitly contradicted, for with the development of his ideas and the growth of his experience Jung came to regard the antagonism between consciousness and the unconscious as an all-pervasive feature of civilized life, and so as 'natural'. Antagonism is not essential to the development of consciousness, but it has the appearance of being an inevitable concomitant of that development, simply because in fact a developed consciousness always does tend to overvalue itself. The difficulty of making a distinction between what is necessary and what appears inevitable accounts for much of the confusion which we found in connection with the question whether or not the division of the opposites was a bad thing; it also results in psychology, as well as theology, in a double sense for the words 'nature' and 'natural'. The encounter with the unconscious 'brings us up against the hard dilemma in which nature had placed us', yet, as we shall see, there is another sense of 'nature' in which unity and not antagonism is 'natural'.

The parallel with the Christian myth could hardly be closer. In the Christian story the relative autonomy of the creatures called 'men', is essential to the kind of creation that God wanted. If this was the creation which He desired it was necessary, we say, that He should create beings with such a relative autonomy. Why He wanted this kind of creation and no other we cannot explain, any more than we can explain why the unconscious should want to flow into consciousness, but when either of these premises is granted the relative autonomy of man, or the division of the opposites, follows necessarily. On the other hand it is only because, being men, we know what a man does with his autonomy that we can understand that it was in one sense 'inevitable' that man should disobey God and follow his own judgements: it seems reasonable enough to us that this should happen, but there is no logical contradiction in the idea of a creature not only having a relative autonomy, but also living in obedience to its Creator. In the same way it is because we are men, in whom the opposites are divided, that we can understand that it is (in the same sense as before) 'inevitable' that a developed consciousness should overvalue itself, and suppose that it was absolute and not relative; it seems reasonable enough to us that this should happen, but there is no logical contradiction in the idea of divided opposites which should be complementary and not antagonistic. Both myths do justice to the fact that there is something 'wrong' with 'natural man', and both indicate the possibility and hold out the hope of correcting what is wrong. The theologian says that the true nature of man (as opposed to the nature of man as we know him to be) is expressed by obedience to God rather than by disobedience. Jung says 'In nature the opposites seek one another . . . and particularly in the archetype of unity, the self' (*Alchemy*, 30).

This account of Jung's myth has been given for three reasons. First, in order to bring out further parallels between psychology and theology. Secondly, in order to show that the division of opposites and the antagonism between consciousness and the unconscious is to be regarded as a feature of human existence as a whole, applicable to the development of thought and civilization over long periods of human history. Thirdly, because what is true of mankind in general is said, by Jung, to be true of the individual man as well, so that the principles of the myth apply to the development of the individual as much as they do to that of the race. Under the second of the heads of our account of the natural man according to Jung we shall consider the process whereby the 'opposites' are rejected and the antagonism between consciousness and the unconscious is formed, paying attention to the individual rather than to the human race as a whole.

2. *The Individual and the Opposites*

From his birth, and throughout his life, every man is a member of many societies. A man is born into a family and into a social group; he is born a member of a country and nation, of a wide cultural society (such as Western Europe or China), and of the human race. The circumstances of a man's birth are usually such that some of the societies into which he is born influence his development more than others; for example, in a village in an undeveloped country the smaller, more immediate groups will have more influence upon their individual members than the wide cultural society of which they are a part, whereas there have been periods of European history when a member of the ruling or student classes was more influenced by the culture of Europe than by the local societies to which he belonged. Although the effects upon him of the different societies into which a man is born vary a great deal, his social environment as a whole exerts a great influence upon his life and development: in particular the 'psychic state' of that environment will have a determining influence upon his own psychic state.

Every society has a 'psychic state', and the psychic state of a society is the result of the process of the development of consciousness in its past history. Behind any social group, whether it is large or small, there is a history, in the course of which opposites have been divided, elements synthetized in consciousness and more opposites divided (as set out in the myth), and the result is that the psychic state of a society is one which is marked by antagonism between the opposites: consciously synthetized elements are opposed by unconscious elements.

The antagonism in societies is reflected in the psyches of their individual members.

To speak of psychic elements being 'conscious in a society' is an extension of the idea of 'conscious'. Examples of elements which are to be called 'conscious' in this sense are ideas which are generally accepted as true by the individuals who make up a society; basic principles upon which the laws and customs of a society are founded, and which are generally unquestioned by the members of that society; attitudes and patterns of behaviour generally approved by members of a society. For instance, the idea of the power of men to manipulate the physical world by magical means was a 'conscious' idea in medieval Europe but it is not 'conscious' in England today; the feudal system has been a basic principle in many societies at one time or another, and the principle of the equality of man is 'conscious' both in communist and democratic societies; it was considered appropriate behaviour when Victorian ladies fainted at the sight of blood, and 'keeping a stiff upper lip' is an approved attitude in English Public Schools. Such things are, or express, complexes of psychic elements which are conscious in a society. Similarly, the idea of psychic elements being 'unconscious in society' involves an extension of the concept of 'unconscious'. This idea will be constructed from 'odd' things which happen in a society as a whole, and these odd things may be of many kinds: they may be customs which contradict the basic principles of a society, like the Carnival in Christian Europe; they may be archaistic ideas and behaviour patterns, representing an attempt to return to ideas which belong to an earlier stage of the development of consciousness, like the ideas of the Rechabites in Israel, or those expressed, for instance, in the *Idylls of the King* in Victorian England; they may be elements which are 'unconscious' in a larger society, but 'conscious' in a smaller society within it, as the idea of the value of polygamy was 'conscious' in Mormon society, but not in America as a whole. Just as odd things in the life of the individual are the material from which elements said to be 'in his psyche, but unconscious' are constructed, so these odd things in societies are the material from which elements said to be 'unconscious in a society' are constructed.

The individual man is surrounded by the elements which are conscious in the societies into which he is born, and also by manifestations of the elements which are unconscious in those societies. In general it is natural that he should be most aware of those elements which are conscious in the societies which most influence him, and in the course of his development he will tend to select as his own some of those elements of which he is most aware. Everyone has to select, because the elements which are conscious in a man's social environment are far more numerous than one man can cope with at once at any stage of his development, and this is particularly true of the early stages. The individual does not 'take over' a whole synthesis of conscious elements ready made, but makes a selection for himself from the elements which he finds around him, and Jung says 'individuality manifests itself partly as the principle which selects, and sets limit to, the components adopted as personal' (*Essays*, 506). A man's conscious character is largely derived from the psychic elements which are conscious in his environment, but, on the other hand, 'inasmuch as the newborn child is presented with a ready-made, highly developed brain which owes its differentiation to the accretions of untold centuries of ancestral life, the unconscious psyche must consist of inherited instincts, functions, and forms that are peculiar to the ancestral psyche' (*Practice*, 61), and, moreover, 'In so far as differentiations exist that correspond to race, tribe, or even family, there exists also a collective psyche limited to race, tribe, or family over and above the "universal" collective psyche' (*Essays*, 235); so that consciousness in the individual is, from the start, opposed by unconscious elements. In selecting as his own some of the elements conscious in his environment, the individual leaves a further (and larger) range of elements unconscious, and the elements remaining unconscious in the individual will be, on the whole, unconscious in his environment. Thus each individual reflects in his own degree and in his own way the 'psychic state' of the societies in which he lives.

A man's character is largely determined by the psychic state of the societies in which he lives, but although Jung claims that much that appears individual and personal is really collective, he does not deny that the individual bears considerable responsibility for his own particular psychic state. On the one hand, he remarks, 'One grows more and more astonished to discover, from attentive observation, how much of our so-called individual psychology is in reality collective' (*Essays*, 462), but on the other hand he admits 'It would be wrong to leave the matter as it stands without at the same time recognizing that there is, after all, something individual in the peculiar choice and delineation of the persona' (ibid., 247), and it is in the selection of psychic elements from among those which are conscious in his environment that the individual is able to influence his own development, and on the whole, in the process of selection, a man tends to aggravate the opposition between consciousness and the unconscious. Although he 'finds' psychic elements already conscious in his environment, we are to think of the unconscious of the individual as the source of the elements which he makes his own, so that it is as though the presence of an element in a man's environment wakes an echo within his own psyche, and to say that a man 'accepts a certain element from among the ideas around him' and to say that 'an element becomes conscious out of his unconscious' are two ways of referring to the same event. In accordance with the myth the unconscious is thought of as prepared to 'throw up' pairs of psychic elements, and the acceptance of an element is thus to be regarded as a division of the opposites. In the course of a man's life, and particularly in the early stages of his development, psychic elements are, as it were, 'offered' to him all the time: ideas are suggested to him by the serious and casual remarks of his friends, his acquaintances, his teachers, and of anyone else with whom he may come into contact; attitudes and emotions 'come upon him' as he reacts to the situations in which he finds himself; a man observes the behaviour and the attitudes of other people; and emotions and moods and ideas come to him from within, without any apparent external cause. As psychic elements are 'offered' to a man in these and other ways he has to take up some attitude towards them: he may accept them, and relate them to his other ideas and to his conscious attitude and character; he may accept them, but being unable to synthetize them for the present he may leave them at the 'back of his mind', for future use; or he may refuse them; that is, he may regard them as of no value for his own development. This does not mean that a man makes a careful study of each psychic element which is 'offered' to him, and comes to a specific conscious judgement about it (although he may sometimes do so), but that he takes up an attitude to psychic elements without giving thought to the question what his attitude should be. To say that a man takes an attitude of acceptance or refusal to a psychic element means that he treats it in a certain way: if he accepts it, then he makes it his own, and relates it to other conscious elements; if he rejects it he does not give it any serious attention at all, and directs his life on the assumption that that element does not exist, or is irrelevant.

Every time a man refuses a psychic element he contributes to the antagonism between the opposites in his own psyche. When a man refuses a psychic element he puts it aside as one which is of no use to him. It is like a man doing a jig-saw puzzle, who decides that a certain piece does not belong to the puzzle which he is doing, and throws it away. In a similar way the man who refuses a psychic element is building a picture of himself, and when he refuses an element he decides that it has no place in the picture which he wants to form. When an element is refused it is not put aside for use later, as the man doing the jig-saw puzzle might put aside one piece while he does a corner where it does not belong, knowing that it will be wanted at a later stage, but it is put aside for ever. If a man's attitude were fully conscious and deliberate he would say that the element which he refuses 'will never be of any use', whereas of an element merely 'put aside' he would say 'it is no use yet'. When a psychic element has been refused it is no longer simply unconscious, it is also said to be 'repressed'.

Strictly speaking repression is only one of the ways in which psychic elements may be refused. It has, however, come to be regarded as the normal way of refusing psychic elements, and the word repressed is often used of all elements which have been refused, whatever the mechanism of refusal may have been; but it is possible to distinguish three ways of refusing psychic elements, and they may be called 'repression', 'refusal' and 'devaluation'. Repression and refusal are very much alike, and they both result in unconscious elements which are repressed, but they differ in that an element may be refused before it becomes conscious at all, whereas it cannot be repressed until after it has become conscious: devaluation, on the other hand, does not directly involve elements becoming unconscious, and a devalued element may remain conscious; but an element which is devalued has very much the same kind of influence on conscious life as elements which have been repressed or refused. It is as well to consider each of the three ways of refusing psychic elements.

Repression is a mechanism for getting rid of a psychic element which has become conscious, and we may represent the process by using the analogy of the man doing a jig-saw puzzle again. Suppose that he starts with all the pieces on the table, and that he makes the picture on a tray. A piece on the table represents an unconscious psychic element, pieces on the tray represent conscious elements, and pieces joined together on the tray represent a conscious synthesis of psychic elements. Repression could then be represented by the following sequence: (1) the man takes a piece off the table and puts it on the tray; (2) he tries to fit it to the pieces already on the table, and finds that he cannot do so; (3) he decides that it does not belong to his puzzle; (4) he puts it back on the table face downwards, or throws it into the dustbin, and does not consider it again. A psychic element is repressed when a man has become aware of it and decided that it has no part in his idea of what he should be, and when he then ceases to be aware of it. The following hypothesis presented by counsel in a court of law describes the process very well: 'Even politicians', he said, 'sometimes said or did something which they afterwards wished they had not done. All that he, counsel, suggested against the plaintiff was that his mind had worked in the following way: It was a silly thing to do; I wish I had never done it: I could not have been such a fool; of course, I did not do it. . . . And finally the plaintiff had come into the witness box fully persuaded that he had not agreed to go.'[1] The process of repression is a process of forgetting: a psychic element and the circumstances in which it was 'offered' are forgotten, and in this way a man may forget that he said something, that someone else said something, that a certain incident occurred, that he thought some-thing, or that he had this or that emotion. By forgetting such things men repress psychic elements which do not fit with the synthesis of elements which form their conscious minds.

What I have called 'refusal' of a psychic element is a process like repression, except that a refused element does not become conscious. Jung says 'Although Freud always speaks of the incest fantasies as though they were repressed, further experience has been shown that in very many cases they were never the contents of the conscious mind at all, or were conscious only as the vaguest adumbrations, for which reason they could not have been repressed intentionally' (*Practice*, 140); in other words there are elements which 'nearly become conscious', but which a man refuses to allow into his conscious mind. Freud is fully aware of this, and he lays it down as a principle that 'memories' recovered in the course of analysis are to be treated on the same principle whether they are veridical or not, so that we may say that an incident which is 'remembered' although it never occurred repre-sents what the patient thought would have happened if a certain

[1] *The Times* Law Report, 27 January 1955: Drayson *v.* London Express Newspapers Ltd.

psychic element had become conscious. In the terms of the myth we are to think of elements pressing upon consciousness and being refused admission. Since elements which are refused do not become conscious, refusal is not brought about by forgetting, because there is nothing to forget. The simplest ways of refusing a psychic element are by failing to understand the words in which an idea is expressed, the implications of a man's behaviour, or the logical implications of his opinions; or by failing to acknowledge that certain things take place, even when it is apparent to everyone else that they do: for example, a mother may refuse to become aware of the evil behaviour of her son by a failure to notice when he behaves in evil ways. The refusal of a psychic element may be represented by the man doing the jig-saw puzzle, when he decides that a certain piece does not belong to his puzzle without taking it off the table or examining it, and pushes it away, turns it over, or throws it out. Refusal, however, involves the same attitude to a psychic element as repression, the attitude that that element does not belong, and will never have any place in one's developed conscious character.

In the last passage cited Jung speaks of repression as 'intentional'. It is impossible not to speak in this sort of way, both of repression and refusal. We cannot help saying that a man 'deliberately' forgets an unfortunate incident, or that he 'deliberately' fails to understand what is said to him, but when we talk in this way we are using 'deliberately' in a special sense. When 'deliberately' is used in this sense to say that a man deliberately fails to understand an idea when it is explained to him, for example, it does not mean that he really understands but pretends that he does not, but that he really does not understand although we can see no reason why he should not do so: that is, it means he does not understand although judging from what we know of the man's intelligence, and from what he has understood in the past, we think that it is reasonable to expect that he would understand. It is the same with forgetting, and when we say that when a man represses a psychic element he deliberately forgets the incident which gave rise to it, we do not mean that he really remembers the incident and pretends to forget it, nor that he went through a conscious process of thought 'I do not like remembering that incident, I shall forget it, it never occurred', but we mean that he 'ought' to have remembered it, but did not do so: that is, judging by what we know of the man's capacity to remember, and in view of the importance of the incident in question we say 'deliberately' to indicate that we think that he might reasonably have been expected to remember it. It is important to realize that in the ordinary sense of 'deliberate' it is impossible either to 'deliberately forget' or to 'deliberately fail to understand': repression and refusal may be called 'deliberate' but if they are they are not to be thought of as 'deliberate' in the sense in which 'deliberate' is used to distinguish between deliberate and accidental acts, they are both very like accidental acts in that they are things which happen to a man and are not things which he sets himself to do.

The devaluation of an element may also be represented by the man doing the jig-saw puzzle. We must now suppose that he puts a piece on the tray, studies it, decides that it does not belong and that he will not consider it any further, and then leaves it on the tray. Like the piece of puzzle a devalued element is still 'there' (i.e. conscious), but it is regarded as useless. An element can be devalued without anything being forgotten or misunderstood; it may remain conscious, but it is not allowed to influence conscious decisions. An element is devalued when it is characterized as 'evil' or 'false' or 'inappropriate' or 'trivial'; that is, when it is regarded as irrelevant to the development of a man's idea of himself. There are, as the words used show, degrees of devaluation: in particular, it is easier to change one's opinion about whether or not a psychic element is trivial than it is to decide that what one thought was evil is not. When an element has been devalued it is no longer an element for which a place must be found in the conscious synthesis, but one which has been sifted and found wanting, and a violent modification of consciousness is necessary before an element which has been devalued can be accepted on an equality with other conscious elements. Devalued elements are not directly repressed, but they tend to fall out of consciousness. For example, if 'evil tendencies' are acknowledged as a feature of one's nature but do not appear to have any influence upon one's life it is easy enough to forget that one ever had occasion to acknowledge their existence in oneself at all, and in this way elements which are devalued frequently become unconscious; but whether they become unconscious or not devalued elements influence conscious life in the same way as repressed and refused elements because they are not allowed to exert their rightful influence on conscious decisions, and Jung often seems to speak of them as 'repressed' even when they are still conscious.

The refusal of an element in any of the ways which have been discussed is equivalent to the declaration 'this element shall have no influence on my life'. Jung appears to be ready to agree that there are some elements which it would be nice to be able to do without, and it is probable that if he thought that it were possible to refuse a psychic element successfully he would encourage us to do so, but he claims that the refusal of psychic elements can never be wholly successful. In the terms of the myth, if an element is refused (that is, if it is not taken into account in forming conscious decisions), then it will have a baleful effect upon conscious life, because if an activated psychic element is denied its proper influence it gives rise to odd things which interfere with conscious purpose. Thus a repressed element functions in a different way from that of an element which is simply unconscious: an unconscious element gives rise to odd things, but the odd things which manifest it will 'compensate' conscious life, and not oppose it; whereas the odd things which manifest repressed elements oppose conscious purpose. Intuitions, ideas which 'come into one's mind', emotions and moods which have no clear external cause may all be the effects of unconscious elements, but if they are taken seriously, and allowed to play their part in conscious life they do not oppose consciousness but provide it with further points of view which it would otherwise be in danger of overlooking; whereas if one attempts to pass them by or to ignore them they become stumbling blocks, and they are then said to manifest repressed elements. Whether an unconscious element compensates or opposes conscious life depends upon the attitude which consciousness takes to it, and this attitude is shown by the view which a man takes of such an element when it appears in the lives of others, and by his attitude to the odd things in his own life to which it gives rise. It should be noticed that the refusal of a psychic element may not have any noticeable results at the time, since the element which is refused may be one which must, at that time, be put aside if consciousness is to develop; but the act of refusal determines the attitude of consciousness towards the element which is refused, not only at the time, but for the future as well, so that when the time comes that the element which has been refused is needed, consciousness is committed to the view that it has no place in the proper conscious synthesis. As we have seen in chapter 2 it is when an element 'ought' to become conscious and does not that it has the most apparent evil effects upon conscious life.

A man starts with a tendency to develop a state of antagonism within his psyche as a result of his membership of human societies.

In the course of his life a man may refuse psychic elements in one or another of the three ways which have been discussed. When a psychic element is refused, consciousness is committed to an attitude of antagonism towards it, and the element itself interferes in the conscious direction of life. Refused elements are mainly unconscious and so they are contaminated with other unconscious elements, since psychic elements cannot be distinguished so long as they remain unconscious. As a result of this contamination the antagonistic attitude of consciousness to the refused elements spreads to the unconscious as a whole. This is the diagnosis of the disease of natural man in mythical terms: to consider the symptoms which mark this state of antagonism, and the conscious attitude which perpetuates it, is to analyse the mythical account.

3. *The Symptoms*

In giving an account of the development of a disease the medical theorist begins with the remote cause of the disease, gives an account of the effects which this cause has on the organism (degeneration of the liver, or the growth of an ulcer, for examples), and explains how the disease gives rise to symptoms. When a patient complains of certain symptoms the doctor makes use of such an account in order to decide what present activities of the patient aggravate and maintain the disease, and to suggest other activities which he thinks may mollify it. For instance, a doctor might say 'the pains in your chest and your fits of giddiness are due to weakness in your heart, caused by lifting over-heavy crates: by digging your allotment and walking up steep hills you strain your heart more, and in order to get rid of the pains and giddiness you must stop digging and take more rest'. From the point of view of the patient the value of such diagnoses lies in the fact that they relate symptoms to a means of cure: if the doctor is right the activities which he prescribes will bring about the cessation of the symptoms, and this is what the patient wants. In respect of health the purpose of a diagnosis is to answer the question 'what must I do to be saved?' and if the doctor gives an answer to this question, and if his answer works, then it does not matter to the patient what he tells him about his liver, or stomach, or heart, none of which things he can see.

The psychological myth is diagnostic in the same way that the doctor's account of a physical disease is diagnostic, and the psychological terms imply pictures like those implied by medical accounts. But psychological diagnosis differs from medical diagnosis in a very important respect. Although when the diagnosis is made neither patient nor doctor can see the disease of the liver, the ulcer in the stomach, nor the weakness of the heart it is possible for the surgeon to operate, and to confirm or reject the physician's account of what has happened inside the patient's body. It is only so long as the physician prescribes a purely medical cure that, if the cure works, it does not matter very much whether the story he tells is 'true', and if he has to advise an operation the truth or falsehood of his account of normally invisible organs becomes important. In psychology, however, there is nothing which corresponds to an operation, because the unconscious elements of which the analyst speaks are not things like the heart and liver and stomach, and there is no means of looking at them to see if they are doing what the analyst says they are doing. It has already been pointed out that this is not just a practical difficulty, and that to speak of 'seeing what unconscious elements are doing' is meaningless; and this means that the 'truth' of a psychological diagnosis depends upon the relations between the remote cause of the disease, the activities said to aggravate the disease, the prescription based upon the diagnosis, and the symptoms, so that a psychological diagnosis is 'true', in the only sense in which it can be said to be true, if:

(a) In general the sort of remote cause indicated is frequently followed by the particular symptoms of which the patient complains.

(b) The symptoms become worse so long as the 'aggravating activities' are continued.

(c) The carrying out of the prescription is followed by the cessation of the symptoms.

These remarks apply to all psychological diagnoses, but the diagnosis which is being considered in this chapter is the diagnosis of a very special disease, because that disease is universal.

Medical diagnoses and most psychological diagnoses are concerned with the diseases of some individuals. Normally the symptoms of a disease distinguish the diseased individual from other men and women, and the patient's complaint is that the things which happen to him did not happen to him before, and do not happen to most people. The disease examined in this chapter, however, is not one which some people get sometimes, but one from which everyone suffers all the time. It is as though a doctor were to diagnose the disease which prevents men running faster than about 15 miles an hour for a distance of a mile and to prescribe a remedy for it. In other words the symptoms of the state of antagonism between consciousness and the unconscious are not strange happenings which beset one or two unfortunate individuals, but occurrences which are normal features in everyone's life.

The symptoms of the disease of natural man (that is, of the state of antagonism between consciousness and the unconscious) may be divided into three groups and, by means of the myth it may be shown how the symptoms of each group arise from the existence of repressed elements. According to the principles of psychological diagnosis which have just been laid down, this means that the symptoms are related by the concept of repressed elements to a remote cause in the past (called 'the rejection of psychic elements'), and to activities in the present (called 'the continued repression of rejected elements') which aggravate them. This means that the symptoms are said to result from the fact that an idea, belief, desire, or inclination has been conscious, and then forgotten ('rejection'), and that they are said to continue because the man cannot recall the forgotten psychic elements ('continued rejection'). The three groups of symptoms are (a) errors of behaviour, (b) errors of judgement, and (c) narrow-mindedness and mental sterility.

(a) The first group of symptoms comprises those things which we do, which we did not mean to do, and which we wish we had not done. Things of this kind, which interfere with conscious purpose, may be trivial, like slips of the tongue; or serious, like besetting sin which we commit even though we set ourselves not to do so. They may be evil or distracting thoughts, or behaviour patterns like the fussiness which caused the man in the illustration to miss his appointment. To a greater or lesser degree things of this sort happen to all of us, but they must be distinguished from things which are also 'odd', but which do not interfere with conscious purpose: passing fancies in an idle moment, valuable intuitions, and actions which we cannot explain but which we are glad to have done, are things which 'happen to us', but they are not symptoms of any kind of disease: they are signs of psychic health.

The psychological story implies that all odd things are effects of unconscious elements, but only those which interfere with conscious purpose are effects of repressed elements. According to the psychological diagnosis the errors of behaviour are manifestations of those elements which have been rejected by consciousness, so that the construction of 'repressed elements' relates such errors to the forgetting of certain ideas, attitudes and so on, and of the incidents connected with them.

(*b*) The second group of symptoms includes those errors of judgement which involve the mistaken imputation of motives or attitudes to other people. Such errors of judgement are common: a shy man is thought by others to be supercilious or 'stand-offish'; a man with a guilty conscience supposes that other people are condemning him when they are not; the prudish person thinks that innocent people are sexually impure; the careful father thinks that his son is extravagant; the libertine supposes that ordinary people are more narrow-minded than they really are. In small things and great it is very easy to make such mistakes, and such mistakes are often found to be systematic.

Psychotherapy gives an account of systematic errors of judgement about other people in terms of 'projection'. This concept is highly complex, and it is discussed more fully in chapter 9. Briefly, it is said that when a psychic element is repressed (that is, when a man refuses to acknowledge it in himself), it is 'projected' upon other people (and, occasionally, things) as a picture is projected on to a cinema screen. Thus the guilty man 'projects' his own self-criticism; the prudish person 'projects' unadmitted sexual desire; and the licentious man 'projects' repressed morality. In this way the errors of judgement are related by the idea of projection to repressed psychic elements, but it must be borne in mind that 'projection' is not an explanation of how something happens, but only the statement that it does.

(*c*) The third group of symptoms consists of things which are quite different from those in the other two groups. Errors of judgement and behaviour are things which go wrong, but the symptoms of the third group are things which fail to go right. Among these symptoms are the inability to accept new ideas, or even to consider them seriously; the tendency to become fixed in habits of thought or behaviour; the inability to adjust oneself to changes in routine; lack of interest in life and general dullness. These symptoms are usually delayed, and they do not usually occur before the middle period of a man's life.

The symptoms of the third group are explained by the myth easily enough. They are due to the fact that 'repression' is like throwing away a piece of jig-saw puzzle. If a man throws away pieces of the puzzle which he is doing, because he has mistakenly decided that they do not belong, he cannot complete the picture and sooner or later he will get 'stuck', although he may not realize this until he has put together most of the other pieces. So the man who has rejected psychic elements eventually becomes 'stuck' because he cannot continue to develop new ideas without the elements which he has rejected, and his character cannot move towards completeness so long as he rejects elements which 'ought' to belong to it. Narrow-mindedness, fixed routine and dullness are the forms which 'getting stuck' takes, so that the symptoms of the third group are not explained as the effects of particular repressed elements, but as the results of the fact that some elements are repressed.

The symptoms of the disease of natural man can be generally covered by the formula 'the things that I would not, those I do, and the things that I would, those I do not', but this assertion is different from that of St Paul, not only because it refers to trivialities like slips of the tongue, which are not sins, but also because it takes no account of the moral character of conscious purpose. Failure in an evil purpose due to the interference of good elements which have been repressed is as much a symptom as failure in a good purpose because of repressed evil elements. 'There are men', says Jung, 'who to all appearances are very disreputable and do not put the least restraint upon themselves, but basically this is only a pose of wickedness, for in the background they have their moral side which has fallen into the unconscious just as surely as the immoral side in the case of the moral man' (*Essays*, 428). On the other hand many of the things which are symptoms for the psychologist are also sins from the point of view of the theologian. Much that we do which is contrary to our purpose is also wrong, as when we fail to overcome a besetting sin, or when we are 'carried away', against our will, by some evil tendency: errors of judgement about other people may not be sins in themselves, but they are closely connected with sins of pride, uncharitableness and hypercriticism: sterility of mind has a close relation with sloth, and narrowmindedness with the thoughtless condemnation of people and ideas. The 'man' with whom psychologists and theologians are concerned is clearly the 'same man', and though each selects a different set of symptoms both select them from the same common 'pool', and their two sets overlap to a considerable extent.

The psychological diagnosis is designed to indicate how the

undesirable symptoms of the disease of natural man can be got rid of. The main prescription to which it leads is that man should cease those activities which aggravate the disease, and the 'aggravating activities' comprise the ways in which a man thinks about the unconscious, and about unconscious psychic elements generally. An account of man's disease must include an account of the attitude of consciousness.

4. *The Attitude of Consciousness*

The psychological diagnosis relates the symptoms of man's disease to past acts of repression of psychic elements, and to the continued repression of those elements in the present. This continued repression of rejected elements is the present activity which maintains and aggravates the disease, and it arises from the antagonistic attitude of consciousness to the unconscious. The symptoms express the antagonism of the unconscious to consciousness, but since the unconscious is not under the conscious control this antagonistic 'attitude' of the unconscious cannot be directly influenced: on the other hand 'The mask of the unconscious is not rigid—it reflects the face we turn towards it. Hostility lends it a threatening aspect, friendliness softens its features' (*Alchemy*, 29), so that the attitude of the unconscious can be indirectly influenced by that of consciousness. The antagonism between consciousness and the unconscious continues because of the conscious attitude, and the psychological prescription is that this attitude should be changed. The prescription itself is not part of the account of the disease, and the discussion of it does not belong to this chapter, but in order to complete the account of the disease the conscious attitude which needs to be changed has to be examined.

The attitude of consciousness which maintains the disease of natural man is one of antagonism towards the unconscious and this antagonism is expressed in some or all of five ways: the unconscious may be thought of as evil, dangerous, sub-human, divine, and numinous, and the myth explains why we should think of the unconscious in these ways, and why they are likely to involve antagonism towards it.

(a) *The Unconscious as Evil*. 'A man's unconscious', says Jung, 'is likewise feminine and is personified by the anima. The anima also stands for the "inferior" function and for that reason has a shady character; in fact she sometimes stands for evil itself' (*Alchemy*, 192): 'The shadow corresponds to a negative ego-personality and includes all those qualities we find painful or regrettable' (ibid., p. 169, n.). It is inevitable that the unconscious should seem to be evil because many elements are unconscious just because they have been rejected from consciousness as 'evil', and because unconscious elements are 'contaminated' with each other: that is, so long as elements remain unconscious they cannot be distinguished, so that although it is only the rejected elements which have been characterized as evil we tend to think of all unconscious elements in the same way.

(b) *The Unconscious as Dangerous.* 'To let the unconscious go its own way and to experience it as a reality is something beyond the courage and capacity of the average European. He prefers simply not to understand this problem. For the spiritually weak-kneed this is the better course, since the thing is not without its dangers' (ibid., 60): 'the remarkable potency of unconscious contents, therefore, always indicates a corresponding weakness in the conscious mind and its functions' (*Practice*, 374). In so far as a man thinks of himself as identical with his own consciousness the opinion that the unconscious is dangerous is entirely justified. Odd though the language would be it might be said that 'the unconscious' is the name of the fact that no conscious standpoint has absolute validity. The unconscious is to be thought of as standing over against every conscious synthesis as the possibility of further development, and such development can only take place at the expense of the synthesis already formed, since the old pattern must be broken up if room is to be made for new elements. If any conscious synthesis is taken as final and absolute, then consciousness must reject the unconscious, because the unconscious is then a very real danger to it.

(c) *The Unconscious as Sub-human.* Jung comments on a dream: 'But if the life-mass is to be transformed a *circumambulatio* is necessary, i.e., exclusive concentration on the centre, the place of creative change. During this process one is "bitten" by animals; in other words, we have to expose ourselves to the animal impulses of the unconscious without identifying ourselves with them and without "running away"' (*Alchemy*, 186). The unconscious includes all those instincts and tendencies most closely connected with our physical, 'animal', nature, so long as we are not conscious of them. If we are to be fully human such elements must have their place in our life, but the man who strives exclusively after 'higher' and 'more spiritual' ends regards the 'animal impulses' as evil and debasing, and in most civilized minds there is a tendency to think in this way, although it may not be marked in particular individuals, and it is an aspect of the antagonistic attitude of consciousness to the unconscious.

(d) *The Unconscious as Divine.* The unconscious 'holds possibilities which are locked away from the conscious mind, for it has at its disposal all subliminal psychic contents, all those things which have been forgotten or overlooked, as well as the wisdom and experience of uncounted centuries which are laid down in its archetypal organs' (*Essays*, 196). This sounds a not unattractive description of the unconscious, but whether or not it is attractive depends upon what a man wants. The man who is content with his conscious synthesis wants to have nothing to do with possibilities 'locked away' from consciousness, and to such a man this aspect of the unconscious is as unpleasant as any other. In this respect the unconscious may be said to be 'divine', since it is as though it said 'get thee out of thy country, and from thy kindred, and from thy father's house, unto the land that I will show thee' but there are many for whom this is not a recommendation: such a call is not always welcome, even when it is spoken by God Himself.

(e) Finally, the unconscious, as all that is not conscious, is 'wholly other'. Even in reading about the unconscious in the books of psychologists one can become aware of that mixture of fascination and dread which is the mark of encounters with the 'numinous', and Jung says 'The other centre of personality lies on a different plane from the ego since, unlike this, it has the quality of "eternity" or relative timelessness' (*Alchemy*, 135), and, more explicitly, he says that all unconscious elements exhibit 'a numinous—"divine" or "sacred"—quality' (ibid., 448). In virtue of its 'otherness' the unconscious provides us with a convenient scapegoat, and it is easy to accuse it of all that we think is evil, undesirable and unwanted.

Jung brings together all these attitudes to the unconscious in a description of the 'Mercurius' of the Alchemists. 'The unconscious', he says, 'is not just evil by nature, it is also the source of the highest good: not only dark but also light, not only bestial, semi-human, and demonic but superhuman, spiritual, and, in the classical sense of the word, "divine". The Mercurius who personifies the unconscious is essentially "duplex", paradoxically dualistic by nature, fiend, monster, beast, and at the same time panacea, "the philosophers' son", *sapientia Dei*, and *donum Spiritus Sancti*' (*Practice*, 389).

The erroneous attitude to the unconscious can be stated easily

enough in terms of these five ways of thinking about it. The unconscious is thought to be evil because psychic elements have been
wrongly rejected as evil; it is thought to be dangerous, because a
conscious synthesis is wrongly regarded as absolute; it is thought to
be sub-human by those who wrongly ignore the physical basis of
human nature; its 'divinity' is a menace to those who are wrongly
content with themselves as they are; and its otherness induces us to
treat it with the suspicion with which we are wrongly accustomed to
face the unknown. Yet it may be asked if this is more than verbiage,
unless it can be shown that there is some sense in speaking of the
attitude which a man takes to a conceptual construct like the unconscious. Since the unconscious is not a thing, but a way of talking about
events, it must be shown what meaning is to be given to the idea of an
attitude of consciousness to the unconscious.

Suppose that a man were in a tropical forest, and that he occasionally
heard tigers roar, that he sometimes found the recent spoor of a tiger,
and that his companion told him stories about tigers. If the man showed
fear on all occasions of this sort it could be said that he was afraid of
tigers, and in this way it could be true that a man was afraid of tigers
even if he had never encountered a tiger. Now suppose that there were
no such things as tigers, although roars were heard and spoor was
found, and that 'a tiger' had become a conventional name used to
refer to a putative source of roars and spoor, and that the man's
companion still told stories about something which he called 'a tiger'.
In the first situation 'fear of tigers' would include fear at the idea of
tigers (the companion's stories), and at the signs of tigers (roars and
spoor) but it would also include something more—the probable
reaction of the man if he encountered a tiger. In the second situation,
on the other hand, 'fear of tigers' would mean fear at the idea of
'tigers', at roars and recent spoors, and at any other observable things
said to be 'effects of tigers', and it could have no further meaning,
because there would be no tigers which the man might some time
encounter. There is no 'thing' called 'the unconscious', and the
'attitude of consciousness to the unconscious' is the attitude which a
man takes to the idea of the unconscious, and to the things called
'effects of unconscious elements'.

Antagonism to the idea of the unconscious may take the form of
the rejection of the whole concept, or of the insistence that it is
unimportant, or of the feeling that it is not 'nice'. Such an attitude is

found among those who reject psychotherapy, and oppose it. It may also take the form of an unnecessarily ugly or derogatory elaboration of the idea of the unconscious, and this is the attitude of some people who accept psychotherapy but think that the unconscious is evil and iniquitous. These forms of conscious antagonism to the unconscious can only arise when the idea of the unconscious has been put forward, but the antagonism also takes other forms which do not involve the idea of the unconscious at all. Antagonism to the unconscious may take the form of the opinion that those things which interfere with conscious purpose are evil, dangerous, and so on, and that they must be opposed, and such an opinion may be held by people who have never heard of 'the unconscious', and who would not describe the odd things as 'effects of the unconscious': the antagonism may take the form of the condemnation of ideas and attitudes which are expressed in the lives of others or which are thought to be expressed in their lives (projection), and which are not acknowledged by the person who condemns them as features of his own life: and the antagonism may take the form of opposition to ideas or complexes of psychic elements considered in the abstract; that is of the condemnation of view-points and 'isms'.

The psychological account of natural man is that he makes errors in behaviour and judgement, that he is liable to become 'stuck', that this is a universal but intrinsically unnecessary result of the only process by which consciousness can develop, and that societies and individuals both suffer in a similar way. The errors of behaviour and judgement, and the tendency to 'stick' persist as long as an individual takes an antagonistic attitude to psychic elements in the lives of others, odd things in his own life, and the idea of the unconscious if and when it is presented to him.

Jung and St Paul both begin with man as he is. Jung sets out to 'explain' the general facts that men sometimes frustrate their own conscious purposes, that odd things which they regard as undesirable happen to them, and that they are liable to get stuck in habit or routine. St Paul 'explains' sins, and a great many sins are included among the things which Jung 'explains'. Jung provides a myth which shows how men in general have got into a state of antagonism between conscious-ness and the unconscious, and teaches that this state is the source of the things which he explains: St Paul accepts the Jewish myth which shows how men in general got into a state of bondage to sin, and teaches that this state is the source of the actual sins of men. The discussion of the state of antagonism between consciousness and the unconscious provides a clue for the understanding of the state of bondage to sin.

It is natural that we should think of the odd things over which we do not have direct conscious control as things which ought to be prevented, and this seems to be an attitude which is altogether right when the odd things are sins. Jung, however, insists that the primary fault in human nature lies in the fact that we take an antagonistic attitude to the odd things which happen to us, and he implies that unconscious elements have an evil effect because we have already wrongly stigmatized them as evil. Within the system of Analytical Psychology there are sufficient checks to prevent this view leading to antinomianism, but if it were imported directly into theology this could hardly be avoided. What Jung's theory does suggest is that we may be mistaken if we see man's problem as nothing more than the need to overcome 'evil inclinations' in the name of the 'good will', and that it may be that the 'good will' makes an important contribution to the state of bondage to sin. In the following chapter this clue is to be applied to the theologians' account of the state of natural man.

5

THE BONDAGE OF SIN

(Man's need according to St Paul)

JUNG teaches that the unconscious, which appears to be evil, is
really as good as consciousness. This does not mean that either
the unconscious or consciousness is good at any particular time,
but that both must contribute to the full Individuated man. The
unconscious is 'good' in' the sense that it must not be thrown away,
not in the sense that it cannot be improved; and one could say that
consciousness is as bad as the unconscious in that consciousness too
must be changed before the full man can be formed. In fact, as we
have seen, the 'badness' of the unconscious is largely the result of the
badness of consciousness. The conclusion is that, in relation to the
goal of the individual, consciousness and the unconscious have equal
value, and when this conclusion is applied to theology it should mean
that in relation to salvation the good will has no more value than the
evil inclinations. In this chapter it will be argued that this is what
Christian theology does teach.

In making a detailed comparison between the process connected
with Justification by Faith and that connected with Individuation it is
important to proceed step by step, and not to be put off by the antici-
pation of difficulties not directly relevant to the particular step with
which one is concerned. In this chapter, for instance, St Paul's description of natural man is compared with that of Jung and in making
this comparison it is impossible not to notice that it is unlikely that
St Paul and Jung would agree about which individuals should be
described in this way and which should not. St Paul's account of
natural man must be inferred from what he says about Jews and
Gentiles, that is about all who are not Christians, and it is certain that
Jung would not accept the implication that all non-Christians are still
in the state of natural man and all Christians are not. Behind this
disagreement there lies a very important contrast between the two

processes and this contrast will be considered in later chapters, but it is not directly relevant to the discussion in this chapter which is concerned with what Christians say about the state of natural man, and not with whether or not certain people should be regarded as being in that state. The comparison of the Christian and Jungian accounts of natural man is a necessary preliminary to a discussion of the application of those accounts to this or that group of individuals, and nothing more than this preliminary comparison is attempted.

According to St Paul natural man is 'in bondage to sin': he says, 'Our old man was crucified with [Christ] that we should no longer be in bondage to sin', and that Christians are 'free from sin', and there is no doubt that he means that natural man inevitably sins. Yet when this has been said there are still two very different ways in which St Paul can be understood: on the one hand he may be taken to mean no more than that, in general, a man's evil inclinations prove stronger than his good will, so that however much he may sometimes do what is right he also inevitably does wrong as well; on the other hand it may mean that even when a man's good will directs his life he yet fails to do what is right. St Paul's account of natural man only resembles Jung's if 'being in bondage to sin' is understood in the second way, because it is only if it is understood in this way that it involves (like Jung's account) a revaluation of the value-judgements which a man ordinarily makes. Understood in the second way to say that natural man is in 'bondage to sin' means that natural man sins even when he thinks that he is doing what is right, and it will be shown in this chapter that this is how what St Paul says ought to be understood. It may be noticed that this is how the Christian view is understood in the 13th Article of the Church of England where it is said of good works done before Justification, 'We doubt not but that they have the nature of sin.'

To accept what St Paul says and to understand it in the second way is not to condemn all who are not Christians, but it does mean to believe that in general those who are not Christians are in bondage to sin, and that they are therefore failing to follow a road which leads to salvation *even when they are doing what they think is right*. In other words those who believe this are committed to the view that the *principles* of non-Christian religions and societies are wrong. The Christian argument is not that there are no good men who are not Christians, nor that Christians as a whole are better than others, nor yet that there is nothing to be learnt from other religions and systems; what the Christian believes is that Christianity points along the right road and that nothing else does. Individuals who have never heard of Christianity may be guided along the right road by God, and another religion may teach much that is very good, but the Christian believes that the One Way is the way of Jesus Christ.

In this chapter the belief that all men who are not Justified are in bondage to sin (which implies that Christianity is the unique way to salvation) will be set out as convincingly as we can make it from three points of view. First the belief will be stated in a way which will show that it is neither absurd nor illogical; secondly it will be shown that it is implicit in many theological assertions which do not usually cause offence; thirdly it will be argued that the belief as it is stated here is in accordance with what St Paul says.

1. *Restatement of the Idea of 'Bondage to Sin'*

St Paul (and all the New Testament writers) saw the world as a world gone wrong and on the wrong road, and Jesus as the only light which could guide men on the right road. One difficulty in accepting this view today is the tendency to think of Christianity as one religion among many—a religion like other religions—even among those who also think that it is better than most. The early Christians, on the other hand, thought of Christianity as unlike other religions: they supposed that Christianity was the truth revealed by God Himself, and that all other religions were the creation of perverted human reason or the invention of devils. If we look carefully at the modern view we see that it implies that the Holy Spirit merely corrects and strengthens the 'good will' in men, whereas in the thought of St Paul He is regarded as an 'alien' third—an addition within a man's nature standing over against that man's good will as much as He stands over against his evil inclinations. For St Paul what we think of as 'good will' on the one hand and 'evil inclinations' on the other make up 'the flesh', because Dodd is surely right when he says that to St Paul 'The "sinful body" is the self as the organization of the sinful impulses inherent in the flesh' (*Dodd*, 90), and if this is so the 'sinful body' must include what a man calls his 'good will', because this is necessarily prominent in his *organized* self. The ideas suggested by these remarks may be set out as follows:

(i) Natural man knows himself as a dichotomy of his 'good will' on the one hand and his 'evil inclinations' on the other, each part opposed to the other.

(ii) St Paul regards the Justified Christian as being a dichotomy of 'the Spirit' and 'the flesh'.

(iii) At first sight it would seem that these two ways of looking at man are very much the same, with different names used in the two descriptions—that is, that what St Paul calls 'the Spirit' corresponds to what natural man calls his 'good will'. This cannot be correct, however, because the second term ('the flesh') of St Paul's dichotomy includes *both* terms of the first dichotomy. The explanation offered here is that for St Paul the coming of the Spirit into the life of a man causes that man to revalue all else that is in him, so that what he before regarded as his 'good will' he no longer thinks to be good. Put another way: according to St Paul, the Christian judging in the light of Christ can no longer accept the good will of natural man as truly 'good'. The 'flesh' is still to be thought of as divided in itself, but neither part is to be regarded as satisfactory, because the true goodness is only found in man to the extent that the Justified man is indwelt by the Holy Spirit. Since St Paul rarely has occasion to refer to the dichotomy of 'the flesh' (as it appears to the Christian) he does not provide us with terms by which to speak of it, and for lack of such terms we may as well speak of 'the high impulses of the flesh' on the one hand, and 'the low impulses of the flesh' on the other. We should then say that what natural man regards as his 'good will' the Christian calls 'the high impulses of the flesh', and that what he regards as his 'evil inclinations' the Christian calls 'the low impulses of the flesh'.

According to this view the Christian should not put his trust in his own good will, but should put it in the Holy Spirit, and the only *human* attitude which he could properly describe as a 'good will' would be the readiness to be guided by the Spirit in all things. Such a good will is unlike that of natural man in that it has no specific content; that is, it is not directed to this or that particular end, but to a general submission to the Holy Spirit of God. This does not mean that the Christian will not use his ability to examine and consider all the features of a situation, nor even that he will not make tentative moral judgements: what it does mean is that he will not commit himself beforehand, either to action, or to some particular result of his action. For example, the Christian may decide that a certain act is right, but even so he will pray that in the moment of action he may be guided by the Spirit, and he will be ready to find that, under the guidance of the Spirit, he does not do what he previously thought would be right. Again, the Christian may judge what will be the best result which his action could have, but he will be willing to find that he has been used by the Spirit for some quite different purpose, knowing that all things work together for good to them that love God. The Christian will use his natural faculties, but he will use them with a general mistrust, and pray at all times 'Thy will, not mine, be done'. To say that the good will of natural man is sinful is to say that it is finally determined by other considerations than bare obedience to God; that is, it is determined by what man himself judges to be right and good.

A second source of difficulty in accepting the view that the good will may lead to sin arises from a misunderstanding of what is meant by 'sin', due to a lack of precision in the language of theology in relation to wrong-doing. It is clear, on the one hand, that there is an important difference between doing wrong knowing that it is wrong, and doing wrong believing that it is right; but, on the other hand, it is also clear (if only from the fact that the last statement can be understood) that there is a sense of 'wrong' in which we may do wrong without knowing it. Yet neither theology nor morality is provided with a precise and generally accepted terminology by which to distinguish between the two senses of 'wrong', and, in particular, 'sin' is sometimes used of all wrong acts, and sometimes only of those acts for which a man is morally culpable. We find, however, that St Paul uses 'to sin' in parallel with 'to fall short of the glory of God', and the second concept is entirely objective, since any creature which fails to reflect God's glory in its own proper measure falls short of that glory, whether moral guilt is applicable to it or not. It is in this sense that 'sin' is used here, so that it applies to any act which neither springs from loving obedience to God, nor is aimed at bringing men to the goal of knowledge and love of God, and in this sense of sin it will be argued that natural man sins when he follows his own 'good will'.

If the preceding argument is correct, then the assertion that natural man sins even when he follows his own good will is a Christian dogma intended to have universal application, and this means that it cannot be proved by bringing instances in support of it. Nevertheless, particular instances of its truth will help to encourage acceptance of the dogma, and they will show that it is not *prima facie* absurd. We may begin with three extreme instances. The order of 'Thugs' in India regarded ritual murder as a sacred duty, and a member of the order under obedience to slay a close friend would regard the act as being in accordance with moral duty, and would suppose that any shrinking he might have revealed the weakness of his flesh. Some tribes have supposed that it was a duty to eat their defeated enemies, in order to incorporate their virtue within the tribe. In many cultures religious prostitution has been enjoined as right and proper. The point of these instances is not that things which we believe to be wrong were permitted, but that they were actually enjoined as being in accord with social or religious principles, and that they would have appeared to those who accepted those principles to be acts in accordance with their 'good will'. We may, and we should say that in acting in these ways those who did so were not morally blameworthy,[1] but there is no reason why we should say that what they did was right: we do not think that it was, and we are entitled to our own beliefs. It has been pointed out that in such extreme instances we must judge that those who followed their good will did wrong in order to prepare the way for a similar criticism of those whose good will is less clearly opposed to our own views. In these extreme instances few of us would want to say that it was right for men to do what they believed to be best, and if this cannot be said in such cases it cannot be laid down as a general principle as some people would wish.

Aristotle's well-known description of the magnanimous man can hardly be left out. Once again, it is not a question of what a man did, but of how a good and honest man thought that the best people ought to behave: 'He is thought', Aristotle wrote, 'to recollect those whom he has benefited, but not those from whom he has received benefits: for the receiver is inferior to the giver: but the magnanimous man wishes to be superior, and the benefits which he confers he hears of with pleasure, but those which he receives with pain' (*Aristotle* iv; iii, 13). We can see easily enough what Aristotle is getting at and we should be inclined to condemn it lightly as 'going a bit far', but in the light of Jesus we ought to condemn it far more strongly as opposed to a major part of his teaching. Similarly the Jewish Rabbis were some of the most earnest exponents of one of the highest ethical religions the world has known, and yet it was against their attempts to live according to their principles that Jesus hurled His fiercest denunciations.

---

[1] It is often said that they should be morally blamed because 'they ought to have known better'. But *why* ought they to have done so?

Buddhism no doubt demands heights of self-renunciation, but, in common with its parent Hinduism, it is orientated to a world-rejecting ideal in direct contradiction to the Christian belief that God saw His world to be very good. Confucianism is shot through with a concern for the respect of men wholly at variance with the teaching of Jesus. Islam incorporated expansion by force as an ideal, and did not (like Christianity) fall into the use of force by historical accident. In all these instances the actual ideals to which the good will is directed are wrong from the point of view of the Christian, and this means that from that point of view however good the particular acts which they enjoin they necessarily lead in the wrong direction. Finally, what are we to say of the ideals of West European humanism? and of the moral judgements based upon those ideals? Much that is included in them, and much morality based upon or associated with them has been, as it were, 'deposited' by the centuries of Christianity, and to this extent it partly represents the will of the Holy Spirit, but if it is to be regarded as representing the good will of natural man it is to be judged as it is presented by those who no longer accept the Christian basis. Taken at its best the ethic of humanism aims at the temporal good of mankind, considered in its widest sense: that is, it is directed not only to bodily health and comfort, but also to the development of the mind, to amity between individuals and nations, freedom from the un-necessary coercion of the individual, trustworthiness, and honesty, and all these things are good. Many people even think that the Christian ethic is the humanist ethic with 'religious' duties added, but nothing could be more mistaken.

Those things for which the humanist aims are good from a Christian point of view, and whenever it is simply a question whether an act will lead to the temporal good of man or not the Christian's moral judgement will coincide with that of the humanist. But the Christian believes that there are other things which are more important than the humanist's good, and if a choice has to be made (as it well may have to be) between such things and temporal well-being then the Christian's judgement will differ from that of the humanist. For example, it is not always clear that, from the Christian point of view, a dying man should be preserved from all pain by drugs if the result must be that he is unable to make final preparation for death. For the Christian, health of body should be regarded as subordinate to health of soul; development of mind is less important than the turning of the mind to

God, and amity is not worth the denial of Jesus; converting a slave to the true faith will bring him greater benefits, in the eyes of the Christian, than winning freedom for him. There can be no assurance that we shall not be faced with choices between such things, and in so far as we are Christians we must differ from humanists who do not accept God. In a world in which men do evil, temporal good may have to be sacrificed for the sake of spiritual good; why else did Jesus not only endure the suffering and death of the Cross Himself, but also set His closest friends on a road which would bring them to a similar fate? It is true that we believe that if all men were to seek first the Kingdom of God, then all temporal goods would be added unto them, but the Christian ought not even to seek the Kingdom for this reason, let alone to regard such goods as more important than seeking for God: the Kingdom of God is to be sought for its own sake, and for no other reason. It may, of course, be said that we ought not to try to preach the Gospel until we have relieved the temporal needs of men (as Satan suggested to Jesus that He might begin by turning stones to bread), or, more mildly, it may be said that the relief of temporal need is a help to the evangelist. This may be said—in fact, it is said—but very little can be added in support. The remarkable increase in the general standard of living in this country during the last hundred years has hardly resulted in an increased concern for God, and, in general, when men are most contented with their life on earth, and when they feel most secure they are least likely to worry their heads about God.

On the whole, natural man is likely to be led by his good will to do particularly things which the Christian believes are contrary to the will of God. On the other hand, it is perfectly possible to conceive of a natural man acting, in certain circumstances, in exactly the same way as a Christian would act, under the guidance of the Spirit, in the same circumstances. Yet even in this hypothetical instance it could still be maintained that the acts of natural man are 'of the nature of sin'. After all, although God does will that men should do certain things, His primary purpose is that men should know Him, love Him, and obey Him, and no amount of external conformity to His will can be a valid alternative. Devotion to duty or to the common good of mankind, for instance, involves idolatry, for it is to give the devotion due only to God to something or someone else, and because it involves idolatry it is sinful. We may honour disinterested sacrifice of self, but such sacrifice alone is not enough; it is all-important what it is for which we sacrifice ourselves: it is quite possible for the worship of the devil to be carried out with as much devotion as the worship of God. If it is suggested, however, that a man who has had no opportunity of hearing of the Father of Jesus Christ may do the will of God while giving his devotion to Him by another name, then the case is more complicated. We dare not confine the Holy Spirit, and we cannot say that such devotion is never unwittingly given to the true God, but we must ask how far what such a man believes about his God is compatible with what Jesus revealed, and the ultimate question must be whether if such a man hears the Gospel he receives it with joy or persists in his old beliefs—just as this was the question with which the coming of Jesus confronted the Jew. And it may well be that the higher and more worthy the pagan's conception of God the less ready he will be to set his own beliefs aside.

This needed to be said in defence of the doctrine that the 'good will' of natural man must be rejected by the Christian. It has now to be shown that this view is implicit in the writings of Christian theologians, and that it is the teaching of St Paul. This doctrine is bound up with the common division of sins into sins of pride on the one hand, and sins of sensuality on the other, and this division of sins will be considered in the next section.

2. *Pride and Sensuality*

The Christian teaching that the good will of natural man is perverted may be shown by direct quotation from Christian writers, and by considering the judgements of Christians upon their behaviour before they were converted. It is also implicit in the division of sins into two great classes which may be called 'sins of pride' and 'sins of sensuality'.

St Paul says, 'We know not how to pray as we ought', and then goes on to explain that Christian prayer is only adequate because 'The Spirit Himself maketh intercession with our spirit'. In other words, even when a man is Justified his high impulses (in this case the impulse to pray) do not lead him aright, and if this is so the high impulses of natural man must be even less trustworthy. St Paul's comment also shows that Justification is not to be thought of as in itself a process of transforming the good will of natural man: the presence of the Spirit of God does not transform the spirit of man so that a man may do what is good, but the Spirit does in the man the good things which he cannot do himself, if the man will let Him. St John of the Cross says explicitly: 'At every step we consider evil to be good, and good evil, and this arises from our own nature' (*Ascent*, 44). The Christian teaching has always been that the good will of natural man cannot be trusted, and this teaching can be easily illustrated from modern writers.

'Paul', writes Bultmann, 'is of this opinion: *Man has always already missed the existence that at heart he seeks*, his intent is basically perverse, evil' (*Bultmann*, 227). 'Our will is evil,' says H. R. Mackintosh, 'It is not wholly evil . . . but evil taints it in every element' (*Mackintosh*, 52). Nygren remarks that 'in the concept "flesh" is included all that belongs by nature to man's life, from the lowest to the highest' (*Nygren*, 320). In Kittel's word-book we read 'Practical reason, the power to make judgements and act on them, which exalts man to a divine sovereignty in the sphere of his own affairs—that is the germ of sinful behaviour' (*Sin*, 26). Niebuhr writes: 'In the same way it is not possible to exempt "reason" or any other human faculty from the disease of sin' (*Niebuhr*, 277). Again, the condemnation of the good will of natural man is implied by what is said of the new life of the Christian: Anderson Scott says that, according to St Paul, 'There was to be a continuous renewing of the mind and the result was to be expected in the recognition or discovery of that will, namely, what is good and well-pleasing and perfect' (*Scott*, 176), implying that the Spirit does not only bring to man the power to do the good which he knew before, but could not do, but also brings to him a new understanding of what is good; to the same effect Vincent Taylor says 'the mind, the feelings, and the will are stimulated and engaged, no longer at the behest of purely self-regarding purposes, but in obedience to motives which are "baptized into Christ"' (*Taylor*, 118), from which it follows that before this occurred, that is in the natural man, mind and will were infected as much as the rest of a man.

The formal assertion that the good will of natural man is perverted can be reinforced by considering the self-criticisms of St Paul and St Augustine. Before their conversion both men did things which were wrong, and both have left a record of their later condemnation of their past. From the 'Confessions' it is clear that St Augustine regarded his readiness to be a 'fellow-traveller' of the Manichees with a disapproval greater than that with which he viewed his sensual sins, and when St Paul said that he was not 'meet to be called an Apostle', he added, 'because I persecuted the Church of God'. Yet in listening to the Manichees St Augustine was following the truth as he then saw it, and striving to distinguish truth from error; and in persecuting Christians St Paul, as he then believed, was giving himself to the service of God: in other words, both men condemned themselves for those things which were in accordance with what, at the time, they considered to be their good will. St Paul and St Augustine would both insist that by doing what they believed to be right they fell into grievous sin. Nygren, in my opinion, goes too far when he says: 'There actually is a righteousness which is to be achieved by virtue of the law; and in relation to that he had *not* failed, but was a "man without reproach"' (*Nygren*, 13), but the comment is a useful corrective to the view that St Paul's only complaint against the law was that it could not be kept. Bultmann also says: 'For just this is what his conversion meant: In it he surrendered his previous understanding of himself; i.e. he surrendered what had till then been the norm and meaning of his life, he sacrificed what had hitherto been his pride and joy (Phil. 3 : 4–7). His conversion was not the result of an inner moral collapse. . . . It was not rescue from the despair into which the cleavage between willing and doing had allegedly driven him' (*Bultmann*, 188).

Sin (whatever we may say of 'moral wrongdoing') is a man's failure to do what is according to the will of God, and not his failure to do what he himself believes to be right, and since the judgement of natural man is perverted by the disease of being in bondage to sin, what a man believes to be right is frequently contrary to the will of God. This is not only the expressed opinion of theologians, but is also implicit in the Christian insistence that pride is both the root and the flower of sin. 'Sin', writes Niebuhr, 'is the self's undue pride and exaltation' (*Niebuhr*, 277), and H. H. Farmer says, 'in the assertion of the will against God's, all other self-assertion is included. All these are taken up into the religious sense of sin, and are, as it were, overtones within it, sometimes one, sometimes another, being more dominant. Yet the ground-tone, which abides throughout, is the sense of being in conflict, through a refusal to obey, with the Eternal Personal' (*Farmer*, 189). Pride is that attitude which expresses itself in refusal to obey, but this view is only possible if the acts which spring from pride are acts which the sinner believes to be right. The pride of Lucifer may have expressed itself in the assertion of the creature, in deliberate revolt against the known will and power of God, and in the

Christian myth of the Fall Adam knows the command which he transgresses, but human pride is rarely conceived on so grand a scale: the man who suffers from pride is more often blind, and his pride is expressed in his assertion of the validity of his own judgements, and in his rejection of criticism. Pride is not vanity, but a deep-rooted confidence in oneself and in one's own ability to judge what is right. In the majority of instances acts which Christians regard as refusal to obey God are not the refusal to obey a known command but the inevitable consequence of men thinking that they know what is right. The proud man relies upon himself, and by doing so he rejects God whether he knows it or not, and if a man relies on his own belief that he knows the will of God, then he rejects God when he supposes that he is being most obedient. 'Pride' is not the name of certain particular sins of thought or act, but refers to an attitude of mind: at the same time the acts which spring from a man's reliance upon himself may be called 'sins of pride', whatever their individual character. The reason why sins of pride are said to be acts of deliberate disobedience is that they are deliberate acts, even though they may not be deliberately disobedient acts. By definition sins of pride are not 'accidents', and if a man is carried away by his instincts, for example, he does not commit a sin of pride. To be proud a man must succeed, or think that he succeeds, in his conscious aims, and this means that sins of pride are those sins which a man does not acknowledge as sins. 'Pride' refers to a whole class of sins, and the sins to which it refers are those which a man commits when he most fully follows what he calls his 'good will'.

It is natural to contrast sensuality with pride. Pride goes with 'strength of will', sensuality with 'weakness of will'. In its primary meaning 'sensuality' refers to those sins which a man commits when he gives way to physical desires, but it is a legitimate extension of the term to apply it to all sins which 'happen' to a man; that is, to the sins which he does not wish to commit, but 'finds himself' committing. The sins of sensuality are those sins for which a man is loth to take responsibility, and from which he would like to dissociate himself by using phrases like 'I was carried away', or 'I was not myself at the time'. 'Sensuality' stands for the sins which men commit despite themselves, and the sins of sensuality stand in sharp contrast to the sins of pride. Sins of pride are acts which a man does with full and deliberate intent; they are not only acts which he does not know as sins, but also they are the acts to which a man points when he wishes to show his own worthiness. Sins of sensuality, on the other hand, are acts which a man commits contrary to his intentions, they are acts which he acknowledges to be wrong, and acts of which he is ashamed. 'Pride' and 'sensuality' are the two forms in which the good will of natural man, on the one hand, and his evil inclinations on the other, manifest themselves in his life.

Pride and sensuality, as they have been explained here, are to be distinguished from vanity and libertinism. When a man is momentarily carried away by thoughts of his own importance, for example, he may think that he has been guilty of pride, but his sin was one of vanity, not pride. In so far as a man is aware that he sins he does not assert his infallibility, and he is carried away against his own judgement, and when this happens he is not proud. In other words vanity, although it may look like a sin of pride, ought to be included among the sins of sensuality. Similarly, if a man consciously and deliberately takes the satisfaction of physical lusts as the aim of his life, then he does not regard his sensual sins as sins, but as acts which are in accordance with his purpose, and such sins should be regarded as sins of pride and not sins of sensuality. In general, pride arises in connection with moral success, sensuality in connection with moral failure. For the practical purposes of evangelism the distinction between these two great classes of sins is of great importance: put concisely, if you want to convince a man that he is a sinner, then you must point out to him the sins of sensuality which he commits, but in order to lay bare the extent of his sinfulness you must also make him aware of his sins of pride. Further, so long as man is only aware of sins of sensuality he attempts to avoid them by relying more upon his good will, and so falls deeper into sins of pride. The sins of sensuality are known as sins, both to the sinner and to the Christian observer, but the sins of pride can only be known as sins to the Christian. This means that in any discussion of sin it is of first importance to make it very clear when one is speaking of sin as it is known to natural man, and when one is speaking of sin as it appears to the Christian. This distinction is of great importance in following St Paul's discussion in the Epistle to the Romans, as will be found in the next section of this chapter.

The picture of the sinner which has been presented is that of a man whose deliberate purpose to do what is right is perverted. It does not matter how he would analyse the term 'right'; it is wholly indifferent

6—J.S.P.

whether he says that his aim is to do the will of the gods, to fulfil his destiny, to develop his personality, to act for the greatest good of the greatest number, or to gain greatest physical pleasure for himself: the Christian teaching is that whatever the ends and means which natural man sets before himself, and however he justifies them to himself, they are not those ends and means which God has chosen for him. In other words, natural man deliberately chooses evil instead of good, even though he does not deliberately choose it as evil. At the same time natural man is not (or not as a rule) unswerving and unerring in carrying out the purposes which he has set himself, but is beset by errors and failures which he is forced to admit arise from what he himself is, and which he must acknowledge to be sinful—although he may prefer some other more or less equivalent term by which to speak of them. The account which such a man gives of himself is that of a man divided between his good will and his evil inclinations, and his desire is that the evil inclinations should be subordinated to the good will. Such a man is in bondage to sin, but this does not primarily mean (as he supposes that it does) that he fails to bring his evil inclinations under the control of his good will, but rather that the alternatives before him lead equally to sin. If, on the one hand, he ceases to strive after his purposes, and lets the evil inclinations have their way, then he commits sins of sensuality, and he knows that he sins. If, on the other hand, he succeeds in controlling his evil inclinations by his good will, he may imagine that he no longer sins, but he commits sins of pride which he does not recognize as sins. Apart from his evil inclinations and his good will, natural man has nothing to which he can turn, so that, turn as he will, he is condemned to sin. This appears to be what is meant by saying that natural man is 'in bondage to sin', and Justification saves a man by providing the third term which he lacks—the Spirit of God, which offers him a new way, between the Charybdis of his evil inclinations and the Scylla of his good will.

3. *St Paul's Account*

Jung's account of the antagonism between consciousness and the unconscious, his insistence that the unconscious must be treated with respect, suggested the possibility that St Paul's account of bondage to sin might involve the assertion that the good will of natural man was no more worthy of respect than his evil inclinations. It has been shown that this idea is not *prima facie* absurd, that it is implicit in much theological thought about sin, and that some commentators understand St Paul in this sense. It has now to be shown that this way of understanding what St Paul says is legitimate.

In any examination of St Paul's account of natural man attention must be given to the seventh chapter of the Epistle to the Romans. Unfortunately, however, there is not any general agreement whether the last part of this chapter is an account of the state of natural man, or of the state of the Justified sinner. Worse, the main arguments offered for one or other of these opinions depend upon the opinions of those who offer them about how St Paul thought of these two states. This means that one cannot decide to whom these verses refer until one has understood what St Paul meant by 'being in bondage to sin', and it follows that they cannot be used as evidence for a particular opinion about St Paul's conception of that state: at most they are a negative test in that no account of what St Paul meant by 'bondage to sin' is acceptable unless these verses can be understood in the light of it. It is as well to begin, therefore, by showing how chapter 7 would be understood in relation to the view of St Paul's thought put forward here.

It has been suggested that the state of being in bondage to sin appears to the sinner as a dichotomy of good will and evil inclinations, and that the natural man knows that there is something wrong with that state because the evil inclinations often overcome the good will. It has also been said that the man who is in bondage to sin cannot know the full extent of his sinfulness because he regards the high impulses of the flesh as good (and calls them his 'good will'). In the Justified sinner the opposition between the high and the low impulses of the flesh continues but when a man is Justified he knows, as the natural man cannot, that both high and low impulses of the flesh war against the Spirit. If this is correct it means that although natural man can be shown that he is a sinner it is not until he is Justified that he can understand the full extent to which he was in bondage to sin before. In order to describe, in its full hopelessness, the state of the man who is in bondage to sin, it is not enough to describe that state as it appears to the man who is in it, because the only man who knows the truth about it is the Christian, and he is not in it. In order to give an adequate account of the state of the man who is in bondage to sin one must point to the flesh, which in the Christian opposes the Spirit, and say 'before you were Justified there was nothing but this: all that is now true of what you call the flesh and recognize as evil, was before true of you'. It is easy to understand chapter 7 of the Epistle to the Romans if this is the sort of thing that St Paul was doing.

Verses 7 to 13 of Romans, chapter 7, are clearly an account of the natural man from his own point of view, and it is also clear that St Paul has his own past life much in mind. The failure of the good will is pressed, and the account ends with the remark that sin and law combined together 'that sin might become exceeding sinful'. This conclusion represents a transition from the account of the state of being in bondage to sin as it appears to the man who is in that state, to an account of the same state as it is known from the standpoint of the Justified sinner. In order to develop the 'exceeding sinfulness' of sin St Paul turns to the experience of those who have received the Spirit, and he marks this by his change from past to present tense. From verse 14 onwards St Paul is speaking of life after Justification, but, it is suggested, his purpose is still to show the hopeless state of man before Justification, and not, primarily, to describe the new life. If this suggestion is correct, what St Paul is doing is to draw his readers' attention to the 'old man' which they still know (despite the presence of the Spirit) so that they can see how miserable was their state before the Spirit came. Elsewhere, when St Paul speaks of the new life in Christ, he fixes attention on the new thing, the Spirit of Christ, which has come into their lives, because in relation to the new life this is all that matters; here he concentrates on the flesh which wars against the Spirit, and this is some indication that his thought is still turned to the old life, rather than the new. Just as the coming of Jesus into the world reveals the sinfulness of mankind, through His rejection by men, so the coming of the Spirit to the individual reveals his sinfulness by the opposition to Him in the man's flesh. If St Paul is understood in the way suggested, then the last two verses of this chapter fall into place.

The suggestion is that St Paul has been using his own experience since his conversion, in order to bring out the full hopelessness of natural man who has not received the Spirit. The opposition of his flesh to the Spirit reveals the full sinfulness of that flesh, so that in effect St Paul is to be thought of as saying: 'Imagine, this, without the Spirit, was what I was before I was Justified', and it is from this imagined state of knowing the truth about human nature, and yet not having received the Spirit, that the cry 'O wretched man that I am! who shall deliver me out of the body of this death?' goes up. In itself this is not a real cry at all, because no one is in a position to make it: natural man does not cry like this, because he relies upon his own good will, and cannot see his full wretchedness; the Christian does not, because he has already been redeemed, and he relies upon the Spirit. This cry can only be made by a Christian who imagines what it would be like if, *per impossibile*, knowing what he now knows he should return to his previous state, but in making such a cry the Christian immediately awakes to reality, and knows that this is only imagining —so St Paul recalls himself, and adds immediately, 'I thank God through Jesus Christ our Lord'. Then, having as it were dramatized the situation, he glosses it with a straightforward comment: 'So then, I myself with the mind serve the law of God; but with the flesh the law of sin.'

This analysis of these verses proves nothing: all that it does is to show that the view taken in this chapter is one which can be applied in such a way that these verses can be understood. The reasons for believing that this view is a correct one have yet to be given. They are to be found in chapters 1, 2 and 10 of Romans, because it is in these chapters that St Paul is speaking directly of those Jews and Gentiles who have not received the Gospel, and it is from these chapters that St Paul's account of the state of natural man must be collected. It is suggested that in chapter 1 St Paul criticizes the Gentiles from two different points of view, which may be distinguished as their own and the Christians': that in chapter 2 he criticizes the Jews from their own point of view, and that in chapter 10 he again criticizes the Jews, this time from the Christian's point of view. The following preliminary points may be taken in support of this suggestion:

(i) In chapters 1, 2 and 3, St Paul is preparing the ground for what he has to say about Christ; that is, he is showing that both Gentiles and Jews do stand in need of redemption, and that they cannot claim to be so thoroughly contented with their way of life that they can despise the salvation which is offered to them in Jesus. This is clearly St Paul's purpose here, and it is also clear that for such a purpose an argument *ad hominem* is stronger than any other. It is not illogical to say to a man, 'You do wrong, because you do not do what I think you ought to do', but it is very much more effective to say, 'You do wrong because you do not do what you think you ought to do.'

(ii) St Paul, having himself been a Jew of some repute, was in a specially strong position from which to argue in this way with Jews, and it would be surprising if he did not do so. The whole tone of the discussion in chapter 2 makes it clear that St Paul is there setting out to condemn the Jews out of their own mouths, according to their own principles, and his transition to the second person at the beginning of the chapter also indicates it. This means that there is no reason to suppose that in chapter 2 we have all the heads of St Paul's criticism of the Jewish way, and all we can expect to find in that chapter is as much of his criticism as he thinks that a Jew ought to accept. In other words, this chapter cannot be regarded as a specifically Christian account of the Jews, but should be thought of as nothing more than the account which St Paul considers a Jew might give of himself if he were sufficiently honest.

(iii) On the other hand, in respect of the Gentiles, it is not surprising that St Paul does not confine himself to an argument *ad hominem* because everything is against his making such an attempt. St Paul never showed himself particularly expert at 'getting inside' the mind of the Gentile as he was able to 'get inside' that of the Jew, and, as a Jew, he already had to hand a criticism of the Gentiles, which, seeing them from 'outside', could well be used by a Christian.[1] If St Paul had used an *ad hominem* argument against the Gentiles he would have to have begun by accepting, for the sake of his argument, the Gentiles' conception of God and their idolatry, and it may be doubted whether even for the sake of an argument he could have done that consistently. Further, St Paul's historical situation was one in which the prime enemy was the Jew, and by criticizing the Gentiles as a Jew would criticize them, and not merely as they might criticize each other, he was able to give added force to his criticisms of the Jews. There were many reasons why St Paul might have been content with the weaker argument, 'You do wrong because you do not do what I know you ought to do' writing of the Gentiles in chapter 1, and yet he used the stronger, 'You do wrong, because you do not do what you think you ought to do', when writing about the Jews in chapter 2.

(iv) At the same time, an examination of chapter 1 shows that St Paul's criticism of the Gentiles does fall into two parts, and that he was himself conscious of a distinction between two general heads of

[1] The argument in chapter 1 of Romans has close association with a similar argument in the book of Wisdom.

criticism. The two parts are marked by phrases like 'they refused' on the one hand, and 'God gave them up' on the other, and the most obvious distinction involved is that between sins which they deliberately committed on the one hand, and sins which, as it were, 'happened to them' on the other; that is, the same distinction as that made above between 'sins of pride' and 'sins of sensuality'. Further examination suggests that sins of the second sort were sins which the best Gentiles would have acknowledged to be wrong, whereas those of the first sort were sins which Christian or Jew would condemn, but which good Gentiles would not. If this is correct, then the criticisms of the Gentiles in chapter 1 can be divided into those criticisms which the Gentiles would accept on the one hand, and those which they would reject on the other.

(v) In chapter 10, St Paul is not arguing against the Jews, but examining the state of the Jew and seeking reasons why the Jews had failed to accept Christ. The whole discussion is written from a Christian point of view, and there is no question of confining it to those sins which the Jew himself would admit to be sins.

St Paul's account of those who are in bondage to sin can be divided into four parts, made up of two kinds of criticism of the Gentiles, and two of the Jews. One kind of criticism the Gentile or Jew who was criticized might be expected to accept, the other he would reject, and the four parts of the account may be tabulated:

(a) Specifically Christian criticisms of the Gentiles   Chapter 1
(b) Criticisms which honest Gentiles would accept   Chapter 1
(c) Criticisms which honest Jews would accept   Chapter 2
(d) Specifically Christian criticisms of the Jews   Chapter 10

What is to be shown is that (a) and (d) both refer to the same kind of sins, and that these are of the kind called above 'sins of pride' and that (b) and (c) both refer to sins of the kind called 'sins of sensuality'.

(a) *Specifically Christian Criticisms of the Gentiles* (Rom. 1: 18–22, 25, 28)

If verses 18–31 of chapter 1 of the Epistle to the Romans are divided according to the introductory phrases which St Paul uses, and the criticisms introduced by 'God gave them up' are omitted, then the account of the Gentiles which remains is this: they knew God, but did not give Him glory or thanks; thinking that they were wise they fell into the foolishness of idolatry; they perverted the truth; and they refused to accept the truth about God which they knew. It is easy enough to see that, whereas this criticism is unexceptionable from the point of view of St Paul, it is altogether absurd from the point of view of the Gentiles themselves: it needs to be examined from both these points of view.

St Paul's condemnation expressed in these verses rests upon his premise that 'the invisible things of (God) are clearly seen'. God may be thought of like a man who says, 'I made myself perfectly clear, and if you did not understand me, it is because you don't want to understand': anyone, St Paul implies, *could* have understood, so that since the Gentiles did not understand this was because they *would* not. So long as this is not regarded as a reference to what actually went on in the minds of the Gentiles it is a perfectly valid criticism, but if such words and phrases as 'refused' and 'knowing God' are taken to refer to actual processes of thought in the minds of the Gentiles, then the criticism will not stand. The Gentiles had not seen what God was like (i.e. what St Paul knew Him to be like) and then refused to admit what they had seen, nor had they ever known God in the way that St Paul knew Him. What St Paul calls 'refusal to have God in their knowledge' would look, from any other point of view, like a serious attempt to discover God, leading to conclusions about Him which happened to be different from St Paul's, and it may be noticed that the idea of 'deliberate refusal' implied by St Paul in this connection raises precisely the same linguistic difficulties as that of 'deliberately forgetting' in relation to repression.[1] Nevertheless, St Paul's view is clear: anybody who took the least trouble could see the truth, the Gentiles had taken trouble, but they still failed to act in accordance with the truth, therefore they had refused to accept the truth. If we say this sort of thing at all, today, we prefer to say that men have failed to see the truth that they 'ought' to have seen, and this is probably the nearest modern equivalent to what St Paul says.

If, however, the features of Gentile life on which St Paul bases these criticisms are now considered from the point of view of the Gentiles themselves, it is clear that their account would contradict his at every point. The Gentiles would say that so far from rejecting the truth which is revealed 'through the things that are made' they had reasoned correctly, and that they had the truth but St Paul had the lie:

1 cf. p. 135.

they would say that the use of idols was the true and acceptable worship of the gods: they would insist that their failure to acknowledge the God of the Jews and of St Paul was not a perverse rejection of the truth, but a clear understanding that the God in whom the Jews believed was not the true God: and, in general, they would deny that their wisdom was foolishness, and claim that it was wisdom in truth and in fact. Especially in the matter of the wisdom of idolatry the Gentiles would directly contradict St Paul: in just this, they would say, lay their good will, the highest known to them, which they strove to follow with all that was best in them. An excellent example of what the Gentiles would have said in answer to these criticisms, although in a somewhat sentimental form, was provided by Julian the Apostate, centuries later. In these matters St Paul is criticizing the Gentiles in just those things in respect of which they would claim to be strongest: he is criticizing the wisdom in which they gloried, and the way which they tried to follow as the right road, and in doing this he is bringing into question what they would call their 'good will'.

(b) Criticisms which the Gentiles would Accept (Rom.1 : 24, 26, 27,29–32)

Although St Paul's criticisms of the Gentiles can be divided into two groups, and although his language shows that he was aware of this, he does not change his point of view in chapter 1. Put in a slightly different way, St Paul is not concerned whether Gentiles would accept his criticisms or not, because he is writing to Christians with a side-glance at Jews, and his attitude to the Gentiles remains that of a detached observer throughout (as his attitude to the Jews does not). Neverthe-less, just as it has been pointed out that the good Gentile could not accept the criticisms discussed in the last section, so also it must be said that the best of them would accept the criticisms which St Paul introduces with the repeated phrase 'God gave them up', and there is reason to think that he was well aware of this.

All those evil things which St Paul introduces with 'God gave them up' are evil doings which would be stigmatized as evil on the basis of that 'wisdom' of the Gentiles which he calls 'foolishness'. The Gentile philosopher might not hold such things in the same extreme horror as a Jewish Rabbi, but he would still characterize them, more or less strongly, as undesirable; just as Plato, for example, can allow that physical homosexual relationships are, in certain circumstances, 'a coarser habit of life, and one unfriendly to wisdom, though not to honour' (*Phaedrus*, 244). It is very likely that St Paul points this by his use of the phrase 'not fitting', for the Greek word occurs only here in the whole New Testament, and a cognate word only once in Ephesians and once in Philemon, and it appears that this word was used by the Stoics as a technical term, for expressing moral judgements (*Sanday*, 47). The use of this word may well suggest that it was in St Paul's mind that these were criticisms with which the good Gentile would agree. In any event, when he condemned the Gentiles for these things St Paul was condemning those sins which occur when the evil inclinations of natural man triumph over his 'good will'.

The account of the Gentiles in chapter 1 accords very well with the description of the state of natural man suggested earlier in this chapter. On the one hand there is the 'good will', the deliberate setting of oneself to follow after wisdom, and to worship the gods of one's fathers, and, on the other, there is the failure to live up to that wisdom, the gross sins, which the Gentiles themselves would acknowledge to be 'unfitting'. The wisdom which the Gentiles would not allow to be anything other than wisdom, however, is treated as a sin, which they have deliberately committed (though not as sin), and so corresponds to the 'sins of pride'; and the unfitting behaviour is treated as something which 'happens' to the Gentiles (something to which they were 'given up') and so corresponds to 'sins of sensuality'. The Gentiles would acknowledge the dichotomy of their wisdom on the one hand, and their tendency to do unfitting acts on the other, but they would regard the first as their good will, whereas St Paul, from a Christian point of view, rejects both as sin. It has now to be shown that what has just been said of St Paul's criticism of the Gentiles is also true of his criticism of the Jews, and for this a longer argument is necessary.

(c) *Criticism which the Jews would Accept* (Rom. 2)

In chapter 2 the Jew is criticized on the basis of his own Law, and it has already been pointed out that this is the most effective kind of criticism in respect of St Paul's purpose in this chapter. The Jew is condemned by the Law which he accepts, and by which he judges the Gentiles, and there is no need for St Paul to raise the question of the status of that Law, because the failure of the Jews can be demonstrated by showing their inability to keep it. But the desire to keep the Law is what the Jew thinks of as the expression of his good will, so that as there is no need to raise the question of the status of the Law, so the good will of the Jews need not be questioned either. In this chapter the Jew is described as he might see himself, and that means that no account of sins of pride can be expected. What is found in this chapter is an account of sins of sensuality which is in accord with the description of the man who is in bondage to sin given above, and the fact that no criticism is directed against the Jews' good will is no indication that St Paul had no criticism to make of it.

The Jew, in so far as he accepts St Paul's rather gloomy account of the behaviour of Jews, recognizes a dichotomy. On the one hand the desire to keep the Law expresses his 'good will', and, on the other, his 'evil inclinations' assert their mastery when he steals, commits adultery, 'robs temples', and transgresses the law generally. In this chapter St Paul is concerned with only one criticism of the way of the law, and that is the purely pragmatic one that it does not work, and the Jews' way is shown to be unsatisfactory simply because the Jews as a whole find that they are unable to live according to the law. For the present this is all that St Paul needs to say, but that does not mean that it is all that he has got to say, as will be shown later. When he has said this St Paul has shown to his own satisfaction that both Gentiles and Jews stand in need of something which they have not got, and that neither can claim perfect satisfaction with their way of life, and he can now go on to speak of the new way offered by Christ. In chapter 3 he sums up what he has said, and then, putting the question of the state of the sinner on one side, he explains what it is that Christianity offers. It is not until chapter 10 that he returns once more to the situation of the Jew.

Transition to (d)

The good will of the Jews was expressed as zeal for their Law, so that to show that St Paul condemned their good will, as well as that of the Gentiles, it has to be shown that his criticism of the Jews included criticisms of their attempt to keep the Law, as well as criticisms of their failure in that attempt. It cannot be said that this is generally agreed by commentators. All that can be taken as established is, on the one hand, that St Paul never ceased to regard the Law as holy, righteous and true, expressing the will of God; and on the other hand, that he believed that his Jewish contemporaries were mistaken in seeking righteousness by trying to keep it.

Many theories about St Paul's attitude to the Jews in their attempt to keep the Law have been suggested from time to time. For examples:

(i) Since, in chapter 2, his criticism is directed only at the Jews' failure to keep the Law, it is often thought that this was his only criticism of them. Accordingly it is said that he believed that if a man were to keep the Law he would achieve righteousness, and, at the same time, that no man was able to keep it. This would mean that St Paul accepted the good will of the Jews as truly good, but criticized them because they failed to live up to it, and it has already been pointed out that no argument of this kind can be based upon St Paul's acceptance of the Jewish attitude in chapter 2, because it may well be that in that chapter he was using an argument *ad hominem*.

(ii) Against this first view Nygren and Bultmann, for instances, insist that St Paul's reason for rejecting the way of the Law was not merely that it could not be kept, but that it was misconceived from the beginning. This would mean that he rejected the attempt to keep the Law on the grounds that even if a man did keep it he would not become truly righteous in the sight of God, and the difficulty in accepting this view is that it hardly does justice to St Paul's insistence on the divine appointment of the Law.

(iii) It may also be suggested that St Paul regarded the way of the Law as the only divinely given way which a man could follow until the coming of Christ, but that the revelation of the new way in Christ superseded the old way of the Law. This would mean that the fault of the Jews was simply that they failed to recognize the Messiah in Jesus of Nazareth, and this is not easily reconciled with St Paul's insistence that the 'righteousness of God' offered through Christ is 'witnessed by the law and the prophets', nor with his appeal to the promise to Abraham, taken from the Torah itself.

The common assumption behind these three suggestions is that St Paul made no distinction between the Law as revealed by God, and the Law as understood by the Jews, but if chapter 10 of Romans is read with the possibility of such a distinction in mind, it is hard to come to any other conclusion than that St Paul did make it. It can, then, be suggested that:

(iv) St Paul believed that God had revealed His will to the Jews by declaring the Law, and that the Jews had failed to understand the true sense of the Law. This would mean that the Law (as revealed by God) showed the true way of righteousness, but that the attempt to do the works of the Law (i.e. the Law as it was understood by the Jews) was a misunderstanding of the way which it showed. In other words, it would mean that St Paul's controversy with the Jews was not a controversy about whether the Law did or did not express the will of God, nor about whether or not it has been superseded, but a controversy about how the Law which revealed God's will ought to be understood. For St Paul the Law properly interpreted revealed the way of Christ, for the Jew it revealed Judaism.

The *prima facie* difficulty in this suggestion is that it means that St Paul thought that God's revelation of His will through the Law was so obscure that the Jews as a whole failed to understand it, and we have trouble in believing that he could have meant that. But this is a 'pseudo-difficulty' which arises from a failure to appreciate the differences between our modern outlook and that of St Paul. If, for example, we show a certain piece of writing to a large number of people and they all find it hard to understand, then we say that it is 'obscure'; and, contrariwise, if we say that a passage is obscure we mean that most people would have difficulty in understanding it: but St Paul does not use words like 'clear' and 'obscure' in this way, and this is shown by what he says about the Gentiles, for he has no difficulty in saying both that the Gentiles, as a whole, have failed to understand the 'invisible things of God', and also that they are 'clearly seen . . . through the things that are made'. In other words, for St Paul the clarity of the revelation 'through the things that are made' is an objective quality of the revelation, which does not depend upon any consideration of how easily men understand it. By 'the revelation is clear' St Paul must be understood to mean 'if men were not in bondage to sin they would understand the revelation', so that the failure of all men to understand it does not show that the revelation is not clear, but that all men are in bondage to sin. Thus there is no difficulty if St Paul thought that the Law clearly revealed the will of God, and also that the Jews failed to understand it, since this would mean that he regarded the revelation through the Law and the Jews' attitude to it in the same kind of way as he regarded the revelation through the 'things that are made', and the Gentiles attitude to that.

It may seem, at first sight, that St Paul's assertion 'Apart from the law, a righteousness of God has been manifested' weighs against the view put forward, but this is not so. If men who are in bondage to sin cannot accept the truth which is clearly revealed by the Law, then the

Law is not practically effective to reveal the will of God to men. Something else is needed, which we should call a 'clearer' revelation, but which is not, from St Paul's point of view, clearer in itself, but only more suited to the sinfulness of men. The new revelation is thus 'apart from the Law', because it is, unlike the Law, a revelation which can be understood and accepted by sinners; at the same time, by adding that the righteousness of God that is manifested is 'witnessed by the law and the prophets', St Paul indicates that although the new revelation is 'apart from the Law' it does not, in itself, reveal anything not already revealed in the Law. In other words, if the revelation of the Law had been understood, then the revelation in Christ would have added nothing to it, and it is for this reason that St Paul appeals from Sinai to Abraham: both are Torah, but whereas the assumption of the Jews was that the Covenant at Sinai was central and determinative for the whole, St Paul, from whose eyes the scales had fallen, claimed that the true key, within the Law, for the understanding of the Law, is the promise to Abraham. This controversy with the Jews about how the Law which reveals God's will is to be understood inevitably causes a certain obscurity of language, because when St Paul has the Jews in mind, or when he is addressing Jews he can speak of 'their Law', or 'the Law' with reference to the Law as the Jew interpreted and understood it; but when he is thinking of the Law in itself he is referring to the Law as revealed by God; holy, righteous and true.

This view of St Paul's attitude to the Law clarifies several difficult passages in the Epistle to the Romans. The three examples below are not conclusive evidence that it is the correct view but they support it, and lead to the discussion of chapter 10.

(i) The phrase 'having in the Law the form of knowledge and truth', in chapter 2, has caused commentators difficulty. As the English stands it can be taken to suggest that the Law is only knowledge and truth in appearance, but the Greek ($\mu\delta\rho\varphi\omega\sigma\iota\nu$) will not permit this reading. Sanday and Headlam comment: '"$\mu\delta\rho\varphi\omega\sigma\iota\nu$": "outline", "delineation", "embodiment". As a rule $\sigma\chi\tilde{\eta}\mu\alpha$ = outward form opposed to inward substance, while $\mu o\rho\varphi\acute{\eta}$ = outward form as determined by inward substance; so that $\sigma\chi\tilde{\eta}\mu\alpha$ is the variable, $\mu o\rho\varphi\acute{\eta}$ the permanent, element in things.' Yet, as they point out, $\mu o\rho\varphi\acute{\eta}$ and not $\mu\delta\rho\varphi\omega\sigma\iota\nu$ is the word appropriate to a context like this, and they quote Lightfoot: 'in two passages where St Paul does speak of that which is unreal or at least external, and does not employ $\sigma\chi\tilde{\eta}\mu\alpha$, he still avoids using μορφή as inappropriate, and adopts μόρφωσιν instead', adding that they do not think that this can be maintained (*Sanday*, 65, 66). It seems as though St Paul used a word which ought to mean 'form which is determined by inward substance', but used it in such a way as to suggest that he meant 'outward form opposed to inward substance'.

The real difficulty is that St Paul does not need to put in any such word at all, because he is speaking to Jews, and Jews would say that in the Law they had 'knowledge and truth', but if St Paul was not, in the end, prepared to admit this, it can easily be understood how he came to write just as he did. So far as his actual argument is concerned, it has been suggested St Paul is accepting the Jews' own ground, so that to write 'the appearance of knowledge and truth' would be to strike a false note in the context; at the same time, to write 'knowledge and truth' without qualification would be to commit himself too far, and the insertion of μόρφωσιν is particularly satisfactory. It does not spoil the argument, and the Jew can bring no complaint against it, because even if he would leave it out, it only implies (what he cannot deny) that the law is outward and visible, and yet, at the same time, it hints at some kind of distinction between knowledge and truth, on the one hand, and the Law as its outward expression on the other. Although the word does not actually imply that the Law as accepted by the Jews is not a perfect expression of knowledge and truth, it leaves open the possibility of saying this later. It is not suggested that St Paul deliberately thought all this out as he was writing the Epistle, but that the slightly odd expression could well have arisen in his mind as a result of the tension between what he knew the Jew would say, and what he would say himself if he were not, for the sake of argument, accepting the Jew's position.

(ii) In chapter 3, St Paul asks 'what advantage has the Jew?' and the answer which he gives has the same sort of strangeness as his use of μόρφωσιν. The natural Jewish answer would be 'why, we have the oracles of God', and there is no obvious reason why St Paul should not say this, but what he does say is: 'they were entrusted with the oracles of God'. In the same way as before he comes very close to what the Jew would say, without actually saying it. The Jew cannot take exception to what *is* said, while it does not commit St Paul; for having said that the oracles were entrusted to the Jews he is still free to say, if he likes, that the Jews failed in the trust which was given to them. Since St Paul immediately refers to the Jews' lack of faith, there is every reason to think that he does want to say that they failed in their trust.

(iii) After speaking of the Jews' lack of faith, St Paul goes on to speak of 'a lie', and seems to imply that in some sense the Jews have been 'liars' in respect of the oracles with which they were entrusted. He wrote this soon after writing of the Gentiles that they 'turned the truth of God into a lie', and if, as is likely, there is an echo of that here, then it would seem that a similar thought was in his mind. In that case what St Paul says of the Jews may be understood from what he said of the Gentiles: when he was speaking of the Gentiles he said explicitly that although the truth was clear they did not accept it, but turned it into a lie, and that they went astray in their 'reasoning' and in their 'hearts', so there may be a hint in this passage that the Jews also had gone wrong in respect of their understanding, and of the aims which they set before themselves.

The purpose of this section has been to prepare the way for the study of St Paul's criticism of the Jews in chapter 10. Nothing has been proved, but an attempt has been made to show that there is no good *a priori* reason why St Paul should not have held the view suggested, and that there are passages in earlier chapters which are in accordance with it. Chapter 10 has now to be examined.

(d) Specifically Christian Criticisms of the Jews (Rom. 9: 30–10: 21)

In the last verses of chapter 9 and in chapter 10, St Paul criticizes the 'good will' of the Jews, and his criticism is formally and materially parallel to that which he made of the good will of the Gentiles in chapter 1. Not only does he come to the same conclusion about the Jews as he does about the Gentiles, but the structure of his discussion is the same in both passages. Thus, at 1 : 18, St Paul opens his criticism of the Gentiles with the general assertion:

'The wrath of God is revealed from heaven, against all ungodliness and unrighteousness of men . . .',

and it is clear from what follows that what reveals the wrath is the abominable behaviour of the Gentiles: 'the wrath of God is revealed' does not mean anything else but 'God gave them up' to a 'reprobate mind', and to the other things which St Paul mentions. In the same way the discussion of the Jews begins at 9: 31:

'Israel, following after a law of righteousness, failed to arrive at law', and it is in this way that the wrath of God is revealed against the Jews. Each opening statement raises a question: Why did the Gentiles do that which was unfitting? on the one hand; Why did the Jews fail to arrive at Law? on the other. The question is implicit in the 'because' of 1 : 19, and explicit in the 'wherefore' of 9 : 32, and in 1 : 19–22 the question about the Gentiles is answered, while in 9 : 32–10 : 21 the parallel answer is given about the Jews. The conclusions are:

> The Gentiles, knowing God, glorified Him not as God
> Israel knowing (by implication of 10 : 19) was a disobedient and gainsaying people.

In chapter 1, St Paul states that God's wrath is revealed against the Gentiles, and then explains why (because they refused the truth) before he particularizes in what way it is revealed; but when he says that the Jews failed to arrive at Law in chapter 10 he has already particularized their failures (chapter 3), and all that remains is to explain why. The two criticisms may be set out:

Gentiles	Jews
Statement that wrath is revealed (1 : 18)	Form which failure takes (3)
Reason for the wrath (1 : 19–22, 25, 28)	Statement of failure (9 : 31)
Form which the wrath takes (1 : 26, 27, 29–32)	Reason for failure (10)

St Paul asserts dogmatically that the Gentiles have rejected the 'invisible things' of God, and that those things are 'clearly seen', but he argues at some length the corresponding assertion about the Jews, and for this reason the discussion of the 'good will' of the Jews is longer—and more confusing—than that of the 'good will' of the Gentiles.

It is so important to see what it is that St Paul is arguing that, at the risk of tedious repetition, the earlier comments on 'clear' and 'knowing' must be repeated. Of the Gentiles St Paul says:

(i) God clearly revealed Himself to them.
(ii) Since God clearly revealed Himself they knew Him.
(iii) They did not worship God as God.
(iv) Since they knew God, but did not worship Him as God, they had rejected the knowledge of God which they had.

This means that St Paul sometimes uses 'to know' as synonymous with 'to have been presented with clear evidence'; as we might say, 'You knew I was going out because you saw me getting my hat', even though the person to whom we are speaking has just shown that he did *not* know by expressing surprise when we said 'goodbye'; and if it is asked by what criterion it is to be decided whether evidence is 'clear', the answer might be (1) that there is *a priori* certainty that if God reveals Himself He will reveal Himself clearly, and (ii) that what the Christian can see clearly in the light of Christ is clear in itself, even though it may never have been seen clearly by anyone before. The parallel criticism of the Jews would be:

(i) God clearly revealed His will to them in the Law.
(ii) Since the will of God was clearly revealed to them the Jews knew that will.
(iii) They did not aim at righteousness according to the will of God.
(iv) Since the Jews knew the will of God, but did not follow after God's righteousness, they rejected the knowledge of God's will that they had.

It has to be shown that this is what St Paul does say in 9: 32–10: 21.

St Paul's short answer to the question 'Why did the Jews fail to arrive?' is given at once in 9: 32. It is that they followed a way 'as it were of works', and not the way of faith. About this it needs to be said that although the failure of the Jews was revealed by their rejection of the Christ, this does not mean that until the Christ came the way of works was right, and that faith was only required of the Jews after He came. The Law and the prophets bear witness to 'the righteousness of God', and since Christ was the expression of that righteousness, He was in the Law, and to 'subject oneself to the righteousness of God' was always to know the Law as the revelation of Christ, and the failure to recognize the Christ at His coming revealed a failure to submit to the Law which stretched back into the Jews' past. It may have been that it was inevitable that sinful man should reject the way of faith offered in the Law, and that only those already 'in Christ' could see that the Law did offer such a way, but even if this were the case it would not alter the fact that the way of the Law, properly understood, was the way of faith. Confronted with the 'either . . . or' of the Law as they knew it, on the one hand, and Jesus on the other, the Jews rejected Jesus, and this was because they already sought the Law of righteousness by the wrong way. The choice of the Law instead of Jesus was the expression, at a particular time, of the choice

which the Jews made at all times, of a way, as it were, of works, instead
of a way of faith: and this 'either . . . or' of works and faith was set
before the Jews in the Torah itself.

The Torah offered both precepts and a promise. According to St
Paul the purpose of the precepts was to show the Jews the extent of
their sinfulness, in order that they might rely upon the promises of
God that He would 'cure' them. The 'condition' attached to the
promise was simply that it should be accepted; that is, that the Jews
should rely upon nothing but the promise, and that was the way of
faith. The danger for the Jews was that they should rely upon the
precepts as a way of works, and suppose that the condition attached
to the promise was that the precepts should be kept, and to misunderstand in this way was fatal, because by relying upon the precepts the
Jews excluded themselves from the promise. Nevertheless, when the
Torah is misunderstood in this way the purpose of the precepts can
still be achieved, and they can still convict men of sin, although they
are powerless to bring men to righteousness, and although, regarded
as a way of righteousness, they actually exclude men from the promise:
this is why in Galatians St Paul can allow the Law (even as misunderstood by the Jews) a place as 'pedagogue' in the divine economy, and
yet, in this passage in Romans, claim that the Law properly understood
declares promise and not precepts, and that the promise which it
declares is Christ.

Having given his short answer in chapter 9, St Paul elaborates it
in chapter 10. The reason why the Jews confront him with a problem
which the Gentiles do not is that he himself knows that they 'follow
after a law of righteousness', and he repeats this in another form when
he says: 'I bear them witness that they have a zeal for God'. There
is an implicit note of approval in this statement, which is lacking in
what he says of the Gentiles, but the difference in his attitude is more
apparent that real. The situation of Gentiles and Jews can be set out
as follows:

Gentiles	*Jews*
They had a zeal for wisdom	They had a zeal for God
They professed to have wisdom	They professed to have righteous-ness through the law
The wisdom that they professed was foolishness	The righteousness which they pro-fessed was not according to knowledge

St Paul passes over the Gentiles' zeal for wisdom (as later, the Greek Apologists did not), and speaks only of its fruit, the professed wisdom which was not wisdom. He acknowledges the Jews' zeal, but equally rejects its fruit as 'not according to knowledge', and, in the next verse (10:3), he emphasizes the parallel. The Gentiles, knowing God, 'changed His glory into the likeness of corruptible man': the Jews, having the Law of God, were 'ignorant of God's righteousness', and 'sought to establish their own'; that is, they changed the righteousness of God into the righteousness of man. Gentiles and Jews alike have 'exchanged the truth of God for a lie', and St Paul goes on to establish this in regard to the Jews.

St Paul supports his assertion that the Jews failed to submit to the righteousness of God by stating that 'Christ is the end of the law unto righteousness to everyone that believeth' (v. 4). He touches the question 'Why did the Jews reject Christ?' but that is not the main consideration here: the argument is (i) the only way to righteousness is Christ, (ii) the Law, in so far as it leads to righteousness is thus concluded and included in Christ, therefore (iii) anyone who submitted himself to the Law as a way to righteousness would (if he did not pervert the Law) recognize Christ, and (iv) inversely, if anyone failed to recognize Christ, that meant that he had already refused to submit to the righteousness of God revealed in the Law. Those who believe in Christ know this, and no arguments are needed to convince them, but it is as well that they should be able to show, from the Torah, that the Law properly understood does teach the way of faith, and St Paul argues this in vv. 5–8.

St Paul does not quote Moses in v. 5 in order to abrogate him in favour of Christ. That is not his style, nor the style of any New Testament writer, and if it is supposed that he did it must also be argued that although he echoes Deuteronomy in vv. 6–8 he does not intend a direct reference to a book of Moses—as it is argued at length, and unconvincingly, in Sanday and Headlam (*Sanday*, 289). In the light of Christ, St Paul revalues the Torah as a whole (that is, he is able to see its true meaning) and what happens is that he shifts the emphasis from the precepts of Leviticus to the promise in Deuteronomy, and in the process the phrase 'the man that doeth the righteousness of the Law shall live thereby' is changed from a promise to a warning. Those who live by the Law are under the Law, and there is no doubt that St Paul held (1) that 'as many as have sinned under the Law shall be judged by the Law', and (11) that 'all have sinned', so that any man who is judged by the Law will be condemned by it. Since it follows that if a man chooses to live by the Law he chooses to be condemned, Moses' comment on the precepts becomes, for St Paul, most necessary advice not to choose to live by the Law.

In the Epistle to the Galatians, St Paul explains what value the Law, wrongly considered as a system of precepts, had had; that is, he considers the purpose of the precepts. The Law had 'shut up all things under sin', so that the promise might be given to them that believe: inevitably he is speaking of the giving of the promise through Christ, but the promise which is given in Christ was as much a part of the Torah as the precepts which made ready for it. As in Romans, so in Galatians, St Paul distinguishes two aspects of the Torah: the precepts on the one hand, and the promise on the other; and these two aspects are related in that the precepts make way for the promise. The failure of the Jews was that they thought that the way to the promise was by keeping the precepts, whereas St Paul teaches that the way to the promise was by failing to keep them. The purpose of the precepts was to reveal man's sinfulness and his need, but although this was their purpose, when they were set before a man he might choose to treat them as themselves the way to righteousness: this choice was open to the Jews, but against it stood Moses' warning that to choose in this way was to choose to be condemned. It may be said once more that the Jews' choice of the precepts as the way to righteousness, and their perversity in understanding warning as though it were promise was both natural and inevitable, because all men have fallen short of the glory of God, and all are in bondage to sin; and yet, at the same time, the choice was inexcusable, because God had clearly revealed His will.

Moses did not offer the precepts as the way to righteousness, but actually warned Israel against the mistake of taking them in this way. Moses gave the precepts to reveal sin, and, in the same Torah, he gave them the promise. In Romans 10: 6–8, St Paul demonstrates that Moses had given the promise, and that the promise was Christ. In order to show that Moses teaches faith in Christ St Paul could hardly have done better than write such a paraphrase as we read here. The old word and the new (Christ) are interwoven in such a way that he makes his point without further comment: Moses declared Christ, and Christ is the word that Moses declared. Rooted and grounded in faith, St Paul can read clearly the revelation offered to Israel in the Law, and misinterpreted by men in bondage to sin. The 'word is nigh thee', Christ is nigh thee, this has been the truth from the beginning, but it is a truth that those who were in bondage to sin refused. Having shown how the Justified sinner sees this truth in the Law, St Paul then turns to show that the Jews had no excuse for failing to see it, and that the cause of their failure was their sinfulness. Verses 11–21 may be paraphrased as follows:

The teaching of Scripture, which the Jews have rejected, is that anyone (without qualification) who calls upon the Lord will be saved. Thus to be saved a man must call upon the Lord, and before he can do so he must believe on Him: before a man can believe on the Lord he must have heard of Him: a man can only hear of the Lord if someone preaches the Lord to him: only those who are sent by God can preach the true word. These are the conditions of salvation, and, in so far as the Jews are concerned, these conditions have been fulfilled: first, preachers have been sent, since we read in Scripture of those 'that bring glad tidings of good things', so the word was preached, although as Isaiah says, not everyone believed. Does this mean (since belief comes from hearing) that the preachers who were sent failed to declare the word? No, because, secondly, the word was preached so that the 'sound went out into all the earth'; nor can it be said that the word was obscure in itself, because Moses says that it will be understood by 'a nation void of understanding', and Isaiah that it will be received by 'them that sought me [God] not'. There is no excuse which Israel can offer, and their failure to receive the word, as Isaiah has already pointed out, is due to the fact that they are 'a disobedient and gainsaying people'.[1]

The wheel comes full circle. The wrath of God was revealed upon the Gentiles because they refused God and rejected Him for idols, and the Gentiles' rejection of God led to the sins and wickednesses which they committed. The Jews also committed sins and wickednesses, and when the cause of this is sought it is found that it was because they were disobedient, and rejected God for their own righteousness. The wisdom of the Gentiles was foolishness, the righteousness of the Jews not according to knowledge; instead of submitting themselves to God as He had revealed Himself, both Jews and Gentiles in their sinful pride have sought to establish man—the Gentiles worship the human image, the Jews seek for human righteousness. In that Jews

---

[1] The idea for this exegesis is taken from Nygren's commentary on Romans.

and Gentiles sin, their evil inclinations overcome their good will, but this is because both Jews and Gentiles misconceive the nature of their good will and what natural man calls his good will is not good in the sight of God. The 'wisdom' of the Gentiles and the 'righteousness' of the Jews both lead to wrath and judgement, and this is the tragedy of natural man: he has no guide which will lead him where he would be, nothing within himself can bring him to God, and when God reveals Himself to him, natural man perverts the revelation by understanding it in terms of his own wisdom, or his own concepts of righteousness. Natural man is a dichotomy of two evils, and there is no cure so long as he insists on dismissing one term of the dichotomy as 'evil' and relying upon the other as 'good'.

The clue from psychology proves fruitful. The disease of natural man as diagnosed by St Paul is not unlike that disease as diagnosed by Jung. Yet when that has been said, it must be added that the two diagnoses seem to lead to very different prescriptions. St Paul and Jung agree that the trouble with natural man is that he is determined to stand in judgement upon himself, and to declare this 'good' and that 'evil', but whereas St Paul directs attention to the error of calling the high impulses of the flesh 'good', Jung directs it to the error of calling the unconscious 'evil'. St Paul's prescription is 'penitence', the recognition that natural man is 'carnal, sold under sin', but Jung's prescription is that natural man should see that he cannot reject elements of himself as 'evil' if he would be made whole. It will be shown, in the next two chapters, that behind these prescriptions there lies a common principle. Whether a man rejects his good will or accepts his unconscious the dichotomy within him is overcome and he ceases to know himself as 'good' and 'evil'; the man who follows St Paul's prescription comes to know himself as wholly 'evil', the man who follows Jung's knows himself as wholly 'good', but because 'good' and 'evil' are relative terms neither can retain its old meaning when qualified by 'wholly'. In any event, both prescriptions lead a man to an awareness of the unity of his nature, and they have a great deal in common, as is shown in the two following chapters.

6

ACCEPTING THE UNCONSCIOUS

THE conclusions of the two previous chapters may be summarized :
    1. Natural man recognizes a dichotomy in his nature. This
dichotomy may be called a dichotomy of 'good will—evil
inclinations', or described as a failure, through one's own fault, to
carry out the aims which one sets before oneself. Natural man sees his
problem as a straightforward matter of strengthening one side of the
dichotomy (the good will, or conscious purpose) at the expense of the
other.

2. Jung criticizes the view that the so-called 'evil inclinations'
have simply to be got rid of, and insists that they have their part to
play in the man's life. He says that the unconscious is not evil, but only
produces undesirable effects because consciousness persists in taking
a wrong attitude to it.

3. St Paul criticizes the view that the 'good will' is able to lead a
man to true righteousness, and insists that it is marred by human
sinfulness. He says in effect that the good will as well as the evil
inclinations must be 'modified'.

Jung's cure for the disease which he diagnoses is discussed in this
chapter, St Paul's in the next.

The account of natural man which one gives determines the 'cure'
which one 'prescribes' for his disease, so that because Jung diagnoses
that the disease is due to a man's conscious rejection of the unconscious
the cure which he prescribes is that a man should learn to accept the
unconscious. Acceptance of the unconscious is the aim to which a
Jungian analysis is directed, and in order to show what is involved in
it something must be said about the principles of such an analysis.
The following account is not in any sense an attempt to describe the
course of an actual analysis, and it is two steps removed from what
goes on in the psychotherapist's consulting room, because it is a restatement of Jung's account and that account is not a description but

a schematization of the course of analysis. The account is ideal in that it describes what Jung thinks ought to happen, so that if the restatement is accurate what can be said is that the more closely an actual analysis follows the course set out here the more effective it is likely to be. Even so, any actual analysis necessarily includes the exploration of by-ways and the use of alternative routes which are not mentioned in this outline. The account is highly abstract and theoretical, and it is intended to be so because our purpose is to compare two theories of life and of how living may be improved.

The Principles of a Jungian Analysis

The use or recommendation of a psychotherapeutic technique implies that something has gone wrong, because the purpose of such a technique is to undo the results of errors which have occurred in the course of a man's psychic development, and the principles of Jung's technique can be best understood against the background of what he thinks ought to happen; that is, of how he thinks a man ought to develop. This 'right' process of development may be pictured by applying to the individual the myth of the development of consciousness in the human race as a whole, which was described in chapter 4. To apply the myth to the individual it is necessary to divide a man's life into two stages: the first may be called the 'period of acquisition of conscious elements' (i.e. their differentiation from the unconscious, and their subsequent development), and the second, the 'period of creative activity'; and these two stages are to be thought of as divided by the synthesis (which will take time and so might be said to be an intervening stage) of the psychic elements developed in the first. The ideal for the first stage is that nothing which is acquired, or might be acquired, should be lost to the synthesis which completes it, and the ideal for the second is that nothing which might direct or contribute to creative activity should be prevented from doing so. These remarks are exemplified by the following passages: 'In the morning of life man painfully tears himself from the mother, from the domestic hearth, to rise through battle to his heights. . . . If he is to live he must fight and sacrifice his longing for the past, in order to rise to his own heights. And having reached the noonday heights, he must also *sacrifice the love for his own achievement*, for he may not loiter' (*Unconscious*, 215); 'It is of the greatest importance for the young person, who is still unadapted and has yet achieved nothing, to shape his conscious ego as effectively as possible, that is, to educate his will. ... He must feel himself a man of will, and may safely depreciate everything else in him and deem it subject to his will, for without this illusion he could not succeed in adapting himself socially. . . . It is otherwise with a person in the second half of life who no longer needs to educate his conscious will, but who, to understand the meaning of his individual life, needs to experience his own inner being' (*Practice*, 109, 110). It may be doubted whether the ideal of either stage is often (or ever) achieved, and the reasons why are fairly easy to see.

During the first period of his life it is a species of impatience which prevents a man from achieving the ideal. By forming a final synthesis too early, or by deciding beforehand what shall be included in it, a man may so form his conscious character and attitude that many elements which have been, or might be, acquired cannot be fitted in; and such elements which will not 'fit' are repressed, and they become the personal unconscious. During the second period the error which a man is likely to make is that of relying too much upon the synthesis which was the culmination of the first period, that is, of relying entirely upon his conscious character and attitude to direct his creative activity, and by doing this to create antagonism between consciousness and the unconscious. In order to put right what has gone wrong during the first period, repressed elements must be made conscious and the conscious synthesis widened to include them, and this means that the personal unconscious must be dissipated and its 'contents' made conscious. To correct the error of the second period, the unconscious (which means the 'collective unconscious', since the personal unconscious must be dissipated before anything else can be done) must be accepted, and the antagonism between consciousness and the unconscious thereby destroyed. If a man has lived long enough to make both errors, then each must be corrected in succession. Since there are two aims which can be distinguished in relation to Jung's technique it can be itself divided into two parts: the first part Jung calls a 'reductive technique', and it is a means of dissipating the personal unconscious, the second he calls 'synthetic', and by means of this a man is to be brought to accept the collective unconscious. Brief comments will be made on each part of the technique, although it is with the second part, the 'synthetic technique', that we shall be more concerned.

The Reductive Technique

(1) Since this part of the technique is designed to put right what has gone wrong in the first period of a man's life, it is all that is likely to be required for younger patients. Jung speaks of the techniques of Freud and Adler as 'reductive' and adds, perhaps a little patronizingly, 'both views are eminently applicable to the young, apparently without leaving any disturbing after-effects' (*Practice*, 75). With older patients, while the reductive technique is still usually necessary, it must be followed by the synthetic technique.

(2) The basic 'mechanics' of the reductive technique is the postulation of unconscious elements 'of a psychic nature comparable to that of conscious contents' (*Religion*, 67), and this procedure has been analysed and discussed in chapter 2. It need only be remarked here, first, that 'likeness' to 'conscious contents' means that the terms which purport to name unconscious elements are to be used in the same way that we ordinarily use such terms as 'fear' and 'desire'—except, of course, that a man must not be said to be conscious of them; and, secondly, that it is because they are (by definition) to be used in this way that the terms which name unconscious elements bring the odd things which they organize into direct relation with conscious life. Roughly speaking, the description of the personal unconscious in terms like those used to refer to consciousness suggests the possibility of making it conscious.

(3) The effect of the technique is to 'lift repression', and so to introduce (or reintroduce) ideas, attitudes, and purposes into a man's mind. Jung calls this a 'widening of the personality', and he says, 'This "widening" primarily concerns the moral consciousness, one's self-knowledge, for the unconscious contents that are released and brought into consciousness by analysis are usually unpleasant—which is precisely why these wishes, memories, tendencies, plans, etc. were repressed' (*Essays*, 218). The result of such a technique is that the patient is confronted with the problem of reforming his character and attitude in such a way that he can accommodate the additional elements, and this constitutes what is, in Jung's sense, a 'moral' problem. The reductive technique cannot be said to have been successfully finished unless the problem to which it gives rise is solved, but, at the same time, the solution of this problem is not a matter of analytical technique. The problem is of a kind which every man must solve for himself, when duties and desires and aspirations conflict with one another, and

it is not made any different because it arises in connection with psychological analysis. The function of analysis is to make a man aware of the full range of conflicting elements within himself, and to persuade him not to try to shelve the problems of reconciling them by ignoring those which will not 'fit' with the others, and it offers no simple formula for solving the problems which it forces a man to face: this is not to say that the analyst, who has helped a man to see new problems, should not, or cannot, help him to solve them by giving 'good advice', but only that in doing so the analyst has no special technique to guide him.

The Synthetic Technique

(1) The second, synthetic, part of Jung's technique is appropriate when all the ideas, attitudes, desires and so on which have been acquired during the first period of development have been successfully synthetized (with or without the help of a reductive technique), and when the character and attitude consciously formed in this way is regarded as the only source of creative activity. There is certainly something ideal (in the sense of 'unlikely to occur in real life') about this conception of a full and complete synthesis, and it is to be supposed that the synthetic technique can be used when a man has only approximated to this ideal, but the question how close a man must come to it before the technique is employed is a practical question which does not affect the theoretical considerations of this study. It might seem that all that is required is that a man who has reached the state just described should be exhorted to refrain from over-reliance on consciousness and to allow other forces to guide him, and it may well be that for some people this is enough; but in the West, at least, exclusive reliance on consciousness has been exalted into a principle, and this means that most Western people tenaciously cling to such a way of life. Further, the antagonistic attitude of consciousness in the past will have obscured the true nature of the contribution which the unconscious might make to a man's life, so that until the antagonism has been overcome the unconscious appears evil or nonsensical, and hard work is needed to overcome the natural repugnance to the idea of taking such a thing seriously.

(2) The basis of the synthetic technique, like that of the reductive technique, is the organization of odd things by the postulation of unconscious elements. When the personal unconscious has been

integrated, Jung says, the unconscious 'calmly continues to produce dreams and fantasies' (*Essays*, 205), and the dreams and fantasies and other interferences with the conscious direction of life which occur after the integration of the personal unconscious are the things which have been called 'odd in the second degree' (see pp. 68f.). Such things frequently have a numinous quality and mythical content lacking to those odd things which are organized by the concept of 'unconscious elements like conscious elements', but they are not necessarily different from them in this way: it is rather that they remain un-explained when all that can be done by means of that concept has been done, so that it becomes necessary to introduce a new category of unconscious elements—that is, to postulate unconscious elements (more correctly 'complexes') which are not thought of as being like conscious elements. The further categories needed to organize things which are odd in the second degree are introduced into Jung's system in relation to the synthetic technique. Jung calls these categories 'archetypes', and whereas the elements of the personal unconscious are to be thought of as like conscious psychic elements, the archetypes of the collective unconscious are to be thought of as like people or spirits. The idea of an individual archetype is based on images which occur in dreams, and the name of such an archetype is used in the way that we ordinarily use the proper names of men and women.

(3) There are most important differences between the effect of the synthetic technique and that of the reductive technique. The reductive technique 'widens' the scope of consciousness, and the conscious mind has to evaluate and synthetize the material which is placed at its disposal as a result of this technique, before the newly discovered elements can take their part in guiding a man's life; on the other hand, although the synthetic technique also enables new tendencies to action, hopes, fears, desires and so on to influence a man's life, it does not make them conscious before they do so and this lies behind the whole idea of 'accepting the collective unconscious'. Before one is in a particular situation one may rightly sum up all its relevant features, and judge what one's response to them will be, and yet, when one is in that situation one may behave in a wholly unexpected way, because some hidden capacity or tendency of which one had no knowledge before has come to light. Exclusive reliance upon consciousness involves a determination that this sort of thing shall not happen and a set purpose to act at all times in accordance with one's previous judgement;

'acceptance of the unconscious' involves a readiness to find that one has more capacities than one knows for responding to situations, even though one does not see how these further capacities can be associated with one's rational decisions. Whereas the reductive technique must be followed by a conscious and deliberate synthesis of the new material, a man must not try to bring under conscious direction the new possibilities of reacting to the world which result from the synthetic technique, but must accept such new reactions without seeking to control them. Like the reductive technique the synthetic technique gives rise to a 'moral' problem, but it is a different kind of problem: 'Even when the conscious mind does not identify itself with the inclinations of the unconscious', Jung tells us, 'it still has to face them and somehow take account of them in order that they may play their part in the life of the individual, however difficult this may be' (*Practice*, 522); and, 'The only person who escapes the grim law of enantiodromia is the man who knows how to separate himself from the unconscious, not by repressing it . . . but by putting it clearly before him as *that which he is not*' (*Essays*, 112).

(4) The synthetic technique culminates in the acceptance of the unconscious, and if a man will accept the unconscious he has done all that he can consciously and deliberately set himself to do. When a man has done this he has fulfilled the condition which must be fulfilled before Individuation can occur, and the remainder of the work must be left to that which Jung calls the 'Self'. 'If', Jung says, 'the unconscious can be recognized as a co-determining quantity along with the conscious, and if it can be lived in such a way that conscious and unconscious (in a narrower sense instinctive) demands are given recognition as far as possible, the centre of gravity of the total personality shifts its position' (*Secret*, 123), and: 'If we picture the conscious mind, with the ego as its centre, as being opposed to the unconscious, and if we now add to our mental picture the process of assimilating the unconscious, we can think of this assimilation as a kind of approximation of conscious and unconscious, where the centre of the total personality no longer coincides with the ego, but with a point mid-way between the conscious and the unconscious' (*Essays*, 365). The peculiar use of 'assimilate' in this last quotation should be noted: it is clear from the context that one must understand it to mean 'associate in equal partnership', and this is also its meaning in passages which will be cited below.

Archetypes

A fuller account of the nature and function of archetypes is needed, and this will be given in the form of a summary of the last few chapters of the second essay in *Two Essays in Analytical Psychology*. In these chapters Jung discusses two most important archetypes, 'the anima' and 'the magician', and he is able to present the whole of the synthetic technique as an 'encounter' with the anima, followed, after the dissolution of the anima, by an encounter with the magician. In the summary below the modifications required to make the account apply to women as well as men (which involve the substitution of 'animus' for 'anima', and 'the great mother' for 'the magician') are ignored: the account is divided into two parts, the first of which deals with the anima, and the second with the magician; each part is divided into three sections: (*a*) the construction of the archetype, (*b*) the 'encounter' with the archetype, (*c*) the dissolution of the archetype.

1. *The Anima*

(*a*) *Construction*. The principle which was established in chapter 2 for the construction of personal unconscious psychic elements applies also to archetypes; in other words, archetypes are concepts which are constructed from those odd things which are said to 'manifest' them. Archetypes are also said to be manifested in the same three ways in which other unconscious elements 'express themselves'; that is, by images in dreams and fantasies, in uncharacteristic thoughts and acts when a man is, as it were, 'off his guard', and in projection. Projection is discussed in chapter 8 below, and here it need only be said that when a man 'projects' an unconscious element on to an external object he mistakenly supposes that the projected element is a quality of that object.

It would be impossible to make an inventory of all the phenomena which might be ascribed to the anima, but the following examples give an indication of the sort of odd things from which it is constructed. In dreams and fantasies the anima is usually manifested as a fascinating and desirable woman, and Jung characterizes these manifestations by reference to the 'fatal' women of literature—from Homer's Circe to Rider Haggard's 'She'. Secondly, in the life of the man who outwardly 'plays an effective and powerful role', for example, the anima is manifested in that 'inwardly an effeminate weakness develops in face of every influence coming from the unconscious. Moods, vagaries, timidity, even a limp sexuality (culminating in impotence), gradually gain the upper hand' (*Essays*, 308), and any unexpectedly feminine reaction from the 'masculine' type of man may be ascribed to it. Finally, the man who projects his anima on to his wife 'becomes childish, sentimental, dependent, and subservient, or else truculent, tyrannical, hypersensitive, always thinking about the prestige of his superior masculinity', and the second effect, 'is merely the reverse of the first' (ibid., 316).

(*b*) *The Encounter*. To 'encounter the anima' is to 'do psychology', because it is only under the guidance of psychology that one uses the idea of the anima to cope with the odd things which it organizes. So long as a man does not use this technique (or some equivalent alternative) it is natural that he 'naïvely ascribes his anima reactions to himself' (ibid., 329), and it is against such 'naïvety' (if it really is naïve) that Jung's technique is directed. The archetypes are postulated in order that the odd things from which they are constructed may be ascribed to something or someone other than the individual in whose life they occur—other, that is, than his 'ego'—and the immediate result of postulating the anima is that a man ceases to feel divided in himself, but seems to encounter an alien personality 'within himself'. Instead of saying 'I sometimes do or think, or tend to do or think, odd things which I don't mean to do or think', he says, in Jung's words: 'It [the anima] can put extraordinary ideas into my head, induce in me unwanted and unwelcome moods and emotions, lead me to astonishing actions for which I can accept no responsibility, upset my relations with other people in a very irritating way, etc. I feel powerless against this fact, and what is worse, I am in love with it' (ibid., 325). Yet a man is not to evade responsibility by postulating the anima, he must still resist its undesirable manifestations while he proceeds to apply Jung's technique, which, if it is successful, leads to the dissolution of the archetype.

The idea behind the technique by which the anima is to be dissolved is simpler, and apparently more reasonable, than the technique itself. The anima, as the 'personal representative' of the unconscious, is to be thought of as having been consistently and systematically misunderstood: it is as though someone with large plans and schemes could get no one to listen to more than a small part of what he purposed, or as though one or two of the many interrelated suggestions which he made were put into practice without the others, and, as a result, had the opposite effect to that which he intended, because as a result of the antagonistic attitude of consciousness the unconscious can only get intermittent possession of the mechanism of thought or action, so that the odd things by which it is manifested are all, as it were, torn from their context, and only a small part of what the unconscious 'intends' can be seen from them. Jung's technique is meant to give the anima a chance to explain what it 'really wants', and this is done by deliberately putting the imagination at its disposal.

The principle underlying the technique is that although the anima cannot be allowed to 'act' it must be allowed to 'speak'; this means that although a man must continue consciously and deliberately to control his behaviour he must at the same time take seriously his dreams and fantasies, and try to understand them. 'We have no alternative', Jung says, 'but to hand over the leadership to the unconscious and give it the opportunity of achieving conscious content [i.e. expressing itself] in the form of fantasies' (ibid., 347), and 'the art of it only consists in allowing our invisible opponent to make herself heard, in putting the mechanism of expression momentarily at her disposal, without being overcome by the distaste one naturally feels at playing such an apparently ludicrous game with oneself, or by doubts as to the genuineness of the voice of one's interlocutor' (ibid., 323). To put this technique into practice a man must take his fantasies completely seriously, and he must do this in two ways: first, he must 'live' them, as one may 'live' a good novel, play, or a film, while they are actually taking place; and, secondly, he must set himself to interpret them afterwards, really believing that they have a meaning.

(c) *Dissolution of the Anima.* Jung tells us that 'so long as the affect [i.e. a state of mind thought of as a manifestation of an unconscious complex] is speaking, criticism must be withheld. But once it has presented its case, we should begin criticizing as conscientiously as though a real person closely connected with us were our interlocutor' (ibid., loc. cit.), but there would be little point in the technique if the criticisms were all one-sided, for to take the fantasies seriously is to be ready to let the anima criticize the ego, and so Jung says of a patient that had he taken a certain fantasy seriously 'he would have won a victory over his one-sided intellectualism and, indirectly, would have asserted the validity of the irrational standpoint of the unconscious' (ibid., 350). In this way Jung's technique leads to a criticism of a man's conscious plans and purposes in the light of his dreams and fantasies and this results in a modification both of consciousness and of the unconscious.

Jung describes the modification of consciousness which results from the application of his technique to the anima as 'a change of personality', and he says, 'This change of personality is naturally not an alteration of the original hereditary disposition, but rather a transformation of the general attitude. Those sharp cleavages and antagonisms between conscious and unconscious, such as we see so clearly in the endless conflicts of neurotic natures, nearly always rest on a noticeable one-sidedness of the conscious attitude, which gives absolute precedence to one or two functions, while the others are unjustly thrust into the background. Conscious realization and experience of fantasies assimilates the unconscious inferior functions to the conscious mind—a process which is naturally not without far-reaching effects on the conscious attitude . . .' (ibid., 359). There are two reasons why such a 'change of personality' affects the description which must be given of the unconscious; first (and this needs to be established empirically), it is accompanied by an actual change in the odd things which occur; and secondly, even though the same things as before happen many of them will no longer be odd, because if a man's general attitude is altered some things previously 'uncharacteristic' become natural to him, so that the 'change of personality' means that many things previously called 'anima reactions' can be ascribed to the ego, that is 'explained' as expressions of a man's conscious character. For example, if a man plays the part of a stern husband and father, who is never wrong and whose word is law, his anima may express itself in occasional odd things which involve pathological dependence upon his wife; but if such a man accepts the anima's 'criticisms' of his behaviour, then he will realize that his earlier picture of himself was at fault, and that there is a place for some element of dependence in his relations with his wife, and, in so far as he lives in accordance with his new ideas, this element will be a normal feature of his life, and the odd pathological aspects of it will cease.

The anima is a concept which relates together a wide range of odd things, and when a 'change of personality' results from the encounter with the anima some of these things cease to occur, some are modified, and some cease to be odd. Since it is those odd things which are most

'typical' of the anima which are affected in this way the odd things
which continue to occur (and any new varieties of odd things which
did not occur before) are no longer appropriately organized by that
concept, even though they were thought of as 'manifestations of the
anima' before, and the anima is said to be 'dissolved'. In other words,
when the fantasies which express the anima are taken so seriously
that a man's conscious character is changed as a result, then the anima,
as it were, falls apart, and some of the tendencies to which the concept
referred are incorporated into consciousness, while others remain
'unconscious'; Jung says that the goal of the encounter with the
anima is 'the conquest of the anima as an autonomous complex, and
her transformation into a function of relationship between the conscious
and the unconscious' (ibid., 374), but this is not an accurate statement
because 'the anima' is the name of an autonomous complex, and not
of a function of relationship, and Jung's meaning is better expressed
when he says 'The dissolution of the anima means that we have gained
insight into the driving forces of the unconscious, but not that we
have made these forces ineffective' (ibid., 391) and, 'In the hierarchy
of the unconscious the anima occupies the lowest rank, only one of
many possible figures', so that 'her subjection constellates another
collective figure which now takes over her mana [that is, the qualities
of 'power' and 'otherness' which are connected with all manifestations
of the unconscious]' (ibid., 378). The new figure is that of the
'magician'.

2. *The Magician*

(a) *Construction*. The dissolution of the anima brings with it a
change of emphasis in dreams and fantasies, and the magician is
constructed from the images which increase in importance after the
anima has been 'conquered'. Such images are those of a man's father,
and of kings and prophets. In behaviour the magician is 'manifested'
when a man 'puts on a father-mask' and claims unexpected or
arbitrary authority for his opinions, and the projection of the magician
is likely to result in a feeling of inferiority towards those on whom it
is projected, coupled with an excessive championship of their real or
imaginary claims to fame and importance: 'The danger [of possession
by the magician]', Jung tells us, 'lies not only in oneself becoming a
father-mask, but in being overpowered by this mask when worn by
another' (ibid., 390).

(b) *The Encounter*. The magician is to be postulated for the same purpose as the anima, that is to enable a man to ascribe odd things to something other than his own 'ego', but the things which are ascribed to the magician have a quality different from that of those ascribed to the anima. 'Anima reactions' are, on the whole, things of which a man feels ashamed, and if he ascribes them to himself he is liable to fall into self-contempt, but the reactions ascribed to the magician are more impressive than those which are normal to the man, and if one naïvely ascribed the magician's activity to oneself 'one would be [no doubt, in one's own eyes] the fortunate possessor of *the* great truth that was only waiting to be discovered, of the eschatological knowledge that means the healing of the nations' (ibid., 260). The anima is postulated as other than the ego in order to prevent a man from forming too low an opinion of himself; the magician is postulated as other than the ego in order to prevent a man from becoming 'puffed up'. Jung says that to encounter the magician is to be 'obliged to face the fact that we both know more and want more than other people' (ibid., 396), but his whole argument rests upon the insistence that this knowing and wanting is a function of the whole psyche, and not of consciousness (the man as he knows himself) alone: that is, it is a potentiality in every man, it never becomes any man's actual possession, and yet it is a potentiality that those who reach the stage represented by the 'encounter with the magician' have to take into account.

Jung says that 'in differentiating the ego from the archetype of the mana-personality [the magician] one is now forced, exactly as in the case of the anima, to make conscious those contents which are specific of the mana-personality' (ibid., 393), but 'to make conscious' must be taken in a weak sense of 'become aware of the existence of', and not in the strong sense of 'bring under the control of the ego', since he has already said that 'the anima has forfeited her tyrannical power only to the extent that the ego was able to come to terms with the unconscious. This accommodation, however, was not a victory of conscious over the unconscious, but the establishment of a balance of power between the two worlds' (ibid., 381), and 'if the ego presumes to wield power over the unconscious, the unconscious reacts with a subtle attack, deploying the dominant of the mana-personality, whose enormous prestige casts a spell over the ego. Against this the only defence is full confession of one's weakness in face of the powers of the unconscious' (ibid., 391). The magician as an autonomous complex (i.e. an archetype) is, as it were, the form which the collective unconscious takes when it is opposed by consciousness and, as has been pointed out above, so long as consciousness is antagonistic to it the unconscious manifests itself only intermittently, so that archetypes are constructed from odd things which are 'out of context'. When the magician is allowed to 'state his case' and a man becomes aware of the 'context' of the odd things from which this archetype is constructed, the autonomous complex is dissolved and the man no longer has to postulate a 'person' opposing his ego, but to become aware of instincts and tendencies which he has not consciously anticipated arising within him in response to the situation in which he happens to be. Before the dissolution of the magician a man does not become aware of these tendencies at all, and after the magician has been dissolved he only becomes aware of them when they are activated; he cannot take them into account before he is in the situation in connection with which they are evoked.

(c) *The Dissolution.* Through the dissolution of the magician a man comes to understand that he may respond to events in ways which he cannot expect or take into account beforehand, and in ways which he does not consciously and deliberately plan: it would also be true to reverse this statement, and to say that by becoming aware of this a man 'dissolves' the figure of the magician. The state which results is that in which the unconscious is 'accepted', and, as it has been said above (e.g. p. 190), this is the only goal at which a man can consciously aim, so that, in this sense, it is the goal of Jung's technique. One further quotation which refers to this state, and points beyond it to Individuation itself may be added to those given on p. 190: 'The dissolution of the mana-personality through conscious assimilation [see the comment on p.190] of its contents leads us, by a natural route, back to ourselves as an actual, living something, poised between two world pictures and their darkly discerned potencies. This "something" is strange to us and yet so near, wholly ourselves and yet unknowable, a virtual centre of so mysterious a constitution that it can claim anything—kinship with beasts and gods, with crystals and with stars—without moving us to wonder, without even exciting our disapprobation' (*Essays*, 398). This 'something' is the Self, and it will be discussed further in chapter 10, for the account of Jung's technique comes to an end with the mention of the goal of conscious effort, 'acceptance of the unconscious'.

The effects of Jung's technique

Jung's diagnosis of natural man differs from that of St Paul in that Jung criticizes man for neglecting one side of his nature, whereas St Paul criticizes him for putting his trust in the other side. Jung does not require men to reject their conscious plans and purposes, but only to acknowledge other (unconscious) plans and purposes as well, and for this reason a Jungian analysis requires the conscious co-operation of the analysand. The analyst is a guide and director, but throughout the analysis the patient's conscious mind is in control, since the analysand must deliberately turn his attention to the unconscious, must deliberately allow the unconscious to 'speak', restrain the conscious to prevent it taking over too much control and scrutinize and evaluate what the unconscious has 'said'; all of this is the activity of consciousness. The Christian theologian is forced to conclude that this is a new 'legalism':[1] instead of the Law of Moses Jung offers his psychotherapeutic technique, and although that technique is very different from the Jewish Law, and far more flexible than any law, and although it is said to lead to Individuation and not to righteousness, the underlying principle is the same: man, by setting himself to follow certain precepts, may work out his own salvation and, sighing over the troubles of the world, Jung does not hesitate to say, 'Everything now depends on man' (*Job*, 745).

Jung's 'prescription' for natural man is basically 'legalistic' and is opposed to the essential Christian principle that we must be saved by grace and not by law, but although this assertion is true as far as it goes it does not go very far because, although the analysand is consciously in control of the development brought about through Jung's technique, the technique is not directed towards a strengthening of consciousness, and so is unlike all religious legalism. The religious way of law aims at strengthening the good will, so that a man is able to carry out his (good) purposes, but Jung's technique aims at the voluntary abrogation of authority by human consciousness, and in this Jung marches with Christianity.

If it is successfully carried out Jung's technique affects conscious-

---

[1] 'Legalism' is commonly supposed to consist in the multiplication of rules, but this is not of its essence. The mark of legalism is the belief that a man can earn salvation by his own performance of rules—whether those rules be many or few, precise or vague. It is in this respect that St Paul opposes the way of grace to Jewish legalism. 'Love thy neighbour' can be commanded in a legalistic sense.

ness in two ways: it causes a modification of the character of consciousness, and it brings a man (consciously) to see that consciousness cannot be the final arbitrator of his life. The integration of the personal unconscious and the dissolution of the anima both result in the introduction into consciousness of psychic elements which were not conscious before, and so cause a 'widening of consciousness': the dissolution of the anima and the encounter with the magician confront consciousness with aspects of human nature which it cannot expect to control. In other words, although consciousness directs the development consciousness itself develops, and is very different at the end from what it was at the beginning. The aims, purposes and ideals with which a man begins the Jungian adventure are widened, modified, and even abrogated in the course of analysis, and further, the new consciousness which results does not presume to think that it always knows what is best—which means that a man who has reached the end of the process is ready to wait upon events, without prejudging the issues of right and wrong. Thus although the achievement of accepting the unconscious is the result of conscious effort it ultimately involves a rejection of the conscious aims and purposes of natural man and the dethronement of consciousness itself, and Jung's technique, if it effects its purposes, brings a man to the point at which St Paul would have him begin.

We have now found a broad agreement between Jung and St Paul. Jung begins by demanding that natural man should acknowledge the value of the unconscious, but he ends by showing a man that he cannot hope to work out his own salvation by conscious purpose and effort, and that all he can do is to look to some 'centre' which transcends his conscious mind—that is to what Jung calls 'the Self'—to do for him what he cannot do for himself: St Paul demands from the beginning that natural man should see that of himself he can do nothing, but that he must look to a power which transcends him, the Spirit of Christ, to bring about his salvation. Yet Jung's technique is not merely a complicated mechanism for bringing about that attitude of mind which Christian preachers try to induce by direct exhortation, because it not only leads a man to realize the inadequacy of his conscious mind, but also prepares him for the 'arrival' of the 'Self'. Jung says that Individuation is something which happens to a man and not something which he sets himself to achieve, but it is clear that a Jungian analysis is designed so to develop a man's conscious mind that it is ready for Individuation, and that one who has reached the end of such an analysis (or of its equivalent) is in a position to expect Individuation to occur because of the development that has taken place, even though he cannot claim that it must. On the other hand, the bare acknowledgement that the good will cannot lead him to salvation does not involve any development of character, and it is St Paul's central claim that Justification by Faith occurs before a man is prepared for it at all, and that it is a gift of grace which no man can claim, or expect, and for which no man is ready, because he says that it was 'while we were yet sinners' that 'God justified the ungodly'. It follows that if there is any development on the Christian way which is like that brought about by Jung's technique it is a consequence of Justification by Faith and not a preparation for it, whereas on Jung's way the development precedes Individuation. This means that although the development involved in accepting the unconscious cannot correspond to anything which prepares a man for Justification by Faith, the understanding of the nature of that development may still help the understanding of the nature and aims of the Christian life itself, and that it is, therefore, worth while examining the purpose of postulating the archetypes.

The things which have been called 'odd' are largely of a kind which have, in the past, been described as effects of 'possession' by spirits or demons, and such a phrase as 'I don't know what got into me' shows how hardly the idea of possession dies. Throughout human history attempts have been made to 'explain' phenomena of this kind, and the concept of 'archetypes' is in direct line of succession to that of gods and demons, thought of as able to enter into and to take possession of men. Jung is fully aware of this, and he says, for instance, 'Only in the age of enlightenment did people discover that the gods did not really exist, but were simply projections. Thus the gods were disposed of. But the corresponding psychological function was by no means disposed of; it lapsed into the unconscious, and men were thereupon poisoned by the surplus of libido that had once been laid up in the cult of divine images' (*Essays*, 150). A consideration of the difference between the idea of gods and demons on the one hand, and of archetypes on the other, however, shows that whereas the former makes possible the abrogation of human responsibility, the latter is designed to search out the true nature of man. A demon is thought of as a being with a life of its own which, from time to time, may manifest itself in the life of a man, and the same demon may successively take possession of several men; but although it is true that archetypes are said to be 'collective' this need only mean that different men have to cope with the same problems, and archetypes are not thought of as having some 'existence' of their own 'outside' the men in whose lives they manifest themselves. In other words, the use of 'archetypes' to 'explain' odd things relates those odd things to hidden powers and tendencies within individual men, and the purpose for which they are postulated is to bring those hidden powers and tendencies to light, so that the 'dissolution' of an archetype refers to the fact that the hidden things connected with the idea of the archetype which has been 'dissolved' have been acknowledged for what they are—potentialities within a man.

There are two sides to the unveiling of the true nature of man, and Jung speaks of both in connection with his technique, and with techniques which he regards as equivalent to it. The hidden things have to be discovered, and the false appearances have to be swept aside. The first of these is effected by what Jung calls 'a descent into the unconscious'; and of this he speaks (for examples) in the following passages:

(i) Of a picture in an alchemical treatise: 'coming now to [its] psychology, it is clearly a descent into the unconscious. . . . The modern equivalent of this stage is the conscious realization of sexual fantasies which colour the transference accordingly' (*Practice*, 455 . . . 456).

(ii) Of the end of the reductive technique: The freed libido 'follows its own gradient down into the depths of the unconscious, and there activates what has lain slumbering from the beginning. It has discovered the hidden treasure upon which mankind ever and anon has drawn, and from which it has raised up its gods and demons, and all those potent and mighty thoughts without which man ceases to be man' (*Essays*, 105). The purpose of bringing to light the hidden character of man is also well expressed by the model of 'the circulation of the light', which Jung finds in a Chinese treatise, and of which he says, 'Psychologically, this circular course would be the "turning in a circle about oneself", by means of which, apparently, all sides of the personality become implicated' (*Secret*, 101).

The other side, the removal of false appearances, is referred to in the following:

(i) 'Psychologically we can say that the situation has thrown off the conventional husk and developed into a stark encounter with reality, with no false veils or adornments of any kind. Man stands forth as he really is and shows what was hidden under the mask of conventional adaptation: the shadow' (*Practice*, 452).

(ii) 'The aim of individuation is nothing less than to divest the self of the false wrappings of the persona on the one hand, and the suggestive power of primordial images on the other' (*Essays*, 269).

In a word, the purpose of Jung's technique is to bring the whole man, as he really is, into full activity, and this is to be done by removing his false conceptions of himself, and by bringing to light the hidden things, so that 'all sides of his personality may be implicated', and this purpose has affinities with that of Christian penitence, for to be penitent is to see oneself as one truly is, that is to say it is to strip off the veils and masks which one wears in order to appear better than one is, and to understand the real sinfulness of one's own nature. Penitence, however, is usually thought to be a way of getting rid of the evil in us, and if this is correct it has a very different purpose from that of accepting the unconscious. The present discussion suggests a new approach to penitence, and raises the question whether penitence also may not be seen as a means of bringing the whole man into full activity. That this is the purpose of penitence is argued in the next chapter, but it may be noticed here that such a view is in accord with the Christian insistence upon 'wholeness' and 'abundance of life'.

The examination of Jung's technique whereby a man is brought to accept the unconscious has led to the following conclusions:

1. Although Jung begins by positive insistence upon the value (or 'goodness') of the unconscious, his technique leads to the rejection of consciousness as the guide of life, and this is equivalent to the Christian insistence that man, being a sinner, cannot work out his own salvation.

2. Whereas Jung's technique prepares a man for Individuation by developing his character, there is no corresponding preparation for Justification by Faith, and if there is some feature in the Christian way which corresponds to accepting the unconscious it must be looked for in the Christian life itself; that is, it must be a consequence and not a condition of Justification by Faith.

3. Jung's technique involves the stripping aside of conventional masks and the 'discovery' of one's true nature, and in this it has obvious affinities with Christian penitence: since Jung's technique also leads to the full activity of the whole man the parallels suggest that one may find that penitence has a similar result.

Dangers and Safeguards

Before leaving Jung's technique and turning to penitence two subsidiary topics require discussion. The first refers to the dangers which beset a man who travels on Jung's way, and the second to the function of the analyst in protecting a man from those dangers. In the next chapters it will be shown that similar dangers beset the Christian way, and that it is one role of the Christian Church to protect men from these dangers.

Dangers

Like many other good things, Jung's technique has its dangers. A way of salvation might be compared to walking across a tight-rope which was the only way of getting over a chasm. If one wants to cross such a chasm, then one must risk the danger of falling to death, but that does not mean that one will fall to death, nor that one may not do so without starting to cross. Similarly, the dangers inherent in Jung's technique can be avoided and they may happen to a man who has never even heard about that technique, but, like falling off the tight-rope, they are real dangers for all who travel on Jung's way. The four dangers discussed below are not only specific dangers in relation to Jung's way, but they also beset the way of the Christian, and the headings under which they are discussed here refer more directly to the form in which they beset the religious than the psychological progress of a man.

(a) *Abandonment.* In the sense in which 'abandonment' is used here it is applied to the man who willingly does what he believes to be evil or unfitting, giving himself up to tendencies which he has despaired of controlling, and who by 'wallowing' in such things seeks to put out of his mind his sense of their wickedness. Modern psychology has often been accused of encouraging behaviour of this sort by teaching that the instincts should be given free expression, but although it is now generally accepted that this is hopelessly wide of the mark as a criticism of most psychotherapeutic systems, and although Jung hardly gives any attention to it, there is no doubt that even in relation to his system (in which morality is taken very seriously) abandonment is a very real danger for those who err from the right path. How this comes about can be easily shown.

Jung's technique is expressly designed to make a man aware of tendencies and powers within him which he has ignored in the past, and since they have most often been repressed because they were disliked the result is that 'The unconscious contents that are released and brought into consciousness by analysis are usually unpleasant' (*Essays*, 218). The patient needs to be persuaded that, with the help of the analyst, he can cope with the newly 'released' powers, and if, for some reason, he is not convinced of this, then he is liable to feel 'as though he were a helpless object caught between hammer and anvil' (ibid., 224); that is, between the demands of the external world (largely constituted within him as 'conscience'), on the one hand, and the potentialities awakened by analysis, on the other. From such an experience a man who is pessimistically inclined easily concludes that he has no hope of controlling the evil tendencies within him, and this leads directly to abandonment, for if one believes that one's evil tendencies are the strongest forces within one it must seem pointless to go on trying to restrain them; but this does not mean that 'conscience' is stifled, and the result is the paradoxical state of 'abandonment', in which a man disapproves of his own ways, and yet seems driven to worse and worse behaviour.

In psychological terms this state of abandonment arises when consciousness is 'overthrown' by the unconscious, and it may also be described as 'possession' by the unconscious, or by unconscious elements. This danger arises particularly in connection with the beginning of the synthetic technique, when failure to postulate the 'anima' in the right way as a person other than the ego, and the consequent ascription of 'anima reactions' to oneself, results in 'possession by the anima'. Of the states resulting from such 'possession' Jung writes: 'They are characterized by one and the same fact that an unknown "something" has taken possession of a smaller or greater portion of the psyche and asserts its hateful and harmful existence undeterred by all our insight, reason, and energy, thereby proclaiming the power of the unconscious over the conscious mind, the sovereign power of possession' (ibid., 370). To give up conscious purpose and control is to give oneself up to forces which lack unity and order, for although the unconscious may be said to have 'purposes' of its own these 'purposes' are directly related to conscious purposes, which they extend, modify, oppose or compensate, and it is only in relation to conscious purpose that the odd things which manifest the unconscious 'make sense'. However inadequate consciousness may be as a guide to salvation it is essential to the unity of a developed nature, nd the man who abandons conscious direction of his life is 'possessed' by forces which are in themselves wholly chaotic and senseless, and he is 'dissipated' in every sense of the word.

(*b*) *Despair*. Despair is the alternative to abandonment. Jung says, 'since human nature is not compounded wholly of light, but also abounds in shadows the insight gained in practical analysis is often somewhat painful, the more so if, as is generally the case, one has previously neglected the other side' (*Essays*, 225), and also 'When a man recognizes [Jung can hardly mean to imply that he rightly recognizes this] that his ideal persona is responsible for his anything but ideal anima, his ideals are shattered, the world becomes ambiguous, he becomes ambiguous even to himself. He is seized by doubts about goodness, and what is worse, he doubts his own good intentions' (ibid., 310). Despair is divided from abandonment by an extremely thin line: the inward state is hardly to be distinguished but whereas the man who abandons himself to his evil tendencies gets some apparent pleasure from the things that he does, the man who despairs gets no pleasure, whether he lets his evil tendencies influence his behaviour, or whether he restrains them. Despair might be characterized by saying that the man who despairs knows that he cannot be good, and yet will not be bad; he sees and abhors the full power of his unconscious, he believes that he can do nothing against it, and still he holds on to his conscious direction of his life without any hope at all.

Abandonment and despair may both be regarded as the result of a failure to dissociate the ego from the anima; that is, a failure to regard the latter as an 'autonomous personality'. In Jung's technique the idea of the anima is a defence against these dangers, and it not only enables a man to distinguish between his deliberate intentions and his instinctive tendencies, but it also enables him to see that the tendencies which distress him are not peculiar to him but 'collective'; that is, that they occur in the lives of all men. From a slightly different point of view it may be said that these dangers arise as a result of the reductive technique, and that they arise when a man refuses to adjust himself to the new discoveries which he has made about himself, for abandonment and despair arise when a man fails to modify his conscious attitude, because consciousness cannot cope with new ideas and attitudes unless it allows itself to be modified. Abandonment occurs when, refusing to allow his conscious character to change, a man finds that it is too weak to oppose the new potentialities; despair when he is able to restrain them, but still unable to fit them into his life. The third danger to be considered results when, by a greater effort, a man preserves his conscious character unchanged by once more relegating to the unconscious the psychic elements activated by analysis.

(c) *Pride*. When a man who is confronted with tendencies which he has previously repressed refuses to modify his conscious attitude he does not necessarily abandon all hope of controlling those tendencies, and he may set himself to oppose and overcome them. This answer to the challenge of the unconscious represents a reaction against the analytical technique, and it is described by Jung as the 'regressive restoration of the persona'. Although Jung does not explicitly connect this with pride it bears a close resemblance to it, because in order to overcome the tendencies released by analysis without modifying his conscious attitude a man is driven to that aggressive assertion of his infallibility which goes with inward uncertainty, and if this is successful it eventually deceives the man himself; and the tacit assumption of the infallibility of one's own judgements is properly called 'pride'.

Jung connects the 'regressive restoration of the persona' with those psychologies which 'explain' the phenomena of the unconscious by exclusive reference to infantile tendencies. The reason for this is that such 'explanations' provide the patient with the opportunity of dismissing the unconscious as childish and contemptible, so that, Jung suggests, he may say: 'It was all nonsense of course. I am a crazy visionary! The best thing to do would be to bury the unconscious or throw it overboard with all its works' (*Essays*, 257). Whatever the man gives as his reason, the effect is that 'Rather than face the conflict he will turn back and, as best he can, regressively restore his shattered persona, discounting all those hopes and expectations which had blossomed under the transference. He will become smaller, more limited, more rationalistic than he was before' (ibid., loc. cit.). It may be added that Jung continues, 'One could not say that this result would be an unqualified misfortune in all cases, for there are all too many who, on account of their notorious ineptitude, thrive better in a rationalistic system than in freedom', but this has more bearing upon Jung's 'gnosticism' (in the sense of advocating a 'higher way' for the privileged few) than upon the danger considered here.

The man who restores his persona in this way—that is, the man who turns back on his new knowledge of himself—and reinstates his old conscious attitude, 'With diminished personality . . . turns back to the measure he can fill' (ibid., 259), but this is not likely to be his own account of what has happened: it will seem to the man concerned that he has resisted temptation and successfully opposed the evil tendencies within him, and however much his conscious personality may be 'diminished' he will suppose that he has every reason to have confidence in it. It will seem to him that he has won a great victory and he will not escape from taking pride in his achievement, and relying yet more exclusively than before upon his conscious character to guide his life.

(*d*) *Antinomianism.* By derivation 'antinomianism' means 'against the law', but the word is not used of all who flout the law, but of those who oppose a generally accepted law by appealing to some special insight of their own of a law which they think is 'higher' than the one which they flout, or to a new status of being 'above the law' which they claim for themselves. Outwardly the antinomian may behave in ways similar to those of the 'abandoned' man, but his inward attitude is the exact opposite since the abandoned man flouts a law which he believes is The Law, whereas the antinomian flouts a law which he rejects. Since the mark of antinomianism is that the antinomian claims for himself authority over the law, it is irrelevant, psychologically considered, whether he uses this authority to abrogate the generally accepted religious or moral law or to establish that law, because antinomianism arises from, and rests upon, the claim to be able to declare the true law on one's own authority. A man makes a claim of this sort when he is, in Jung's terms, 'possessed by the magician'.

Just as abandonment and despair (possession by the anima) may be due to a failure to postulate the anima in the right way, so antinomianism may be due to failure to postulate the magician as an autonomous personality. 'Possession by the magician' arises at a late stage of the technique, when the anima has been dissolved, and it represents an over-confidence in one's ability to order the new-found tendencies, so that one takes them as expressions of one's personal character. This state may also be called 'identification with the collective psyche', whereby 'One would be the fortunate possessor of the great truth, that was only waiting to be discovered, of the eschatological knowledge that means the healing of the nations', and 'This attitude does not necessarily signify megalomania in direct form, but megalomania in the milder and more familiar form it takes in the reformer, the prophet, and the martyr' (*Essays*, 260). On the whole Jung tends to stress the good intentions of those who suffer this fate and to represent them as pathetic figures, but this is only a proper attitude to those who find that the 'mana' does not work on others, for if the 'mana' does work, that is, if other people take the man who is possessed by the magician at his own valuation, then the consequences may be devastating, and however much compassion one may have for the unfortunate individual concerned that compassion must be mixed with some element of condemnation. For example, of Nietzsche one may say, with Jung, 'Can the neurotic philosopher prove to us that he has no neurosis? he cannot prove it even to himself' (ibid., 397), and feel nothing but sympathy, but despite the obvious similarities between Nietzsche and Hitler one can hardly feel in exactly the same way about the latter. To be possessed by the magician is to wear a 'father-mask', and that is to take upon oneself the role that (in past ages, at least) the child ascribes to the father: the role of one who is above law, and the source of all authority. The man who takes this role upon himself becomes the lawgiver, and if the law which he enunciates conflicts with accepted morality, then so much the worse for that morality! Analysis certainly brings with it the danger of 'inflation' of this sort, and such inflation is the source of antinomianism.

It is of some interest to note that what Jung says of possession by the magician is directly related to the function of the king in early civilizations. In such civilizations the 'father-mask' is fixed, by common consent, upon the king, and because he wears it he is able to maintain the order and prosperity of society. 'Behind the later stage [of the civilization of the ancient East]', it has been said, '. . . there lies an older stage, dimmer but still distinct, when the focus of the attempt to secure the well-being of the community was a single individual possessing qualities of strength, or knowledge, or both, which indicated him as the centre of the ritual life of the community. He was both king and god, the term god implying nothing more at that stage than the king in his ritual aspect with all the magical potencies which he embodied' (*Labyrinth*, 214). In Jung's terms this is to speak of a collective projection of the magician on to the king, and if this account of the past is correct, it can be seen how the projection of the magician upon a god distinct from the king ultimately leads to a weakening of the authority of the king (maintained for centuries by the assumption first of a physical relationship between god and king, and then by that of a special divine selection of the king), and how the rejection of gods leads to a 'vacuum', so that the magician can no longer be projected at all. In such a 'vacuum' the danger that individuals will become possessed by the magician is very great, and in the West this danger seems to have been largely avoided by the personification of Justice and Law as carriers of the projection: yet how tenuous a defence this may be has been shown by the German acceptance of Hitler as the embodiment of the 'magical potencies' ascribed to ancient kings.

The four dangers which have been discussed also arise in connection with penitence, and the way in which they do so will be shown in the next chapter. Analytical psychology and Christianity both include safeguards against these dangers, and in the former the safeguard is the analyst. In the last section of this chapter this function of the analyst is examined.

The Analyst

It is probably true that the analyst is popularly thought of as the high priest of the unconscious, evoking the forces of the unconscious by his incantations and spells, and that with this picture of his work there goes a tendency to dismiss the whole thing as so much mumbo-jumbo. Up to a point this idea is correct, because the analyst is concerned to persuade his patients to become aware of tendencies which they prefer to ignore, and his technique is designed to bring those tendencies into play: nevertheless, the most important function of the analyst is to bind, not to loose, for his incantations and spells (that is, his psychological terms and his curious language) are designed to enable the patient to arrange the unconscious forces into some sort of pattern, so that he can come to terms with them. Once the resistance of consciousness to the unconscious has been overcome, and the unconscious forces have been released, then the analyst's influence is thrown in to support and strengthen consciousness, and about this Jung is altogether explicit.

The function of the analyst in helping the patient to order and relate the released tendencies, and in supporting him against them, is indicated by the following passages:

(i) 'I help the patient to understand all the things which the unconscious produces during the conflict' (*Alchemy*, 37).

(ii) Of abreaction: 'The intervention of the doctor is absolutely necessary. One can easily see what it means to a patient when he can confide his experience to an understanding and sympathetic doctor. His conscious mind finds in the doctor a moral support against the unmanageable affect of his traumatic complex. No longer does he stand alone in his battle with these elemental powers, but some one whom he trusts reaches out a hand, lending him moral strength to combat the tyranny of uncontrolled emotion. In this way the integrative powers of his conscious mind are reinforced until he is able once more to bring the rebellious affect under control' (*Practice*, 270).

(iii) 'Here [i.e. in an alchemical treatise] we seem to have a hint about the treatment required: faced with the disorientation of the patient, the doctor must hold fast to his own orientation; that is, he must know what the patient's condition means, he must understand what is of value in the dreams, and do so moreover with the help of that *aqua doctrinae* which alone is appropriate to the nature of the unconscious' (ibid., 478).

(iv) 'Therapy aims at strengthening the conscious mind, and whenever possible I try to rouse the patient to mental activity and get him to subdue the *massa confusa* of his mind with his own understanding, so that he can reach a vantage-point *au-dessus de la mêlée*' (ibid., 479), though to this Jung adds the note: 'Remembering the rule that every proposition in psychology may be inverted with advantage, I would point out that it is always a bad thing to accentuate the conscious attitude when this has shown itself to be so strong in the first place as to violently suppress the unconscious.'

Thus the analyst provides understanding, strength and, most important, hope for the patient. Behind all the technique lies the implicit assurance that however confused, evil, or over-powering the unconscious forces may appear, in the end 'all shall be well, and all shall be well, and all manner of things shall be well' (Julian of Norwich). Understanding, strength, and hope are equally necessary for the penitent sinner, and like the analyst the Christian Church provides them. It is a mistake to think that it is the actual confession of sin in the confessional that corresponds most closely to analysis, for the above remarks show that in so far as there is a parallel between analysis and sacramental confession the work of the analyst is to be compared rather to the giving of absolution by the priest, than to the hearing of the confession itself: 'Mere rehearsal of the experience' Jung says of the trauma, 'does not itself possess a curative effect' (*Practice*, 269). The true parallel, however, is between the analyst on the one hand, and the Church, as the Company of all Faithful People on the other, and both defend men against the dangers which beset them upon the way of salvation by the implicit or explicit declaration that evil can be controlled, and that chaos shall not have the last word.

7

PENITENCE

IT was mentioned in the last chapter that accepting the unconscious appears to correspond, in different ways, to two features of the Christian scheme of salvation. It will now be shown why this is so, and what are the features in Christianity which correspond to accepting the unconscious, and it will be found that, although they are different, both features are properly called by the same name: 'penitence'.

Accepting the unconscious is Jung's prescription for natural man, and, as has been shown, it is something which a man can do by his own conscious effort; but although a man can set himself to accept the unconscious, and so prepare himself for Individuation, he cannot set himself to become Individuated, because Individuation is something that happens to a man, and the most that can be said is that, so far as we know, it does not happen to men who have not accepted the unconscious (by means of Jung's technique, or in some other way). It cannot even be said that every man who has accepted the unconscious becomes Individuated. To think of accepting the unconscious in this way is to think of its place and function in Jung's system, and to ignore what it is in itself, and if anything has a corresponding place and function in the Christian scheme it must be something which a man can set himself to do, something which is (so far as we know) a condition which must be fulfilled before a man is Justified and something which prepares a man for Justification by Faith, yet at the same time something which does not, itself, effect a man's Justification. Thought of in this way, accepting the unconscious corresponds to the prior condition which must be fulfilled before a man can be Justified, but there is another way of thinking of it, and thought of in this other way it corresponds to a feature in the life of the Justified Christian.

Just as it is possible to ignore what happens when a man accepts the unconscious, and to think only of the place and function of accepting the unconscious in Jung's system, so it is also possible to pass over the place and function of accepting the unconscious, and to think only of what is done when a man accepts the unconscious, and from this second point of view accepting the unconscious is a process of development, which leads from a state of antagonism between consciousness and the unconscious, to a state in which all sides of a man's personality are 'implicated'. Such a development cannot correspond to the condition which must be fulfilled before a man is Justified, because Justification by Faith is a gift which God gives to those who have not yet begun to develop in the right way. Thus, whereas accepting the unconscious corresponds in respect of its place and function to the prior condition of Justification by Faith, it also corresponds in respect of what it involves to a development initiated by God's Justifying act, and this double correspondence occurs because of an important difference between the Christian system and that of psychotherapy. This difference has been noticed already, but is of sufficient importance to be mentioned again.

Accepting the unconscious corresponds to two distinct features of the Christian way because of a fundamental difference between Individuation and Justification by Faith, and this fundamental difference can be represented symbolically:

(i) Individuation   ●————————→| ⨯

(ii) Justification by Faith   ●—| ⨯————————→

The black circle represents natural man, the ⨯ the goal, and the arrow a process of development. In Jung's scheme the development is the activity of natural man, and the goal is reached after the development has ended, but in the Christian scheme the goal of Justification is reached before the development begins, and the development is made possible by the presence of the Spirit in a man. At the same time, as was remarked in chapter 3, not every man who hears the Gospel is Justified, so that there must be some condition which is fulfilled by those who are Justified, but not fulfilled by those who are not Justified: this condition is represented in (ii) by the short line between ● and ⨯. It can be seen from the diagram that formally, as that which intervenes between natural man and the goal, the arrow in (i) corresponds to the short line in (ii), while in respect of its content, as a process of development, it corresponds to the arrow in (ii). We have now to consider what in the Christian way are represented by the short line and the arrow in (ii): that is, what is the prior condition which must be fulfilled by a man before he is Justified, and what development in the Christian life corresponds to the development which should take place during a Jungian analysis.

Penitence as the Prior Condition of Justification by Faith

It was argued in chapter 3 that before a man can be justified he must be ready to accept God's gift, and that this is to say that he must be penitent. The arguments used in that chapter will be recapitulated and extended here.

There is a general agreement among most theologians that there is a condition which a man must fulfil before he can be Justified. It is acknowledged that God offers and gives His gift freely to men, but it is also thought that the giving of the gift depends in some way upon man's response to God's offer of it. As was shown in chapter 3 there are many theologians who believe that the response which man must make to God's offer is 'faith', but reasons were given in the same chapter for rejecting this view, and for thinking that penitence is the prior condition of Justification by Faith. The short way of rejecting the assertion that faith is the prior[1] condition of Justification by Faith is to point out that the Church has always held that Christian Faith is impossible without the prior activity of God, and that the assertion that 'as far as faith is concerned, the meaning is . . . that men are gripped and constrained by God's power' (*Nygren*, 78) is only another way of expressing the scholastic doctrine that faith is a 'supernatural' virtue, which depends upon grace. 'Supernatural' should direct us to see faith as something achieved by man's encounter with the Gospel, and it should also instruct us that faith is something which happens to us, and not something which we can set ourselves to get, so that it cannot be a condition which a man must fulfil. More simply, to have faith is to have accepted Christ, and this is to be Justified, so that if faith were the condition of Justification by Faith it would be a condition of itself.

One example may be given of the view that penitence is the condition which a man can and must fulfil before God gives His gift: F. P. Harton writes, 'Repentance is the one essential condition upon which God opens to us the treasures of His grace' (*Harton*, 158), and although he does not explicitly mention Justification by Faith there is a clear identity of meaning between his statement that 'The

---

[1] It is, of course, a logical condition, in that if a man is Justified he also has faith.

power of Christ lifts us out of the sin-ruined life of the flesh and enables
us to live in the Spirit, as God means us to do' (ibid., loc. cit.) and,
for example, 'That I am justified means that through Christ I have
become possessed of the new righteousness which comes from God,
and am incorporated as a member of the kingdom of God' (*Nygren*,
18). This view can also be argued from Dodd; it is true that he says
that it is in response to faith that God acts, and that he also seems to
have serious doubts about penitence, since he writes 'A sense of sin,
although it is often recommended and cultivated by the religious, is in
itself not a help, but a hindrance, to the growth of personality'
(*Dodd*, 145), but he goes a long way to cancel his own claim when he
comes to define 'faith'. Dodd says that 'for Paul, faith is that attitude
in which, acknowledging our complete insufficiency for any of the
high ends of life, we rely utterly on the sufficiency of God' (ibid.,
15), and this sentence is ingenious, because the use of the adverbial
clause obscures the fact that Dodd has brought together two distinct
attitudes in his definition of one word, and that it is possible for a man
to hold these two attitudes one after the other. A man may begin by
acknowledging his inadequacy and then go on to rely upon God, and
although it is impossible to rely utterly upon God until one has seen
one's own 'complete inadequacy' one may acknowledge one's
inadequacy without relying on God: in other words, Dodd's assertion
fits better with the view that penitence is the condition of Justification
by Faith than it does with his own view that 'faith' is the condition,
in that it can be said that when a man, through penitence,
acknowledges his complete insufficiency, then God, through grace,
gives him that faith whereby he relies utterly upon the sufficiency
of God.

If one now turns from modern writers to the New Testament itself,
and if one makes the assumption (as one must, if one believes that
Christianity is one) that there is an agreement between the New
Testament writers overriding all differences, it is clear enough that
penitence is to be regarded as the condition of entry upon the
Christian way. St Mark tells us that Jesus' first demand upon men was
'Repent, and believe in the Gospel', and St Luke that St Peter's reply
to the question 'What must we do to be saved?' was 'Repent, and be
baptized'. Again, the first three Evangelists all teach the same lessons,
in that they present St John the Baptist's preaching of repentance as
the proper preparation for the coming of Jesus to men, and although

it is true that St Paul himself does not make any explicit statement of this kind, a consideration of his criticisms of Gentile and Jew in the Epistle to the Romans leads to the same conclusion. In the Epistle to the Romans St Paul is writing about those whom he criticizes, but if we imagine him saying the same things to Gentiles and Jews themselves, and ask ourselves what result he would wish his remarks to have, the answer to our question is clear: St Paul would wish his hearers to realize that their best efforts came to nothing, that their way of life was undesirable, and that they should turn from it to something better. Although it goes beyond the available evidence there is considerable truth in Harton's assertion that 'St Paul preached Christ crucified and so did St Peter, and the practical result which each desired to bring about was Repentance' (*Harton*, 160).

Penitence is the condition which a man must fulfil before he can be Justified, and the Greek word for 'repent' suggests, by its derivation, that penitence is primarily a 'turning of the mind'. Harton, for instance, says of repentance, 'Not until sin is realized as hateful is there any chance of overcoming it', and adds that this is the 'negative side', and goes on, 'Sin cannot be recognized for what it is until it is seen against the background of the love of God, and for gaining of a new mind with regard to sin ($\mu\epsilon\tau\alpha\nuo\acute{\iota}\alpha$) the soul must turn to God' (ibid., 159), but in saying this Harton, like Dodd but in the reverse sense, overthrows his own position. Harton says that repentance is the condition which man must fulfil before God 'opens the treasures of His grace' but if the above definition were right penitence would depend on faith, because it would not be possible before the soul had turned to God. This view of penitence ignores the fact that men may be exhorted to repent before they have received Christ and even, as the coming of St John the Baptist shows, before they have heard the Gospel. Penitence is a 'turning of the mind' as has often been pointed out, but there is insufficient reason for the common view that it is a 'turning *to* God': by itself it may be no more than a turning *from* one's past way of life. Unless such a turning from the past is coupled with a turning to Christ it is valueless from a Christian point of view, but the two 'turnings' can be considered separately, and this is shown by the New Testament formulae: man is to 'repent and believe', or 'repent and be baptized', and this is to say that penitence alone is not enough. Penitence is the condition of Justification, but the Christian life does not begin until the man who is penitent is also

Justified, and the sign that he is Justified is that faith is added to his penitence.

Penitence, as the condition of Justification by Faith, is a turning from the past. It involves a recognition of the fact that one is sinful, that one's best efforts are inadequate, that one's sinful desires and acts are hateful, and that one has 'no profit' in one's behaviour: in a word, it is the realization that something needs to be done about oneself, and a readiness for something to be done. Penitence of this sort does not Justify a man, nor does it involve a change of character, but it does involve a clearer understanding of what one's character is, and, in particular, it involves the rejection of the 'good will' as a guide. Such penitence may be compared and contrasted with accepting the unconscious.

Like accepting the unconscious, penitence of this sort involves a change of attitude, but whereas the former requires an intense self-investigation the latter is relatively superficial. It is uncertain whether all men can endure the rigours of a full analysis, but anyone can see that his life is unsatisfactory. Secondly, although both accepting the unconscious and penitence are things which natural man does, the man who accepts the unconscious *does* something to himself (in that he widens and modifies his conscious character) whereas the man who is penitent merely sees himself more clearly: in other words there is an important sense in which it can be said that to be penitent is not to contribute anything to one's own salvation, whereas this is not true of accepting the unconscious. Thirdly, neither accepting the unconscious nor penitence by themselves bring a man to salvation, and both need to be followed by some event which a man cannot bring about by his own efforts; but whereas accepting the unconscious may be said to make a man fit for Individation, penitence does not make him fit to be Justified. The man who accepts the unconscious is like a man who says 'I want a cake, I have weighed and mixed all the ingredients, and now I am waiting for someone to cook it'; whereas the man who is penitent is like a man who says 'I want a cake'.

The comparison made in the last paragraph refers to penitence as it is demanded from natural man before he is Justified: that is, to that penitence which has the place and function in the Christian way which corresponds to the place and function of accepting the unconscious in Jung's way. Christians who are Justified, however, are also exhorted to '*be* penitent', and to increase and develop their penitence, and that penitence which is a feature of the Christian life itself corresponds to accepting the unconscious considered as a process whereby a man's character is developed.

Penitence in the Christian Life

Mention was made in chapter 5 of our modern difficulty in accepting the New Testament view that Christianity is generically different from all other religions and ways of life, and the same problem arises in connection with penitence. If we accept the New Testament position we can avoid much of the confusion which besets the discussion of penitence. The fact is that 'penitence' is now used in two different senses: it is used of the first turning from a false way of life which precedes Justification (in accordance with New Testament usage) and also of the sorrow for sins committed after Justification which is expected from Christians. 'Penitence' is not used in the second sense in the New Testament, and it may be unfortunate that as we have no other word for this 'post-Justification' sorrow we cannot mark the distinction between the two forms of penitence. If, as Christians believe, Justification means a fundamental change in a man's status before God it follows that 'penitence' cannot mean the same thing when it refers to one who has not yet accepted Christ as it does when it refers to a Christian. For the non-Christian, penitence is a turning from an established way of life and the rejection of all those things in which he has been wont to put his trust, but for the Christian it is a turning back from things which have led him astray to that in which he has already put his trust.[1] Penitence as a prior condition of Justification by Faith is negative, whereas penitence within the Christian life is meaningless except in relation to the positive purpose of surrendering oneself to Christ; the non-Christian may be penitent and yet not have faith, but for the Christian penitence presupposes faith and when this distinction is kept in mind, the 'portmanteau' statements quoted from Dodd and Harton are easily understood.

Dodd writes, 'Faith is that attitude in which, acknowledging our

[1] This is in accordance with New Testament teaching, but does not fit well with modern conditions. The New Testament writers never envisaged our situation in which we are confronted by many who must be acknowledged as Christians (and so as being Justified) who have never consciously put their trust in the Holy Spirit. It seems that unless we wish to deny that such people are Christians we must still say that the 'turning' demanded from them is somehow different from that demanded from those who have no prior claim to be called 'Christians'.

complete insufficiency for any of the high ends of life, we rely utterly upon the sufficiency of God'; Harton that 'Sin cannot be recognized for what it is until it is seen against the background of the love of God, and for gaining of a new mind with regard to sin ($\mu\epsilon\tau\alpha\nuo\iota\alpha$) the soul must turn to God'; and both statements emphasize the close association of penitence and faith in the Christian life. Faith only leads to a full reliance upon God in so far as it is coupled with a realization of one's own inadequacy, and the extent of one's own inadequacy can only be known in the light of the knowledge of God which is given by faith, and Dodd and Harton would be perfectly correct in describing the *Christian life* as an organic unity of faith and penitence, but they are mistaken in so far as they are speaking of the condition required of natural man before he becomes a Christian. Penitence has already been considered in relation to the natural man, and it has now to be examined as a feature of the Christian life.

Penitence and faith are the continuing marks of a truly Christian life, and no life can be called truly Christian if these two elements are not both present in their proper degree. In the course of such a life both penitence and faith develop, they are not acts which must occur once and for all at the beginning of the way. It is possible to say that the goal of the Christian life is the perfection of these two things, but if we say this we must remember that in the ultimate Christian ideal both are transformed. The Christian ideal is neither penitence, nor faith, but love, and in love faith is transformed in the possession of God, and penitence in a contemplation of the beloved which leaves no room for any thought of the inadequacy of self. On this side of such an ideal the transformation of penitence has already begun: penitence looks to oneself and one's own inadequacy, faith looks to the adequacy of God, and so, as the Christian life deepens and God is more fully known, penitence becomes more and more a mere background for faith—there, but hardly present to consciousness. The more aware we become of the adequacy of God, the less heed we have to consider the inadequacy of man. It follows that in speaking of the development of penitence we are speaking of an abstraction, for we are turning our attention to only one aspect of the development of the Christian. The reason for selecting this aspect is that it corresponds to the development which occurs in the course of analysis, and it does so because it is that feature of the Christian life which is concerned with a man's attitude to himself.

Much Christian penitence is inevitably 'ambulance work': the
Christian who has turned from lust, or pride, or selfishness finds that
he has been led again into sin, and that he must return to the true way:
similarly a man who has become conscious of unpleasant psychic
elements may find that he has repressed them once more, and that the
process of making them conscious must be gone over again. In other
words, even though penitence and accepting the unconscious are
processes of development the development does not always proceed
smoothly and may be subject to many setbacks, but in comparing
the two such setbacks may be ignored because what has to be
considered is the process which takes place when penitence comes to
its full flower, or a man fully accepts the unconscious. It has been
shown that in accepting the unconscious a man passes through three
marked stages:

(a) By attention to odd things which manifest the personal unconscious he modifies his conscious attitude by 'widening' it.

(b) By encountering the anima he further 'widens' his conscious
attitude, and also becomes aware of unconscious elements, which
he must take into account.

(c) By acknowledging the collective unconscious he comes to a
state in which he realizes that a full life must, somehow, involve
both his conscious purpose and, also, the apparently contradictory purpose of the unconscious.

In the development of penitence as Christian theologians speak of it
it is also possible to detect three stages, and when the basic difference
between St Paul's and Jung's diagnosis of natural man is remembered
it can be seen that the stages in the development of penitence are
parallel to those in the process of accepting the unconscious. Jung
says that what natural man thinks is 'evil' is as good as what he calls
'good', so that his system has two complementary aims: on the one
hand psychic elements are to be taken from the 'bad' side, and incorporated in the 'good' (unconscious elements are to be made
conscious), and on the other hand those elements which cannot be
'transferred' are to be recognized as 'good' in themselves (the
collective unconscious must be accepted). St Paul says that what
natural man calls 'good' is no more use than what he calls 'evil', and
so the aims of the Christian system are, first, to 'transfer' from the
'good' to the 'bad' side (that is, a man is to recognize that many

thoughts and acts regarded as harmless or good are rooted in evil inclinations), and, secondly, to convince a man that he cannot put his trust in those activities which cannot be 'transferred' (that is, to convince him that the 'good will' cannot lead him to salvation). Thus the stages of penitence which correspond to the three stages of accepting the unconscious are:

(a) By careful scrutiny of one's acts, to recognize the extent of one's sinfulness (to widen one's awareness of evil inclinations).

(b) The realization of the incompetence of the good will as a means of controlling the evil inclinations. (In Jung's system the second stage begins the 'rescue' of the unconscious, in the Christian system it begins the rejection of the 'good will').

(c) The recognition that nothing in man can bring him to salvation.

It has to be shown that it is the general view that penitence does develop in the way suggested by the above scheme.

(a) *Extension of Penitence.* That there are degrees of penitence, and that penitence should develop, does not need to be argued, but two quotations from William Law may be given in illustration: 'Natural religion' he says, 'if you understand it rightly, is a most excellent thing, it is a right sentiment of the heart, it is so much goodness in the heart, it is its sensibility both of its separation from and its relation to God; and, therefore, it shows itself in nothing but in a penitential sentiment of the weight of its sins, and in an humble recourse by faith to the mercy of God. The Gospel calls you to nothing but to know and understand and practise a full and real penitence, and to know by faith such heights and depths of the divine mercy towards you, as the religion of nature had only some little uncertain glimmering of' (*Law*, 3, 4). This not only indicates the possibility of degrees of penitence, but also emphasizes the unity of penitence and faith in the Christian life which has already been noticed. The second quotation gives some indication of what 'full and real' penitence involves: 'Repentance is but a kind of table talk till we see so much of the deformity of our inward nature as to be in some degree frightened and terrified at the sight of it' (ibid., 13).

The encounter with Jesus, or the Gospel, brings about, or should bring about, an increase of penitence, and one form which this increase takes is an extension of our awareness of our sinfulness. Vincent Taylor, for example, remarks, 'The more fully we understand what

[Jesus'] suffering was . . . the more living our penitence becomes, not merely because our feelings are stirred and our pity stimulated, but because we perceive how evil sin is, and how much more deeply it is entrenched in our hearts than we had supposed' (*Taylor*, 197); Harton says 'Face to face with Christ crucified, the soul realizes the heinousness of its sin' (*Harton*, 161); Mackintosh that if 'we are confronted with Jesus Christ, if in Him we discover how awful goodness is and how great is the love we have violated . . . the gravity [of our consciousness of guilt] is painfully increased by the new perception of sin as antagonism to utter goodness' (*Mackintosh*, 73, 74 modified). Two things are involved, on the one hand if his penitence deepens in this way a man sees that his sins are more serious in themselves than he supposed, and, on the other, he realizes that many more things are sins than he thought before, because as he becomes aware of the immensity of God's demands so he realizes how often he falls short of them, even when he is not doing anything evil in itself; and this is why, in the lives of the Saints, increase in holiness is always accompanied by increased awareness of sin. This increased awareness of the extent of sin represents a 'transfer' from 'good' to 'evil', in that it means that as we judge ourselves by the standard of Jesus we come to see more of our life as 'evil', and less of it as 'good', and, as we have already seen this (inversely) corresponds to the 'widening of consciousness' in Jung's scheme. Thus both Jung's reductive technique, and the extension of our awareness of sin brought about by the knowledge of Jesus tend to bring more of a man's life and character, as it were, under the same 'label', but whereas increase of penitence means an increase in what we think of as evil, analysis increases what we think of as good. The first stage in the increase of penitence is an extension of it, and it is comparable with the first stage of Jung's technique, and when this extension of penitence is coupled with an increased awareness of the seriousness of sin it has a further result, which corresponds to that of the dissolution of the anima.

(*b*) *The Incompetence of the 'Good Will'*. So long as a man thinks of his good will as what he really is, and regards his evil inclinations as extraneous tendencies which sometimes interfere with his life, he supposes that his problem is nothing more than one of overcoming his evil tendencies and strengthening his good will, but according to most Christian writers the deepening of penitence involves the realization that he must describe very much more of himself as evil than he thought, and that the evil side of his character is far more powerful than he thought. Mackintosh, for example, tells us that 'all who reach moral personality learn, on the faintest self-scrutiny, that their moral being is somehow wrong and crooked; that alongside of the commanding sense of obligation there are fermenting within them a set of half-blind and half-perverted instincts, evil tendencies which solicit their choice, lead their will astray, and often master it shamefully' (*Mackintosh*, 52), and if a man does learn this, he can no longer put much trust in his good will. Penitence, as it deepens, marches with Jung's psychotherapy, because both systems lead a man to doubt his ability to follow his own purposes, and to bring them to a satisfactory conclusion. Jung requires us to see that we 'ought' to allow the unconscious a place in the direction of our life, simply because it is as much 'ours' as any other aspect of our nature; Christianity asks us to see that we cannot hope to overcome our evil tendencies for the same reason—that they are ours and express what we are. Behind the difference of emphasis (Jung presents the unconscious as the source of new possibilities for good, penitence merely destroys the hope of overcoming evil) is the common principle that we are what we are, that whatever we do we must do as ourself, and that we must begin by seeing ourselves as we are, with all masks and hypocrisies put aside.

Penitence may deepen to this extent without any specific Christian influence. It is, perhaps, too strong to say that 'all who reach moral personality' realize the extent of their evil inclinations or the futility of their good will, and, as the quotations above suggest, the encounter with Jesus is an important way in which penitence is brought to such an intensity, but penitence as intense as this may sometimes be an element in that 'natural religion' of which Law speaks, and so might be called 'natural penitence'.[1] Natural penitence may vary in degree from the mere admission that something goes wrong with one's life and that it is one's own fault, to the realization that there is in one more wrong than right and that there is little that one can do to put right what is wrong. The encounter with Jesus increases the intensity of penitence, but it is not the only thing which may do this, and in so far as this is

---

[1] This 'natural penitence' must be sharply distinguished from that penitence which is a turning entirely from the old way, which is what is meant in the New Testament by 'penitence' and which was discussed at the beginning of this chapter.

what it does it does not change the character of penitence. That true
Christian penitence which *follows* Justification involves more than an
increase in intensity, and penitence is not fully Christian until the
third stage is reached.

(*c*) *Rejection of the Good Will.* There is not the least question that the
intensification of penitence which is brought about by the Gospel is
of first importance, or that to understand the real horror of sin is an
essential step on the way to self-knowledge, yet it may easily lead by
its very importance to a failure to realize an even more important
extension of penitence which is effected by the Gospel, whereby the
value of the good will itself is brought into question. Yet this further
extension of penitence is implicit in all talk of Jesus as the 'revelation
of perfect humanity', of Jesus as judge of men, and of the imitation
of Christ, because if man already knew how to detect his sin, if he
could already judge how and how far he fell below the ideal of human
nature, then there would be no great value in a new pattern by which
he could judge his success. A new pattern would be unnecessary unless
it were the case that there are sins which we are systematically unable
to know, either as sins or mistakes, apart from our knowledge of
Jesus, and this most important consideration is too rarely stressed,
although it is not completely neglected: 'We now detect and measure
sin by its unlikeness to the spirit of Jesus; we know sin when we see it
by its difference from Him', writes Mackintosh (*Mackintosh*, 53), and
in *Sin* Hempel is quoted 'that is how revelation works: it brings the
real situation to light, and so begins the destruction of Satan's
kingdom' (*Sin*, 73, n. 3). The 'real situation' is not merely that
our errors were worse than we supposed, nor that we had failed
to see numerous minor errors which we now acknowledge, but that
sins have been brought to light which we could not have known as
sins were it not for our encounter with the perfection which Jesus
reveals.

'Natural penitence' is entitled to the name 'penitence', but Christian
penitence is not merely natural penitence tremendously intensified by
a new understanding of the nature of our sins. Christian penitence
involves a 'qualitative' change in natural penitence, because it means
the discovery of a whole class of sins which were not before acknowledged, even as errors; sins which, in fact, we cannot know as sins
without being confronted by a criterion of perfection from outside
ourselves. This new class comprises all those sins which, it was

suggested in chapter 5, should be described as 'pride'. Natural penitence is penitence for those sins and errors of which we may be aware as the result of 'purely human considerations', that is penitence for acts and thoughts for which we are responsible and which conflict with our settled purposes and ideals; and whether we are as it were 'taken by storm' by some emotion or 'evil inclination', or whether we deliberately purpose to do some wrong act, it remains true that so far our 'sins' (that is, what we naturally acknowledge to be sins) are essentially those things which we condemn when we would say that we are 'most ourselves'. We condemn them precisely because they are out of harmony with the hopes and ideals which we regard with approval. The encounter with the Gospel means an extension of penitence because through the Gospel we come to see that our sins are not only those acts which we deplore because of their contrast with the hopes and ideals which we value, but that we also sin when we act in the most complete accord with those very hopes and ideals. Through the encounter with Jesus we are able to see that what we thought was our highest good is sin: ' . . . our will', says Mackintosh, 'is evil. It is not wholly evil . . . but evil taints it in every element' (*Mackintosh*, 52). Again, the assertion 'Practical reason, the power to make judgements and act on them, which exalts man to a divine sovereignty in the sphere of his own affairs—that is the germ of sinful behaviour' (*Sin*, 26) is a judgement which the natural man could never make, because it is only by his 'practical reason' that he is able to judge at all: only in the presence of Jesus is it possible for a man to see that 'at every step we consider evil to be good, and good, evil, and this arises from our own nature' (*Ascent*, 44).

Fully to appreciate what is involved in Christian penitence one must look to the goal to which it is directed, but Christian penitence, as it was said above, is only one aspect of the Christian life, and it is closely bound up with faith. Moreover, as penitence develops it becomes less a thing in itself, and more a background of faith, so that in seeking for an account of the development of Christian penitence it is necessary to look for an account of faith which pays particular attention to its negative aspect. St John of the Cross has provided us with just such an account of the way of faith in the *Ascent of Mount Carmel*, and it will help to an understanding of Christian penitence if we notice one or two points about that account.

The dominant concern which runs through the whole of St John's

8—J.S.P.

work is to teach his readers to put aside every human faculty upon which they might be tempted to rely. He is speaking of faith, because the only reason for this rejection of human faculties is to increase a man's dependence upon God, but he is speaking of the 'negative side' of faith because it is only on that side that human initiative has any meaning. Man may set himself to put aside all that is his on which he might rely, but he must leave it to God to provide the divine power to replace the human 'will'. It is natural enough that St John should be very conscious of the danger of confusing human tendencies, or tendencies due to the activity of the devil, with the acts of God in the human soul, and this is what we should expect, but we should also expect that he would provide his readers with careful criteria by which they could be distinguished, and with detailed rules for the application of those criteria. This is not St John's plan at all, and what we find is that he urges his readers not to make any such attempt. So far from insisting upon the necessity to distinguish for ourselves between those things whose source is God and those whose source is man or the devil St John has a short way with everything—all is to be put aside, and no human affirmation of anything is to be allowed. If, he says, an imagination, or a thought, or an ability is indeed from God, then it will work its way with us whether we acknowledge it or not, and he claims that it will be even more effective if we do not make any affirmation of it.

The modern reader may well be inclined to regard St John's rejection of 'imaginary visions' as 'enlightened'. When St John says, 'I say, then, that with regard to all these imaginary visions and apprehensions and to all other forms and species whatsoever . . . whether they be false and come from the devil or are recognized as true and coming from God, the understanding must not be embarrassed by them or feed upon them . . .' (*Ascent*, 132), the modern man easily agrees—not because he agrees with St John, but because he is liable to doubt whether such 'imaginary visions' are more than expressions of the human mind (or 'psyche'). Again it may seem to him sensible, even if a little overcareful, to avoid the danger of mis-interpreting divine revelations by refraining from putting any reliance in them, as St John teaches when he says, 'from this it is clear that, although sayings and revelations may be of God, we cannot always have confidence in them; for we can very easily be greatly deceived by them because of our manner of understanding them' (ibid., 155).

The wide divergence between any modern 'enlightenment' and the religion of St John only becomes apparent when we go further, to the proper attitude to knowledge. True knowledge, we feel, must be and ought to be something which can guide us through the intricacies of life, but St John treats knowledge as cavalierly as he treats 'imaginary visions': 'and thus it seems to me that there is no reason to describe here either the effect which is produced by true knowledge, or that which comes from false knowledge. . . . In saying that all should be rejected, we have said sufficient for the soul not to go astray' (ibid., 203).

The same sequence which St John follows in respect of interior matters 'occurs in the same way with respect of outward effects, and in the same way we should agree (for our own reasons) with his earlier comments and find the latter surprising. We do not find any difficulty in understanding the danger of shouting our good works from the housetops, and would be quite prepared to see the point of the following passage: 'These persons, then, in order to flee from this evil ['of sounding of the trumpet'], must hide their good works so that God alone may see them. And they must hide them . . . even from themselves. That is to say they must find no satisfaction in them, nor esteem them as if they were of some worth, nor derive pleasure from them at all' (ibid., 295). We do, however, in England at least, feel rather strongly about the human duty to make fullest possible use of our natural talents, and especially of the gifts of grace which God gives us, but to St John this is also error: 'He then', he says, 'that has supernatural gifts and graces ought to withdraw himself from desiring to practise them, and from joy in so doing, nor ought he to care to exercise them . . .' (ibid., 304). The reason for this is made clear enough; St John would not have us fall into the mistake of regarding the gifts which we have received from God as 'ours': we might put his point by saying that God does not give us an ability or a power which is a mere instrument which, when He has given it to us, is ours to use, but that His gift is His own activity in our lives, and He is still the user of it; 'for God', says St John, 'who gives Himself to such persons, by supernatural means, for the profit of His Church and of its members, will move them likewise supernaturally in such a manner and at such a time as He desires' (ibid., loc. cit.).

From this brief glance at St John of the Cross we see that the end of penitence is a complete and utter reliance upon God, whereby He is acknowledged as the sole effective source of all that is good, and whereby He is permitted to act as He will, without the least inter- ference from the 'will' of the individual in whom and through whom He acts, and if this is so we can see why Christian penitence must extend to the whole of a man, for so long as there is anything which the man claims to be both 'his own' and 'good' he will seek to follow that 'good' which is his, and not give himself wholly to God. Penitence is the self-ward element in Christianity, and that element is an attitude of complete rejection of self, good will as much as evil inclinations. Martin Luther is in complete agreement with St John of the Cross when he says 'here it is vital that our own righteousness and wisdom be brought to nought and rooted out of our hearts'.

The development of penitence has been considered in three stages which broadly correspond to the stages of accepting the unconscious, but penitence seems to lead to a rejection of the whole man, good will as well as evil inclinations, whereas Jung's technique leads to an acceptance of the whole man, the unconscious as well as conscious- ness. This was to be expected in view of the difference between the diagnosis of St Paul and Jung, since one claims that what we think good is really evil and the other that what we think evil is really good. At the end of chapter 5 it was remarked that as 'good' and 'evil' are relative there is little to choose between the two statements, and this remark will now be explained in order to show in what way the purpose of penitence is like that of accepting the unconscious.

The Purpose of Penitence

Jung's claim that what we think is 'evil' is really 'good' is one which arouses the suspicions of theologians and, on the other side, the theologians' claim that much that we call 'good' is really sinful always irritates psychologists, but this mutual suspicion and irritation is due to a misunderstanding about what is meant. Jung does not mean that the unconscious elements which seem to be evil need no alteration, nor that consciousness as it is is perfect, and what he means by calling both 'good' is that each has its proper place in a man's nature. The very existence of Jung's technique shows that he believes that both consciousness and the unconscious need to be altered before they can play their proper part in a man's life. On the other hand to say that the whole man is sinful does not mean that he can have no place in God's good world, but that his whole character needs to be changed before he can take his proper place in that world. Jung uses 'good' to mean that all aspects of human nature must play their part in the life of a 'full man', and, theologically speaking, this is equivalent to saying that everything in man can be redeemed. Theologians use 'sinful' to mean that nothing in man is right as it is, but that the whole man needs redemption, and, psychologically speaking, this is equivalent to saying that in their state of mutual antagonism neither consciousness nor the unconscious is what it ought to be. There is no basic conflict between the two views, and as it has been seen that the purpose of Jung's technique is the 'implication' of the whole man, so it has now to be shown that this is also the purpose of penitence.

Prima facie penitence is the rejection and not the 'implication' of all parts of a man, but although when it is carried to its extreme penitence is absolutely rejection of self, it is more than mere rejection. Penitence is paradoxical, because it is a man's rejection of himself, and this means that in the act of rejection there is also an affirmation of the self which rejects. The rejection of self takes place only in the sphere of judgement, and a man who comes to the extreme of penitence does not put himself aside as worthless, but judges that he is the sort of person who ought to be put aside as worthless. Penitence leads to a new understanding of oneself, and to the realization that as one is one can do nothing that is worthwhile, but in understanding this one affirms one's own existence, and one affirms oneself as one really is. Nothing but harm is done to the Faith by those who shrink from pressing Christian penitence to its extreme point. It is not merely that to do so is to leave human 'goods' in which sinful man will too willingly trust, and so to open the way to the sin of pride, although this is serious enough, but such shrinking also gives point to the charge sometimes made that Christianity is dualist. If we say that a man is a battle-ground between forces of good and evil within himself, and that the object which he must set himself is the victory of the good and the rejection of the evil: if, that is, when satan and his angels have been 'thrown out' of the 'heaven' of the soul there remain 'good angels' (the human elements which make up the good will) then, in respect of the individual and of morals, Christianity is most clearly dualistic, and this is the true criticism of Pelagianism which is constantly missed. It is not that Pelagianism sets man up as an equal with God (which, on the whole, it does not do), but that it makes an absolute principle of the dichotomy in the natural man, of which the sinner is, anyway, only too conscious; it is not especially that 'pelagian man' comes to God glorying in the goodness which is his own, but that he comes with only half, or less than half, himself; it is probable that he comes to God seeking more strength to reinforce his own good will, rather than to receive divine commendation, but he still comes 'leaving behind' his 'evil inclinations', and so deliberately divides himself into two parts, for the more we assert the goodness of one part of ourselves at the expense of the rest the more certainly we divide ourselves. True penitence overcomes the dichotomy within the sinner, by bringing him to see that his whole self is sinful.

Whatever else we may say about the absolute rejection which is penitence we cannot say that it divides the man. There is certainly something rather grim about the way in which penitence 'makes a man whole', but the fact remains that it does. The pain of natural man when he knows that he sins is that he feels within himself an absolute opposition between his good and his evil; his sinfulness is inwardly manifested by a division in his own nature, and he presents that division to himself as a division between that which is good and which is to be retained and strengthened, and that which is evil and which is to be mortified and rejected. Christianity teaches such a man that this account which he gives of himself is false, that he is not nearly so divided as he supposed, because what he calls 'good' is affected by his sinfulness as well as what he calls 'evil', for to come to penitence is to see that '... our will is evil. It is not wholly evil ... but evil taints it in every element' (*Mackintosh*, 52). Yet we may, if we are wilfully blind, still fall into the old error, for we may suppose that the 'tainting' of the will is a matter of some 'foreign body' added to it and that not being 'wholly evil' there are 'parts' of the will that are good, and which can be disentangled from the rest. What we are to understand is not a division of 'the will' into good and bad 'parts', but a characterization of 'the will' (that is, ourselves in decision and action) as 'relatively evil'. In other words we do not claim to be the epitome of evil, we are not each a little 'devil' in complete and absolute opposition to God, we are merely 'sinful' and find no joy in our sins. There is some value in regarding our sinfulness as basically more an 'inadequacy for the ends of life' than as downright wickedness, because to do so is to provide a useful corrective to that inverse pride which, when it is denied all hope of affirming a man as 'good', runs to the other extreme and glories in its depths of evilness. In the end Christian penitence is

not so much the rejection of oneself, as the Christian version of
the Greek advice 'know thyself', because to say 'I am a sinner'
is quite as much to accept oneself, for what one is as it is to reject
oneself.

Augustinian theology rooted in platonism has always maintained
that 'value' (or 'goodness') and 'existence' are mutual criteria, but
according to the account just given Christian penitence involves the
denial of this, because it brings a man to say 'I am, and I am not good',
affirming his existence and his lack of value at the same time, so that
penitence is both the affirmation of one's existence and the denial of
one's value. So long as we think in moral terms penitence is complete
and utter rejection, but in terms of existence it cannot be, because the
'we' who, in the moral field, reject 'ourselves' are the same individuals
who, in doing so, affirm that we are: there is not some other 'we' which
stands outside the self which sins, and we both sin and know that we
sin, perform the sin and condemn the sin. In the field of existence
Christian penitence is acceptance and not rejection and the position
can be expressed as follows: if you would be something, if you want
to be anything at all in the universe you can only be what, in fact, you
are; to accept yourself, to be yourself is to know yourself for what
you are; to know yourself for what you are is to know that you are a
sinner, so that to be yourself is to be a sinner. Such acceptance of
oneself is certainly sinister enough, but it has the tremendous advantage that it enables a man to see that he is a man, and not an angel and
a devil fighting inside a human body, and it is certainly the first
requirement which must be fulfilled before a man can not only see
that he is one, but also begin to grow into a true and organic unity.
Through penitence we assert the existence of ourselves as evil,
and so posit the question of how good can be done with that which
is evil.

Since penitence, in the moral field, is the rejection of the whole man
there is nothing left in man with which he could do good, and that is
why the thirteenth article of the Church of England declares that 'good
works done before justification have the nature of sin'. Further, since
penitence is concerned with our judgements about ourselves, the
problem of how good may be done with what is evil cannot be solved
in the sphere of penitence, so that the examination of Christian penitence
is really over when we have seen that true penitence is to assert both
that we are, and also that what we are is 'evil'. It is well, however,

to conclude the account by going beyond the strict limits of penitence, because to do so is to indicate the purpose of penitence in the Christian life. The core of Christianity is that God calls sinners to Himself, so that the condition of answering God's call is that we should be sinners, and know that we are sinners. Since all men are sinners this is simply to say that the condition is that we should acknowledge our sinfulness. It was 'while we were yet sinners' that 'God justified the ungodly', so that the question which is posed by penitence is not 'what can we do that is good, seeing that we are evil', but 'what can God do with us, even though we are evil?' and, first of all, He can do nothing with us unless we will come to Him, and allow Him to use us: if we wait until we cease to be sinners before we dare to come to God, then we shall wait for all eternity. Mechthild of Magdeburg expresses perfectly the fact that when we come to God we must come as sinners: 'When I, the poorest of the poor, go to my prayer,' she says, 'I adorn myself with my unworthiness and clothe myself with the mud which I myself am. I shoe myself with the precious time I have lost all my days and gird myself with the suffering I have deserved. Then I throw around me the cloak of wickedness of which I am full. I put on my head a crown of the secret sins I have committed against God. After that I take in my hand a mirror of true knowledge and see myself therein as I am, so that I see nothing but alas! and alas! But I am happier in these clothes than I could be if I had every earthly gift, even though I am often sad and impatient, for I would rather be clothed with hell and crowned by all devils than be without my sin' (*Mechthild*, 167). This is not to be dismissed as an oddity of medieval mysticism; rather it should be understood as representing an accurate understanding of the text, 'Come unto me all that are weary and heavy laden, and I will refresh you.' We are sinners, but Jesus is the friend of sinners.

Dangers of Penitence

In the last chapter four dangers into which a man may fall in the course of a Jungian analysis were considered. It was shown that two (abandonment and despair) beset a patient on the early stages of the analysis, that the third (pride) is the result of a reaction against the principles of psychotherapy, and that the last (antinomianism) arises from misconceptions near the end of an analysis. These four dangers stand in a similar relation to the development of penitence. Abandonment and despair are liable to result from what has been called 'natural penitence', that is from self-criticism based upon the failure of one's good will, and the danger of both may be increased by mistaken ideas of the Gospel; pride results from a reaction against penitence; and antinomianism is a misconception likely to occur when a man has begun to advance in the understanding of Christianity. Pascal's remark, 'It is equally dangerous for man to know God without knowing his own misery, and to know his own misery without knowing the Redeemer' (*Pensées*, ii; quoted *Knox*, 202), may stand as a warning against the dangers which beset the penitent. Abandonment and despair are alternative aberrations closely related to each other, and whereas it was convenient to consider abandonment first in the last chapter, it is easier to begin with despair in this.

(*a*) *Despair.* Harton speaks of 'sorrow for sin based upon merely human considerations' and says that it 'may operate in either of two opposed ways: it may lead to remorse which partakes of the hopelessness of Hell and has led many a soul to despair and, in extreme cases, to self-destruction, or it may lead to *Attrition*' (*Harton*, 161), and the same thought is expressed by Jung when he speaks of those who are '. . . depressed, even crushed by the contents of the unconscious' and who 'finally give up all sense of responsibility in an overwhelming realization of the powerlessness of the ego against the fate that rules it from the unconscious' (*Essays*, 221). In relation to sorrow for sin a man is in danger of despair when he realizes the strength of his evil inclinations and his inability to control them, and this is the condition which has been described as the second stage of penitence. It is to those who have reached this stage that the Gospel comes with its offer of a Saviour, and by this offer Christianity provides a defence against the danger of despair, but if this offer is not accepted, or if it is misunderstood, despair is almost unavoidable. The Christian message is 'you have seen the weakness of your good will, and you know that it is no use relying upon it, but if you will commit yourself to Him you can rely with confidence upon Jesus', but many refuse to listen to the end of the message, and many cannot receive it, because they will not give up their habit of relying upon themselves.

The misunderstanding of the Gospel frequently occurs in the following way. When a man accepts Jesus as the pattern of human goodness he realizes 'how evil sin is, and how much more deeply it is entrenched in his heart than he had supposed', and so becomes more aware of the weakness of his good will than before. It has been pointed out that he should also distinguish his own good will from the goodness of Jesus, and rejecting his good will he should put his trust in his Saviour, but this does not always happen, and instead of rejecting his good will a man may try, as it were, to 'touch it up' in accordance with the precepts of the Gospels, and continue to rely upon it, and this seems to be what he will do if he holds a merely 'exemplary' theory of the Atonement. The result of doing this is that the man's ideal becomes harder of attainment, and his failure to achieve it more marked, so that he has even more reason to despair than before. Christianity increases the danger of despair when a man fails to distinguish what is 'his' (his good will) from what is not (the goodness of Jesus), just as analysis increases it when a man fails to distinguish between ego and anima. The danger of despair is close to every penitent, and many who travel the Christian way pass so close to it that they seem to fall into it for a time. Of many instances that of Martin Luther may be taken as an example: 'I thought that I was utterly cast away,' he says, 'if at any time I felt the lust of the flesh: that is to say, if I felt any evil motion, fleshly lust, wrath, hatred, or envy against any brother. I essayed many ways to help to quiet my conscience, but it would not be . . .' (quoted *James*, 126, 7).

(*b*) *Abandonment.* The following remark (written by a psychologist about the sadist) describes remarkably well the way in which abandonment is connected with penitence: 'He is one of those who, despairing of ever being able to measure up to such standards [sc. those of their "idealized image" of themselves], have consciously or unconsciously resolved to be as "bad" as possible. He may succeed in being "bad" and wallow in it with a kind of desperate delight . . . he develops the recklessness of a person who has nothing to lose' (*Horney*, 204). The genesis of abandonment is the same, whether it is consciousness or the good will which a man finds impotent to achieve its own standards, but as with despair a mistaken acceptance of Christianity may make the danger of abandonment greater. A man who accepts Christianity may realize that it promises strength and power and happiness, but he may be unwilling to believe that the promise is for the present and think of it as a promise for the future, which is conditional upon his 'measuring up' to the standards of Christ. If a man does misunderstand the Christian promise in this way his acceptance of Christianity intensifies his sense of loss when he fails to 'measure up', because he has not only failed his own ideals, and lost (perhaps) the respect of his fellow-men; he has also, he supposes, thrown away all that God offers him, and nothing that he can do can make his condition worse, so that seeing himself already damned he may decide that he may as well enjoy whatever delights are still possible to the damned. This danger is particularly liable to beset one who has been brought up in some strict and uncompromising Christian sect, when he finds himself guilty of some grave sin.

Justice to the danger of abandonment cannot be done here, but one or two things can be noticed. There are, first, many different arguments which may lead a man into this danger: he may say, for example, 'being damned I must behave accordingly', or 'being damned anyway there is no point in trying to be good' or he may say 'all my efforts to do well fail, what use in trying further', or 'Seeing that the powers of evil overcome the power for good within me, it is as well to be on the winning side.' Secondly, abandonment may take many forms: for examples, the excesses of amoral 'bright sets', satanism, sexual licence (normal or perverted) and deliberate and systematic criminal behaviour of the less 'respectable' kind. Thirdly, secret societies with nefarious purposes may make use of abandonment in order to cut off the initiate from the rest of society, and they do this by including in the initiation one or more acts held in particular abhorrence at the time. For example, in the Middle Ages apostasy was enough to make a man feel himself cut off from all hope of salvation, and apostasy was invariably included in initiations into the covens of witchcraft. Finally, the sense of having 'crossed over' may be accompanied by a feeling of release, and increased power or knowledge. Charles Williams gives an account of a confession at a witch trial: the only act demanded of the men had been apostasy, then 'there was given to him a skin full of that grand brew. He drinks; immediately he feels within himself a knowledge of all our arts and an understanding of all our rites and ceremonies' (*Witchcraft*, 136), and with this may be compared 'The process of assimilating the unconscious yields some very remarkable phenomena. In some patients it leads to an unmistakable, and often unpleasant, accentuation of ego-consciousness, a heightened self-confidence; they know everything, they are completely *au fait* with their unconscious, and they believe themselves to be fully acquainted with everything that comes out of it . . .' (*Essays*, 221).

Abandonment, like despair, is not far from anyone whose penitence becomes deep. Bunyan, perhaps, provides an example. 'But my original and inward pollution', he writes, 'that was my plague and

my infliction. . . . Sin and corruption, I said, would as naturally bubble
out of my heart as water would bubble out of a fountain', and 'sometimes I would tell my condition to the people of God, which, when
they heard, they would pity me, and would tell of the Promises. But they
had as good have told me that I must reach the Sun with my finger as
have bidden me receive or rely upon the Promise' (cited *James*, 155, 4).
Bunyan, of course, is not ready to have any truck with 'sin and
corruption', but not only does he find it naturally arising within him
(that is, an expression of what he is), but he describes its presence by
using an image appropriate to what is thought desirable, and to a
Christian it suggests the 'fountain of living waters'. In other words
Bunyan's infliction included a feeling of the attraction as well as of the
horror of the evils of which he speaks.

(c) *Pride*. Jung says that the process of assimilating the unconscious
is often unpleasant, and it is partly because it can be unpleasant that
a patient may react against it by the 'regressive restoration of his
persona'. This reaction may also be partly due to a sense of the
absurdity of the technique, especially when it means holding con-
versations with hypostasized unconscious complexes, and such a
reaction leads to pride. A man may react against penitence for the
same two reasons, and the reaction against penitence also leads to
pride. Penitence is always unpleasant, because it means admitting that
one fails to do what one thinks is right, and natural penitence alone
may lead to the realization that the good will is weak, and cannot
enable one to live up to the demands that one makes of oneself, but
for every man there is a way of escape back to the good opinion of
himself which he had before penitence began. Some men can so
deceive themselves that they believe that they succeed in all that they
set out to do, but anyone can reinstate himself in his own eyes by
comparing himself with other people, for by careful study of other
people's failures a man can convince himself that he is no worse than
others and better than most, and if he does this two results follow.
First, he again relies upon himself, for by concentrating upon his
successes he decides that he can after all achieve something, and that
there is real merit in what he does, and such reliance in oneself is the
core of pride. Secondly, when a man is content to be as good as other
people he has accepted a lower standard than that with which he began,
because instead of aiming at his ideal he now aims to get as near his
ideal as most people get to theirs. This means a narrowing of his

personality with respect to his ideals, which corresponds to the
'diminished personality' connected with the 'regressive restoration of
his persona'.

Christian demands may easily emphasize the natural tendency to
react from penitence to pride in two ways. The specific demand which
gives rise to true Christian penitence is that a man should see that even
the ideals of the good will are affected by human sinfulness, and there
are many people who would be ready to admit that they fail of their
ideals but to whom it must seem as absurd to ask that they should
criticize them, as Jung's technique seems absurd to others, and such
people would say, 'If penitence means that I must give up my ideas
of what is good and right it is all nonsense.' At the same time their
ideals themselves may be 'touched up' and brought more into accord
with the ideal which is Jesus, and the 'improved' ideal may result in
some improvement in performance, so that those who reject the full
demands of Christianity may have been provided, by their Christianity,
with more reason to trust in themselves.

John Wesley may be said to have contemplated such a reaction as
that described when he wrote '[I saw that] alienated as I am from the
life of God, I am a "child of wrath", and heir of hell: that my own
works, my own sufferings, my own righteousness, are so far from
reconciling me to an offended God . . . that the most specious of them
need an atonement themselves' (*Journal*: under Jan. 29, 1738). This is
Christian penitence, but one can hear behind it the regret that penitence
should mean this; the unuttered cry from the human heart, 'I have
worked, I have suffered, I have done right—why may I not rest upon
these things, and take comfort in them?'

(*d*) *Antinomianism*. Antinomianism is an 'advanced' danger both
in a Jungian analysis, and in the development of penitence. In the
former it arises when the deepest tendencies of the unconscious are
discovered, and a man fails to realize that they are not his own personal
and private desires and ideas; in the latter it arises when a man begins to
understand the nature of the ideal which Jesus sets before him, and fails
to see that it is 'supernatural'; that is, that it cannot be formulated in
terms of mere human hopes and aspirations. A man who fails to understand Christianity in this way supposes that he himself, of his own
human ability, has accepted for himself the full Christian ideal, and
when this happens it is as though he says 'I am Christ' when he should
say 'Christ lives in me'. In *Enthusiasm* Ronald Knox has noted

occasions when this has taken place, and of antinomianism in general he says, 'On the opposite slope lies the peril of pure antinomianism; a single false step, and your evangelical enthusiast is over the precipice. St Paul, with his *Omnia mihi licent*; St Augustine, with his *Ama, et fac quod vis*; Luther, with his *Pecca fortiter*—is it certain that any natural law of morals is binding on a soul which has emancipated itself from the natural, and lives now by a law of grace? Indulgence of the passions is culpable in the unregenerate soul, helps it on its road to perdition; but the children of predestination are emancipated from the bondage of law; not their actions, but the merits of their Redeemer, avail to justify them. May it not be that actions which the world counts sinful are, for them, like all their other actions, sanctified?' (*Knox*, 583).

The Christian, St Paul says, is free from the law, but this freedom is in exact proportion to the extent to which he has submitted himself to Christ; it does not arise because a man knows more and seeks more than other people, but because he no longer directs his own life, but allows Christ to direct it for him. If, however, a man has not seen the full inadequacy of his good will, but has, as it were, remodelled it, in an attempt to make it into the will of Christ, then he takes upon himself the role of Christ. Such a man lays claim to a freedom from law which is really an authority over law, and, declaring the law for himself and others, is a true antinomian. As has been hinted already, the antinomian may not, in practice, contradict the established law, but may appear to be a fanatical upholder of it: the essence of antinomianism is the claim to be oneself the source of the true law, whatever the character of the law which one dictates and, once again, the connection with old ideas of kingship can be seen.

The Church

The examination of the dangers which beset the path of penitence shows what needs to be done to preserve a man from them. First, he must be persuaded to be thorough in his self-examination, in order that he may see the full extent of his sin; secondly, he must be taught to have a sure hope in the Saviour. Not only are these two things what the Christian Church has always tried to do, but they are also very like the two functions of the analyst during the course of psychological treatment. The thorough self-examination, like the lifting of repressions, brings to light the tendencies which a man prefers to hide or ignore; confidence in Christ, like confidence in the ultimate success of the analytical treatment, prevents the man from being swamped and overcome by those tendencies. This broad similarity, however, is modified by two important differences.

Christian penitence requires the criticism of the good will because in order that he may rely wholly upon Christ a man must put aside his own conscious plans and purposes. It may be that he will find that what he does under the guidance of Christ is what he believed to be right before, but he must not expect to find this, and of true knowledge as well as false St John of the Cross says, 'in saying that all should be rejected we have said sufficient for the soul not to go astray' (see above, p. 227). In analysis, on the other hand, 'the values of consciousness' are to be retained, and hope for ultimate success depends upon retaining them, together with the newly discovered 'values' of the unconscious. There is little to choose between the unpleasantness of the two ways, for whereas penitence demands that one should give up what one holds most dear (that is, one's highest ideals), analysis requires one to endure the tension of apparently incompatible aims, and give precedence to neither: on the other hand, penitence requires less sophistication, and there are many who would soon be lost in the intricacies of advanced analysis but who would have no difficulty in understanding what is required by penitence.

Secondly, no Christian director offers himself as a support to the penitent. His function is to point to Jesus as the 'strength and stay' on whom the penitent must lean. No doubt some directors are more able than others, but it remains true that the more able the director is the less he will suggest that he has anything to offer of himself. In principle the director points to Jesus, and his own personality is of no great importance: ideally it is true in this respect, as in others, that the 'unworthiness of the minister does not diminish the grace of God's gifts' (Article 26 of the thirty-nine Articles of the Church of England). On the other hand, Jung says, 'The great healing factor in psychotherapy is the doctor's personality' (*Practice*, 198), and it seems that the psychotherapist is forced to take upon himself a burden which the Christian minister is mercifully spared.

It is natural to compare the work of the analyst with that of the spiritual director (not, it should be remembered, the confessor), but the director plays his part as a minister of the Church, and it is rather the 'company of all faithful people' which, supporting the penitent

so far as men and women can, should be compared with the analyst.
Something of this can be seen by considering how the three men
already quoted were supported in their trials.

Bunyan, in his hopelessness, did not cut himself off from Christian
fellowship: he called together the 'people of God' and told them of
his troubles, and they 'recited the Promise'. Thus the group to which
he belonged set before him a hope, and although, at the time, he could
not accept it he must have derived support from it, or he would not
have come back for more. Luther 'essayed many ways' to quiet his
conscience, which meant that he made use of the mortifications
customary in his community, and again, although he appeared to
derive no benefit from them they undoubtedly kept before him the
hope of the end to which they were directed. Thirdly, Wesley continued to perform the good works which 'needed atonement themselves' and this is not only the way to salvation commonly accepted
by Anglicans but also that specifically proposed by Wesley and his
friends at Oxford (see the opening letter of his *Journal*). In other words,
throughout the period in which these men were exposed to the dangers
which have been discussed they followed the practice accepted by the
Christian groups to which they belonged, and by doing this they were
kept in mind of the Christian hope.

Generally speaking the Christian Church is a company of penitents
who have confidence in their Lord, and the more its members are
aware of this the more effectively it protects the penitent from the
dangers that beset him. On the one hand the sense that all are sinners
is protection against the tendency to react back to pride, and, on the
other, the common faith is a protection against abandonment and
despair, and this is the true analogue of the double work of the
analyst; to convince the patient that the manifestations of the unconscious are not peculiar to him and to hold out the hope that if he
endures to the end he will be saved.

In these two chapters a parallel has been drawn between Jung's
analytical technique and penitence: both demand that a man shall
become aware of deep-rooted tendencies within him, which conflict
with his ideals; both require him to realize that these tendencies do
not divide him from other people, because they are common to all men;
both support him with the hope of ultimate salvation. The hope which
supports the Christian penitent depends upon his faith, and true

Christian penitence is impossible without faith. Jung's psychology bears upon faith in two ways. On the one hand there is a true analogy to Christian faith in the hope of ultimate success which the analyst holds out to the patient, and on the other there is an apparent analogy in the phenomena of the 'transference', which is a transitory feature of most successful analyses. These two analogies are discussed in the next two chapters.

8

PROJECTION

THE comparison between the two ways of salvation in the preceding chapters has led to the following conclusions:

1. Both ways are put forward as ways which lead a man away from the same unfortunate state, which may be called the 'state of natural man', but the two systems with which the ways are associated give different accounts of the nature of that state. Or it may be said that both ways are 'cures' for the same symptoms, although the 'disease' from which natural man suffers is differently diagnosed in the two systems.

2. Each way requires that a man must do something before he can cease to be in his unfortunate state, or, using the other form of expression, each requires that a man must do something before he can be cured of his 'disease'.

3. To follow Jung's way to its goal a man must accept the unconscious, and this involves a long process by which his personality is developed: to enter upon the Christian way a man must be penitent, but the penitence that is required before a man can travel on that way does not involve any development of personality. At the same time, there is also a penitence which follows Justification, and which ought to deepen as a man's character develops.

4. Jung's technique is directed towards the 'implication' or 'acceptance' of all sides of a man's character, whereas Christian penitence is directed to the rejection of all that a man is.

Jung claims that Individuation 'unites the opposites', and it was shown in the last chapter how it can be said that through the deepening of penitence Justification by Faith also unites the opposites, even though it does so in a rather 'sinister' way, by convincing a man that he is wholly sinful. Penitence, however, is only one aspect of the Christian life, and an account of the development which is initiated by Justification is incomplete unless it includes a discussion of that other aspect of the Christian life which is called 'faith'. In one sense

faith implies a further division of the opposites, because it means that a
man acknowledges the holiness of Christ at the same time as he admits
his own sinfulness, and from a psychological point of view it is
possible to suggest that this means that the antimony of good and evil
in man is 'projected' on to the figures of Christ on the one hand,
and of the man on the other, and that in this way faith involves an
ultimate division of the opposites. In another sense, however, faith
brings about a further union of the opposites, because Christian faith
is faith in Christ as a present reality in a man's life, and this aspect of
faith is further considered at the end of the next chapter, after some of
the difficulties which psychology raises about faith have been examined.
There is nothing in Jung's system which exactly corresponds to faith
in the Christian system, but if faith is understood in what is psychologically the most straightforward way of understanding it (that is
in terms of 'projection'), then it appears to be similar in many ways
to what is known as 'the transference', and serious criticisms can be
directed at faith on the basis of this similarity. The greater part of this
chapter and the next is taken up by an examination of such criticisms
of Christian faith.

The assertion that there is no close parallel to Christian faith in
Jung's system requires defending, in view of Jung's claim that 'The
development of personality means more than just the fear of hatching
forth monsters, or of isolation. It also means fidelity to the law of
one's own being. For the word "fidelity" I should prefer, in this
context, the Greek word used in the New Testament, πίστις, which is
erroneously translated "faith".[1] It really means "trust", "trustful
loyalty". Fidelity to the law of one's own being is a trust in this law,
a loyal perseverance and confident hope; in short, an attitude such as
a religious man should have towards God' (*Development*, 295, 296).
No one can take towards a law that attitude which the Christian
should take towards God, and the distinction between faith in an
unseen law and faith in an unseen God is closely linked with the
differences between Jung's system and Christianity which are apparent
from the conclusions listed at the start of this chapter. The development of the Christian does not take place until Justification has
occurred, and, by faith, the Christian is then aware of the presence of
Christ within him, yet other than himself, and because he looks to

[1] It may be noticed that 'faith' has retained the meaning of the Greek original more
accurately in English than in continental theology.

Christ as one who is other than himself to guide his development he can 'afford', as it were, to reject everything that he himself is. The development which occurs during a Jungian analysis, on the other hand, takes place before Individuation occurs, so that whether he thinks of it as other than himself or not, the analysand cannot be aware of the Self as his guide during that development, and all that he can rely upon is himself as he is, so that he cannot 'afford' to reject himself, but must affirm all that is in him. Thus 'fidelity to the law of one's own being' is another way of referring to the fact that in following Jung's way a man must affirm the value of all sides of his nature, and the 'confident hope' that a man must have is that he is on the right road. In other words, Christian faith is faith in a guide, who will lead one to the goal of life, whereas the faith for which Jung asks is faith that one will come to the goal without a guide, or that there is a guide although one is not aware that one is being guided, and there is very little likeness between the two. A man may have 'fidelity' to the law of his own being without having any idea or conception of 'the Self', but no man can have faith in God without, also, having an idea of God, and of the religious man's idea of God, and of his attitude to God Jung has said a great deal, and what he says will be considered in this chapter.

Preliminary Note.

In this chapter the word 'projection' is given a wider sense than that in which it is usually supposed to be used, but the *argument* does not depend upon this extension of the meaning of the word. In psychology 'projection' refers to *false* judgements about an object resulting from the identification of that object with an internal image or idea, and it will be pointed out that this same psychic mechanism (the identification of an external object and an internal psychic element) can also produce true judgements about objects. 'Projection' is used here to refer to the psychic mechanism itself, whether it results in true or false judgements, and three things may be said about this usage:

(i) It is in accord with the idea suggested by the word 'projection' (that is the idea of 'throwing' a picture on to an object as on to a screen) because this idea directs attention to what the subject does, not to the truth or falsehood of the result.

(ii) If 'projection' is only to be used when the judgements produced by the general psychic mechanism are false, then we need another word to describe the mechanism in itself, and there does not seem to be a more suitable word than 'projection'.

(iii) Although Jung and other psychologists would *define* 'projection' in such a way that it applies only to false judgements they are not always careful to *use* the word only when the falsehood of a judgement has been established, and it even happens that a judgement is stigmatized as the result of projection (including the idea that it is false) when all that has been established is that the source of the judgement is the identification of an external object and an inward image. The wider use of 'projection' suggested here would enable the word to be used in such a case, but it would no longer carry the implication that the judgement in question was false.

This can be illustrated by the very important statement often made that an idea of God is formed by the 'projection' of an unconscious image. If 'projection' is defined so that it only refers to false judgements, then this statement can only be made after the idea of God has been shown to be false *for other reasons* than that it is the result of externalizing an inner image. Yet we often meet the argument 'the idea of God is formed by projection and is therefore false' which is an argument in a circle if 'projection' is used in the stricter sense. As 'projection' is used here (in the wider sense) we may say that the idea of God is formed by projection if we have detected an inward image from which it is formed, but we could not then argue directly to the falsity of the idea.

One important conclusion to which we shall come is that the psychological statement that the idea of God is formed by projection is equivalent to the theological statement that we can only know God because He has stamped his image on our souls, and this conclusion is closely linked with a restatement of the very ancient idea that man is a 'microcosm'—that is, it is suggested that the 'archetypes' of the unconscious are images by the projection of which we perceive the objective world.

Jung criticizes a number of religious ideas and practices, and most of his criticisms depend upon the view that the idea of God in men's minds is formed by the mechanism known as 'projection', upon his experience of the 'transference situation' in the course of analysis, and upon his general theory that religion is a form of psychotherapy. Since Jung's theory of religion is, as a whole, unacceptable to

Christians, it might seem that his criticisms could be dismissed without more ado, but this is not so, because although the Christian believes that his religion is more than Jung will allow, he also believes that it has results in this life which are desirable from the point of view of the psychotherapist, and he cannot be indifferent to the charge that his beliefs must inevitably fail to have such results. In order to answer Jung his criticisms are evaluated in this chapter, and in the next it is shown that they are not valid criticisms of orthodox Christianity. In order to form a clear picture of what the criticisms are the following things have to be discussed:

Projection
The Transference
Jung's General Theory of Religion
Jung's Criticisms of certain Religious Ideas
The Application of his Criticisms to Christianity

Projection

The idea of projection is not only of importance for the discussion of faith, but it also helps to clarify the peculiarities of psychotherapeutic language, because projection can be thought of in three quite different ways. First, one can form a picture of projection which is in accordance with the way the word is used in psychology, and with its meaning in more common talk, but this picture is only a model which guides the use of the word and it is not a picture of anything which goes on. Second, one may consider the observable events related by the concept of projection, which means to ask when the word is appropriate, and an account of these events can be given without any reference to the model which guides the use of the word. Third, one may attempt to explain how the state called 'projection' comes about and, if one follows Jung's explanation, this results in a picture of what happens very different from that suggested by the way the word is used.

Jung (whether he is aware of it or not) is speaking in terms of the model which helps us to use the word 'projection' correctly when he says, 'Projection involves a discrimination of the object from the subject, by means of a subjective content transveyed into the object' (*Types*, 567): and '[The concentration of the alchemists] would naturally serve to project values and meanings into the object . . . and to fill it with forms and figures that have their origin primarily in the unconscious of the investigator' (*Alchemy*, 389). The thought behind these statements is, first, that there are unconscious ideas and images 'in' a man's mind, that these ideas and images would reveal something about the man if he became aware of them as 'his', but that because they are unconscious he cannot become aware of them in this way: second, the idea is that the man can, and does, 'throw' such ideas and images on to objects, become aware of them wrongly, as 'belonging' to the objects on which they are 'thrown', and so suppose that the nature of the object and not of himself is revealed by them. Written out this sounds a peculiar procedure, but we do something very like it from time to time with conscious images and ideas: if, for example, we are looking for someone in a crowd we have an image of that person in our mind and we may find that we have a tendency to 'fit' people who resemble the person for whom we are looking to that image; again, if we find a certain subject (algebra, perhaps) simple and straightforward we tend to suppose that it must be simple for other people, so making our idea of them conform to our idea of ourself; if we are naturally honest we have difficulty in believing that other people tell lies, and if we are dishonest we suspect people of deceiving us when they are telling the truth. In all such instances it is as though we attribute something 'in' ourselves to other people, and we may think of projection in this way, remembering that the ideas and images which we 'project' are not known to us in the way that we know we have an image of the person we are looking for in our mind, that we know we find algebra easy, and that we know that we are honest or dishonest; because those things which are 'projected' are unconscious.

The model of projection explained in the last paragraph indicates that projection involves two things, an unconscious element, and the attribution of that element to someone or something else. In other words the concept of projection relates the concept of an unconscious element to mistaken judgements about objects, so that one can say that projection is one way in which unconscious elements manifest themselves. But if one thinks only of the odd things from which unconscious elements are constructed one must say that the concept of projection relates mistaken judgements about objects to the slips of the tongue, dreams, uncharacteristic acts and other odd things which occur in a man's life, and to say 'Everything unconscious is projected' (*Essays*, 31) is to say that if an unconscious element has been rightly constructed from the odd things in a man's life then that man will, at some time or another, wrongly attribute that element to other people or things. For example, if the feminine aspects of a man's character are 'unconscious' (that is, if a man thinks of himself as wholly 'masculine') then he will not only behave in uncharacteristically 'feminine' ways, and have dreams and fantasies which express the feminine side of his character, but he will also be liable wrongly to judge other men as effeminate and to suppose that women have thoughts and feelings appropriate to his own, unacknowledged, femininity.

The odd mistaken judgements which are related to other odd things by the idea of projection are not necessarily false, but only unjustified. If, for example, a man judges that his friend is dishonest it is an 'odd' judgement if he has no cause to think his friend dishonest, whether it is true or not, and, on the other hand, a mistaken judgement that a tree seen through a mist is a man is not an 'odd' judgement if most people would have made the same mistake. In other words, judgements which are properly described as the results of projection have something of the character of what is generally called 'intuition', in that they go beyond what is warranted by the facts which a man knows, and in that they are accompanied by a sense of inward certainty, and a man will frequently maintain such judgements with a perverse disregard of rational arguments. Whether or not a judgement is odd in this way depends entirely upon what a man knows and what he is in a position to deduce, and not at all upon what is objectively true, and, it may be added, there is no reason why a judgement which is psychologically described as due to the projection of an unconscious element should not also represent a true insight into the objective world.

Men do make odd judgements of the kind organized by the concept of projection, and there is no reason to doubt the psychotherapists' contention that such judgements are related to unconscious elements; that is, the contention that if a man imputes certain characteristics to other people or things without having adequate reasons for doing so, then the same characteristics will appear to manifest themselves in his slips of the tongue, dreams, uncharacteristic actions, and so on: but to say this is not to accept the story about 'throwing' invisible psychic elements at other people, or even to accept the idea of projecting an image like a magic lantern. Such pictures are extremely useful (and possibly indispensable) for talking about projection, but they are not an account of what happens, and when Jung does try to explain how projection comes about he tells an entirely different story.

Jung says, 'The so-called *projections* that are familiar enough in

our analytical practice are also mere residua of this original identity of
subject and object' (*Types*, 294), and 'Identity [upon which the
possibility of projection is based] is primarily an unconscious equality
with the object' (ibid., 553), and in speaking like this he is clearly
talking about something quite unlike the 'transveyance' of 'a subjective content into the object'. According to this theory projection is
the result of a category mistake in the process of differentiating one's
environment, whereby psychic features are attributed to the object
instead of to the subject, and the theory depends upon the assumption
(which is a psychological commonplace) that in early childhood (of
individuals or of the human race) man knows himself and his environment as a single, undivided whole. In other words, it is assumed that
it is only by learning and habit that one is able to distinguish what is
'oneself' and what is the 'objective world' in which one finds oneself,
and that before one distinguishes objects one has to distinguish between
subject and object, and on the basis of this assumption projection may
be explained as a failure to distinguish subject and object correctly.
This theory of projection and its relation to the model of 'throwing'
psychic elements can be illustrated by an analogy. Suppose that I have
a large number of books jumbled up in a bookcase, and that I decide
to sort them out according to authors, and then suppose that I overlook one of the books and leave it in its original place. This would
represent the failure to attribute some psychic element to oneself in
the process of differentiating subject from object, but it would be
quite natural for a friend to look at the books, and say 'you've put
this Scott in the wrong place, it's mixed up with the Hardys': in fact,
I have not put the book anywhere, but have simply failed to put it in
the right place, but it is as though I had put it in the wrong place;
and, in a similar way, when one makes a 'category mistake' in differentiating one's environment it is as though one has 'taken' a psychic
element 'belonging' to oneself and 'put' it with the things which are
not oneself.

In ordinary speech we come very near to the 'category' mistake
which causes states of projection. If, for example, we talk of a 'peaceful
place' we ought to mean 'a place in which I or anyone else would
have a feeling of peace', but we usually want to mean that the place is,
somehow, peaceful in itself. On the whole we do not make this kind
of mistake when we are the only sentient being present, but it is very
likely that this is not so much because we are specially good at

distinguishing between subject and object as because we have learnt that such things as feelings and emotions should not be attributed to inanimate objects, since we are by no means infallible when there are other people about. For example, we may be aware of a sense of hatred or irritation in connection with another person, and yet very uncertain whether it springs primarily from him or from us; if two people are in a dangerous place each may be quite sure that he is not nervous, and the other is; at one time or another most of us have been exhorted not to be impatient, when it seemed to us that the impatience manifestly 'belonged' to the person who exhorted us—and either may have been 'projecting'. According to this theory of projection we 'project' a psychic element when we become aware of that element, ought to attribute it to ourself, and attribute it to someone else instead.

It may be that the theory just described is not an account of what takes place but only another picture or model for thinking about projection, and, if this is so, then there is no question of choosing between this picture and that of 'throwing' unconscious elements. This second picture, however, sounds very much more like an account of what people actually do, and it does not involve treating 'unconscious elements' as though they were 'things', so that it is at least a plausible theory of what happens, whereas the story of the 'transveyance of subjective contents' is not, and we may say:

(i) In thinking and talking psychologically we are to picture projection as a process whereby we 'throw' an image or idea 'on to' an object and suppose that the object conforms to that image or 'possesses' that idea.

(ii) In thinking and talking in this way we are referring to the fact that people do make judgements on inadequate grounds, and stick to them with an assurance which is wholly unwarranted.

(iii) If we have to account for such unwarranted judgements we may suggest that they are a result of a 'category mistake', whereby a man mistakenly attributes an element in his environment to an object instead of to the subject (himself).

It has now to be noticed that, whichever way we think of projection, it does not always give rise to false judgements. If we think of 'throwing' psychic elements there is no reason why we should not 'throw' our unconscious fear (say) 'on to' someone who is afraid, and, as we shall see, Jung implies that there is some reason why we should; it has already been remarked that since a judgement is odd (in the sense

in which the word is used in this essay) if it is unjustified, and for no
other reason, it may quite well be both odd and true: and, thirdly, if
both subject and object happen to have the same psychic attribute the
'category mistake' will involve a mistaken judgement that the subject
has not got it, but a true judgement that the object has. Although
Jung notices this and speaks of it from time to time he does not seem
to give it the attention it deserves, for the implication of what he does
say is that projection is an important function whereby we comprehend
the external world, and that what the psychotherapist calls projection
is really the misuse of that function.

It is easy to see why the psychotherapist should be concerned with
the errors which result from projection, and not with its possible value,
because projection always involves a mistaken judgement about the
subject, and the 'subject' is the analyst's patient. One example will
point this. Suppose an analysand has unconscious pugnacious tendencies, and suppose that he projects them on the doctor, and thinks and
speaks of him as aggressive: the analyst is concerned to make his patient
recognize the unconscious aggressiveness in himself, and he will do
this partly by pointing out that the patient has no good reason to
impute aggressiveness to the analyst. What the patient needs to understand is his own nature, and the projection of pugnacious tendencies
on the analyst is only of interest because it can reveal those tendencies
in the patient, and from the point of view of psychotherapy there is
no more to be said. But the point of view of psychotherapy is not the
only point of view, and it might happen that the analysand was a
statistician interested in the incidence of pugnacity among analysts:
in such a case the analysand would not only be concerned with his
own unconscious tendencies but he would also want to know whether
his judgement about the analyst (admittedly based on projection)
happened to be true. Questions of this sort are not of direct interest
to psychotherapists, but they are of great importance in discussing
the relation between Christian faith and projection.

It has been said that projection may accidentally, as it were, give
rise to an idea of an object which is true, even though the man who has
this idea of it is not justified in claiming that he knows it to be true:
a particular psychic element can be attributed to two different people
at the same time, and when a man fails to acknowledge his own 'possession' of such an element and attributes it to someone else, it may
happen that the other person also 'possesses' it. Smith, let us say,

unconsciously dislikes Brown, is aware of the dislike between them, and attributes it to Brown: he will have the same idea of Brown as one who dislikes him whether or not it happens to be true that Brown dislikes him, and to show that Smith had made a 'category' mistake would not help anyone to decide whether what he thought about Brown was true or not. Jung, however, goes further than this, and gives reasons for thinking there may often be reasons why an idea formed by projection should be true: 'Experience shows', he says, 'that the carrier of the projection is not just *any* object but is always one that proves adequate to the nature of the content projected—that is to say, it must offer the content a "hook" to hang on' (*Practice*, 499), and 'Alchemy afforded numerous "hooks" for the projection of those archetypes which could not be fitted smoothly into the Christian process' (*Alchemy*, 40). This idea of 'hooks' is certainly important, but it is not to be pressed so far as to make nonsense of the idea that projection gives rise to unjustified judgements, for the least acquaintance with the works of psychotherapists shows one that almost anything can be a "hook" for the relating together of psychic elements by the unconscious: similarity of appearance, punning meanings, likeness of sound, association in the past, for example, could all give rise to 'hooks', and Jung greatly weakens what he says in the passages quoted when he also says 'everything unknown and empty is filled with psychological projection' (ibid., 332). What the idea does suggest is that there is every reason to suppose that if there is an object handy which already possesses the element which a man 'wants' to project, then that is the object upon which he will project it. In other words there is, in general, a slight balance of probability that in any case of projection the judgement made will happen to be true, but in addition to this Jung seems to say that there are some occasions when the judgements made on insufficient evidence, as the result of projection, are not only true and important, but also judgements which would not have been made without projection having occurred.

Jung cites Robert Mayer's account of his discovery of the theory of the Conservation of Energy, and he then writes: 'whence this new idea that thrusts itself upon consciousness with such elemental force? . . . if we apply our theory here, the explanation can only be this: the idea of energy and its conservation must be a primordial image that was dormant in the collective unconscious' (*Essays*, 108), and this idea could only have been applied to the external world by some 'trans-

veyance' of the 'subjective content into the object'. In the same way
Jung says that it is 'probably true of most creative intuitions' that
'they can also arise from subjective inner causes, opinions, convictions,
where external stimuli play no part at all, or a very insignificant one',
and he shows that he applies this to intuitions about objects by adding
'for we are hardly likely to suppose a purely causal connection between
the falling apple and Newton's theory of gravitation' (ibid., 270).
Nor does Jung confine his theory to 'great occasions', for he also tells
us that 'an inherited collective image of woman exists in a man's
unconscious, with the help of which he apprehends the nature of
woman' (ibid., 301), and the only way in which such an image could
help would be if it were projected on to the women whom a man
encounters. In other words, Jung's theories clearly imply that the
ability to project is an important human faculty, which enables us to
understand the external world, and not merely the cause of gross
mistakes, and it may well be that it is mere chance that the concept of projection arose in the course of psychotherapy, and that
what the psychotherapist is dealing with is the misuse of a valuable
ability.

When Jung's hints are gathered together it can be said, first, that it
seems that sometimes (and perhaps always) we are able to apprehend
external objects by projecting an idea or image which is 'in' the
collective unconscious, and this of course implies a belief in man as a
'microcosm'; that is, the belief that the human psyche reflects the
structure of the Universe—a belief which Jung certainly holds. There
is, secondly, some reason to think that this may be the main purpose
for which collective elements exist, and the suggestion recalls the
scholastic doctrine that 'like can only be known by like'. Thirdly, so
long as there are no repressed elements in the unconscious, and so long
as the collective unconscious is unreservedly accepted (two ideal
conditions, which are probably never fulfilled), it is to be supposed that
no mistakes about objects would be made, but the repression of psychic
elements, and the antagonism of consciousness to the unconscious
'contaminates', or distorts, the collective elements and the result is
that our knowledge of objects is likely to be falsified in one of two
ways. On the one hand, the fact that the image by means of which we
apprehend a particular object is distorted may cause us to suppose that
the object conforms to the distorted image; on the other hand, because
no object exactly conforms to the distorted image we may project it

on to an object which has no proper connection with it. For example, by repressing attitudes to one's mother, say, one may 'distort' the 'collective image of woman' which 'exists in a man's unconscious' so that when one uses it to 'apprehend the nature of' a woman one attributes to her particular characteristics which do not belong to the general image, but only to one's own distorted version of it.

The Transference

The 'transference' situation frequently arises during the course of analysis and when it does the patient 'misjudges' the doctor, and takes towards him emotional attitudes which are inappropriate. This situation is clearly to be understood in terms of projection, and Jung says of it: 'Contrary to certain views I am not of the opinion that the "transference to the doctor" is a regular phenomenon indispensable to the success of the treatment. Transference is projection, and projection is either there or not there. But it is not *necessary*. In no sense can it be "made", for by definition it springs from unconscious motivations. The doctor may be a suitable object for the projection, or he may not' (*Essays*, p. 62, n.). The attitudes which the patient takes to the doctor, particularly in the early stages of the transference, are usually attitudes which he has taken to his parents and teachers in the past, so that it can be said, for example, that 'it is as though the patient's mind tends to re-enact his infantile emotional patterns as though they belonged to his reality relationship to the analyst, rather than exert the necessary mental energy that would be required to convert them into memories of his own early life' (*Berg*, 25). In Jung's terms, the patient projects on to the analyst images of his parents which have become unconscious: that is, he projects elements of his personal unconscious. The Freudian view is that this is a complete account of the transference, but Jung believes that what he calls collective elements are also projected on to the analyst.

There is no great disagreement between Jung's view and that of Freudians so far as the facts are concerned, but there is considerable disagreement about how the facts should be interpreted. When the Freudian analyst finds that 'though the analyst was being fought off as though he were a father-image, still a father-image was being cherished and clung to (religious belief) in the role of the saviour or preserver' (*Berg*, 85), he acknowledges that the 'father-image' which a man projects is liable to correspond as little with his actual father as it does with the analyst, and he must give some account of how this comes about. The explanation which is natural to the Freudian is that in the past the child had, in fact, thought of his father in religious terms, and that in the course of analysis he 're-enacts' the emotional patterns connected with his idea of his father at the time when he did think of him in those terms. Jung agrees that the patient may have thought in some such way, but he does not believe that this is necessarily the origin of the projection of religious images. Rather, he thinks that the religious images are 'in' the collective unconscious, ready to be projected, and that they may be projected upon the father, or the analyst, or both, at different times. 'The transference', Jung says, 'is in itself no more than a projection of unconscious contents. At first the so-called superficial contents of the unconscious are projected . . . the doctor is interesting as a possible lover . . . he appears more in the role of the father . . . sometimes the doctor has a maternal significance . . . all these fantasy projections are founded on personal memories. Finally there appear forms of fantasy that possess an extravagant character. The doctor is then endowed with uncanny powers: he is a magician or a wicked demon, or else the corresponding personification of goodness, a saviour. Again, he may appear as a mixture of both . . . there are no personal grounds in the memory for this kind of projection. It can sometimes be shown that similar fantasies had, at a certain period in childhood, attached themselves to the father or mother, although neither father nor mother provided any real occasion for them' (*Essays*, 98, 9).

According to the Freudian theory the transference is to be entirely dissolved by making conscious the memories which are unconsciously re-enacted during its course, and Jung agrees that these memories must first be made conscious, but he does not believe that this is enough. When the memories of the past are made conscious, then the projection of personal ideas and images is 'withdrawn', and this is one form of the 'reductive technique' discussed in chapter 6; since this technique leaves the collective unconscious untouched, it is to be expected that the projection of collective ideas will continue, and Jung believes that a somewhat different technique must be used to deal with projections of this kind. It is no longer a question of bringing memories to consciousness, but of becoming aware of the images which are being projected without attempting to bring them within a conscious synthesis. From this point of view the doctor is a 'screen' on which the patient is able to see images which would be otherwise invisible to him, and by recognizing what is going on the patient may be able to realize that these images do 'belong' to himself. Jung thinks that the unconscious is, as it were, trying to tell the conscious mind something by means of an image, and that because the patient does not understand this he assumes that the image must be an image of some external object, and the most convenient external object may be the doctor. For example, after describing a case which was clearly of great importance to the development of his views, Jung says, 'Or, I said to myself, was it rather the case that the unconscious was trying to *create* a god out of the person of the doctor, as it were to free a vision of God from the veils of the personal, so that the transference to the person of the doctor was no more than a misunderstanding on the part of the conscious mind, a stupid trick played by "sound common sense"?' (*Essays*, 214).

Jung thinks that the transference has supreme importance for showing the patient what he himself is like, or might be like. In the early stages of analysis (the period of 'reductive technique') the elements which appear on the 'screen' which is the analyst are 'personal', and they should be made completely conscious, but in the later stages (the period of 'synthetic technique') they are not personal elements at all and they should not be made fully conscious, but merely accepted as 'belonging' to the patient and not to the analyst. With reference to Individuation Jung pays special attention to the projection of the idea of God, and he believes that the withdrawal of this projection from the analyst, so that the idea of God is recognized as an image which reveals what the patient really is, is an essential and most important step towards 'salvation'. We have to see in what this idea of an image of God consists and what Jung understands by its 'withdrawal', for he believes that it ought to be 'withdrawn' not only from the analyst, but also from any being 'outside' the psyche.

Jung's General Theory of Religion

Jung claims to be a champion of religion, and he occasionally expresses a kind of hurt surprise that theologians will not consider his views more seriously than they do. The trouble is, however, that Jung does not simply say that religion is a good thing, but also enunciates general principles about what religion is: it can hardly be denied that his full claim is, 'Religion is a good thing, if by "religion"

is understood "religion as I say it should be".' An example of the
confusion which arises in the minds of his commentators, and which,
one sometimes feels, is not entirely absent from his own mind, is
provided by the following quotations taken from the same page of a
pamphlet on his book *Aion*. 'This book', it is said, 'does not show an
anti-Christian bias, on the contrary, Dr Jung joins the front against
materialism . . .', and yet, in the preceding paragraph we have been
told that in the same book Jung propounds 'the view that the era of
Christianity is drawing to its end' (Guild of Pastoral Psychology,
pamphlet 74). It might almost equally be said that Marxism joins the
front with Christianity against all kinds of false spiritualism and
other worldliness, at the same time that it involves the belief that
Christianity will pass away with the capitalist system. There is
no doubt that Christians are not able to accept Jung's theory of
religion without reservation, because if they did they would have
to accept Jung's opinion of what religion ought to be, and not
that of Christianity itself, but, at the same time, this does not mean
that there is nothing that Christians can learn from what Jung says
about religion.

Jung begins with a view which is unacceptable to Christians since
he believes that religions are all, as it were, special 'schools' of
psychotherapy. There can be no doubt that he does hold this opinion
(which is both somewhat naive and somewhat arrogant) because he
has himself said so more than once: 'Not only Christianity with its
symbols of salvation,' he said in a lecture in 1935, 'but all religions,
including the primitive with their magical rituals, are forms of psychotherapy which treat and heal the suffering of the soul, and the suffering
of the body caused by the soul' (*Practice*, 20); 'since the only salutary
powers visible in the world today', he writes in a work published in
1946, 'are the great "psychotherapeutic" systems which we call the
religions . . .' (ibid., 390); and in an article published in 1951, 'For
not only is religion not the enemy of the sick, it is actually a system
of psychic healing, as the use of the Christian term "cure of souls"
makes clear [sic], and as is also evident from the Old Testament'
(ibid., 249; he cites Psalm 147: 3 and Job 5: 18, but the opinion
expressed is more important than the reasons he gives for holding it).
Since Jung holds this opinion, it should cause no surprise that he also
believes that 'religious statements are psychic confessions which in the
last resort are based on unconscious, i.e. on transcendental, processes',

9—J.S.P.

which 'demonstrate their existence through the confessions of the psyche' (*Job*, 555). In other words, Jung thinks that religious statements, when properly understood, are statements which reveal the nature of the human psyche, and he applies this theory particularly to statements about God: but it must be added that he regards the 'psyche' as quite as numinous and incomprehensible as religious people regard God.

Projection may result in false judgements about external objects which a man perceives with his senses, but it may also produce the illusion that there is an object present when there is not. More subtly, men may form the idea of a fantastic object existing in some other place, as they were given to doing when large parts of the earth's surface were unknown, and, in a yet more rarified way, they may form the idea of an object existing in a 'different way'. Jung believes that the idea of God is formed by projecting unconscious elements on to an object thought to exist in a special way, and that statements about God should be understood as statements about the unconscious element which is projected. In 'The Psychology of the Unconscious' for instance, he wrote: 'The religious projection offers a much more effectual help [sc. for solving conflicts]. In this one keeps the conflict in sight (care, pain, anxiety and so on) and gives it over to a personality standing outside of oneself, the Divinity', and, later, he remarks that 'one must not forget that the individual psychologic roots of the Deity, set up as real by the pious, are concealed from him and that he, although unaware of this, still bears the burden alone and is still alone with his conflict' (*Unconscious*, 39, 40).[1]

Jung has never changed this opinion that the idea of God is the projection of an inward image, but in the course of time he has developed the implications of it. When he says that a man's idea of God is the projection of an unconscious image he does not suppose that he is dismissing it as unimportant, but, on the contrary, that he is finally establishing its importance. It is because Jung believes that what is said about God is said about an image in the human psyche that he is prepared to take religion seriously, and since he believes that there is only one archetype in the unconscious which ought to be called 'God', he also believes that statements about God can be true or false. What Jung calls the 'Self' he also calls 'the image of God' and if a

[1] cf. Vol. 5 of Collected Works § 95. The whole passage has been re-written, but the central idea remains unchanged.

man's idea of God is formed by projecting this 'image of God' then it is to be called a true idea of God, although falsely located 'over there', but if it is formed by projecting any other unconscious image it is to be called a false idea. The two criticisms of certain religious ideas which are to be discussed in the next chapter are, first, that some ideas of God are formed by projecting the wrong image, and, secondly, that so long as a man is unaware of 'the individual psychologic roots of the Deity' his idea of God is valueless to him.

According to Jung the Self is the archetype of wholeness, the potential unity of a man's nature, his highest value, and the goal to which his life should be directed, and if he will take it seriously and let it 'work' in him it will itself guide him towards that goal. Although the projection of this archetype into the idea of God is an implicit acknowledgement of its supreme value, however, Jung claims that so long as God is thought of as an object external to a man the archetype of the Self cannot be effective. 'An exclusively religious projection', he tells us, 'may rob the soul of its values so that through sheer inanition it becomes incapable of further development and gets stuck in an unconscious state. At the same time it falls victim to the delusion that the cause of all disaster lies outside, and people no longer stop to ask themselves how far it is their own doing' (*Alchemy*, 11). It should be apparent that not only does Jung believe that religion is a form of psychotherapy but that he also expects it to conform to analytical practice, because it is clear that, according to his theory, the idea of God as an external object performs the same function in religion as the analyst performs in the transference situation. Just as the analyst is a 'screen' upon which the patient may project his unconscious images, and so come to observe them, so this idea of God is a 'screen' upon which a man projects the image of the Self, so that he is able to 'see' it. Just as projection must be withdrawn from the analyst, and the projected elements acknowledged as 'belonging' to the patient, so the image projected into the idea of God must be acknowledged as 'belonging' to the man who projects it. The only important difference is that because the analyst is an actual object the elements projected on to him must be 'detached' from him before they can be accepted by the patient as his own, whereas the idea of God can be accepted as belonging 'in' the psyche, and still be called 'God': in the first case a man must say 'I was mistaken in attributing those elements to the analyst, I should have attributed them to myself', in the second case he says 'I was right to call that image God, but I was wrong in thinking that God is an external object'.

Jung's Criticisms of Certain Religious Ideas

Jung's criticisms of certain religious ideas depend upon the theory of religion which has just been described. Religion, he believes, ought to lead a man to the same goal as analytical Psychology (that is, to Individuation), and it ought to do so by constellating the archetype of the Self in the idea of God, and making that idea effective in a man's life. In this section this theory will be assumed for the purpose of developing Jung's two main criticisms of religious ideas: if the theory were not assumed it would be necessary to keep saying 'if Jung is right'; as it is, these words may stand here as a direction governing the whole section. The two criticisms which will be developed are, first, that some people sometimes project the wrong archetype into the idea of God, and, secondly, that the idea of God, even when it is formed by the projection of the right archetype, is too often allowed to remain external to a man, and so ineffective.

(a) *Self or Magician?* To project an archetype into the idea of God is to treat it as having supreme value. To elaborate a concept of God, and to ask other people to believe it, as religious systems do, is to instruct people to treat the archetype which corresponds to that concept as having supreme value. In theory it can happen that any archetype is projected into the idea of God, but in practice the common, conscious ideas of what God is like usually limit the possibilities. It is true that individuals or groups may form ideas of God very different from that generally accepted in the society to which they belong, as is shown, for example, by the fact that the covens of the Middle Ages could picture a figure based on the current idea of the devil and address it as 'god', but in general the idea which a man has of God bears a close resemblance to that of his neighbours. For practical purposes, in the modern West, the 'choice' of a suitable archetype for projecting into the idea of God may be said to lie between the Self and the magician. The first criticism which we have to discuss is that sometimes the idea of God is formed by projecting the archetype of the magician, and that since this archetype is less important than the Self this means a false valuation of the human psyche.

Jung describes the dire effects of projecting the magician in a passage which must be given at length: 'It is now quite possible that, instead of identifying with the mana-personality, one will concretize it as an extramundane "Father in Heaven", complete with the attribute of absoluteness—something that many people seem very prone to do. This would be tantamount to giving the unconscious a preponderance that was just as absolute (if one's faith could be pushed that far!), so that all value would flow over to that side. The logical result is that the only thing left behind here is a miserable, inferior, worthless, and sinful little heap of humanity. This solution, as we know, has become an historical world view. As I am moving here on psychological grounds only, and feel no inclination whatever to dictate my eternal truths to the world at large, I must observe, by way of criticizing this solution, that if I shift all the highest values over to the side of the unconscious, thus converting it into a *summum bonum*, I am then placed in the unfortunate position of having to discover a devil of equal weight and dimensions who could act as a psychological counterbalance to my *summum bonum*. Under no circumstances, however, will my modesty allow me to identify myself with the devil. That would be altogether too presumptuous and would, moreover, bring me into unbearable conflict with my highest values. Nor, with my moral deficit, can I possibly afford it. On psychological grounds, therefore, I would recommend that no God be constructed out of the archetype of the mana-personality. In other words, he [the mana-personality] must not be concretized, for only thus can I avoid projecting my values and non-values into God and Devil, and only thus can I preserve my human dignity, my specific gravity, which I need so much if I am not to become the unresisting shuttlecock of unconscious forces' (*Essays*, 394, 5). More briefly, Jung says elsewhere, 'To believe that God is the Summum Bonum is impossible for a reflecting consciousness' (*Job*, 662).

To understand this criticism it is first necessary to appreciate what Jung means by the 'summum bonum'. The phrase may mean 'that, whatever it may be, which does in fact have supreme value for man, whether or not men correctly value it', and in this sense it must be a description of God, whatever idea of God a man may actually form. Jung, however, does not mean this by the phrase, he means 'the idea formed by bringing together all those things which men judge to be good', and it is in this sense that the idea of God which results from the projection of the magician is the 'summum bonum', and in this sense that a 'reflecting consciousness' is unable to believe that God is the 'summum bonum'. After this explanation it is possible to explain what 'projecting the magician' means.

In a man there are high possibilities which are manifested in the tendency to do good, the sense of great potential power, aspirations towards high ideals, and so on, but such things are combined with other, contradictory attributes, like selfishness, sloth, carelessness, and vanity, and in most men the two sets of tendencies balance one another. It is possible, however, to form an ideal picture of a man who would possess all the 'good' attributes and none of the 'bad' ones; such a person would be sinless, wonderful, wise, and possessed of power over men and nature, and this is the image of the magician. To be 'possessed by the magician' would be to imagine that one was, oneself, such a person, and to attempt to live appropriately, and this would at once bring one up against the fact that one's own 'bad' tendencies frustrate the good, and also against the intransigence of one's environment; as Jung puts it, the 'mana' would not work on others (*Essays*, 380). Rightly rejecting the aim of living as the magician oneself, one may wrongly project its image on to someone else, a society, or a cause, or one may project it into the image of God, and to project the image of the magician is to suppose that some actual object, or the idea of God has all the attributes of the magician and none of the opposing attributes always associated with them in human nature. In the passage cited Jung claims that to project the magician into the idea of God always has, and must have, certain definite consequences, and if it looks at first sight as though a man's idea of God has been formed in this way it must be very doubtful whether it has if those consequences do not arise.

The consequences of projecting the magician can be easily listed from the passage cited:

(i) By definition, the idea of God that results is that He is the 'summum bonum' in the sense explained above.

(ii) (*a*) A man's own idea of himself is that he is a 'miserable, inferior, worthless, and sinful little heap of humanity', and this must be understood to mean that he thinks of himself as literally 'nothing'. (*b*) To this, however, there is an unlikely alternative, that a man may think of himself as the devil incarnate; that is, that having projected all that he thinks 'good' into the idea of God, he may form his idea of himself from the 'bad' that is left.

(iii) Neglecting the possibility of (ii)(*a*), a man has an idea of a devil which is in every respect as 'bad' as God is thought to be 'good'; one, that is, 'of equal weight and dimension' with the idea of God.

(iv) A man will become the 'unresisting shuttlecock of those unconscious forces' which he thinks of under the figures of God and the devil.

In the next chapter it will be shown that belief in the Christian idea of God has none of these consequences, and that therefore it is unlikely that it is formed by projecting the magician; for to apply the criticism that a certain idea of God was the result of the projection of the magician it would need to be shown that most, if not all, of these consequences did actually result from the acceptance of that idea.

(b) *God as External*. Projection of an archetype into the idea of God is a mixed blessing: it has the very important effect of bringing the image of the archetype before consciousness, so that a man can see what the archetype is, but it also obscures the fact that the archetype 'belongs' to the man who projects it. So long as the archetype is projected it is thought of as 'outside', and so cannot be taken into account as a force acting through the man, and this is what Jung says: 'In an outward form of religion where all the emphasis is on the outward figure, the archetype is identical with externalized ideas but remains unconscious as a psychic factor. When an unconscious content is replaced by a projected image to that extent, it is cut off from all participation in and influence on the conscious mind. Hence it largely forfeits its own life, because prevented from exerting the formative influence on consciousness natural to it' (*Alchemy*, 12). If a man projects that which gives to his psyche its true value, the goal of his life, and the potential unity of his nature, then 'So insignificant does the soul seem that it is regarded as hardly capable of evil, much less of good. But if the soul no longer has any part to play, religious life congeals into externals and formalities' (ibid., 11).

To apply the above criticism to a particular idea of God it would have to be shown:

(a) That God was thought of as exclusively 'outward', standing 'over against' a man, and also

(b) that this idea of God was coupled with a tendency to obey the 'letter' rather than the 'spirit', and

(c) that those who held this idea lacked any aspirations to high ideals, feeling that such things were not for them.

'Religion appears to me to be', says Jung, 'a peculiar attitude of mind, which could be formulated in accordance with the original use of the word "religio", which means a careful consideration and observation of certain dynamic factors that are conceived as "powers": spirits, daemons, gods, laws, ideal, ideals, or whatever name man has given to such factors in his world as he has found powerful, dangerous, or helpful enough to be taken into careful consideration, or grand, beautiful, and meaningful enough to be devoutly worshipped and loved' (*Religion*, 8). He believes that this attitude is founded upon a true instinct, because he believes that such 'factors' exist, and for this reason he takes religion with the greatest seriousness. On the other hand, he also believes that the 'place' where these 'factors' exist is the human psyche itself, and that the belief that they exist somewhere else deprives them of true value. This is particularly true, in his opinion, of the archetype of the Self, and of this he says '[My observations] prove only the existence of an archetypal God-image... but as it is a very important and influential archetype, its relatively frequent occurrence seems to be a noteworthy fact for any *theologia naturalis*' (ibid., 102). All that he says about religion, and all his criticisms of religious ideas, are ultimately to be regarded as generalizations from his experience and observations as a psychologist, and they can be understood in this sense even when his theory of religion is not accepted in its entirety.

In effect, Jung has observed that some attitudes to the 'factors' or 'powers' to which he refers do in general lead men towards the goal that he calls 'Individuation', and that other attitudes impede a man's progress towards it. He does not offer explanations of why this should be, but simply records it as a fact. This means that the two criticisms which have been discussed are to be understood from the point of view of the practical efficacy of religious ideas to bring a man to the goal which Jung believes to be the true goal for him: thus the projection of the magician into the idea of God and the failure to regard the 'factor' represented by the image of the Self as within the psyche are two ideas which Jung claims are found, in experience, to interfere with a man's progress towards the goal, and this is a claim which, whether or not it is true, is well within the competence of a psychologist.

The Application of Jung's Criticisms to Christianity

It is clear that Jung's criticisms would have no validity for anyone who regarded the goal of religion as exclusively concerned with what happens when a man has died. If anyone were to say 'my religion may make a man thoroughly unhappy in this world, it may subject him to all sorts of neuroses, he will fail to be of any value to others, and his life will be entirely disorganized, but he will come to ultimate bliss when he dies', then such a person would not need to concern himself with Jung's criticisms at all. Equally, if one says 'my religion does hold out a goal for men in this life, but that goal is not a bit like the goal to which Jung points us', one would also be able to dismiss his criticisms as irrelevant. The Christian cannot evade Jung's criticisms by saying either of these two things: on the one hand it is certain that the Christian ideal includes an ideal for this life as well as for the next, and if Christianity cannot lead to a full, valuable, unified life in this world, then it is not what it claims to be; and on the other hand, the Christian can hardly reject the ideal of a unified life which Jung sets forward. The goal of Individuation, Jung tells us, is a release from that state in which 'a man can neither be at one with himself nor accept responsibility for himself', and in which 'he feels himself to be in a degrading, unfree, unethical, condition' (*Essays*, 373); he says it is 'at-one-ment with oneself and at the same time with humanity, since oneself is a part of humanity' (*Practice*, 227); that in the process of Individuation a 'patient becomes what he really is', and that 'if the worst comes to the worst, he will even put up with his neurosis, once he has understood the meaning of his illness' (ibid., 11); a mark of being Individuated is 'the consciousness of being a child of God which then frees one from the spell of the blood' (*Secret*, 133); 'The meaning and purpose of the process is the realization, in all its aspect, of the personality originally hidden away, in the embryonic germ-plasm; the production and unfolding of the original, potential wholeness' (*Essays*, 186); Individuation means 'The completest expression of that fateful combination we call individuality, the full flowering not only of the single individual, but of the group, in which each adds his portion to the whole' (ibid., 404); 'Individuation, therefore, is a *process of differentiation*, having for its goal the development of the individual personality' and 'since the individual is not only a single, separate being but, by his very existence, also presupposes a collective relationship, the process of individuation must clearly lead to a more intensive and universal collective solidarity, and not to mere *isolation*' (*Types*, 561, 2; in definition of 'Individuation'). The Christian can hardly claim to be indifferent to the question whether or not his beliefs are of a kind which usually lead men to such a goal.

The Christian cannot accept Jung's theory of what religion is because he believes that it is more than Jung says, but he believes, at the same time, that it is at least what Jung says. A goal such as that to which Jung points us may not be the full goal of Christianity, but it is certainly included in the Christian goal, and it is well for Christians if they can show that their religious beliefs are of the kind which do, in fact, usually lead towards such a goal. In other words, if it can be shown that certain ideas come under the criticisms discussed above it is to be hoped that those ideas are not taught by orthodox Christianity, and that they are not will be shown in the next chapter. Yet in giving this modified acceptance of Jung's views one thing should be added, to avoid misrepresenting him. Although Jung does talk as though he is able to explain the nature and purpose of religion, and although there is no doubt that his terms are all concerned to set before us a goal for this life, he is also at pains to explain that he does not know what he is talking about. 'A scientific term like "individuation"', he says, 'does not mean that we are dealing with something known and finally cleared up, on which there is no more to be said. It merely indicates an as yet very obscure field of research much in need of exploration. . . . These processes are steeped in mystery; they pose riddles with which the human mind will long wrestle for a solution, and perhaps in vain. For, in the last analysis, it is exceedingly doubtful whether human reason is a suitable instrument for this purpose' (*Alchemy*, 564); and, 'I trust I have given no cause for the misunderstanding that I know anything about the nature of the "centre" [that is, the Self]—for it is simply unknowable and can only be expressed symbolically through its own phenomenology, as is the case, incidentally, with every object of experience' (ibid., 327); again, in the introduction to *Answer to Job*, he writes, 'If, therefore, in what follows I concern myself with these "metaphysical" objects, I am quite conscious that I am moving in a world of images and that none of my reflections touches the essence of the Unknowable' (*Job*, 556). This means that although it is not possible for the Christian to admit that Jung's account of religion as a form of psychotherapy is an exhaustive account he must not regard it as an attempt to explain away religious ideas. Jung's opinion reveals his idea of what psychotherapy is as much as it reveals his idea about religion, for he believes that both disciplines lead to an encounter with the 'numinous', and that in the attempt to describe such an encounter words fail and reason is baffled. Christians have faith in a God who exists, somehow, as an external object; Jung speaks of an archetype which is, somehow, in the unconscious; and, because neither can explain exactly what they mean in intelligible terms it is impossible to decide whether or not they mean the same thing by the terms that they do use. So long as Jung is content to say that the reality of God as an external 'object' is a matter which lies beyond his competence as a psychologist Christians have no cause to object, but in so far as he implies that the only importance of the idea of God lies in the fact that it is possible to give a psychological account of it and that belief in God as external inevitably leads to formalism, they cannot be expected to accept what he says.

9

FAITH

JUNG suggests that faith in God as an external being may be an important stage on the way to the goal of human life, but that it can be no more than a stage. Such faith, he would have us believe, corresponds to the projection of important archetypes on to the analyst in the course of the Individuation process, and must be 'withdrawn' from all supposed connection with an external object in order that God and his kingdom may be found where it ought to be found; that is, 'within you'. It has already been shown, however, that faith is a mark of the Justified man, which means that under no circumstances can it be regarded as merely a means, but that it is itself an element in the goal, and an enduring feature in the life of the Christian. Nevertheless, it is also true that a man's faith is an important element in the development of the Christian's life and that a man's idea of God has considerable bearing on the intensity of his penitence, so that faith may also be regarded as a means towards the Christian goal. This means that it is possible to ask whether the idea of God which is set before men by the Church, and the attitude towards God which the Church asks of men, are such that Jung's criticisms apply to them; that is, assuming that Jung's psychological generalizations are correct, it may be asked whether the Christian idea of God, and faith in Him, are likely to advance or impede men's progress towards his goal in this life.

Whether Jung himself thinks that his criticisms apply to the teaching of the Christian Church is not easily decided, and this is mainly because Jung is concerned with the ideas which people hold about God rather than with the explicit teaching of a particular religious body, but it is also partly due to the inevitable difficulty of knowing exactly what is meant by the 'orthodox teaching of the Church' in the present divided state of Christendom. The distinction which Jung makes is not between 'orthodox' and 'heterodox' ideas, but between 'the deepest and best understanding of Christianity' on the one hand, and 'superficialities

and disastrous misunderstandings' on the other (*Alchemy*, 7), and this
can hardly be regarded as satisfactory, for two reasons: first, this
distinction implies that one knows what is the 'deepest and best understanding of Christianity', and it is difficult to avoid the suspicion that
Jung means by it what he has decided ought to be the Christian faith,
and this is a basis for discussion which Christians can hardly accept;
secondly, it seems to ignore the effort which the Church has made, for
over 1900 years, to criticize, sift, and synthetize the work of her
children. There is an understanding of Christianity which, being the
Church's understanding of her own religion, is Christianity itself,
and although any one of us may be mistaken as to what this understanding of the faith is it is this which we should have in mind when
we discuss Christianity, and not something which we happen to think
is 'deepest and best' on the basis of our own opinions.

It seems most likely that Jung does not think that what the Church
teaches represents 'the deepest and best understanding of Christianity',
and the following reasons for thinking this may be given: in the
account of projection of the magician, quoted in the last chapter, he
says that the solution which he condemns 'has, as we know, become a
world view', and it is difficult to think that he is not referring to
Christianity; in a note to that passage he remarks that 'a psychological
God could reach man', and adds, 'The Church seems to be a magical
instrument for protecting man against this eventuality'; with reference
to ideas 'in the body of Protestantism' he says, 'If the supreme value
(Christ) and the supreme negation (sin) are outside, then the soul is
void: its highest and lowest are missing' (*Alchemy*, 9); he remarks,
'So long as religion is only faith and outward form, and the religious
function is not experienced in our own souls, nothing of any importance
has happened' (ibid., 13); and of patients in general he says, 'He needs
"justification by works", for "justification by faith" alone has remained an empty sound for him as for so many others' (ibid., 37).
These things suggest, although they do not prove, that Jung does
criticize the Church's teachings as such, and that those Christians who
are willing to accept his psychology have got a case to answer; but it
is not in the end very important whether Jung does apply his criticisms
in this way, for the criticisms are available and, since they might be
applied to orthodox Christianity, it is as well to show that they are not
applicable, more particularly in that to do so is to turn one's attention
to aspects of the Christian faith which might otherwise be overlooked.

The possibility of applying Jung's criticisms to Christianity rests upon the fact that there is full agreement between Jung and Christians on a matter of central importance in that both believe that God represents the final goal for man. 'The self', Jung says, 'is our life's goal' (*Essays*, 404), and 'it might equally be called the "God within us"' (ibid., 399): 'Be ye holy', say the Christian Scriptures, 'for I am holy'; and 'Be ye perfect, even as your Father is perfect' was our Lord's command to His disciples. Whatever else Christians may say about God, they cannot deny that the idea of God in a man's mind should set the goal at which his life is aimed, nor can they deny that there is in every man a pattern of what God is like, since they declare that God made man in His own image. Because of this agreement, and because, as has been shown, Jung's goal is very like the Christian goal, it is possible to compare Christianity with Jung's psychology by asking whether, on the basis of that psychology, the Christian idea of God is the image of the goal, and whether faith in the Christian God does mean that the 'religious function is not experienced in our own souls', so that 'nothing important' happens; in other words, to ask whether the Christian God conforms to the image of the Self, and whether faith is all outward form. The discussion of these questions leads to the consideration of the following things:

The Ontological Argument
The Character of Jesus
The Effects of Penitence
The Devil
Transcendence
Immanence
Faith and the Opposites

The first four are involved in the answer to the first question, the next two in the answer to the second, and the last arises from the discussion of the others.

The Ontological Argument

It is hardly possible to avoid mention of the ontological argument in connection with Jung's account of 'projecting the magician', but it will be mentioned only to be set aside. The 'mechanism' of this argument conforms in every detail to the psychological account of projecting the magician; for a man selects all that he calls 'good', inflates each thing to infinite proportions, detaches them from all that is evil, and then combines them into the idea of a Being existing 'over there'. Lotze's attempt to justify this argument is of particular interest because it brings out the psychological features of it very clearly: 'This', he says, 'is obviously rather a case where an altogether immediate conviction breaks through [where from?] into consciousness; to wit, the conviction that the totality of all that has value—all that is perfect, fair, and good—cannot possibly be homeless in the world [has it no home at all in man?] or in the realm of actuality, but has the very best claim to be regarded by us as imperishable reality' (*Lotze*, 10). To whatever other ideas Jung's criticisms apply there can be no doubt that what he says of 'projecting the magician' applies to an idea of God formed by means of this argument.

The ontological argument, however, has never been generally accepted by the Church. It has not been formally condemned but for every theologian of stature who has affirmed it another has denied it, and the Church is not committed to it. More important, even those Christians who accept it as an argument to the existence of God would not commit themselves to the view that Christians know what God is like by thinking in this way, and the Christian idea of God can never be formed along these lines. Such a way of learning what God is like is only possible to those who refuse to continue the text 'No man hath seen God at any time' which might be a doctrine of any religion, with the specifically Christian assertion, 'The only-begotten Son, which is in the bosom of the Father, he hath declared him'; or to those who reject the words of Jesus, 'he who hath seen me hath seen the Father'. The Christian idea of God is not (at least not avowedly) modelled upon an image in the mind of man, but upon the man Jesus, as that man is presented to us in the New Testament. Any criticism that the Christian idea of God is unsatisfactory must be directed at the picture of Jesus which is found in the Christian scriptures.

The Character of Jesus

The Christian faith implies that God is like Jesus, and the Christian idea of God cannot be dissociated from Jesus as He is presented in the New Testament: according to Christianity Jesus is God, translated, as it were, into terms which men can apprehend. What God is 'in Himself' or 'for Himself' lies beyond all possibility of human understanding, but the Christian believes that God has manifested, or

expressed Himself within the terms of human existence, and that He
has done so by being made man. We can know Jesus because He is
perfectly man, and, because He is also God, when we know Him we
know God. To go beyond this is to go beyond the teaching of the
Church, and to attempt to 'translate' from human terms into 'divine'
terms is to attempt to go beyond the limits of the human mind: the
Church points to Jesus, and says 'God is like this, to know or to
encounter Jesus, is to know or to encounter God'.

   To say that the Christian idea of God is the idea of One who is
like Jesus does not evade the possibility that that idea may be criticized
as a 'projection of the magician'. The nerve of Jung's criticism is not
that he claims to explain how the idea of God is derived, but that he
claims that if the idea of God (however it may be derived) conforms to
the image of the magician rather than to that of the Self it is an unsatisfactory idea from the point of view of guiding man towards what
ought to be his life's goal. Even though we say that God is like Jesus
it may still be that our idea of what Jesus is like conforms to the image
of the magician, and this may come about in either of two ways.
Projection may falsify not only an object which is actually before us,
but also one which is described to us, so that in reading the records of
the life of Jesus and the comments of the New Testament writers upon
it it is always possible to project upon Jesus one's unconscious idea,
and, by passing over this and emphasizing that, to form a picture of
Jesus quite different from that which is presented in the records; and
this is one way in which it might happen that the idea of Jesus in the
minds of Christians came to conform to the image of the magician:
but it is also possible that Jesus Himself, as He is presented in the
records, should conform to that image either because He himself
conformed to it or because His first disciples projected the image upon
Him. What is perfectly clear is that some people do have an idea of
Jesus which does conform to the image of the magician, but although
this is probably true of the majority of uninstructed Christians today
that does not prove that it is the teaching of the Church, for if the idea
which people have of Jesus is not in accordance with the picture of
Him presented in the Gospels then it is not the Christian idea of Jesus,
and to criticize it is not to criticize the teaching of the Church. If
anyone wishes to claim that the Christian idea of Jesus (and hence the
Christian idea of God) is unsatisfactory because it is like the image of
the magician and not like the image of the Self he must show that this

is true of Jesus as the New Testament presents Him, and not merely that it is true of what some people believe about Him. Jung has shown us how he would set out to criticize the Christian idea of Jesus in this way, and what he says will be examined.

In *Answer to Job* Jung argues at some length that there is something inadequate about Jesus as an incarnation of God. In God, he claims, the 'opposites' are united, but in Jesus only the 'good' or 'light' aspects of God are visible. Before criticizing this claim three things should be noted:

(i) Jung does not reject Jesus: he implies that Jesus did manifest God in a special way, although he does not believe that He manifested God adequately. Moreover, he also implies that whereas Jesus was a good thing at the time when He lived, and during the following centuries, He is less of a good thing today. Put in another way, Jung regards the manifestation of the 'light' side of God in Jesus as an important stage in the development of human consciousness in the western world, but he regards it as a stage in this development, and not final in any way: 'At first', he says, 'God incarnated His good side in order, we may suppose, to create the most durable basis for a later assimilation of the other side' (*Job*, 741). Jung does not want to deny that Christianity is something important and something which works for good, but he does deny that Jesus is 'The fulness of the Godhead bodily'. Unfortunately, to deny this is to reject Christianity and to set up a 'sect', and since we already have sufficient Christian sects it would be preferable if we could treat Jung as an unequivocal opponent of Christianity, but to do this would be very unkind in view of his expressed approval of religion in general.

(ii) Jung's comments are, in the main, true of what masses of un-instructed Christians think about Jesus today, and if he were content to criticize the popular view of Christianity many of us would be only too glad to be associated with what he says, but as it is, in fastening the ideas which he criticizes upon the Church, Jung is shying at an Aunt Sally. It is not Jung who has set up this Aunt Sally but Christians of his generation, yet he can hardly be excused for taking Jesus and Christianity at the valuation of contemporary Christians, for he should know better. What he says will not stand as a criticism of Christianity or of the Church over the centuries, whereas as a criticism of many modern misunderstandings of Christianity it is both true and important.

(iii) From Jung's point of view it is not in the least important whether the Jesus of the New Testament is the same as the man who lived in Palestine, because he is concerned with what Jesus means for men, and when he speaks of 'Jesus' he means 'Jesus as he is presented in the New Testament, and believed in by Christians'. Nevertheless Jung does appear to believe that what he says of Jesus is true of the man as He was.

Answer to Job is a strange book, because Jung deliberately uses the concrete imagery of the Judaeo-Christian tradition in order to speak about the psychology of man. One recognizes the analytical technique at once: just as the 'anima', or any other archetype, in a man's unconscious must be allowed to 'have its say', and as, while it is 'speaking', the man must give himself up to the fantasies which manifest it, so Jung regards the religious ideas of an age as projections of archetypes, and that which is said about them as the way in which those archetypes 'speak', and he is ready to 'give himself up' to the 'fantasies' by treating them as though they referred to objective facts. The justification of this procedure is the fact that men have held certain ideas, the assumption (which is certainly not unreasonable) that this fact reveals some other, deeper fact about the constitution of the human mind, and the further assumption that this deeper fact can only be known in and through the ideas which manifest it. Jung, as has been said before, believes that God is the central image in the unconscious, and that the idea of an objective being called 'God' is 'true' in so far as it is a projection of that image. Individuals may project the wrong image, and so form a false idea of God, but if *Answer to Job* is to be understood it must be supposed that the idea of God formed by a large group of men at any time is not 'false' in the same way, even though it does not conform to the 'God-image'. In other words, in the history of the development of consciousness there have been times when the true 'God-image' was not effectively central for men, and the group concept of God at such times will manifest (and, it might be said, 'ought' to manifest) the image which does happen to be central in the collective unconscious, and Jung seems to suggest that the beginning of our era, when Christianity came into being, was a time when the magician was the most important archetype—not of course absolutely, but relatively, in that the Self cannot be reached until the magician has been dealt with.

'Yahweh', according to Jung, was for many centuries a projection of the collective unconscious in its undifferentiated state. He is 'everything in its totality; therefore, among other things, he is total justice, and also its total opposite', and, 'from the way the divine nature expresses itself we can see that the individual qualities are not sufficiently related to one another, with the result that they fall apart into mutually contradictory acts' (*Job*, 574). Until about the time that the book of Job was written Yahweh remained a projection of mere unconsciousness, but the book of Job represents a striking advance in human consciousness, which involves and implies a reconstellation of unconscious elements, and a change comes over the nature of God—eventually 'As a result of the partial neutralization of Satan,' says Jung, 'Yahweh identifies with his light aspect and becomes the good God and loving father' (ibid., 651). This means, in effect, that at this period the idea of God corresponded to the projection of the magician, and from what Jung says this must be regarded as a necessary stage in the development of consciousness, even though it is a mistake for men today to 'stick' at such a stage. This new concept of God set the stage for an incarnation of His 'good' and 'light' side, and the idea of God as the 'good God and loving father' was objectively manifested in the person of Jesus, or in the idea of Him in the minds of His first disciples and, in this way, Jesus was the incarnation of only one side of God. This briefly, is Jung's argument, and by examining five typical assertions from *Answer to Job* it will be shown that whatever may be said of the rest of it, the conclusion is certainly false.

(*a*) 'God, with his good intentions,' Jung says, 'begot a good and helpful son and thus created an image of himself as the good father—unfortunately, as we must admit, again without considering that there existed in him a knowledge that spoke a very different truth. . . . Where, for instance, did his darkness go?' (ibid., 694).

In other words the 'original' Yahweh was compounded of light and darkness, while Jesus and his Father were wholly 'light'; but this contention will not stand, because when the meaning of 'darkness' as applied to Yahweh is understood it is clear that such 'darkness' does belong to Jesus and to the God of the New Testament. The idea of 'darkness' carries straight back to the Old Testament, and it is in the Old Testament that we must look for passages determinative of its meaning. Amos is probably the most appropriate: 'Woe unto you that desire the day of Yahweh,' he says, 'wherefore would ye have the day of Yahweh? it is darkness, and not light . . . shall not the day of Yahweh be darkness, and not light? even very dark, and no brightness in it?' and the meaning of this is perfectly clear from the context of the whole book. When Yahweh comes he will come to a sinful and unrepentant people, and because they are sinful and unrepentant they will find Him 'very dark', that is, he will be to them a terror and an evil. This is the sense in which Yahweh, in the Old Testament, has a 'dark' side, and it may be pressed a very long way; it may be pressed, in association, with the claim that 'all men have sinned', to the extent of saying that to the very best of men Yahweh will appear 'dark' as well as 'light', and that no man can look for the day of Yahweh to be nothing but 'light'. In this sense[1] Jung is right that Yahweh of the Old Testament has a 'dark' side, but this does not mean that Yahweh is not all light nor does it conflict with the claim that 'in him is no darkness at all', because in these assertions 'light' and 'darkness' are used in a different sense. 'God is light' is as much a definition of 'light' as it is a description of God, and it is equivalent to saying 'whatever you say God is that is light': in other words, to say that God has a 'dark' side when viewed by sinful man is to say that sinful man does not know the true meaning of 'light' and 'dark', and as will appear when the doctrine of evil as *privatio boni* is mentioned below, Jung agrees, by implication, that this is so.

The 'darkness' of Yahweh is a characteristic of God as He appears to men, and it is particularly manifested by His wrath and His condemnation of sinners, and to suggest that Jesus does not also manifest such 'darkness' is to distort the evidence of the Gospels beyond imagining. Jesus Himself tells us that His very coming, like the day of Yahweh, is a judgement which convicts men of sin: 'If I had not come', He says, 'and spoken unto them, they had not had sin . . . if I had not done among them the works which none other did, they had not had sin': Jesus is the 'light of the world', but not all men will recognize Him as light, and He hints that the fate of those who reject Him may be compared to being cast 'into outer darkness'; Jesus speaks of the judgement of the world, and He makes it clear that many will be condemned, and He threatens that those who knowingly do wrong will 'be beaten with many stripes'. Throughout the Gospel record we are

---

[1] Jung would probably claim more than this—that Yahweh's 'darkness' includes downright evil. In so far as he bases this on the text of the Old Testament as it stands I do not believe that it can be maintained.

reminded, again and again, that though God is a loving Father He is yet one who cannot abide evil, and Jesus does not cancel but establishes the 'dark' side of Yahweh which the Old Testament writers had perceived.

(*b*) 'With regard to the human side of Christ', says Jung, 'if we can speak of a "purely human" aspect at all, what stands out particularly clearly is his love of mankind' (ibid., 646).

In relation to Jesus' love for men, what stands out most clearly of all is that the love which He offers is very different from what men want. If the muddled conception of Jesus in England today is any guide, then the love which men seek from God is a love which will condone or forget sin, accept men at their own valuation, and assure them that everything will come right in the end, whatever they may do. Jesus, on the other hand, offered none of these things, and coupled with His burning desire for men was a fierce determination that those who came to Him should come on His terms and not theirs. Even Jesus' call to sinners was double-edged, for to say that He came to call 'sinners, not the righteous' was to say that those who claimed to be righteous could have no part in Him; and, when sinners did come to Him, He required that they should give up all, and follow Him. Jesus made an absolute demand upon men before He promised them salvation, and Jung (with many others) confuses the promises that Jesus made to those who had already accepted His demands with His concern that those who had not accepted them should do so before the wrath of God fell upon them.

Yet it is by no means clear that Jesus' love for men is His plainest characteristic. I had already written in my notes for this chapter that His plainest characteristic was 'obedience to His Father's will', and that 'He expects the same from His followers', when I had the opportunity of asking a group of children 'what kind of a person was Jesus?' Only one girl was prepared to answer at all, and very much to my surprise she said 'He was one who was devoted to the will of God': this, of course, proves nothing, but it raises a doubt as to whether Jung is right about what is 'clearest', and it remains true that it is not only in the order in which He puts the two great commandments but in all His recorded words and acts that Jesus shows that all His life was subordinated to His Father, and that His concern for men stemmed from obedience to God.

(*c*) 'Jesus, it is plain,' says Jung, 'translated the existing tradition into his own personal reality, announcing the glad tidings: "God has good pleasure in mankind. He is a loving father and loves you as I love you, and has sent me as his son to ransom you from the old debt"' (ibid., 689).

None of this is at all plain! It is not plain what Jung means by 'the existing tradition', and from what we know of the 'traditions' of the time, and from the reception which Jesus received from His contemporaries, what seems plainest of all is that if He did 'translate an existing tradition into His own personal reality' He translated it very badly. It is not plain that 'God has good pleasure in mankind' is even a free rendering of the Gospel that 'the kingdom of heaven is at hand', which Jesus announced, and it is quite certain that it distorts the sense. It is only plain that God's love for mankind is unmixed with wrath against sinners when one has already misconceived the nature of Jesus' love for men, and nowhere in the Gospels does Jesus introduce the idea of men having a debt to God, for the force of 'ransom' is 'make free', and not 'pay what is owning'. According to the Gospel record the message of Jesus was quite different from the version which Jung gives; He came into the cities of Galilee preaching 'repent, and believe in the Gospel', and he urged men to be ready, lest He should return in an hour when they were not expecting Him 'like a thief in the night'.

(d) 'When one considers', says Jung, 'with what intensity and exclusiveness not only Christ's teaching, but the doctrines of the Church in the following centuries down to the present day, have emphasized the goodness of the loving Father in heaven, the deliverance from fear, the Summum Bonum, and the *privatio boni*, one can form some conception of the incompatability which the figure of Yahweh presents, and see how intolerable such a paradox must appear to the religious consciousness' (ibid., 685).

(i) The irony of such a passage as this is monumental. For two or three generations there has been a sort of 'conspiracy' (in the Church of England at least) to 'hush up' those aspects of a full Christian faith which might seem unacceptable to the modern world. Suspicion has been cast on the Old Testament, and it has often been quietly ignored; the Apocalypse has been largely set on one side, as not quite fit for a Christian's reading; the psalter has been carefully purged, as in the abortive Prayer Book of 1928; and many 'hard sayings' of Jesus have been weakened. The tide, it may be hoped, has now turned within the

Church, but meanwhile a man of the stature of Jung can take Christianity at modern Christians' false valuation of it, and, having fastened this modern view upon the Church from the very beginning, loose a blasting criticism at the Church for thinking of Jesus as too benevolent. The period of the late Middle Ages alone is enough to provide a complete refutation of Jung's assertion that the Church has consistently emphasized the 'goodness' of God as opposed to His wrath, and insisted upon love without any mention of 'the fear of the Lord', and one need only read an 'enlightened' criticism of Christianity to learn that in that period the Church ruled the masses of Europe by the fear of judgement and of the fires of Hell. However exaggerated some of these criticisms may be there is sufficient evidence to show that they are founded upon fact and that the mind of Christendom at that time was very largely concerned with the danger which God presented to man, and the need to guard against His righteous wrath. It would be hard, indeed, to find any age before the present when the picture of Jesus as the stern judge of men was absent from the teaching of the Church, and it has already been shown that it was not absent from the teaching of Jesus Himself.

(ii) The doctrine of evil as the 'privation of good' has given rise to a controversy of some importance between Jung and his Christian admirers, and it cannot be discussed at length here. There is, however, very good reason to suppose that Jung does not do justice to the Christian doctrine. He seems to suppose that to insist that evil does not, in some sense, exist as a 'thing' in its own right is to suggest that it has no place in the fulfilment of man and creation; that is, he argues that this doctrine requires us to deny that evil has any place in the pleroma of God, and hence in the goal to which we move. No doubt many Christians do understand the doctrine to mean this, but if one turns to St Augustine one finds that he understood it very differently: 'As a picture', he says, 'wherein a black colouring occurs in its proper place, so is the universe beautiful, if any could survey it, notwithstanding the presence of sinners, although, taken by themselves, their proper deformity makes them hideous' (*City of God*, xi : 23, quoted *Confessions*, 73 n.). The point of the doctrine is that one should be able to accept the reality of evil without having to regard it as rooted in some power eternally opposed to God, and St Augustine's comment is, in effect, taken up by the Lady Julian, when she says 'In heaven, sin is turned to worship', and both would seem to be saying exactly what Jung says when he writes: 'The inner voice brings the evil before us in a very tempting and convincing way in order to make us succumb. If we do not partially succumb, nothing of this apparent evil enters into us, and no regeneration or healing can take place. (I say "apparent", though this may sound too optimistic.) If we succumb completely then the contents expressed by the inner voice act as so many devils, and a catastrophe ensues. But if we can succumb only in part, and if by self-assertion the ego can save itself from being completely swallowed, then it can assimilate the voice, and we realize that the evil was, after all, only a semblance of evil, but in reality a bringer of healing and illumination' (*Development*, 319). As already noticed in connection with 'darkness' there are two senses of 'evil': that which we call 'evil' appears evil to us because we mistake its nature and function, but when we rightly regard it, then it is seen to be no longer 'evil'; but, at the same time, the appearance of evil is not mere appearance (in the sense of seeming to be, but not being effectively evil) but can act as 'so many devils' and work havoc in a man—this, it would seem, is the teaching of the Church, and also the teaching of Jung.

(e) Jung's complaints about the goodness of the New Testament figure of Jesus have been answered exclusively from the Gospel record. It is clear that they could have been answered by appealing to the Apocalypse, but Jung has tried to forestall such an answer by dividing the Apocalypse from the rest of the New Testament, and implying that the Christ of the Apocalypse is a second figure 'compensatory' to the Jesus of the Gospels. Jung tells us that the Jesus of the Gospels is marked by love of mankind, but of the 'Christ' of the Apocalypse he writes, 'Out of his mouth goes a "sharp two-edged sword", which would seem more suitable for fighting and the shedding of blood than for the demonstration of brotherly love' (*Job*, 699), and 'This apocalyptic "Christ" behaves rather like a bad-tempered, power-conscious "boss" who very much resembles the "shadow" of a love-preaching bishop' (ibid., 706).

This distinction between two 'Christs' depends upon Jung's assumption that he has correctly characterized the Christ of the Gospels, and when that assumption has been shown to be mistaken it can no longer be maintained with any force. It may be further pointed out, however, that the two-edged sword of the Apocalypse is no more than a pictorial commentary on the evangelical claim, 'I come not to bring peace, but a sword'; that so far from promising 'brotherly love'

Jesus, in the Gospels, declared that as a result of His coming, 'They shall be divided, father against son, and son against father, mother against daughter, and daughter against her mother'; and that the threats and terrors let loose against evil-doers in the Apocalypse only develop Jesus' prophecies of the last days as we have them in the Gospels. The parallels in content between Gospels and Apocalypse destroy Jung's distinction, but even if they did not that distinction would still be difficult to maintain. It is certainly fair to claim, as Jung does, that the visions of the Apocalypse 'rose' out of the author's unconscious, but this does not explain the fact that not only the author but also his contemporaries accepted the picture of Christ in the Apocalypse as a true picture of Him to whom the Gospels bore witness, and that they did this consciously. There was no *a priori* certainty that because the Apocalypse was written it would be included in the Sacred Writings of the Church, and it came to be included partly because the Church believed that it was a valuable contribution to her understanding of the character of her Lord. No doubt many Christians today may wish that the Apocalypse had no place in the New Testament, but it has, and when the Church points to Jesus it is to the New Testament, Apocalypse as well as Gospels, to which she directs men, and the Jesus of the Church is One who included in His person all those aspects which are found in the figure of Christ in the Apocalypse.

To conclude this rejection of Jung's account of the Jesus in whom Christians are asked to put their faith two remarkable statements may be noticed, which reveal how curiously Jung proceeds. He has noted that Yahweh was 'dark' as well as 'light'; 'wrathful' as well as 'loving'; and the Church has always believed that Jesus' anger expressed the wrath of God: but this would not fit with Jung's preconceived notions, and so he writes, 'Besides his love of mankind a certain irascibility is noticeable in Christ's character, and, as is often the case with people of emotional temperament, a manifest lack of self-reflection' (ibid., 647). In other words, when he is confronted with characteristics which might show that Jesus incarnates both 'sides' of the deity Jung has no scruples about finding some other explanation for them. Similarly Jung's 'The sixth petition [sc. of the Lord's prayer] indeed allows a deep insight, for in face of this fact Christ's immense certainty with regard to his father's character becomes some-what questionable' (ibid., 652), only has any force because Jung has already decided for himself in what 'Christ's immense certainty with

regard to his father's character' consists—and he has done so in the
face of such assurances as that God is like the Lord of a vineyard
who, when his authority has been set at naught, 'will come, and
miserably destroy those miserable men'. Jung's complaint that Jesus
is too good to be 'the fulness of the Godhead, bodily' cannot be
supported: in other words, there is no evidence that the figure of
Jesus in the New Testament conforms to that of the magician in the
collective unconscious, and the more positive side of this discussion,
that the Jesus to whom the Church points us conforms to the image of
the Self, must wait until chapter 11. In the preceding chapter certain
consequences of projecting the magician into the idea of God have been
noted, and in the next two sections of this chapter it will be shown that
Christianity does not involve such consequences, which is a further
reason for thinking that Jung is mistaken about the nature of Jesus.

The Effects of Penitence

In his account of projecting the magician which was cited in the
last chapter, Jung says that if one should 'concretize [the magician]
as an extra-mundane "Father in Heaven"', then 'the logical result is
that the only thing left behind here is a miserable, inferior, worthless,
and sinful little heap of humanity', and this, he says, 'has become a
world view'. Whatever Jung means by this last statement, the view
to which he refers is certainly not the Christian view. Penitence, as
has been shown, does result in the admission that one is sinful in all
one's being, but it does not result in the belief that one is worthless,
and the orthodox Christian doctrine of man excludes this result in
two ways. First, the teaching of the Church is that the sinner is a
man who is 'damaged' but not wholly perverted, and that the 'image
of God' in man has been 'marred' but not destroyed, and this
insistence that man, however sinful, retains the essential nature with
which God created him implies that man, however sinful, retains
value in the sight of God. Second, the Good News of Christianity is
that it was for the sake of sinners that God became man, and that Jesus
died upon the cross, and the Church has always rightly insisted that
it is blasphemy to suppose that man, for whom God was prepared to
do so much, can be worthless. Penitence should lead the Christian to
see that of himself he can do nothing, but not to suppose that there is
nothing that can be done with him. If Jung is right, and the projection
of the magician into the idea of God does result in leaving man 'a

miserable, inferior, worthless, and sinful little heap of humanity', then it follows that the Christian idea of God is not one that could have been formed in this way.

The Devil

The same is to be said of Jung's further assertion that having concretized the magician as an extra-mundane Father in Heaven one is 'placed in the unfortunate position of having to discover a devil of equal weight and dimensions who could act as a psychological counter-balance to [one's] *summum bonum*'. The idea that Christianity is fundamentally dualist at heart is very popular with some of its critics, so that Alan Watts, for example, says, in what purports to be an authoritative account of Christian myth, that the conflict between 'good' and 'evil' in man is 'reflected in the irreconcilable war between God and Satan' (*Watts*, 78), and this is a complete travesty of the Christian ideal of the devil. While it is true that Origen was condemned for saying that the devil would finally be saved his error was not that his attitude to the devil was too sympathetic, but that by saying that he *certainly* would be saved he denied him free will to choose to continue to oppose God. According to the Church the 'war' between God and Satan is only 'irreconcilable' so long as Satan will not be reconciled, and this is implicit in the orthodox doctrine that the devil is a fallen creature, which means that he, like men, has no power of his own, but derives his existence from God. The devil is not 'the power of evil' but one who uses the power which God has given him for evil. Moreover, the devil does not do the evil which men do when they listen to his whisper, but he is only the 'tempter' whose work is to suggest to men that they should sin, and in this the devil is not the antithesis of Christ, for whereas when a man gives himself to Christ Christ works powerfully in and through him; when a man gives himself to the devil he continues to order his own life, albeit in accordance with the devil's suggestions. Nor can the devil's claim to be able to give to Jesus authority over the kingdoms of the world be set against this, for not only is the devil 'a liar from the beginning' but the point in the temptation lies in the fact that he was speaking to the incarnate Word, by whom all things were made. The offer of the kingdoms could be made to Jesus, and to no other man, because Jesus *is* Lord of the kingdoms of the world, and the choice before Jesus was whether He would, as the devil suggested, take only to Himself the authority which was His, or whether He would lay that authority at the feet of His Father in eternal self-oblation. The devil has no true power of his own; all that he has he has from God; and if he is not, in the end, redeemed it may be doubted whether God's will that He should be 'all in all' will have been done.

Christianity has not found itself forced to 'discover' a devil of equal weight and dimensions with God, and this is another indication that the Christian idea of God does not conform to the image of the magician in the unconscious.

The first criticism which might be levelled against Christianity, that the Christian idea of God is unsatisfactory because it conforms to the image of the magician, does not apply and it will now be shown that the second criticism, that the idea of an external God inevitably means that the 'religious function' remains 'outside' man, does not apply either.

Transcendence

The Church teaches belief in a God who is both 'transcendent' and 'immanent', but in speaking of God as 'immanent' Christians do *not* mean that He is in any way a part of the human soul, however much they think of Him as active *in* it. This means that the psychological criticism of belief in a God 'external' to man (on the grounds that such a belief leads to an 'outward' form of religion) is not turned by simply pointing to the idea of immanence. The criticism can be pressed by saying, on the one hand, that so long as God is thought of as transcendent as well as immanent the emphasis on His 'wholly-other-ness' prevents belief in His immanence from 'bringing the religious function within the soul', or, on the other hand, that even if this is not so the insistence upon the distinction between God and the soul so impairs the idea of His immanence that the idea loses all practical value. To answer criticisms along these lines without rejecting Jung's psychological findings two things have to be shown: first, it must be shown that on Jung's own principles there is no necessary contradiction between the idea of a transcendent God, and, at the same time, an 'inward' religion: secondly, it must be shown that the Christian doctrine of immanence is effectively equivalent to Jung's teaching about the place of the 'image of God' in the soul. The first will be shown in this section, the second in the next.

When Jung says that 'So long as religion is only faith and outward

form . . . nothing of any importance has happened' (*Alchemy*, 13),
the juxtaposition of 'faith' with 'outward form' strikes strangely on
Christian ears, and in order to give the assertion any meaning it is
necessary to supply the suppressed premise, that faith or belief in a
God thought of as existing apart from man inevitably leads to an
'outward form of religion', wholly concerned with a man's external
relations with God. If this is true then it would have to be admitted
that the Christian insistence upon the objective existence of God leads
to legalism, and that the tendency towards legalism (which certainly
exists) in Christianity is not only inevitable, but a direct result of the
Christian idea of God. Christians can hardly be expected to accept
this, because not only has the Church, in her teaching, found no
difficulty in maintaining both the 'inwardness' of religion and the
objectivity of God, but many Christians have managed to combine
in their living a deep and inward religion with faith in an external God.
The Christian knows that these two things are not incompatible, and
it follows that Jung is wrong when he implies that they are, and the
only question which remains is whether the incompatibility of these
ideas follows from Jung's system as a whole, or not. If it does, then
Christians must reject his system, but since it can be shown that in
making the assumption that faith in an objective God must lead to
mere 'outwardness' Jung goes beyond anything which can rightly be
deduced from his psychological conclusions it is possible for Christians
to take Analytical Psychology seriously.

Jung's argument is well presented in the following passage: 'In
an outward form of religion where all the emphasis is on the outward
figure, the archetype is identical with externalized ideas but remains
unconscious as a psychic factor. When an unconscious content is
replaced by a projected image to that extent, it is cut off from all
participation in and influence on the conscious mind. Hence it largely
forfeits its own life, because prevented from exerting the formative
influence on consciousness natural to it' (*Alchemy*, 12). This is to say,
first, that there are in the psyche certain powers and tendencies which
can have a determinative effect upon a man's life when they are
consciously acknowledged as human potentialities; second, that so
long as these powers and tendencies are unknown to consciousness
they are in a state equivalent to that of repressed elements, and that
they therefore tend to manifest themselves in the ways appropriate
to such elements, one of which is projection; third, that when the

central powers of the psyche are unacknowledged they manifest themselves as the 'God-image', and one form of their manifestation is
projection into the idea of an objective God; fourth, that this projection of the God-image has the desirable result that a man becomes aware
of the existence of these powers, but, at the same time, the undesirable
result that he thinks that they exist 'over there', and not within himself; and fifth, so long as the God-image remains projected the
determinative powers within a man remain ineffective, so that it is
essential for true 'inward' religion that the projection should be
withdrawn.

The parallel between this account and the transference phenomenon
in analysis is clear enough. The implications for religion are that if a
religion is to be effective it must ensure that belief in the transcendence
of God gives way to some form of belief in His immanence: in other
words, although belief in the existence of God as an externally existing
Being has great value, in that it brings to a man's notice the archetype
of Deity, it is only a stage in the development of consciousness, and
it must be followed by the understanding that the archetype is not
'outside' but 'inside' the human psyche so that transcendence and
immanence (in this sense) are not to be regarded as two complementary
ideas about God as they are by Christians, but as ideas which must be
held successively. According to this theory if a man is forced (e.g.
by the Church) to retain his belief in the transcendence of God he will
be unable to proceed to the more important knowledge that God is
'within him'. This argument sounds consistent enough, but the
conclusion is erroneous because it is based upon a mistaken application
of the analogy which the transference provides.

When a patient projects the God-image upon the analyst he not
only 'externalizes the archetype' but, at the same time, he falsifies
the object, because the analyst is a man and to ascribe divine attributes
to him is to see him as other than he is. It follows that when the
projection is withdrawn and the patient acknowledges the archetype
as 'his', he must also admit that its characteristics are not applicable to
the analyst. This situation, in which the God-image is projected on the
analyst, however, is not the true analogy of the religious belief in an
external God, and the analogy to this is the projection upon the analyst
of psyche elements proportionate to a man, such as the projection of
pugnacious instincts mentioned in the last chapter. In such a case the
patient must, for the sake of his own psychic development, come to

understand what he has done, and that the pugnacious instincts 'belong' to him, and, for the sake of his development, it does not matter whether they also 'belong' to the analyst or not, but, as it was said, if the patient is a statistician interested in the incidence of pugnacity among analysts then, from this point of view, he must take into account the fact that his projection of pugnacious instincts upon the analyst may have been 'hung' on the most appropriate 'hook' possible—a pugnacious analyst; that is, according to the other account of projection as a 'category mistake', it may be that in differentiating the elements in the situation the patient should properly ascribe pugnacity both to subject and object, and to acknowledge this need not prevent him from becoming aware of his own pugnacious instincts at the same time. If it happens that projection does not falsify the object, as it was shown in the last chapter that it may not, then there is no necessary reason why the projected elements cannot be acknowledged as being 'within' the subject, and at the same time also ascribed to the object, and when this possibility is taken into account the religious ideas about God take on another aspect.

Let it be supposed that there is no more to be said about the 'archetype of Deity' than that it is an image, which is, somehow, representative of certain powers and tendencies in the human psyche, and let it be also supposed that for a man's own development all that is necessary if he is to reach the goal of his life is that he should acknowledge that this image does represent such powers, and that he should be ready to let them influence his life. It would then be true that the essential step required of him was that he should recognize his idea of God as a projection of the inward archetype, and so recognize the inwardness of that archetype, but this would not mean that the projection of the archetype necessarily resulted in falsehood, and if the man were concerned with the nature of the Universe as a whole then it might well be that the projection of the archetype of Deity was a means of gaining true insights about the objective world. A word about this possibility is added in the last section of this chapter, but all that needs to be established in answer to the criticism that belief in an objectively existing God necessarily prohibits acceptance of the archetype of Deity as an 'inward function' is that it is not a proper conclusion to draw from Jung's theory of projection: if there is an externally existing God who conforms to the archetype in man, then His attributes may belong both to Him and to the unconscious image.

Immanence

By immanence, in this connection, is to be understood the direct activity of God upon the soul of man in general, and the activity of Christ within the believing Christian in particular. In the last section it was shown that there is no necessary contradiction between belief in an objectively existing God, on the one hand, and the acknowledgement of the 'archetype of Deity' as a force within the psyche, on the other. In that section, however, the question of the relation between the idea of an objectively existing God and the archetype (apart from the ostensible similarity between the characteristics ascribed to God and to the inward image) was not raised, and it has still to be asked whether the Christian belief that the effects which Jung is content to ascribe to the archetype are due to the activity of an externally existing God provides a further opportunity for criticizing the teaching of the Church. In other words, it is now to be shown that the effectiveness of Christ within man is not vitiated, from the point of view of Jung's psychology, by the Christian insistence that He is other than the man in whom he dwells. Jung (in apparent contradiction to his account of Jesus in *Answer to Job*) recognizes the similarities between the Christian belief in Christ and his own concept of the Self: 'For psychology', he says, 'the religious figures point to the self, whereas for theology the self points to its—theology's—own central figure. In other words, theology might possibly take the psychological self as an allegory of Christ' (*Alchemy*, 21). There are two reasons why it might be thought that a Christ supposed to be distinct from the man in whom he dwells would not have the effectiveness of the Self thought of as an archetype in the unconscious; the first arises from a verbal confusion; the second depends upon an assumption which might be made, but which cannot be justified from empirical psychology—and which, moreover, is one which Jung either does not make, or else one which he made but contradicts in later works.

The verbal confusion depends upon the difference between theological and psychological language, and it arises when one tries to take a theological statement as though it were psychological, and a psychological statement as though it were theological. Thus the Christian says that Christ in man remains other than man even though he is an effective power in a man's life, and if such a statement is taken psychologically it is self-contradictory because in psychology 'to be effective in a man's life' is synonymous with 'to be in a man's psyche'.

The reason for this is that since the human psyche is the subject matter of psychology the psychologist cannot take cognizance of the source of those powers which he finds active within the psyche, and he can only distinguish between that which is part of the psyche, and effective, and that which is other than the psyche and not effective. On the other hand, when Jung's comment that the God image coincides 'with a special content of [the unconscious], namely the archetype of the Self' (*Job*, 757) is taken theologically it seems to mean that the God image is part of a man, whereas all that it means, psychologically, is that the effects of the 'God-image' are best organized by the concept of 'the Self'. Jung does not, and does not wish to claim that he knows the ultimate source of the effects which he refers to 'the Self' and to attempt to seek for such a source would be to trespass beyond the limits of psychology. In other words both Christians and Jung claim that there are effective powers acting within man which appear to spring from a 'centre' within the man, but Christians claim that this 'centre' also has an existence of its own apart from its effectiveness in the life of men, whereas Jung expresses no opinion about what it is in itself. The only disagreement that can arise comes from Jung's implicit assumption that no knowledge of what this centre is in itself is possible to anyone, but this raises questions about the truth of Christianity which lies beyond the scope of this essay.

The second reason why it might seem that a Christ distinct from the man in whom He dwells cannot be effective in the same way as 'the Self' is that it is easy to suppose that 'the Self' is destined to become fully conscious in men, whereas by saying the Christ is other than the man in whom He dwells one denies that a man can ever know himself as Christ. But the assumption involved which, if it is made, means a serious divergence between Analytic Psychology and Christianity, is that everything properly called 'part of the psyche', or a 'content of the psyche' will ultimately become fully conscious in man and form part of a conscious synthesis, and this assumption is unjustified. Jung seems to imply this when he speaks of the 'goal of higher consciousness' to which mankind, as a whole, should press forward, for he seems to have in mind a state in which all the unconscious shall have 'poured itself' into consciousness, and this same idea is suggested by his description of Individuation as 'The production and unfolding of the original and potential wholeness' (*Essays*,

10—J.S.P.

186), and if this idea is inherent in Jung's system, then what he say of the God-image could not be applied (by Christians) to Christ because the Christian insistence that Christ is other than the men in' whom He dwells is the insistence that the power which He exerts within men can never come under man's own conscious direction. But although there is certainly nothing to prevent anyone making this assumption about the psyche it can be no more than a psychological hypothesis, and Jung does not make it in his later works. The psychologist may observe that in the process of the development of consciousness, both in individuals and in the human race, new psychic elements become conscious from time to time, and he may detect adumbrations, in dreams, fantasies, projections, and 'odd' things generally, of such elements before they actually become conscious; and from observations of this kind he may justly formulate an account such as that which Jung gives of the development of consciousness 'out of' the unconscious, but this account does no more than define terms with which to talk about what has been observed. A psychic element is said to be 'unconscious' when adumbrations of it occur, although it is not itself present to consciousness, and it may be equally said to be 'potential', so that observations of what has happened in the past permit the assertion that 'unconscious elements have frequently become conscious', and the formulation of a working principle that 'unconscious elements strive to become conscious', or in other words that 'when an element is adumbrated it is likely that, under favourable conditions, it will sooner or later become conscious', and while this is unexceptionable as a general working hypothesis it does not justify the dogmatic assertion that everything unconscious must eventually become conscious, because it cannot be shown that this is the invariable meaning of adumbrations. There is, in fact, some reason to think that the adumbrations of the Self, at least, do not have this meaning, because Jung claims to have evidence of manifestation of the Self from Paleolithic times (*Secret*, 105), and this suggests that its adumbrations are not followed by its inclusion within consciousness; that is, that it is 'unconscious' in a different sense from that in which, say, the ability to communicate by sounds was once 'unconscious'; and Jung himself appears to take some such view.

In his later works, so far from claiming that the unconscious must eventually become fully manifest in consciousness, Jung says, for example, 'consciousness, no matter how extensive it may be, must always remain the smaller circle within the greater circle of the unconscious, an island surrounded by the sea' (*Practice*, 366), and, of the images of the Self, '[They] are naturally only anticipations of a wholeness which is, in principle, always just beyond our reach' (ibid., 536). Again, he says, 'The goal is only important as an idea; the essential thing is the *opus* which leads to the goal: *that* is the goal of a lifetime' (ibid., 400), and the conclusion of *Answer to Job* seems unequivocal: 'That is to say, even the enlightened person remains what he is, and is never more than his own limited ego before the One who dwells within him, whose form has no knowable boundaries, who encompasses him on all sides, fathomless as the abysms of the earth and vast as the sky'.

With the two sources of misunderstanding cleared out of the way, it is now possible to indicate the close resemblances between what Jung says of the archetype of Deity within the psyche, and what Christians say of God dwelling in man:

(*a*) Jung is at pains to insist upon the 'reality' of the God-image, but by 'reality' he means 'psychic reality', which does not imply objective existence but effective influence upon human life, and this sense of real can be illustrated by the two following quotations: '[We are] to take [the contents of the irrational function] not as concrete realities—that would be a regression—but as psychic realities, real because they *work*' (*Essays*, 151); 'Presumably the psyche does not trouble itself about our categories of reality; for it, everything that *works* is real' (*Practice*, 111). Of the God-image itself he says, 'Should any of my readers feel tempted to add an apologetic "only" to the God-images as we perceive them, he would immediately fall foul of experience, which demonstrates beyond any shadow of doubt the extraordinary numinosity of these images' (*Job*, 558). In effect, the existence of psychological 'things' lies entirely in their psychic effect: if they are 'psychically effective' they 'exist', if not they do not 'exist'.

The Christian does not think of Christ from the same point of view, and the 'reality' of Christ for him is bound up with the question of His objective existence, but this does not prohibit the Christian from believing that Christ (and God) is also 'real' in Jung's sense, and the attribution of 'reality' of this sort to God is implicit in belief in a 'living God', 'with whom we have to do' not only in our outward behaviour, but also in the innermost recesses of our souls. To say that the God who exists (objectively) is such a God as this is to say that

He 'exists' in Jung's sense as well: that is, it is to say that he may manifest Himself to men in dreams and fantasies and visions and by the inward word of revelation, as well as by outward signs. The Christian says of God all that Jung says of the God-image, but this is only (*pace* Jung) a part of what the Christian has to say about Him.

(*b*) Jung says that the real effectiveness of the God-image depends upon conscious acknowledgement that it exists as a force within the psyche: in other words, so long as it is not consciously acknowledged it only manifests itself in 'odd' things of one kind or another, but when it is acknowledged it begins to have a determining influence (for good) on a man's life. It is to be noticed that this is not so much a characteristic of the God-image, as a definition of it, since it encompasses all that can be known of the God-image, in that 'unconscious' things can only be known in so far as they influence consciousness. In precisely the same way the Christian believes that God only takes charge of a man's life when the man permits Him to do so. God may reveal Himself at any time and in any way to individual men, but if they choose to overlook or reject His manifestations of Himself He never becomes truly effective in their lives; at least they miss the best, at worst God's wrath is manifested in them, perverting their conscious purposes in the same way as the odd things which are said to manifest the archetypes. Again, the manifestations of Himself which God chooses to make, and the influence which He exerts when a man permits Him to 'take charge' encompass all that a man may know of God by looking into his own soul, although the Christian will not say that this is the only way in which God may be known. The evidence all goes to suggest that in speaking of the manifestations of the God-image Jung is speaking of things of the same kind that the Christian speaks of when he talks about the influence of God within him.

(*c*) Jung says that the God-image is an 'archetype of the collective unconscious', and by this he means that its manifestations can be detected in the lives of men and women of all times and in all places and that it is not something which occurs in a few individuals who have special characteristics, but something which is common to men as men. The image is recognizably the same in its manifestations in the thought and behaviour of different people, although it also takes special forms appropriate to the individual in whom it is manifested at any time. Similarly it is one of the most important implications of the Christian belief that God is an 'objective Being', that He is One wherever and however He manifests Himself. This belief has as its corollary the further belief that God is 'there' for every man to meet, and that a man does not have to be specially privileged to encounter God, but at the same time the Christian believes that God treats each man as an individual, and that in His encounter with God every man finds that which is appropriate to his own particular circumstances.

(d) Finally, so far from claiming that the archetype 'belongs' to the man in whose life it is manifested, Jung categorically asserts that it does not. Of the unconscious in general he says that a man is 'to separate himself from [it] by . . . putting it clearly before him as *that which he is not*' (*Essays*, 112), and although of many unconscious elements it may be said that they are what the man may become, he says of the God-images 'the archetypes in question are not mere objects of the mind, but are also autonomous factors, i.e. living subjects', and he continues 'the differentiation of consciousness can be understood [he does not say that it is] as the effect of the intervention of transcendentally conditioned dynamisms' (*Job*, 758). So long as Jung says no more than this his psychology affords no grounds for criticizing the Christian's belief that Christ who dwells in him is other than he, living and reigning with the Father and the Spirit, One God for all eternity—and it is hard to see how, on psychological grounds alone, more than this could be said.

A religion may be criticized if it throws exclusive emphasis on God as an 'outward figure', which can have no direct contact with, or influence on, the human soul, but however much Christianity emphasizes the 'otherness' of God it gives equal weight to His indwelling in man, especially in connection with the Justified sinner in whom Christ chooses to dwell, and it has been shown that (so far as Jung's psychology is concerned) there is no incompatibility between these two beliefs about God, and there is no reason to think that insistence upon the existence of Christ apart from man would be likely to detract from any influence that He might have upon a man's life.

Faith and the Opposites

Possible objections to Christian faith which might be based upon Jung's psychology have now been answered, and it is possible to consider the place of faith in the development of the Christian life. In chapter 7 it was shown how penitence leads to a union of the two sides of natural man's character by bringing him to see that they are both sinful, and in chapter 8 it was mentioned that this appears to result in a great gulf between sinful man and the holy Christ: it has now to be shown that this gulf is bridged by faith, so that the opposites, man and Christ, are also united.

In conjunction with penitence the acceptance of a particular idea of God, considered as an objectively existing Being, gives rise to a new opposition between the sinner and God. This opposition is often thought of in such a way that it merely repeats the original opposition in man, and when it is thought of in this way the psychological account that the man has 'projected' his 'good will' into the idea of God is appropriate to the situation. If a man contrasts himself and God in this way, then all the evil consequences of 'projecting the magician', against which Jung warns us, necessarily follow. Religious language alone, however, is sufficient indication that this is not the way in which the opposition between man and God should be conceived, for whereas the opposition within natural man is to be thought of in terms of the 'moral' opposites, 'good—evil', the opposition between God and man is properly described by the 'religious' opposites 'holy—sinful', and the opposites of good and evil (as men judge) are both on the human side. Sinful man falsely understands the opposition between himself and God, for it seems to him that there can be no union between the two sides, and that he is in a state of 'enmity against God', which can only be brought to an end by his own achievement of a righteousness which will justify him in standing upright before his Creator. Christianity teaches that this is a false seeming, and that it is a man's very sinfulness which makes him suppose that he is unacceptable to God. The Christian knows, by faith, that the Holy God loves sinful man, that He loves him to the extent of acting upon his behalf, and that when a man will accept Him God enters within his life, thereby uniting what appeared to sinful man to be irreconcilable opposites. Thus faith is the mark of the union which has been forged between the supreme opposites sinful man and the Holy God, by the work of Jesus.

This brings out, from another point of view, the difference between the two 'ways of salvation' which has already been mentioned. In the psychological way the new centre does not 'take charge' of a man's life until the opposition between consciousness and the unconscious has ceased, or, more accurately, the 'arrival' of the Self as an active and determinative power in a man's life is the cessation of the opposition, and if 'war' should again break out between the opposites the Self would cease to exist as a determining force. In the Christian way, on the other hand, the 'new centre' is present in the Justified sinner, even though the opposition between 'good will' and 'evil inclinations' continues, and it is as a result of the presence of Christ (despite the 'war' within a man) that the reconciliation of the opposites in his nature may be brought about. Jung, it may be said, could attach no meaning to the idea of 'integrated people, in whom consciousness and the unconscious are still antagonistic to each other', which would appear to be the psychological formula corresponding to 'Justified sinners' in Christian theology.

God as External

This section is more an appendix than anything else, because it goes beyond the limits of this study. By calling upon psychology for help one is committed to consider only those aspects of religion which are concerned with those elements in human life which are the proper subject of psychology, and the truth or falsehood of a belief about objects (as opposed to reasons for and against believing it) is not the concern of psychology. Nevertheless, having had to consider the relation of the belief in the 'objective existence' of God to certain inward processes, and since this belief is an essential part of the Christian faith, it is as well to add a brief note upon what it means.

When the idea of God (as the Christian understands it) is replaced by the idea of the God-image religion does not lose in importance, as Jung is at pains to show, but it loses very considerably in extent. The God-image is known only through the human mind, and its 'manifestations' in human thought and behaviour, so that, as Jung says 'the behaviour of the archetypes cannot be investigated at all without the interaction of the observing consciousness' (*Job*, 758) and, as he also says, if this is so 'religious statements without exception have to do with the reality of the *psyche* and not with the reality of *physis*' (ibid., 752). Christianity, however, is not to be confined within such arbitrary limits, and a God who is not concerned with tables and chairs and the lilies in the field is not the God of Christians, and belief in the existence of God as a self-sufficing Being is essential if one is to think of God as the God of the whole world, and not the God of the human soul alone. Jung is careful not to make any assertions, either positively or negatively, about the possibility that the God-image in the psyche may be the image of someone or something who or which is not in the psyche, but admirable as this is in a psychologist it will not do for the theologian.

Jung himself has been driven to consider the relation of archetypes to what goes on in the physical world, and the following assertion raises considerations of particular interest: 'It is perfectly possible, psychologically, for the unconscious or an archetype to take complete possession of a man and to determine his fate down to the smallest detail. At the same time objective, non-psychic parallel phenomena can occur which also represent the archetype. It not only seems so, it simply is so, that the archetype fulfils itself not only psychically in the individual, but objectively outside the individual. My own conjecture is that Christ was such a personality' (*Job*, 648). In other words, Jung has concluded that his concept of archetypes may be employed beyond the range of the psyche, to order and relate events occurring in the world, and the previous discussion of projection enables us to make two comments upon this:

(1) If, as Jung has said in the past, the archetypes have value as means of enabling us to understand the external world, so that by projecting the archetypes we may derive true knowledge of that which is outside us, then we should expect to find non-psychic phenomena which represent one or another archetype, and this leads to the suggestion that the God-image which Jung also calls 'the archetype of unity', is the appropriate archetype for comprehending the universe as a whole.

(2) At the same time, it is very doubtful whether it can be said, as Jung implies it can, that the concept of an archetype is properly used to order physical events, because the archetype is defined in strictly psychological terms. Yet Jung is surely right when he says, 'The given constitution of the organism, therefore, is on the one hand a product of outer conditions, while on the other it is inherently determined by the nature of living matter. Accordingly the primordial image [sc. 'archetype'] is just as undoubtedly related to certain manifest, ever-renewing and therefore constantly effective Nature-processes as it is to certain inner determinants of the mental life and to life in general' (*Types*, 557); which is to say that the images which represent archetypes are derived from our experience of external objects. Whatever is said, however, the function of the concept of archetypes is expressly bound up with the study of the psyche, and if it is to be related to the

physical world its relation to it must be indirect. This suggests how the idea of God may be employed in a way in which that of the God-image cannot.

If we seek ultimate categories for the comprehension of the physical world we shall not turn to psychology, but to physics. We have seen how psychology may bring us to regulative terms, which, from the point of view of psychology, are indefinable, and we have seen that the most important of these terms, the 'God-image', has brought Jung over the border of psychology into that of religion. Along the psychologist's line of thought, however, there is no need to go beyond this term, and to do so is, in fact, impossible, and all that can be said is that from the point of view of psychology 'the God-image' will do everything that 'God' could do. In other words, so long as it is only a question of psychology the religious idea is no more use than the psychological concept. But suppose that the same thing could be said of physics; suppose, for example (and this is not intended as more than a wholly suppositious example), the only way of accounting for the actual 'choice' made by an electron was to say that it moved 'according to the will of God'; then it would be for the theologian to show, if he could, that the idea of God standing 'behind' the physical concepts was the same idea as that standing 'behind' the psychological concepts, and in this way to reinstate theology as regulative in a new sense of the other sciences.

10

THE SELF

WHEN a man is penitent Christ, or the Spirit, can enter his life; the man cannot conjure Christ to him, but must wait for the 'free gift' of God: when a man accepts the unconscious the Self can rule his life; the man cannot induce the activity of the Self, but must wait for it to 'happen'. Jung's concept of the Self is examined in this chapter, and in the next the conclusions are applied to the Christian teaching about Christ. A full account of the Self cannot be given in a single chapter, because the implications of this concept stretch throughout the whole of Jung's psychological system; nor can the many parallels between the Self and God be examined. After a short discussion of the nature of the concept of the Self two of the many aspects of this idea will be considered: the Self as the goal to which the Individuation process leads, and the Self as it represents itself in imaginative images. In this way it will be possible to show in what sense the Self 'unites the opposites', and what it means to say that it is, in itself, a 'union of opposites', and in the next chapter it will be shown that, in the same way, Christ unites the opposites and is Himself pictured as a union of opposites.

The Concept of the Self

The idea of the Self plays the part in Jung's psychological system which Kant ascribes to the idea of God with respect to 'pure reason'. Reason, according to Kant, 'Does not *form* conceptions of objects, it merely *arranges* them and gives to them that unity which they are capable of possessing when the sphere of their application has been extended as widely as possible' and it 'brings unity into the diversity of conceptions by means of ideas': such ideas of reason 'can never be employed as constitutive ideas', 'they cannot be conceptions of objects. . . . But they are capable of an admirable and indispensably necessary application to objects—as regulative ideas, directing the understanding to a certain aim, the guiding lines towards which all its laws follow, and in which they all meet in one point. This point—though a mere idea (*focus imaginarius*), that is, not a point from which the conceptions of the understanding do really proceed, for it lies beyond the sphere of possible experience—serves notwithstanding to give to these conceptions the greatest possible unity combined with the greatest possible extension' (*Kant*, 373, 4). So 'By admitting these ideal beings [sc. 'ideas of reason'], we do not really extend our cognitions beyond the objects of possible experience; we extend merely the empirical unity of our experience, by the aid of systematic unity, the scheme of which is furnished by the idea' (ibid., 390), and of the conception of God Kant says, 'Reason does not assure us of the objective validity of the conception; it merely gives us the idea of something, on which the supreme and necessary unity of all experience is based. This something we cannot, following the analogy of a real substance, cogitate otherwise than as the cause of all things operating in accordance with rational laws, if we regard it as an individual object; although we should rest contented with the idea alone as a regulative principle of reason, and make no attempt at completing the sum of the conditions imposed by thought' (ibid., loc. cit.).

According to Kant the idea of God is implicit in the possibility of a unified view of the Universe, and from this point of view God is a 'postulate'—a putative source of all things, in the existence of which we have no reason to believe, but the idea of which is necessary to thought if we wish to 'regulate' observable phenomena, and to bring them into relation with each other. At the same time, it should be remembered, Kant does believe in the existence of God (which 'pure reason' can only regard as a postulate) for reasons connected with 'practical reason', so that his insistence upon the status of the term 'God' as an idea alone does not prohibit the possibility of belief in the objective existence of God. In precisely the same way the Self is a concept implicit in the possibility of a unified view of psychic events, which it is necessary to postulate as the source of all such events if Jung's system is to have unity, and it may be noticed that one of Jung's expressions for the Self is 'the archetype of unity'. The Self is a concept which regulates observable psychic phenomena and brings them into relation with each other, and from this point of view we have no reason to believe in the existence of the Self as a 'thing' of any kind: but like Kant Jung clearly does believe that the Self 'exists' in some way. These two ideas, that of the Self as a concept, and that of the Self as an existing 'thing' ('Essence') are brought together in the following comment 'Intellectually the self is no more than a psychological concept, a construct that serves to express an unknowable essence which we cannot grasp as such, since by definition it transcends our powers of comprehension' (*Essays*, 399).

In accordance with the discussion in chapter 2 'the Self' is to be regarded, like Jung's other psychological terms, as a concept which enables us to talk about observable psychic phenomena, but which we are to think of as though it were the name of a 'thing', and which we are to use (grammatically) as we use proper names. This does not necessarily imply the rejection of Jung's view that 'the Self' also names an 'unknowable essence', but many will prefer to suspend judgement upon this opinion so long as nothing more can be said about this essence than that it is 'unknowable' and 'beyond comprehension'. It may also be remarked that the concept of the Self as it is used by Jung is subordinate to the idea of God as that is explained by Kant, because the idea of God 'regulates' all observable phenomena, whereas the concept of the Self is properly psychological, and should only be used to 'regulate' psychic phenomena. In other words, from this point of view we must say that the concept of the Self is one of many concepts 'regulated' by the idea of God, or, positing the existence of God, we should say that 'the Self' refers to the way that one aspect of God appears to us—that is to God in so far as He is the source and controller of the human mind.

Since the idea of the Self is implicit in the existence of Jung's psychology as a unified system it must be relevant, in one way or another, to any and every psychic phenomenon, or, to put the same thing in another way, the enquiry into any psychic happening must lead, if it is pressed far enough, to the concept of the Self. This means that the Self is not only to be thought of as the goal of Individuation but as something which is effective in a man's life at all times, and Jung does, in fact, ask us to think of it in this way. The Self, he tells us, is pre-existent, the source of the existence of the ego, the guiding principle which determines the development of the individual, as well as being that which appears to come into existence as a man proceeds towards Individuation; and in all these ways what Jung says of the Self is identical with what Christians say about God. But Jung also warns us that what he says of the Self is to be understood 'psychologically' and not 'metaphysically', and although we must speak of the Self as though it were a thing we must always remember that we only know the Self as a concept. Further discussion of these many aspects of the Self is not possible here, and in the next section the Self is considered as the goal of Individuation.

The Self as Goal

In Jung's system accepting the unconscious is the goal of conscious effort: it is all that a man can do by deliberate purpose, but it is only a transient goal, and if nothing more happens when a man has accepted the unconscious he cannot be said to be Individuated. Accepting the unconscious is like setting a mouse-trap; we set the trap to catch the mouse, but when we have set it we can do no more and it depends upon the mouse whether it is caught or not. Natural man suffers from a hidden antagonism between consciousness and the unconscious, and the man who accepts the unconscious does not reconcile the two sides of his nature but only brings the antagonism to light, and Jung emphasizes that the state of having accepted the unconscious is one of tension and struggle; for example: 'Nobody who finds himself on the road to wholeness can escape that characteristic suspension which is the meaning of crucifixion. For he will infallibly run into things which thwart and "cross" him: first, the thing he has no wish to be (the shadow); second, the thing he is not (the "other", the individual reality of the "You"); and third, his psychic non-ego (the collective unconscious)' (*Practice*, 470); 'The open conflict is unavoidable and painful' (*Alchemy*, 37); 'One is then confronted with an apparently irreconcilable conflict with which human reason cannot deal except by sham solutions or dubious compromises' (*Secret*, 86); '. . . the fundamental problem of the patient seemed insoluble to me [i.e. to the doctor as well as the patient] unless violence was done to the one or the other side of his nature' (ibid., 88). It is when the apparently irreconcilable conflict is manifest that the Self can 'appear' as the 'solution'.

The Self does not arise as the result of conscious effort. In the state of accepting the unconscious all effort to resolve the tensions between the opposing forces leads one astray, and all one can do is to endure the suffering which the tension brings in the hope that the solution will arise of itself. A word from the Chinese text of the *Secret of the Golden Flower* expresses what happens as well as anything which Jung says, 'But, when no idea arises, the right ideas come. That is the true idea. If things are quiet and one is quite firm, the release of Heaven suddenly moves' (*Secret*, 65). Jung says much the same in many more words: 'When I examined the way of development of those persons who, quietly, and as if unconsciously, grew beyond themselves, I saw that their fates had something in common. Whether arising from without or within, the new thing came to all those persons from a dark field of possibilities; they accepted it and developed further by means of it . . . in no case was it conjured into existence through purpose and conscious willing, but rather seemed to flow out of the stream of time' (ibid., 89). Again he says, 'I have often been asked, "and what do you *do* about it?" I do nothing; there is nothing I can do except wait, with a certain trust in God, until, out of a conflict born with patience and courage there emerges the solution destined—although I cannot foresee it—for that particular person' (*Alchemy*, 37): The Self, as has been said, simply 'happens', one cannot say why it should happen, and although it seems that it does not happen except to those who have already accepted the unconscious (or done something which is equivalent to this) it would be unsafe to be dogmatic even to this extent.

The Self comes to 'take charge'. It is as though a new 'controlling centre' had come into a man's personality, and Jung attempts to indicate (one cannot describe or define it) what this means. 'Sensing the self as something irrational', he says, 'as an indefinable existent, to which the ego is neither opposed nor subjected, but merely attached, and about which it revolves very much as the earth revolves round the sun—thus we come to the goal of individuation'. He continues, 'I use the word "sensing" in order to indicate the apperceptive character of the relation between ego and self. In this relation nothing is knowable, because we can say nothing about the contents of the self. The ego is the only content of the self that we do know. The individuated ego senses itself as the object of an unknown and superordinate subject' (*Essays*, 405; strictly it is the man, not the ego, who is 'individuated'). Speaking of a 'spiritual body' mentioned in the Chinese text Jung says: 'This body is a symbol for a remarkable psychological fact, which, because it is objective, appears at first projected or expressed in forms furnished by the experiences of organic life, that is, as fruit, embryo, child, living body, etc. This fact could best be expressed in the words: It is not I who live, it lives me. The illusion as to the superior powers of the conscious leads to the belief: I live. If, by the recognition of the unconscious, this illusion is shattered, the unconscious appears as something objective of which the ego is a part' (*Secret*, 131, 2): at the end of *Two Essays* he says: 'Thus the dissolution of the mana-personality through conscious assimilation of its contents leads us, by a natural route, back to ourselves as an actual, living something, poised between two world-pictures and their darkly discerned potencies. This "something" is strange to us and yet so near, wholly ourselves and yet unknowable, a virtual centre . . . I have called this centre the *self*' (*Essays*, 398, 9), and he also says, 'The self is not only the centre but also the whole circumference which embraces both conscious and unconscious; it is the centre of this totality, just as the ego is the centre of the conscious mind' (*Alchemy*, 44). So long as we think of the Self as some kind of 'thing' is can be indicated but not defined, but when we remember that it is a concept, that is, a way of talking about observable phenomena, it can be seen that it is possible to describe the state of a man who is said to be 'controlled by the Self'.

From the quotations in the last paragraph four things can be inferred about the state of being 'controlled by the Self'. First, a man in this state will still think and speak of 'I', and by 'I' he will mean what Jung calls his 'ego': second, although a man will say 'I' he will regard this 'I' as encompassing only a part of what he is: third, in the actual process of living what a man does will be the activity of the 'whole' and not only of that part which he calls 'I': finally, it will seem as though the responsibility for his living is taken by some 'centre' other than what he calls 'I'. These four things, taken together, may be explained in the following way: since a man still says 'I' he continues to formulate ideals, make plans, and have purposes just as he has always done, but because he has, *ex hypothesis*, already accepted the unconscious he is aware of the existence of other tendencies, pressures, potencies, or whatever we may call them, which he knows to be there, but which he does not comprehend; the Self is said to be 'in control' when the action (of thought, speech, or muscle) with which he responds to his situation is not guided exclusively by his conscious plans, purposes, and ideals, but also takes into account the tendencies of which he is aware, but of which he is not fully conscious; at the same time, the action determined in this way must not contradict his conscious ideas ('the ego is neither opposed nor subjected' to the Self) but must take them up in a new or unexpected way. 'I have been deeply impressed', Jung tells us, 'with the fact that the new thing prepared by fate seldom or never corresponds to

conscious expectation. It is a still more remarkable fact that, though
the new thing contradicts deeply rooted instincts as we know them,
yet it is a singularly appropriate expression of the total personality,
an expression which one could not imagine in a more complete form'
(*Secret*, 90). We may analyse and judge and plan our life, but if the
Self is in control our behaviour will not be in accordance with our
preconceived plan and yet when we have acted we shall see that what
we have done does not conflict with our conscious reasoning, although
we could not see that it was the right thing to do beforehand. In much
the same way, the Christian is taught to use his reason to the best of
his ability, and then to offer his conclusions in prayer to God, and seek
that God may direct his life in His way, whether or not it is the way
which has seemed best to the man.

The Self regarded as the goal of Individuation refers to a way of
behaving. When the Self is in control, then a man reacts to the external
world as a united whole, and he is not driven this way and that by
conflicting purposes and desires. Although such a man may not be
able to see beforehand how he can fulfil his whole nature, he will find
that when action is called for he truly expresses himself as a whole.
Thus the Self unites the opposites, because it brings unity to the two
parts of a man's nature which before seemed to be hopelessly opposed,
and in the Self the principle that nothing shall be lost is visibly fulfilled.
Conscious and unconscious elements may be modified but, if it is
true to say that a man is wholly guided by the Self, then elements of
all kinds are so brought together that they form a unified human
being, and the unity of an individual, always expressed in his physical
body, is also expressed in his psychic nature.

Images of the Self

'The Self' is a term which is always relevant to what goes on in a
man's life, and its use is not confined to those who are said to be
controlled by the Self; that is, the concept of the Self may be used to
order to 'regulate' all kinds of psychic phenomena, or, in psychological language, the Self is always manifested in some way in an
individual's life. The Self, for example, may be said to be expressed
in the 'compensatory' function of the unconscious, because by presenting another point of view which a man has ignored in his conscious
thought the unconscious bears witness to the ultimate unity of his
nature. Jung has come to the conclusion that the Self is also expressed

by certain images which appear in dreams and fantasies, and these
images, which he calls 'mandalas', have special importance for any
enquiry into the nature of the Self. As a concept the Self has neither
shape nor form so that the nature or character of the Self, as such,
cannot be discussed, but the images which express the Self have form,
and by discussing their form Jung is able to discuss the character of the
Self. Jung's treatment of these images, however, leads to confusion
unless we bear in mind the Kantian background of his thought,
because, according to Kant, one can only know a thing by the
phenomena which express it, and the name of a thing refers equally
to the 'thing-in-itself' and to phenomena. Thus, for instance, suppose
one is run over by a bus: 'something' has encountered us, but we do
not know what that 'something' is in itself, and all we can say is that
it appears to our senses as 'bus'. Strictly we should say 'we have
encountered an unknown essence which appears to us as "bus"',
but we have no name for this essence, and we must use the name 'bus'
for both essence and phenomena. It is the same with Jung's concept
of the Self, and although Jung might well be expected to distinguish
between the Self in itself, and the mandalas which express the Self
imaginatively, because (unlike Kant) he has coined special names for
the 'noumena' with which he is concerned, in fact he does not do so,
and he frequently speaks of mandalas as though they were the Self.
For example, Jung writes, 'The unconscious does indeed put forth a
bewildering profusion of semblances for that obscure thing we call
a mandala or "self"' (*Alchemy*, 247), whereas the mandala is the
'semblance' of the Self. Again he says, '[The Self] is the "uniting
symbol" which epitomizes the total union of opposites. As such and
in accordance with its paradoxical nature, it can only be expressed by
means of symbols [he has just said that the Self is a symbol]. These
appear in dreams and spontaneous fantasies and find visual expression
in the mandalas that occur in the patient's dreams, drawings, and
paintings. Hence, properly understood, the self is not a doctrine or
theory but an image born of nature's own workings, a natural symbol
far removed from all conscious intention' (*Practice*, 474): but, as we
have seen, the Self is a concept, and not an image, and it is the mandala
which is the image of the Self. The terminological confusion exists in
Jung's writings, but if we are on our guard we can avoid being
confused by it.

Before the terminology of 'Self' and 'Mandala' had been elaborated (however confusedly) Jung had already become aware of the phenomena to which they refer, and in an early work he said, 'Through the activity of the unconscious, a content is unearthed which is constellated by thesis and antithesis [consciousness and the unconscious] in equal measure' (*Types*, 608), and he calls this content the 'uniting symbol', 'the transcendent symbol' and the 'mediatory product'. Jung continues on a later page, 'When the mediatory product is preserved [by the refusal to give primacy to either opposite], it fashions a raw product which is for construction, not for dissolution, and which becomes a common object for both thesis and antithesis; thus it becomes a new content that governs the whole attitude, putting an end to the division, and forcing the energy of the opposites into a common channel' (ibid., 610). In a treatise published in 1946 he wrote, 'The self is the total, timeless man and as such corresponds to the original, spherical, bisexual being who stands for the mutual integration of conscious and unconscious' (*Practice*, 531). So that in his early work and in his later elaborations, Jung insists that the uniting symbol is characterized by participation in all sides of a man's nature, and that it is a symbol of unity; that is, that it is (visibly) a union of the opposites. The mandala is of so much interest that it will do no harm to give more attention to it than may be strictly necessary: four aspects of mandalas will be examined:

(a) Their place in the process of development
(b) Their function
(c) The attitude of consciousness towards them
(d) Their character, or form

(a) *Their Place.* Mandalas appear in fantasy when the individual is nearly ready to move forward to the achievement of the goal of unity, but this is not to say that they never occur at any other time, for '. . . they do not invariably indicate a subliminal readiness on the part of the patient to realize that wholeness consciously, at a later stage; often they mean no more than a temporary compensation for chaotic confusion and lack of orientation' (*Practice*, 536). What it does mean is that when these images do indicate a 'subliminal readiness' to realize wholeness they press upon consciousness with great 'force', and almost compel it to take note of them. In other words, a 'casual' mandala, as it were, will only be recognized by someone who already knows what to look for, but a mandala 'in its proper place' is something which one cannot help noticing even though one may have no idea what it is: the dream which contains it, or the fantasy concerned with it, will seem important, and 'make an impression' in a way that other dreams and fantasies do not.

Mandalas belong to the period immediately preceding and including the state of accepting the unconscious, and they arise when the individual is stuck in the state of tension already referred to, for 'When the opposites are given a complete equality of right, attested to by the ego's unconditioned participation in both thesis and antithesis, a suspension of the will results' (*Types*, 608: the reference to 'ego' needs to be corrected—if we read 'man's' for 'ego's' the account is accurate). In the analytical situation this state of being stuck frequently takes the form of 'being stuck in the transference' and from the way he presents it Jung's experience (already mentioned) with a young lady who was stuck in the transference situation seems to have had great significance for him in this connection. Not knowing what else to do they watched her dreams, and Jung gives one of them at length, continuing, 'A careful examination and analysis of the dreams, especially of the one just quoted, revealed a very marked tendency— in contrast to conscious criticism, which always seeks to reduce things to human proportions—to endow the person of the doctor with super-human attributes. He had to be gigantic, primordial, huger than the father, like the wind that sweeps over the earth—was he then to be made into a god?' (*Essays*, 214). Eventually Jung concluded that a god was being sought beneath the unlikely appearance of the doctor (in other words, that the god-image was activated, and was being pro-jected upon the doctor), and when he assumed that this was the case, and persuaded his patient to entertain the idea (despite a certain amount of conscious resistance to it), the whole situation began to change, and the state of being stuck gave way to further development.

The appearances of the images of the Self mark a readiness to go forward, but they arise before the individual is consciously ready to do it. The first requirement for an advance is that the images should be taken seriously and not dismissed by rationalistic conscious criticism, and taking the images seriously is, in essence, the admission that consciousness cannot have the last word. So much of what Jung has written suggests that all that is needed is this readiness to take the images seriously that it is as well to point out that this is by no means his intention, and three quotations from the discussion of a series of

dreams in *Psychology and Alchemy* show this. In this discussion he is
concerned almost exclusively with the images that appear in dreams
and fantasies and he purposely omits references to the 'outer' life of
the dreamer, yet in 170 pages there are 15 references to the fact that
such a life exists, and it is important that attention should be drawn
to them, because they indicate that its importance is not forgotten by
the author. For instance, Jung says, 'From the dreams that come in
between the ones we have quoted here it is evident that the dreamer is
finding the insistent demand for wholeness somewhat disagreeable,
for if he takes it up it will have far-reaching practical results the
personal nature of which, however, lies outside the scope of our
study' (*Alchemy*, 239): 'He cannot get out of the chthonic prison
because he is not yet ready to do something that he should. (This is an
important matter, a duty even, and the cause of much misgiving)'
(ibid., 277): 'It is a three-dimensional mandala—a mandala in bodily
form signifying realization. (Unfortunately medical discretion prevents
my giving the biographical details. It must suffice to say that this
realization did actually take place.)' (ibid., 308). In the *Development
of Personality* more detail is given of a young man who analysed his
own neurosis 'showing really remarkable insight', and yet remained
completely uncured: having discovered that he was getting large sums
of money from a financially poor woman with whom he said he had
'a liaison', Professor Jung remarked, 'don't you think that the fact
that you are financially supported by this poor woman might be one
of the chief reasons why you are not yet cured?' The young man did
not. 'He was one of the many', the final comment runs, 'who believe
that morals have nothing to do with neurosis and that sinning on
purpose is not sinning at all, because it can be intellectualized out of
existence' (*Development*, 182).

The apparent overlooking of the outward life of patients is not so
much due to the fact that the analyst is primarily concerned with
fantasy material as that this side of the process is more amenable to a
general treatment because it does not depend upon the actual individual
situation of the patient but upon the common structure of human
minds, so that it is possible to discuss it without revealing too much
of the private life of patients. There is, perhaps, the further reason that
Jung is specially concerned to establish the truth of his view that the
psyche is, to a very great extent, collective. The fact remains that most
of his work is concerned with the inner world and not with the outer,

although, as we have seen, the two march together. So in connection with the further development of the girl who projected the god-image on him he continues to keep the image in the centre of his attention, but he mentions, almost parenthetically, what was happening 'outside': 'There now occurred something which at first I alone perceived, and with the utmost astonishment, namely a kind of subterranean undermining of the transference. Her relations with a certain friend deepened perceptibly, notwithstanding the fact that consciously she still clung to the transference' (*Essays*, 217). It is interesting to contrast this with a Freudian analyst, referring to the same point, of the 'undermining' of the transference, who, by contrast, keeps his eye firmly on the outer events: 'His heterosexual libido, never entirely absent, became enormously energized, and he found himself with an increasing drive, impulse, or incentive towards female acquaintances, who had previously meant very little to him from an emotional point of view' (*Berg*, 233). The contrast will be even clearer when we consider the rest of what Jung says in connection with this case in the next section.

The appearance of the mandalas is to be expected when the patient is stuck, and when he is somehow ready to go forward. They indicate the possibility of going forward if the patient is ready to fulfil two conditions: on the one hand he must be prepared to take the images seriously, and not dismiss them as 'mere fantasy'; on the other, he must be prepared to take account of the 'life duties' which press upon him from the world outside, and as he fulfils these conditions, so he advances. Inwardly his psyche becomes harmonious, outwardly he responds to the world as a whole man.

(*b*) *Their Function.* The images of the goal, like all unconscious images, stress the limitations of consciousness, in that they bring to its notice the presence of that which is other than it, but these images do much more as well; because to all appearances they actually perform the function which is ascribed to the Self. 'The raw material [sc. the "uniting symbol"] when elaborated by the thesis and the antithesis', Jung tells us, 'which in its process of formation reconciles the opposites, is the living symbol' and 'it governs the whole attitude' (*Types*, 610). This is the same confusion which we noticed above: so far as appearances go it is the 'symbol' which unites the opposites, and since the Self is only 'visible' as expressed by the symbol it is not possible to say 'it is not really the symbol, it is really the Self', but it still remains true that as Jung uses 'Self' this is what we ought to say. When we speak of the 'Self' we are using conceptual terms; when we refer the work to the symbol we are giving an account of what is to be observed: sometimes one point of view is best, sometimes the other.

The account begun earlier can now be rounded off. When the girl acknowledged the faint possibility that she was 'seeking a god', then the transference was 'undermined', and Jung says, 'I saw how the transpersonal control-point developed—I cannot call it anything else—a *guiding function*, and step by step gathered to itself all the former personal over-valuations; how, with this afflux of energy, it gained influence over the resisting conscious mind without the patient's consciously noticing what was happening' (*Essays*, loc. cit.). In more general terms, 'The steadfastness of the ego and the superiority of the mediatory expression over thesis and antithesis are to my mind correlates, each mutually conditioning the other. It would appear at times as though the fixity of the inborn individuality were the decisive factor, at times as though the mediatory expression possessed a superior force prompting the ego to absolute steadfastness. But, in reality, it is quite conceivable that the firmness and certainty of the individuality on the one hand, and the superior force of the mediatory product on the other, are merely tokens of one and the same fact' (*Types*, 609, 610). In the light of the later developments we must understand that the 'steadfastness of the ego' does not lie in initiating anything, but in accepting the opposites, and—yet more important in accepting the guidance of the 'mediatory product'—the Self, or the mandala.

Thus the function of these images is to take charge of the development. They can and do do this in so far as consciousness will 'let them', and that means, in so far as it will turn towards them as bearers of high value and look to them as a source of life and power; and this explains why it is that in those religions where mandalas are in use they are instruments of meditation.

(c) *The Attitude to the Images*. 'The known attitudes of the conscious mind have definable aims and purposes. But a man's attitude towards the self is the only one that has no definable aim and no visible purpose' (*Alchemy*, 247); in other words, you accept the mandala, or you reject it, you do not try to put it to any use, for it is the mandala which, in the goal, will put consciousness to use. But this does not mean that the appearance of the mandala does not evoke any response from the conscious mind. It is not enough to say that the chief characteristic of the response which the mandala evokes is that it is 'numinous', because all unconscious elements tend to evoke this kind of feeling to a greater or lesser degree. The mandala evokes such a feeling to an exceptional degree, and it seems to be of very great and special importance even though we cannot say what it is important 'for', and many of Jung's patients have felt great compulsion to express the mandala in drawing, painting or dancing. A mandala seems strange, but infinitely worthwhile. Finally, the whole-hearted acceptance of the mandalas brings a new attitude altogether, and on the final vision in the series examined in *Psychology and Alchemy* Jung comments, 'This remarkable vision made a deep and lasting impression on the dreamer, an impression of "the most sublime harmony", as he himself puts it' (*Alchemy*, 308).

(*d*) *Their Character*. Formally, the typical mandala is based upon the number four. The arrangement may be that of a circle, a square, a sphere, or a cross, or it may be a complete individual. Whatever the precise form, the mandala includes two features. On the one hand it brings together many diverse elements into a single unity, thereby signifying its character as a 'union of opposites', on the other hand it points to a centre or goal. One or other of these aspects may be emphasized and one or other may be lacking in any particular goal-image.

The theme, of a fourfold arrangement with emphasis on the centre, has the widest imaginable distribution in space and time. Jung finds it playing an important part in the dreams and psychic development of his patients, but it is also to be found in Egypt, in the religions of the East, and in medieval Christianity, and it is very difficult to reject his opinion that it must be something of great significance for the human psyche. The following illustrate this distribution. 'The term "mandala" was chosen because this word denotes the ritual or magic circle used in Lamaism and also in Tantric yoga as a *yantra* or aid to contemplation. The Eastern mandalas used in ceremonial are figures fixed by tradition; they may be drawn or painted or in certain special ceremonies, even represented plastically' (*Alchemy*, 122): '*Mandala* means a circle, more especially a magic circle ... *mandalas* are amply represented in the Middle Ages. . . . For the most part, the *mandala* form is that of a flower, or a cross, or wheel, with a distinct tendency towards four as the basis of structure. . . . *Mandalas* of this sort are also to be found in the sand drawings used in the ceremonies of the

Pueblo Indians' (*Secret*, 96, 97): 'The oldest *mandala* known to me, is a paleolithic so-called "sunwheel", recently [the book was published in England in 1931] discovered in Rhodesia. It is likewise founded on the principle of four' (ibid., 105). For the Christian mandalas, he says of those from the Middle Ages, most 'show Christ in the centre, with the four evangelists, or their symbols, at the cardinal points. This conception must be a very ancient one because Horus was represented with his four sons in the same way by the Egyptians' (*Secret*, 97).

The religious mandalas almost invariably point the emphasis on the centre, by placing the figure of a deity there. 'The mandalas used in ceremonial,' Jung says, 'are of great significance because their centres usually contain one of the highest religious figures: either Shiva himself—often in the embrace of Shakti—or Buddha, Amitabha, Avalokiteshvara, or one of the great Mahayana teachers, or simply the *dorje*, symbol of all the divine forces together, whether creative or destructive in nature' (*Alchemy*, 125), and this goes some way to justify the parallels which Jung adduces between the Self and God. From his psychological studies he has come to postulate the Self as that which lies behind the mandala, or that which is seen as the mandala, and from his excursions into comparative religion he finds strong reason for thinking that there, behind the mandala, lies the god, and this is in keeping with the numinousness of the mandalas in modern fantasies, and with the high significance which seems to be attached to it. '. . . the mandala symbolizes either the divine being hitherto hidden and dormant in the body and now extracted and revivified, or else the vessel or the room in which the transformation of man into a divine being takes place' (*Religion*, 166), Jung says; and, 'The place of the deity [in the modern mandala] seems to be taken by the wholeness of man' (ibid., 139): '. . . it is evident', he continues later, 'that in the modern mandala man—the complete man—has replaced the deity.[1] There is no reason to reject these conclusions, and yet there may be some doubt as to their true interpretation. Jung implies that this shift from cultic god to the 'complete man' is a mark of higher development, but it may be

---

[1] This passage was taken from the original *Psychology and Religion*, and the comments following made before I had opportunity of seeing the revision in Vol. 11 of the collected works. The passage there reads 'it is clear that in the modern mandala man—the deep ground, as it were, of the self—is not a substitute but a symbol for the deity' (*Religion*, 157). This is in close agreement with my comments.

that it is no more than an expression of the manward-looking tendencies of the modern age, and that these are as much a passing phase as any god who has been worshipped and forgotten centuries ago. The mandala is the Self. But what is the Self? Jung says that he does not know. Psychologically it is the new man, who will be one in whom the ego is no longer the final arbiter, but this may simply mean that psychology cannot go further without ceasing to be psychology. On the evidence there is nothing which excludes the view that the centre 'ought' to be the deity, and if this were so then it might well matter, and be a matter of first importance, how and in what form the deity was represented. The Christian will say that there is one 'image' of God which is the true image: the figure of the God-man, Jesus Christ his Lord.

II

CHRIST

JUNG treats 'the Self' as a concept which stands above the turmoil of religious controversy, and it would seem that he thinks that what he says of the Self embraces all that is significant in what men say of Tao, Nirvana, Brahman, Christ or any other central religious concept. One result of the preceding enquiry has been to show that this is not true in relation to Christ, whatever may be said of other religious figures, and that Christ in the Christian scheme of salvation does not exactly correspond to the Self in Jung's scheme. The Self is all form without content, and, in its visible manifestations, it takes protean shapes, whereas Christ is known in the one definite figure of Jesus, as He is presented in the New Testament; The Self is only adumbrated as a man travels on Jung's way of Salvation, and does not come into full flower until the goal is reached, whereas Christ in his fulness enters a man's life before he can begin his journey on the Christian Way. At the same time, despite these differences, many important parallels have been found between Jung's way and that of Christianity and among them are parallels between the Self and Christ. In this chapter the differences between the two ways are put on one side, in order that it may be shown that Christ is like the Self in that He unites the opposites, and in that He is, in Himself, a union of opposites.

The Function of Christ

It is a theological commonplace that St Paul fastened a legal analogy on his concept of Justification by Faith, and that those who give an account of it in terms which are exclusively legal can cite very good authority for using those terms although they are hardly true to St Paul in that they reject other models which are just as prominent in his writings. It has been pointed out, for example, by Vincent Taylor, that the legal language is not pressed by St Paul; and that though he uses his forensic terminology, as it were in passing, he does not use it more, or even as much, as he uses quite different terms to express the same truth. It would seem that of all his models the legal is the most easily grasped, and that this accounts for the excessive weight which has been given to it in later theology. In chapter 3 we have already noticed that if we must use a legal model, then the least objectionable is that which takes the legal concept of 'status' as the central concept in the analogy with Justification by Faith, but that although this model is less objectionable than the model of reward and punishment, it is still liable to lead to a formalistic account, and the best recent example of this is Nygren's commentary on Romans. Nygren could hardly use stronger language in his insistence upon the change of status which is involved in becoming a Christian; he shows how it affects man in his relationships to God, to Wrath, to Sin, to Law, and to Death: and as one reads, one does feel the authentic Pauline note of wonder at the great change which has taken place. If one asks, however, 'And what is the visible result of this change of status?' the answer which Nygren gives is 'nothing'—not even at the Last Judgement, for 'by justification by faith God has not abolished the judgement of the works of men' (*Nygren*, 127).

The tendency to reduce all St Paul's models to the legal model of a change of status is well illustrated by an essay of G. W. H. Lampe. Lampe rightly states a large number of Pauline models when he says, '*In* Christ the believer receives in his own measure, like Christ at His Baptism, the indwelling of the Spirit, for being in Christ he is in the Spirit, or the Spirit dwells in him, or Christ dwells in him, for from the point of view of the Christian life all these expressions signify the same thing' (*J—Lampe*, 56), but in order to explain the meaning of these models he continues: 'Spirit-possession is, of course, synonymous with the assurance of sonship towards God' (ibid., loc. cit), and on a later page he relates this assurance to a change of status, saying 'Christ's righteousness is imputed to the sinner who is devoid of any inherent righteousness, because he is *in* Christ. He has put on Christ, and so has confidence before God because by free grace he has received a new status in Christ, for no merit of his own' (ibid., 59). This is a reversal of St Paul's thought, because St Paul fills out the idea of a 'new status' by means of other, more dynamic, models, whereas Lampe seems to imply that the other models mean no more than that the change of status has taken place. 'Spirit-possession' may bring with it an 'assurance of sonship' (indeed, it must) but to say that the two expressions are synonymous is to confine the activity of the Spirit to the narrowest of limits, and to replace St Paul's conception of a new power active in a man's life by the idea of a changed attitude (the acknowledgement of a new status) on the part of man.

The one-sided emphasis on the legal model is easily understood. It arises from a real and right fear that men should suppose that they could be justified by works. The danger which it avoids is that if we rejoice that Justification by Faith makes possible 'good works' that were not possible before, and if we regard this as an important result of Justification, we may go on to think that we are to have confidence before God by virtue of those works. This danger is no chimera, as the history of theological controversies shows clearly enough, but it is not an inevitable consequence of the idea that Justification does bring about a change in the actual life of men, because it is possible to rejoice in 'good works' for their own sake, and not for any contribution that they make towards our 'confidence before God'; and it is not only possible, but also essential to a full Christian outlook. If, on the one hand, you insist that Justification by Faith must result in good works, because if it did not it could not give us confidence before God; or if, on the other hand, you insist that it must not result in good works, because if it did then something more than Justification is required to give us confidence before God, you fall into the same error, of supposing that the only matter of real significance is the individual's confidence before God, and you reduce both 'Justification' and 'works' to nothing more than means to this end. In other words, you forget that God has a plan for the world, as well as for men, and that He purposes that His plan for the world should be put into effect through man. Man is the 'steward of nature', and if 'salvation' merely affects our status before God, and does not make us better stewards, then it loses a very great part of its meaning.

It is of interest to notice that the denial that Justification by Faith, 'receiving the Spirit', 'being in Christ' means being a better 'steward', is curiously paralleled by Jung's account of religion in *Answer to Job*. In effect this denial means that the work of Jesus, and the whole paraphernalia of Church and Sacraments, is directed to nothing more than to bring about a changed attitude of men and women to God, so that the world which God created and saw to be 'very good' is reduced to a stage set on which the drama of man is carried out. In *Answer to Job* Jung asserts that 'religious statements' are important assertions made by the 'archetype of deity' through the conscious minds of men and women, and he then denies that these statements ever have important reference to physical events, and this, in effect, means that they are always about the archetype of deity, as well as originating in it. In the theological version it is difficult to avoid the conclusion that God is rather like one of the *nouveau riche*, perpetually concerned with being treated properly by his servants, and in the psychological version He is clearly a bore, who can talk about nothing but Himself; neither offers us a god whom we can greatly respect.

In *The Doctrine of Justification by Faith* two other essays provide a salutary correction to the emphasis on the legal model with which we have been concerned. Thus: '[the doctrine stresses] the need of grace, and grace regarded not merely as divine favour, but as the life of Christ and His Spirit working within us' (*J—Symonds*, 80); and 'The result of incorporation into Christ or of being justified by Christ is not to destroy but to perfect nature' (*J—Maycock*, 94). In Pauline terms, the Justified sinner is not merely 'free from wrath' and it is not merely that the 'enmity with God' is destroyed, but the Justified sinner is also 'free from Sin' and new possibilities of life and action are opened to him. Again, the redemption of men and women is not only effective for themselves, it has its repercussions upon the whole world, for 'The whole creation groaneth and travaileth in pain until now' (that is, the natural order is also to be redeemed), and its redemption is dependent upon the 'redemption of the sons of God', because it is through man that it will come to pass. Again, Christ is Lord of 'both the living and the dead'; His coming to men is a matter of importance for their life here on earth as well as for their status before God. In Johannine terms, Jesus came in order that we might have life, and 'have it more abundantly', and such a claim becomes meaningless if Justification by Faith has no visible effects here and now.

The 'this-world' emphasis of modern times in the West, which is spreading over all the world, is a serious over-emphasis, but it is the emphasis of a truth which Jesus clearly enunciated, and which His Church has too often forgotten in the past, and the Christian does well to take note of it, because it will remind him that God created man to live in the physical world which He had made, that His gifts to man are gifts for life in the world, and that this is as true of the 'gift' of the Spirit as it is of anything else. The Spirit is 'given' to work in and through men living in the world, and it is to suggest a serious limitation to imply that the work of the Spirit is only, or even primarily, to 'put men right' with God: it would be more correct to say that we are 'put right with God' so that we can do God's will in this world, but it is better still to say that being right with God and being effective in His world are parallel effects of the Spirit, or two aspects of a single effect. We are being told more and more frequently that what is demanded of the Church in the world today is a recovery of the doctrine of Justification by Faith, and nothing could be more important, but that doctrine will make no impact on the world of today if it is not presented in such a way that it gives hope of new possibilities of life and action here and now. R. L. Stevenson laughed at the pretensions of the 'formalists' in his parable of the *Yellow Paint*. Shaken by the death of his friend a young man submitted to be coated with the yellow paint, so highly spoken of by his friends and relations. As each catastrophe fell upon him he complained to the physician, to be told in turn that the paint had no power against physical ills, moral evil, or the inevitable punishment of the criminal. The fable ends with the young man condemned to death, but assured that all is well because no fleck of the paint is out of place. The Roman Church followed a sure instinct in condemning the Reformers' teaching on 'sola fide', in so far as that teaching rejected any idea that Justification brought with it new possibilities for life in this world, but the objection was wrongly formulated, and so distorted. Justification by Faith is more than an intangible change of 'status', but it is not, what seems the inevitable alternative, a transformation of the sinner.

F. H. Maycock sets the 'Catholic-Protestant' controversy as follows: 'the Catholic view is that Justifying Faith brings about a double change. It does away with sin and it imparts to the person a new status, causing an interior change and conferring new powers', and in this connection he quotes S. L. Frank, 'Christ's sacrifice would be in vain if the human soul did not receive it and were not inspired by it with readiness and the strength to imitate Christ...': 'The Protestant view is that Justifying Faith cancels sin; the sinner is accounted righteous before God . . . Man is always undeserving and will remain so' (*J—Maycock*, 89). Here, he adds, is a 'direct conflict'. This is not a conflict which depends merely upon the terms used, but one that rests upon the acceptance of a mistaken premise on both sides, and this premise is that what a man does expresses the nature of the individual concerned, and that if he does certain acts it is because he possesses the powers necessary to do those acts. This is a very natural premise, but it is not one which St Paul would accept, and if it is not accepted the conflict between 'Catholic' and 'Protestant' loses its force. It is one of the lessons which theology can learn from Jung, that an act may be a man's act, and yet not depend upon powers which can properly be called 'his'.

Jung claims that it is an empirical fact that much that we do cannot be regarded as determined solely by what we are. If we leave aside the psychological postulates his claim is that there are 'powers' which, acting through men and women, determine much of their behaviour, and that individuals have not 'directive' control over behaviour determined in this way. We are able to limit the effect of those powers to a certain extent, but we are unable to take them into ourselves, as it were, and use them for whatever purpose we may choose. We may inhibit 'powers' of this sort, but we cannot control them. St Paul implied the same thing when he 'personified' 'Sin' as an external power, exercising sway over individuals from 'outside', and it is the only view which does justice to those models other than the legal which he uses to present Justification by Faith. With Jung's conclusion in mind the meaning of such phrases as 'I live, yet not I, but Christ liveth in me', and 'work out your own salvation with fear and trembling, for it is God that worketh in you, both to will and to do', present no difficulty at all, and their meaning becomes perfectly clear: yet the true significance seems to have been overlooked by Protestant and Catholic alike in the controversy over Justification by Faith.

In this connection the scholastic distinction between 'natural' and 'supernatural' should have preserved theologians from error. It would seem, however, that of the two possible models for this distinction the wrong one was consistently chosen. The wrong model makes it a distinction between the origin of the powers which a Christian possesses, and so gives rise to the assumption that what he has is his, however he has acquired it: the right model applies the distinction both to the origin and the operation of the Christian's powers and abilities. The two models have the same background; they start with the same account of man as created by God, and as modified by sin. The 'natural man' in his original created nature was a creature of God, and he had certain human powers, which were given to him by God; God also gave him the further ability to direct the powers which he possessed into the world; that is, God gave him a relative autonomy which enabled him to initiate actions. Man used his autonomy to

misuse his powers, and this misuse of his powers resulted in 'damage'
to his nature—amongst other things, man lost the full autonomy
which God has given him, so that his nature became divided by warring
'factions' within him. Since man is 'damaged' he cannot possibly
recover the lost harmony of his own nature, in which his various powers
would compensate and reinforce one another, and so long as this
harmony is destroyed the powers of man oppose and frustrate one
another, and none has free and full effect in the world. So much is
common ground to both the models.

Both models of the distinction between 'natural' and 'supernatural' are concerned with the recovery of the lost harmony of
human nature, and with something else as well. Both accept the
necessity of God's grace, in order that that may be done which man
cannot do in his own strength. The wrong model visualizes a double
act on the part of God: first God reinstates the original harmonious
nature of man, so that he can act freely and rightly in the world; then
God gives him further powers which were not given to man at his
creation, and these further powers are 'supernatural'. The model
implies these two separate acts, but not in the crude succession suggested above. 'Supernatural' powers may be given before the original
nature is restored, and they may well help in the restoration of that
nature, but the essential error of this model is that the 'supernatural'
powers are called 'supernatural' simply because it is inconceivable that
a man, however perfect, could acquire them for himself: they are not
inherent in man as he was first created by God, but were 'added' after
the redemption of man by the death of Jesus, but, when they are given,
they enter into the autonomy of man: that is, they become his powers.
Theoretically this should mean that the 'supernatural' powers are as
liable to be misdirected by man as his natural powers were misdirected,
but because such a conclusion is clearly absurd, the model must be
completed by the assertion that these 'supernatural' powers cannot be
misused. This addition reduces the whole model to nonsense, but the
way of thought, implied rather than anything else, remains—the
'supernatural' powers are conceived of as a gift with strings attached:
they are thought of as really given—but on condition that they are
used in the right way.

The right model, on the other hand, indicates that a 'supernatural'
power is something which is not only acquired in a different way from
a 'natural' power but something which operates in a different way,

here and now: that is, there is no sense in which a 'supernatural' power ever comes within the autonomy of the individual man, but it remains a power acting on and through the individual, and never becomes a power or ability of the individual. A 'supernatural' power is a divine 'gift' in that it is something which man could never have achieved for himself, but it is not a 'gift' that is 'given' to the man for him to use since it is not given to a man, but comes upon him. The 'supernatural' powers have an autonomy of their own, and the most that man can do is to frustrate them or allow them full expression through him: he can never presume to use them, and the possibility of the misuse of such powers cannot conceivably arise, as it does with natural abilities, because man does not use the Spirit, the Spirit uses him.

The conclusion is that the 'Protestant' is right to insist that man remains 'undeserving', for so far as Justification by Faith is concerned the Justified sinner retains his sinful, damaged nature unchanged, and the gift which he has received is not, in itself, a return of the harmony of created human nature which has been destroyed by sin. On the other hand the 'Protestant' is wrong if he suggests that nothing has been changed, here and now, or that the change cannot have visible expression in the life of the man. Although man is not changed, something new has come into his life, and that new thing brings with it possibilities of change in the future. The man has 'received the Spirit', and that means that his nature is no longer the sole determinant of his actions, because the Spirit is also able to control his mind and his body. In the Justified sinner there are two sources of thought and action, the undeserving, damaged human nature, and the undeserved Holy Spirit of Christ. Again the 'Catholic' is right to insist that new powers may and ought to be seen at work in the life of the man who is Justified, because Justification by Faith does mean that the Spirit can become a force in the world through the man, and to deny this is to denude the doctrine of all point and value, but the 'Catholic' is wrong if he goes on to claim that to be Justified is to possess new powers which we did not possess before, because the Justified sinner has no new abilities which he did not have before under his control, and in himself he is in no better position than the simple sinner to recover the lost harmony of created human nature. If the Justified sinner does good where he did evil before that is not because he is different, but because the Spirit now acts in him and if he slowly acquires a greater harmony in his human nature that is not because of anything which he does; it is the effect of the Spirit of God dwelling in him—and this is not to be understood as a 'way of talking' but as an actual effect, which a man may experience in his own life. Justification by Faith introduces new possibilities, which are not to be understood as possible achievements for the man, but as possibilities which may be achieved 'in the man', though not by the man himself.

In the light of these considerations the Pauline models become transparent, and extraordinarily clear. The first set of models is grouped around the phrase 'we have the Spirit', and nothing, surely, could be clearer than that St Paul pictures the 'Spirit' as within us, and yet, at the same time as lying 'alongside' our spirit. The two are both present 'within' the Christian, but they are distinct, and it is always possible that there may be conflict between them. This is what has been said above. The second set of models are clearly to be taken as parallel accounts of the same thing: they involve such phrases as 'in Christ', 'member of his body', 'Christ is the head', and up to a point the implications of this second set are the same as those of the first. Christ has a control over our bodies, comparable to the control which we have been used to exercise over them,[1] so that there is another source of human activity which is not 'I' but which can use my mind and body in the way that 'I' can use it. 'The Spirit in us' is, in fact, the rule of Christ over us, seen from within the individual, but the second models go beyond the first, in such a way that they exclude the 'enthusiastic' tendencies which might be encouraged by them. So long as I claim to possess the Spirit there is the possibility of conflict with others who make the same claim, but if each simply accepts the rule of Christ then there is no conflict, because the same Christ rules the lives of all Christians, and He remains distinct from each. Christ controls (or can control) our bodies, but each individual body is only one part of the whole organism which is His. It is also possible to see clearly how it is that Justification by Faith can be 'something', and yet not be sanctification. Sanctification is the goal in which our 'spirit' has become wholly and completely subject to Christ, or to His Spirit; Justification is the essential preliminary, the formation of a relationship with Christ which introduces His Spirit into our lives as a determining force: it means the effective presence

---

[1] Not necessarily because He is the 'head' (which may have the sense of 'source') but because our bodies are part of 'His body'.

of the Spirit of Christ, even though the goal of complete subordination to that Spirit has not been reached.

This rather long introduction enables us to see how it is that Christ 'unites the opposites'. It has already been pointed out that Christian penitence unites the nature of a man by bringing him to see that all he is is sinful, and it has also been remarked that in seeing himself as sinful a man sees himself as divided from God. All that a man does of himself 'has the nature of sin', and in all that he does a man fails to conform to the will of God; a man encounters God as one who opposes his aims and purposes, because God wills that he should be other than he is; God cannot abrogate the consequences of what a man does, and as the Controller of the Universe He dispenses those 'punishments' which are the result of sin; sinful man stands 'over against' the holy God, and the relation between them must be described as 'enmity', marked by disobedience on one side, and 'wrath' on the other. In these ways the 'opposites' are divided, and it is this division of the opposites which is overcome by the Atonement wrought by God.

Justification is the uniting of sinful man with Christ in the person of the man, and for this reason it is also at-one-ment. If it were not this it would not bring the opposites together, because the opposition 'sinful—holy' is a fact about the nature of God and man which can never be merely 'thought' out of existence. The Old Testament, for example, teaches us that God does not desire the death of the wicked, and that He would rather that he turned from his wickedness, but this is of little comfort so long as man remains a sinner and cannot turn from his wickedness. It is not enough to know that God wills that the 'enmity' should be destroyed, one must also know that He has Himself done something to destroy it, and the coming of Christ into the life of a man, which is the meaning of Justification, is the thing which God has done. Yet Justification alone does not bring the opposites into effective unity unless and until the Justified sinner permits it, and the entry of Christ into a man does no more than establish conditions necessary for a full union of the opposites. Before he is Justified a man can only strive with his inadequate (sinful) nature to do the impossible, to lift himself out of the mire by his own pigtails, but after Christ has come into his life a man may, if he will, cease from striving and hand himself over to the control of Christ. Justification is thus the possibility of a full union of the opposites if only the man who is Justified will 'stand still, and see the salvation of God'.

Justification makes unity between man and Christ a possibility, and by doing this it also overcomes the disunity in the nature of man. So long as a man strives to lift himself out of his sinful state he must set out to assert some part of himself at the expense of another, but Christ comes to the man who sees that no part of him is truly trustworthy and, as we have seen, to accept Christ is to put one's whole self, evil inclinations as well as good will, at His disposal. Whereas we learn by penitence that our whole self is sinful, and that in itself, under our direction, our nature is opposed to God in every way, we learn by faith that Christ comes to use the instrument which is useless in our own hands: under the guidance of Christ the evil which seems to us to be 'so many devils' is transformed, and we are healed and illuminated. In Christ, and only in Christ, can sinful man live as one.

If we ask how the presence of Christ is revealed in the life of the Justified sinner, the answer given will be very like what was said in the last chapter of the man who is guided by the Self. The Justified sinner judges good and evil, right and wrong; he examines and evaluates his circumstances; he makes plans and decisions; in general he uses his faculties to the best of his ability, and he does all this of himself: but when he has done this he offers himself and his decisions to Christ with the prayer 'nevertheless, not my will but thine', and he looks to Christ to guide his actual behaviour. He should not, himself, seek to imitate Jesus but, trusting Christ to guide him, he will expect that when he has acted he will see that what he has done was the sort of thing which Jesus would have done in similar circumstances.

The state of the Justified sinner might be compared to that of a cyclist on a steep hill, or a sailing vessel in a gale. By the use of brakes or by furling the sails considerable resistance may be offered to the force of gravity or the power of the wind, but if these forces are not resisted, then they, and not the cyclist or the helmsman, determine the direction and speed of motion. The cyclist will go downhill, and the ship in the general direction of the wind, and powers of this sort are essentially different from the power developed by a motor-car engine, for instance, which can be applied to carry the driver in any direction which he may choose. The picture of the ship is a particularly good illustration, because to spread the sails and to try to steer across the wind is to court danger and catastrophe, so that that which might be for good becomes a source of evil.

Justification means that the Spirit is with man, that Christ has access to the man and can exercise control over him. 'Mortification' and 'sanctification' then fall into place as two sides of the process whereby control by Christ replaces human autonomy. 'Mortification' refers to our own renunciation of authority over ourselves, and this renunciation is altogether necessary in order to 'make room' for the activity of Christ. 'Sanctification' refers to the growing influence of the Spirit in our lives which is made possible by our renunciation. The Justified sinner still lives in a world of 'crisis', at every moment he is confronted with the choice whether he will act, or whether he will let Christ act through him.

The Nature of Christ

Like the Self, although not in the same way, Christ unites the opposites when a sinful man is Justified, and it may be said that the figure of Jesus is a 'reconciling symbol'. 'Jesus', with His visible existence in history, stands to 'Christ', who enters invisibly into men's lives, very much as the mandala figures stand to the Self, and just as Jung hardly distinguishes between mandala and Self so Christians identify Him who comes upon them in power with Jesus Christ born at Bethlehem in the reign of the Emperor Augustus and crucified under Pontius Pilate. The mandala takes many shapes but whatever its shape it serves to express the unity of the opposites which characterize the Self; there is one Jesus, and it has now to be asked whether He, in Himself, is also a unity of opposites, and it will be shown that He is, from whatever point of view He is considered.

1. '*Metaphysical*'. By 'metaphysical' here is meant the use of broad high-sounding words like 'heaven', 'light', 'darkness' in a semi-poetic way to carry ideas of things which are certainly 'experience-able', and yet which we cannot strictly define. Words of this sort cannot be analysed satisfactorily, and they easily make for confusion, and yet they have some sort of use and value. To consider Jesus from this 'metaphysical' point of view is to ask how such words as these are used of Him, and in relation to words of this kind His character as a 'union of opposites' is straightforward.

Jesus unites 'heaven' and 'earth', in that He 'came down from heaven' to live upon earth and in that at the Ascension He returns from earth to heaven, and yet He is with His disciples on earth 'always, even unto the end of the world'. Jesus belongs equally to both these 'realms', which is a more poetic way of saying that He is 'perfect God, and perfect man'. At the same time, as the 'creating Word', He is the maker of the whole world: thus He unites in His own person 'all the corners of the earth', there is no extent in created space which does not come within the unity of His nature. Finally, in His pilgrimage, He also descends below the earth, into hell. Jung will refer to the descent into hell when it suits him,[1] but he can also write, 'in the Christian projection the *descensus spiritus sancti* stops at the *living body* of the Chosen One, who is at once very man and very God, whereas in alchemy the descent goes right down into the darkness of inanimate matter whose nether regions, according to the Neopythagoreans, are ruled by evil' (*Alchemy*, 413), which is but another example of the confusion into which so many great ones fall when they approach the Christian mysteries.

2. *Human*. It is only for completeness that one need give instances of Jesus as the uniter of the whole human race, because this aspect of His character is obvious to anyone. The 'righteous' (if there be any) belong to Him of necessity, and in going forth to the sinners He brings them together into the same 'fold'. 'Lifted up' He will draw all men unto Him. 'In Christ', St Paul assures us, there are no divisions of colour, race or sex. The love of Jesus goes out to all men whoever they are, whatever they are, and wherever they are, but most particularly we learn from the New Testament that Jesus unites Jew and Gentile.

It is possible that the Pauline idea of the unity of Jew and Gentile in Christ is, in part, a paradigm of the wholeness which Jesus brings to a man. For St Paul the primary division of the world is that between 'Jew' and 'Gentile', and this division is primarily based upon circumcision and acceptance of the Law, but there is some reason to think that it is 'over-determined' in St Paul's mind, and that he also thinks of it as a division between those who follow after a moral code and those who give way to their evil inclinations. We may notice, for example, that at the beginning of the Epistle to the Romans both Gentile and Jew are first introduced as unnamed 'types', since St Paul refers to the Gentiles as those who 'hold down the truth in unrighteousness', and introduces the Jew as 'O man, whosoever thou art that judgest'. This would mean that the union of Jew and Gentile in Christ may be taken not only as a union of two well-marked groups, but also as the union of 'good' and 'evil' men, and it may be suggested that beyond this there lies yet another level of interpretation. St Paul was

---

[1] e.g. *Religion*, 149; *Alchemy*, 440.

well aware that these two 'directions' (the 'law of the flesh', and the 'law of the mind') existed in himself, and so in every man, so that it is possible to understand the division of 'Jew' and 'Gentile' with reference to the division of every individual. That this idea is expressed in the Epistles is a tentative suggestion which gets some support from the well-known passage in Ephesians, where the three levels of interpretation are all applicable: 'wherefore remember, that aforetime ye, the Gentiles in the flesh, who are called Uncircumcision by that which is called Circumcision, in the flesh, made by hands; that ye were at that time separate from Christ, alienated from the commonwealth of Israel, and strangers from the covenants of the promise, having no hope and without God in the world. But now in Christ Jesus ye that once were far off are made nigh in the blood of Christ. For he is our peace, who made both one, and brake down the middle wall of partition, having abolished in his flesh the enmity, even the law of commandments in ordinances; that he might create in himself of the twain one new man, so making peace.' The Church as the 'body' is common enough, but only in one other place (Gal. 3 : 28) is there reference to 'one man'—and there also the unity of Jew and Gentile is in question.

3. *'Pictorial'*. Jung says, 'Yet it cannot be denied that the great symbol of the Christian faith, the Cross, upon which hangs the suffering figure of the Redeemer, has been emphatically held up before the eyes of Christians for nearly two thousand years. This picture is completed by the two thieves, one of whom goes down to hell, the other into paradise. One could hardly imagine a better representation of the "oppositeness" of the central Christian symbol', writes Jung (*Job*, 659). I have already remarked that it is sometimes difficult to tell what is his attitude to Christ as a 'union of opposites'; at first sight this seems to affirm that He is, but on the whole, in view of the context, it seems that it should be taken as an assertion of a conflict, rather than of a union of opposites. Within the frame of the picture, as it were, both interpretations are possible, for on the one hand one may emphasize the fact that the two thieves are brought together, one on each side of Our Lord, and read this compresence in one 'picture' as a reference to unity; or on the other hand, one may point out that the thieves are 'vector qualities' even within the framework of the picture (that is, that they are already 'pointed' in the direction in which they will move), so that the picture represents a division of the opposites:

and it is probably in this sense that Jung means us to take it. If this is so, he has again omitted the descent of our Lord to Hell, for if the thieves are about to 'split apart' Our Lord is also about to make a journey to the two places to which they have gone, so reminding us that He is not a symbol of division, but brings unity to the opposites.

This is not the only pictorial representation of Jesus as a union of opposites. Professor Jung takes the Christ of the Apocalypse as equally one-sided with the Jesus of the Gospels (as he interprets Him), but as a figure of the 'other side'. Yet the two-edged sword in the mouth of the opening figure is hardly to be disposed of with the casual comment that it seems 'more suitable for fighting and the shedding of blood than for the demonstration of brotherly love' (*Job*, 699) : it is quite as much a symbol of opposites united in one image as it is of war.

I add a further image. Whether it has any universal significance I do not know but in attempting to relate Professor Jung's findings to Christianity it has struck me with some force, and for that reason it seems worth putting it before others. It may well be that to many it will seem no more than nonsense, and a hopeless straining of the facts. The mandala which represents a union of opposites is usually drawn, but it may also be danced, and sometimes takes the form of a sacred enclosure or garden; it often involves an arrangement of four figures round a central representation in the deity; in the series of dreams referred to in the last chapter one stage of the development of a mandala is represented by four figures arranged so that three of them represent the more differentiated 'superior' conscious functions, and the fourth represents one, less differentiated, 'inferior' function, which is 'contaminated' by the unconscious, and has an 'evil' character. It may be suggested that the account of the betrayal of Jesus presents us with such a stage in the development of a mandala.

The betrayal takes place in a 'garden'; we do not read of this garden before, but St John tells us that it is a garden to which Jesus often went, and Matthew follows Mark in calling it a χορίον, whereas Luke alters this to the more natural word for a 'place', τόπος: the Revisers felt the need of pointing out that χορίον would be more exactly rendered by 'an enclosed space'. Here is the perfect setting for a mandala, a garden, in a sense 'sacred' to the deity, which is an enclosed space. Jesus enters the garden, accompanied by three faithful disciples, who show themselves to be not up to what is expected of them, and from the 'other side' the fourth figure of the evil disciple approaches, and he is accompanied by a very shadowy crowd of 'soldiers and servants'—and an undistinguished crowd of this sort is a typical dream symbol of the unconscious. The movement which takes place is a movement of the centre, over towards the evil figure, and it is clearly Jesus' wish that the faithful disciples should accompany Him. Jesus receives the kiss of the traitor (Mark and Matthew), and is submerged unresisting in the crowd; the others take up an aggressive attitude, but opposition is hopeless and deplored by Jesus, and they flee away. The appearance of an abortive mandala seems very marked and reading it in this way it represents Jesus' will to unite the 'opposites', frustrated by the failure of His closest friends. What would have happened if they had stood firm beside Him, as He passed over to the 'other side', we cannot guess.

4. *Moral.* The points of view from which Jesus has been shown to appear as a union of opposites are relatively trivial, and it can only be claimed that He is a 'union of opposites' in Jung's sense of the phrase if it can be shown that He unites the moral opposites, 'good' and 'evil'. At first sight the attempt to show that Jesus unites good and evil must appear doomed to failure, if not actually blasphemous, but this is due to systematic difficulties in the way of understanding what it means to unite moral good and evil, and these difficulties arise from the perverse human assumption that Christianity is 'morality plus'. Something of what needs to be said has already been said in Chapter 5, but it is as well that it should be said again. Human morality depends upon the judgements which men make about what is 'good' and what is 'evil', and it is assumed that if men judge correctly what they judge to be good always shows what is best for them to do or to seek. This assumption is perfectly right so far as it goes, but it is restricted by the fact that morality is concerned with what men do and with what men are able to do, so that if there is (as Christians believe there is) a 'good' for men which a man himself cannot possibly do or attain then moral judgements cannot take this into account. This may be illustrated by a man on a desert island, who might say to himself, 'it would be good to make a raft with a sail and set out on it, it would be bad to try to swim to the mainland—it would be best of all if I had an aeroplane": the best, being unavailable, cannot enter into his estimate of what is best, so that he must decide 'it is best for me to build the raft'. So moral judgements (if they are correct) show men what is best for them to do within the limits of what it is possible for sinful

men to do, and they do not take into account the Spirit of God, which 'bloweth where it listeth' and brings about that which is 'best', without any limitation, so that he who has the Spirit is free from Law.

There is a 'good' which is higher than moral good, because moral good is relative to man, and sinful men cannot do what is best, so that all purely human choice of action is a choice between acts which are less than the best. This higher good is not an extension or intensification of moral good, but a good in a different way, and because it lies beyond the capacity of a man it cannot even be visualized by man, for only in the Spirit does a man do what is good in this sense, and only in doing so does he recognize it for what it is. It is in this sense of 'good' that Jesus is 'good' and because this is a sense of good which is altogether different from the moral sense of the word it is not impossible for such goodness to unite moral good with moral evil.

What has been said may be put in a different way. Man judges good and evil from his own point of view, and man's point of view is the point of view of one who is in bondage to sin. Because he is in bondage to sin and divided in himself man sees his own inward division reflected in the external world, and his moral judgements depend upon the way in which he has already differentiated his environment into separate things, states and events. If, however, a man were 'whole' he could see the external environment as a whole and so understand how each part was related to the rest, and if he could understand this he would no longer judge each thing in isolation from the whole, and his judgements of good and evil would be seriously affected. To suggest that Jesus unites the moral opposites is to suggest that in Him all the elements of human nature are brought together into one man in such a way that what in us is evil finds, in Him, its proper place and meaning. In other words, to show that Jesus unites the moral opposites it does not have to be shown that His character is made up of opposing elements but that elements which are opposed in men are united in Jesus, and it is obvious that by being brought into unity with their opposites such elements will be in some way transformed, so that we cannot expect to distinguish them in the same way as they can be distinguished when they oppose one another in a man. What will be shown is that in relation to Jesus human judgements of good and evil become hopelessly confused, and that, in particular, much that men call good is condemned by Jesus, and much that they call evil is found in Him.

Jesus condemned the Pharisees of His time, and Christians are liable to accept His condemnation of them without giving due consideration to what they were really like. It is natural that we should form a picture of the Pharisees as manifest hypocrites, who would be judged and condemned as such by the best men, and that we should suppose that Jesus only expressed what all good men thought; but to think in this way is to go against what little we know about the Pharisees from non-Christian sources, and, more important, to misread the Gospels. The study of Rabbinic sources from a period not long after the time of Jesus suggests (it cannot prove) that the Jewish teachers of His time were among the best men (as men judge "best") of any age, and that their teaching was very much more like that of Jesus than we should think from the Gospels, and this alone should make us reconsider the meaning of Jesus' condemnations, even if there were not supporting evidence in the Gospels themselves. It cannot be that the Pharisees were manifestly bad men, because if so Jesus could never have said 'except your righteousness exceed the righteousness of the Scribes and Pharisees . . .' because this demand only has point if it can be taken in the sense 'this is good, but even more is required', and the parable of the Publican and the Pharisee is conclusive. Jesus puts before us a Pharisee at prayer and asks us to condemn him, and we condemn him for self-righteousness and pride, yet as Jesus describes the men's prayer there is nothing in it which justifies us. The Pharisee was almost certainly better than many other men, and in admitting this he was simply accepting the truth, and, having stated this truth he goes on to give thanks and glory to God for the gift of righteousness that God has given him. We should hardly be surprised if a Christian preacher were to exhort us to count our blessings, remembering particularly the gifts of grace which God has given us whereby we are able to overcome temptations, and to thank God for them, and yet, in telling us to do this the preacher would be telling us to behave exactly like the Pharisee in Jesus' parable. In general Jesus' condemnation of the Pharisee was a condemnation of what men judge to be good, and shows that for Him 'good' is somehow different from what we, morally, judge as good.

From the other side we may consider the reaction of men and women to Jesus. We begin by believing that Jesus was 'good' and 'perfect', and so we naturally suppose that only those who were perversely blind could fail to see His goodness, but those among whom He lived saw Him as just a man, and we have to consider how He must have appeared to them. When we consider the condemnation of Jesus from this point of view it can be seen, even from the biased accounts of the Gospels, that there were many among His enemies who honestly judged that He was a bad thing: put at its lowest, it was clearly not the case that all who met Jesus judged that He was one who was 'good above all other'. We have no reason to reject the evidence that those who were responsible for the crucifixion believed that they were doing what was best for the nation with whose welfare they were charged, just as Saul once believed that Christianity was an evil threat to the true worship of God. Confronted with God in Jesus there were those who, judging as men, judged Him an evil thing, and this means that what seems to men to be evil may have its place in Jesus.

Less strong, but to the same effect, Peter's rejection of Jesus' plan to die at Jerusalem had much to recommend it from a human point of view and it would seem to anyone that a prophet could do more good by a continuing ministry ('that I should live is better for you', wrote St Paul to his converts) than by putting his head into the noose, and Jesus condemned Peter's arguments as 'savouring of the things of men'. Jesus deliberately courted rejection and crucifixion, and it is only because He did, and because His act was sealed by the Resurrection that we know that this was good—for such behaviour, in itself, we should naturally regard as foolish, or even wicked. Further, it is not possible to dissociate Jesus from the 'evil man' among His disciples, because Jesus chose Judas and kept Him among the inner circle of His followers, knowing, we must believe, 'what was in him'. What is more, however obscure to the other Apostles, the words with which Jesus sent Judas into the night had a clear meaning between the two of them, and as they stand they constitute a mandate to Judas to carry out the work on which he had resolved. No satisfying account of the relations between Jesus and Judas has ever been given, but it may be remembered that Jesus was 'the friend of sinners', so that it is perhaps not strange that so great a sinner should be included in His fellowship.

The mystery of Judas may suggest a slightly different approach to the Apostles as a whole. The treason of Judas and the weakness of Peter are usually regarded as exceptions, but it may be that these things are the clue to the nature of the chosen band. The Apostles may, perhaps, be taken to represent aspects of human life which Jesus unites into one whole, and if this is so it is certain that what they represent is not exclusively what we call 'good'. We know of figures in myth and legend whose companions represent their virtues, strength, courage, long sight, wisdom and the like, but if we are asked what attributes we naturally connect with the companions of Jesus we must reply, 'treason, avarice, weakness, anger, ambition, fear, envy and doubt'. Of Judas we know that he was a double-dealer who stole the common funds; of Peter that he was ambitious for His master, and a broken reed in a crisis; of James and John that they would have had Jesus call down fire from heaven when they were angry at a slight, and that they sought for themselves the highest places in His Kingdom; Thomas will be known as 'doubting' for ever: the disciples as a whole were envious of James and John, and after Jesus' arrest 'they all forsook Him and fled'. Such were the men from whom Jesus formed, 'by His death and passion . . . and by the sending of the Holy Ghost', the New Israel, the Church of God.

St Paul presents the unity of 'good' and 'evil' in Jesus in a figure. Jesus was 'born under the law', which is to say that He belonged to the group of men marked off as 'Jews'; on the other hand He became a 'curse' under the Law which is itself 'Holy and righteous and true', and He was thus thrown out of that group, and in this way the idea of the union of moral opposites is perfectly expressed. Again, the temptations teach that Jesus had within Him the seeds of sin, because temptation is impossible unless the outer voice can find an echo in the inner depths, and the story of the temptations is nonsense if Jesus did not have within Him the instincts and tendencies which could (if released from the harmony of His nature) have led Him into evil. So St Paul says that He came in 'the likeness of sinful flesh', that is, possessed of all those human elements which, in us, express themselves in evil ways; St John assures us that 'He knew what was in man', and such knowledge of others can only be had by those who can in some way experience in themselves what is in those whom they know. In the light of the remarks at the beginning of this section there is enough to give us reason to regard Jesus as a union of the moral opposites of 'good' and 'evil'.

The attempt has been made to show that in relation to Jesus human moral judgements are turned upside down, and that this is because Jesus unites all human characteristics in His own person, so that the common divisions which we make between good and evil are not applicable to Him. When we say Jesus is 'good' we should not mean that He possesses only those attributes which we call 'good' in man, but rather that all that is found in man is found in Jesus and that in Jesus human characteristics do not oppose each other, as they do in men, but reinforce one another. This may be called a 'higher' sense of good, or it may be said to be 'beyond good and evil', but however it is expressed it refers to a human nature in which there is no opposition between good will and evil inclinations, and which is whole because the opposites are united, and this is what we should mean when we say that Jesus was born free from original sin. Our problem is to bring the opposites into unity, but Jesus began His life whole, and His temptation was to allow the opposites to 'escape' from the unity of His nature, by following some human aim instead of submitting in all things to His Father's will.

5. *Love and Wrath.* Jung attempts to give us a picture of the Jesus of the Gospels as one who is wholly characterized by love and benevolence, and then to oppose to this picture the wrath of the 'lamb' revealed in the Apocalypse. It cannot be denied that there is a change of emphasis, but it is very questionable whether there is anything more, for the figure of wrath in the Apocalypse is largely built up of hints scattered everywhere in the Gospels: the outpourings of the plagues are only a different figure of the horrors of the last days which Jesus recounted to His disciples outside Jerusalem; the angels of judgement and the harvest at the end of the world are foreshadowed in the parable of the tares; the judgement of the world is referred to again and again in the Gospels; and the lake of fire and the final divorce from God is presented by the 'fire where their worm dieth not', 'outer darkness', and the condemnation 'depart from me, ye cursed'; the two-edged sword, which distresses Jung, is itself only a version of 'I come not to bring peace, but a sword'. It is only by the most drastic mutilation of the Gospels that it is possible to offer a contrast between the 'two Jesus' such as that which Jung suggests, and once the contrast between Gospels and Apocalypse is seen to be an illusion, all that Professor Jung says about the two figures may be turned to show that Christ is a union of opposites. If we are dealing with two aspects of the one figure, then that figure is one in which love and wrath are strangely combined, so that love is something more than what we call love (be it *eros* or *agape*), and wrath is something different from our wrath.

From every point of view Jesus is a union of opposites, and what has been said may be summarized in Charles Williams' words: 'There had appeared in Palestine, during the government of the Princeps Augustus and his successor Tiberius, a certain being. This being was in the form of a man, a peripatetic teacher, a thaumaturgical orator. There were plenty of the sort about . . . but this particular one had a higher potential of power, and a much more distracting method.[1] It had a very effective verbal style, notably in imprecation, together with a recurrent ambiguity of statement. It continually scored debating-points over its interlocutors. It agreed with everything on the one hand, and denounced everything on the other. For example, it said nothing against the Roman occupation; it urged obedience to the Jewish hierarchy; it proclaimed holiness to the Lord. But it was present at doubtfully holy feasts; it associated with rich men and loose women; it commented acerbly on the habits of the hierarchy; and while encouraging everyone to pay their debts, it radiated a general disapproval, or at least doubt, of every kind of property. It talked of love in terms of hell, and of hell in terms of perfection. And finally it talked at the top of its piercing voice about itself and its own unequalled importance. It said that it was the best and worst thing that had ever happened or ever could happen to man. It said it could control anything and yet had to submit to everything. It said its Father in Heaven would do anything it wished, but that for itself it would do nothing but what its Father in Heaven wished' (*Descent*, 1-2).

The claim which has been made is that Jesus of Nazareth Himself was, in His own person, a manifest 'union of opposites': that those who knew Him on earth were more or less consciously aware of this, or that, at any rate, they introduced into their records of His life, and into their comments upon Him, enough material to make this clear to us: and that 'Christ', in whom the Christian is exhorted to put his trust, having a character determined (for our knowledge) by the nature of Jesus, is inevitably also such a 'union'. That is, that our idea of the nature of Christ as a union of opposites is not simply the result of a projection of an 'archetype', but depends upon the Gospel account of Jesus.[2] Yet this is not to say that we may not apprehend the Gospels

---

[1] C.f. 'One thing, anyway, cannot be doubted: Christ is a highly numinous figure' (*Job*, 93).

[2] The account itself may, of course, have been influenced by projections made by the writers upon the central figure.

and understand them by means of the mechanism of projection, and it does mean that, if we do understand them in this way, then the 'archetype' projected is the 'Self', or the 'archetype of deity' and not the *magician* or any lesser figure in the hierarchy of the unconscious.

It has also been claimed that the way of salvation, set forth by the Christian Church, called 'Justification by Faith', and determined at all points by a man's relationship to Christ, can be seen to involve a highly sophisticated and complex process, marked by the repeated differentiation and union of 'opposites', although this is not to say that no one can follow this way without being conscious of the 'opposites' as such, and of their union: rather, the Christian process 'wraps up' the whole question of the 'opposites' in terms closely related to the terms of human morality. This has two results: on the one hand, it opens a wide door to misunderstanding, both by Christians and by opponents or critics of Christianity, and on the other, it brings the Christian way within the reach of the great majority of men and women who would be utterly excluded by the demand that they should understand the somewhat esoteric concepts involved in such a system as Jung's.

12

CONCLUSIONS

IF this study has any value, that value does not lie in the conclusions to be drawn from it so much as in the comparisons which have been made. What is important is that we should learn how to compare psychology and religion, and how to use one to aid the other, and the conclusions to which one individual is led have only transient value. Nevertheless, it is well that one who has made some attempt, however inadequate, to compare a psychotherapeutic system with the Christian way of salvation should also set down what he has himself concluded from that attempt. If, in this chapter, such conclusions are set down dogmatically it is not to be thought that they are offered as final: work on the relation between modern psychotherapy and religion has only recently begun, and nothing can yet be certain.

The conclusions to which we have come in the course of this study may be stated under three heads. First, the clear and direct parallels between Justification by Faith and Individuation: second, those features which appear to be very different, but which prove to have much in common when more closely examined: third, the contrasts between the two ways. Of the parallels, whether clear or hidden, little more will be said, but some further discussion of the contrasts is needed.

1. *Clear Parallels*

The two systems which we have been considering are clearly alike in four important respects: (i) They are both means whereby a man is brought from a state considered to be unsatisfactory to one which is thought to be desirable, and (ii) both the state from which a man is led and the goal to which he is led are alike in the two systems; (iii) the goal of the Christian way and that of the psychotherapeutic way are both said to 'happen' to a man, and in regard to both it is said that a man cannot achieve the goal by his own conscious effort alone;

(iv) in both systems there is a continual emphasis on the unity of human nature.

The original state of 'natural man' of which Jung and St Paul both speak may be described, in 'neutral' language (that is, ordinary language which does not involve specifically religious or psychological terms), in the following way. A man is aware of 'himself' as having a specific character, which is expressed in his ideas, ideals and purposes, and he thinks of his behaviour as being in a special way 'his' when it is in accord with his ideals and purposes. At the same time a man is aware that he frequently fails to carry out his plans and purposes as he intends, and that he often does things which are 'out of character'; in other words, although we realize that we are one man, we find that the man who is ourself is divided in himself and divided against himself. All a man's efforts to overcome the tendency to fail in his ideals, plans and purposes, are ineffective and he is unable, left to himself, to express in his behaviour the unity of his nature. When this state is described in religious or psychological terms the accounts given not only sound different, but also are different, because the religious or psychological account is more than a bare description: either the one or the other involves a diagnosis which points to a means of cure.

The religious account of the state of natural man is that he is in 'bondage to sin'. The failure to do according to one's ideals and aims is explained as a result of the power of sinful tendencies within one, but further examination of the idea of 'bondage to sin' led to the conclusion that it means more than this. When we say that natural man is 'in bondage to sin' we mean that his whole character is infected by sin, and that the source of his failure to do what he wills lies as much in his failure to will to do what is truly right in the sight of God as it does in the presence of tendencies within him opposing his will. In this way the religious 'diagnosis' points to a unity of the (sinful) nature of man, and, at the same time, hints at the possibility of a cure if a man will cease to put his confidence in his good will and in his own purposes. Jung describes the state of natural man as an antagonism between consciousness and the unconscious, and, although this is said to be partly due to the presence of undesirable complexes in the unconscious, the fundamental source of this antagonism lies in the rejection of the unconscious by consciousness. In suggesting that this is an error Jung points to the unity of the nature of man, and hints at the possibility of a cure if a man will cease to think of the unconscious as evil. The apparent differences in the cures to which the two diagnoses point belong to the group of 'hidden parallels'.

The goal to which each system leads may also be described in 'neutral' language, in such a way that the same account may be applied to each. Natural man is to be led to a state in which he is able to respond consistently with his whole being to the situations in which he finds himself, without any sense of being divided against himself or of being at odds with his environment. This response of the whole man is, at the same time, felt as being the response of something which transcends the man, so that although he can describe the act in no other way than as 'my act' he seems to be the instrument by which the act is performed, rather than the agent who performs it. The religious account of the new state to which a man is brought is that he is indwelt by Christ and that he lives by the power of Christ, according to the will of Christ and not according to his own will. The psychological account of the new state is that his ego is subordinated to the Self and ceases to be the origin of his acts and decisions, although the activity of the ego makes a contribution to the activity of the whole man. The difference implicit in the description of the 'new centre' as Christ, on the one hand, and 'the Self', on the other, is further discussed under the third head—'differences' between the two systems.

The feature common to Christianity and Analytical Psychology, that the new state is brought about by the activity of something beyond the conscious thinking and willing of the individual concerned, and that no amount of set purpose can bring a man to the goal unless such activity takes place, has been discussed more than once in preceding chapters. It need only be remarked here that, once again, the something beyond individual consciousness is described as 'God' by St Paul, and 'The Self' by Jung. Both systems consistently hold before us the idea of the unity of man. The goal which each sets before us is one in which a man behaves as a real and effective unity, and each appeals to natural man to recognize the unity of his nature from the beginning. Jung exhorts natural man to realize that the unconscious is not, as he imagines, evil, St Paul exhorts natural man to realize that his good will is not, as he imagines, good.

2. Hidden Parallels

There are two main 'hidden parallels' between the systems, both connected with what may be called the 'treatment'. The first lies behind the apparent conflict between the view that man is wholly sinful, on the one hand, and the view that he is wholly good on the other; the second behind the fact that in Jung's 'treatment' a long process of development lies between the state of natural man and the goal, whereas in Christianity the goal is reached before any real development begins.

The Christian diagnosis of the state of natural man implies that natural man's own simple account of himself as a dichotomy of good will and evil inclinations is mistaken, and that it is mistaken because natural man wrongly calls his 'good will' good. Jung's diagnosis implies that he is mistaken because he wrongly calls the unconscious evil. It would seem, at first sight, as though these two diagnoses could not be reconciled, but when we consider the implications of each it can be seen that they come to what is effectively the same thing. By saying that the unconscious is not evil Jung means that it can play its part in the life of the man, and that if it is allowed to do so it will be a source of strength and goodness, and this determines the nature of the 'treatment' which he prescribes: Jung's treatment is designed to bring a man to see how the unconscious can be allowed its proper place, but we have seen that in order to do this a man must allow his consciousness to be modified, and stop putting his whole trust in it. In other words, although the *statement* of Jung's diagnosis involves this assertion that the unconscious is good the practical implications are that both the unconscious and consciousness require to be changed, and this implies, in turn, that neither consciousness nor the unconscious are what they should be in natural man. On the other hand, by saying that the good will is sinful, the Christian means that if a man puts his trust in his good will he will not come to salvation, and we have seen that penitence, by bringing the good will down to the level of the evil inclinations, enables a man to come to God as he is, and put his whole self, evil inclinations as well as good will, into the hands of God. The implication of this is that although neither good will nor the evil inclinations are able to bring a man to salvation both the evil inclinations and the good will are material which God can and will use; in other words, that properly employed (by God) the evil inclinations can be so modified that they have a part to play in the life of the redeemed. This means that the parallel between Christianity and Analytical Psychology in this connection is exact: both say that neither part of natural man (good will and evil inclinations, or consciousness and the unconscious) is what it should be, but that both can take their place in the goal.

The parallel connected with the apparent contradiction that in Christianity no development of character is necessary before God justifies a man, whereas in Analytical Psychology a long process of development preceded Individuation, is only partial and it can only be detected because theology uses the word 'penitence' ambiguously. Nevertheless, it remains true that the process of development involved in analysis does have a parallel in Christianity, even though the parallel is not straightforward. On the one hand, as that which a man must do before the Self can take over a man's life, accepting the unconscious is paralleled by penitence considered as the condition of Justification by Faith; on the other hand, considered as a process of development of character it is paralleled by penitence, as an enduring and developing aspect of the Christian life. These parallels have been discussed at some length in chapter 7 and further comment is not needed, but the difference (that is, the fact that development of character precedes Individuation but follows Justification by Faith) will be considered in the next section.

3. *Differences*

A marked difference between Individuation and Justification by Faith which has been noted from time to time in previous chapters is that Justification by Faith precedes all advance towards a full life whereas Individuation crowns an advance which has already taken place, and this is closely associated with the fact that the goal of the Christian life is known from the beginning, whereas the goal of Jung's psychotherapeutic system is not known until it is reached. The examination of this difference leads us to consider two further points about Jung's system which have not yet been discussed at any length, the strongly 'gnostic' element involved in it, and some curious remarks which Jung makes about the goal of Individuation. The consideration of these points leads to the conclusion that as a way of salvation for all men the Christian way is very much more satisfactory (always supposing that it is a way which can be travelled) than the psychotherapeutic, whatever value the later may have.

St John begins his Epistle: 'That which was from the beginning, which we have heard, which we have seen with our eyes, which we have looked upon, and our hands have handled, of the Word of life';

and from the very beginning of the Christian life a man's thought is directed to Jesus who lived on earth, and who was seen and known by men. This Jesus, known to His first disciples in the flesh and known to others in the word of Scripture, is the goal of Justification by Faith, and this means that the nature of the goal is known before it is reached. Jung, on the other hand, says of the goal of Individuation: 'In no case was it conjured into existence through purpose and conscious willing, but rather seemed to flow out of the stream of time' (*Secret*, 89); and of the mandala motif in a dream series: 'it only *appeared* more and more distinctly and in increasingly differentiated form' (*Alchemy*, 329). Jung does say that the Self is in some sense 'there' from the beginning, but it is not there in the sense of being known by a man before it becomes effective in his life, as Jesus may be known even before a man is Justified, and as He is known to the Justified before He becomes the effective controlling centre of the man's life. In other words, salvation as it is understood by the Christian has, it might be said, two parts: first the new centre is accépted, and then it is given more and more control over the individual; Individuation, on the other hand, means the acceptance of the new centre as the controlling principle, and the new centre is not known until it is in control, and it is in control as soon as it is known. This means that the assumption made in the introductory chapter that Individuation is paralleled by Justification by Faith must be modified, because although Individuation is like Justification by Faith in that it involves the coming of a new centre it is unlike it in that it also involves the effective control of a man by that centre, whereas Justification by Faith is only directed towards the eventual control of a man by Christ and has taken place before that control is complete. It is from this contrast that the other differences between the two systems arise.

The psychotherapeutic process is not only a movement towards the goal, it is at the same time a search, for neither analyst nor analysand knows the nature of the goal to which the latter is moving: 'The new thing,' Jung tells us, 'seldom or never corresponds to conscious expectation' (*Secret*, 90), and this means that the work proceeds in 'blind faith' that there is a goal and that the goal is worth while. Since the goal of analysis is unknown the man who journeys towards it cannot begin by putting his trust in it, and it is necessary that he should have confidence in something else. For this reason it is impossible to ask him to begin by setting aside those values in which he has been accustomed to trust, so that although in the course of the process he will come to see that his conscious values were not all that he supposed them to be, he must at first hold fast to them, at the same time as he begins to learn of the compensatory values of the unconscious. Thus it is essential that Jung's diagnosis of the state of natural man should emphasize the value of what is in man (consciousness as well as unconscious), because if it did not there would be nothing else in which a man could trust. On the other hand Christianity offers Christ from the beginning and can point to Christ as one in whom a man should trust, and for this reason it is not necessary that the man who travels on the Christian way should trust in anything else, for if a man accepts Christ he can be told from the start that he must not trust to his good will to lead him to salvation, and the Christian diagnosis can safely be negative, emphasizing the fact (implicit as we have seen in the Jungian diagnosis) that all that there is in man needs to be redeemed. All that the man has been asked to put aside as useless in his search for salvation will ultimately be used by Christ, but there is no need to emphasize this aspect, which is emphasized by Jung, because Christ can be trusted to do what is right with all that is in a man. As St John of the Cross insists, we need not worry as to the use to which God's gifts should be put because God who gives them will see that they are rightly used, if we will let Him.

Secondly, because the goal of Individuation is not known until it is reached, and because it appears to arise from the equal association of consciousness and the unconscious, there can be no question of the effective presence of the new centre before a man's character has developed. The effective existence of the goal depends upon the acceptance of the unconscious by consciousness, and such acceptance is impossible at the beginning of the psychotherapeutic way. It may well be, as Jung frequently hints, that behind all that takes place the Self is obscurely active, but if this is so it is something of which the man concerned knows nothing, and something which can hardly enter into his conscious appreciation of his situation. Theoretically, Jung remarks, the mandala motif (i.e. the expression of the Self) should be universal. 'In practice, however, it is only to be met with in distinct form in relatively few cases, though this does not prevent it from functioning as a concealed pole round which everything ultimately revolves' (Alchemy, 330). On the other hand, because the goal of the Christian way is already known at the beginning the man who travels on that way can take into account its existence and character, and may enter into relation with Christ before Christ is in full control of his life. Knowledge of Christ and the conscious purpose of putting one's trust in Him is possible from the very beginning, and from this point of view (which is the point of view of 'faith') Justification by Faith is marked by a man's discovery that Christ is trustworthy, and that Jesus, who lived and died many years ago, may be an effective power in his life today.

From this account of the differences between the two ways it can be seen why it is that, for the majority, the Christian way is far easier than the psychotherapeutic. First, natural man, before he begins on either way, is aware that there is something wrong with his life, and he must already realize that his own attempts to put right what is wrong are largely inadequate; in other words, natural man already judges that he is partly 'bad' and that what is 'good' in him is largely impotent; but whereas Christianity asks him to take these two judgements more seriously Jung, in effect, asks him to reverse them. The Christian diagnosis of his state implies 'you are right, there is something very wrong with you, and there is nothing that you yourself can do about it', and though this may be hard for a man to accept, it is at least more or less what he has already come to see. Jung's diagnosis, however, implies, 'You are wrong in thinking that you are impotent, and you are even more wrong in thinking that part of you is really bad: your troubles all come from your misjudgements about yourself', and although this may be more acceptable to human pride, it appears so contrary to the apparent facts that it requires considerable faith for natural man to believe it. Secondly, Jung holds out to man the hope that he will become his 'true self', but he can offer a man no account of what that 'true self' will be like and he asks men to go blindfold to the end of the way, in faith that the goal can be reached, and, more important, that it will be worth while when it is reached. If we may judge from the fact that many people turn to the last page of their detective story or novel long before they have read the intervening pages, it seems that for large numbers it is more satisfactory to know where they are going, and Christianity teaches them this from the beginning. The man who starts on the Christian way has been presented with the goal in the figure of Jesus, and he knows that his final state (if he travels the whole road) is to be 'made like unto Christ'. Thirdly, Jung repeatedly assures us that the full process of his analysis involves great effort and determination, and that although the analyst may guide and suggest the analysand, in the later stages at least, must himself choose the way, and make the critical choices which confront him: 'the patient', he says, 'must be alone if he is to find out what it is that supports him when he can no longer support himself' (*Alchemy*, 32). In other words, Jung's way requires a man to work and purpose and plan and decide for himself, and it is precisely man's trouble that he finds that his best-laid schemes go awry: the Christian way, on the other hand, requires a man to recognize that he cannot succeed by his own effort, and that he should cease to try to purpose and plan and decide correctly. Christianity holds before man the possibility that another, Christ, may purpose and plan and decide for him, so that his own inability to carry out his purposes need not interfere with his advance towards salvation. In all these ways it is clear that Jung demands more of men than Christianity does, and we should be justified in thinking that as a way of salvation for the 'common man' Christianity was more satisfactory than a Jungian analysis, even if Jung himself had not told us that many people cannot travel the road to which he points.

Jung has never accepted the description 'gnostic', which is one which is occasionally applied to him by others. Whether the epithet is correct in other respects may be uncertain, but he is certainly 'gnostic' in the sense that he does believe that his way is only for the select few who are called to travel on it. There cannot be two opinions about this, because he is explicit, and whether or not it justifies the use of the term 'gnostic' is relatively unimportant. One or two passages are quoted in illustration of this side of Jung's thought: Jung mentions that there are many who 'enjoy a surplus of unconsciousness' but who 'never get anywhere near a neurosis', and goes on, 'The few who are smitten by such a fate are really persons of the "higher" type who, for one reason or another, have remained too long on a primitive level'; 'Individuation', he says, 'is indispensable for certain people, not only as a therapeutic necessity, but as a high ideal, an idea of the best we can do' (*Essays*, 291, 373); in one place he tells us that he is 'speaking of the border-line cases, and not of the less valuable, normal, average folk for whom the question of adaptation is more technical than problematical' (ibid., 236); 'Such a change [from a state of unconscious possession]', he writes, 'can begin only with individuals, for the masses are blind brutes, as we know to our cost. It seems to me of some importance, therefore, that a few individuals, or people individually, should begin to understand that there are contents which do not belong to the ego personality. . . . Very few people care to know anything about this' (*Alchemy*, 563); 'Fortunately, in her kindness and patience, Nature never puts the fatal question as to the meaning of their lives into the mouths of most people. And where no one asks, no one need answer' (*Development*, 314). It is true that like Christianity Jung offers a universal panacea (*Alchemy*, 563), but unlike Christianity he does not expect many men to receive it, and he tells us that the development towards Individuation only occurs when it springs from 'inner necessity' (*Essays*, 369), and to this extent Jung looks to the salvation of a few 'higher' types, rather than to that of every man.

One final question remains. It may be asked, 'granted that the Christian way is offered as a way which any and all men can and should travel, and that it does not require the moral and intellectual equipment which is needed to travel to the end of Jung's way, is it not also true that the man who is Individuated has gone very much further than the man who is Justified? in other words, is it not the case that Individuation corresponds rather to that salvation to which Justification points than to Justification by Faith itself?' On what has been said so far the answer to this question must be 'yes', but there is something to be added about Individuation which leaves the answer to the question in considerable doubt. Although Jung speaks of Individuation as the true goal of life and as that which all men should desire, and although this way of speaking of it has been followed in the preceding chapters, he raises questions in *The Psychology of the Transference* (1946) which must modify this view.

In the introduction to *The Psychology of the Transference* Jung hints at a doubt whether the man who sets out on his way will come at last to the true goal: 'The goal,' he says, 'is only important as an idea; the essential thing is the *opus* which leads to the goal: *that* is the goal of a lifetime' (*Practice*, 400), and he returns to this at the end of the treatise. The goal of Individuation is a unity of opposites, and from much that Jung says we might be led to believe that this means a harmonious functioning of the whole, but having put before us images of the goal he proceeds to criticize them in such a way as to suggest that the goal to which they point is not entirely satisfactory. He remarks, for example, 'In John Gower's *Confessio amantis* there is a saying which I have used as a motto to the Introduction of this book: "Bellica pax, vulnus dulce, suave malum" (a warring peace, a sweet wound, an agreeable evil). Into these words the old alchemist put the quintessence of his experience. I can add nothing to their incomparable simplicity and conciseness' (ibid., 523), and he expands his theme in relation to the hermaphrodite symbol of the goal. Jung describes the alchemists' symbol as 'the misshapen hermaphrodite' marked by 'crude embryonic features', and partly explains these features by reference to the 'dark origins' of alchemy, and the 'immaturity of the alchemist's mind' (ibid., 533): he remarks that the problem was left at this stage from the time of the alchemists until Freud 'dug up this problem again', and that then the archetypes behind the alchemical symbol blossomed forth 'into the theory of infantile sexuality, perversions, and incest, while the *coniunctio* was rediscovered in the transference neurosis' (ibid., loc. cit.). Jung admittedly says that we have to see that 'the alluring sexual aspect is but one among many—the very one that deludes our judgement' (ibid., 534), but it seems that even if we can do this it remains true that the images of the goal retain some element which eludes us, for '[The] images are naturally only anticipations of a wholeness which is, in principle, always just beyond our reach' (ibid., 536), and 'we can see how the *opus* ends with the idea of a highly paradoxical being that defies rational analysis. The work could hardly end in any other way, since the *complexio oppositorum* cannot possibly lead to anything but a baffling paradox' (ibid., 532).

The fact is that Jung's system, from the beginning, involves a repeated process of synthesis, disintegration, expansion and re-synthesis (cf. chapter 4, above), and this process is carried forward to Individuation itself. Individuation is the name of the ultimate goal, but as when one climbs a mountain one sees false summits, so at any moment the goal that one can see is not the final goal but a ridge or lesser peak. The goal to which one moves is called 'Individuation' because, until one reaches it, it is the furthest one can see, but when it is reached a new goal, also to be called 'Individuation', lies ahead. This must be so, because the unconscious is, according to Jung, illimitable, and even when it is 'accepted' and a man acts, for a moment, as a 'Self' it still presses forward into consciousness. The 'Self' is a synthesis of consciousness and the unconscious, but the synthesis cannot be final because once more 'detached opposites' tend to flow over from the unconscious into consciousness, and the old synthesis must be destroyed and reformed to accommodate them. In other words, Individuation is no more a goal in which a man can rest than Justification by Faith: the man who reaches Individuation must begin once more to modify his consciousness and again accept the unconscious; the man who is Justified must seek to allow Christ more and more control over his life. Neither the one nor the other offers us the finality which we seek, and it is not true, after all, that Jung's way leads to a goal to which Justification by Faith does no more than point. Rather, both point to a continuing striving to reach a goal: just as the goal which a man may reach under the direction of Analytical Psychology always points forward, so Christian theology teaches that the fullness of the Beatific Vision is not given to any man in this world, however close to it he may come, and from this point of view there is little to choose between the two ways.

An attempt has been made to compare Christianity and Analytical Psychology without too much prejudice or bias. Naturally, however, it is impossible to set out upon such a task without a point of view, and no secret has been made of the fact that any bias that exists is on the side of Christianity. It remains to state in a few words what the Christian, speaking as a Christian, may say about the two ways which have been discussed.

First, it must be very clear that Analytical Psychology is not Christianity. It may be that it can be shown that 'Be penitent' and 'Accept the unconscious' are precepts which turn out to be practically equivalent, but they are still quite different precepts, and although their equivalence may teach the Christian pastor much about what he is doing when he preaches 'penitence' he cannot treat them as alternatives. Christianity requires a man to put aside all that is his, and to put his trust wholly in Christ, and no other demand is Christian—nor, as we have seen, is any other demand strictly universal. Unto us who are Christians the way of Christ has been committed, and we believe that this alone is the way which can bring any and every man to God and to salvation, and whatever we may learn from Jung we cannot learn a new way.

But, secondly, what are we to say about Jung's way? Where, in Christian terms, does it lead? The answers to these questions are not difficult. The Christian may not offer Jung's way as an alternative to that of the Church, but, at the same time, he cannot deny the possibility that God might use psycho-analysts and pyscho-analytical techniques to bring a man to Himself. We dare not limit God, or ignore the possibility that God will use this or that unexpected means, and we dare not say that Jungian psychology cannot be used by God. The test is one that can only be applied in individual cases: when a man claims that he has come to be his full self, and that he has begun to live a 'whole' life, then the Christian can ask what is the quality of the life which he lives; and the criterion for the Christian is conformity to the life of Jesus.

God, who rules all things, is not limited by man's thought, and His activity is not changed by the names which men use to speak of it. If God acts in the lives of men, then the activity of God on men is known only in and through the thoughts and acts of the men in whose lives He acts, and the psychologist who studies the thoughts and acts of men cannot put on one side those which the theologian claims have their origin in the direct activity of God, but must try to bring all within a single system. Some psychologists have reduced all human thoughts and acts to the same level and whatever strange names Jung may use, and whatever doubtful claims he may make, the Christian should be grateful to him for one thing at least, that he insists that there are some acts and thoughts which can only be 'explained' by appealing to something (whatever it may be called) which passes the bounds of human thought, and so directing us (again) to the Epistle to the Romans: 'O the depths of the riches both of the wisdom and knowledge of God! how unsearchable are his judgements and his ways past finding out'—and what more fitting conclusion could there be to any theological enquiry.

BIBLIOGRAPHY

(Books cited in the Text)

(1) *Theological*

BICKNELL, E. J, *A Theological Introduction to the Thirty-nine Articles* (Longmans, 1919)

BULTMANN, R. C., *Theology of the New Testament*, Vol. I (trans. Kendrick Grobel: S.C.M., 1952)

DODD, C. H., *The Epistle of Paul to the Romans* (Hodder & Stoughton, 1932)

FARMER, H. H., *The World and God* (Nisbet, 1935)

HARTON, F. P., *The Elements of the Spiritual Life* (S.P.C.K., 1932)

HOOKE, S. H. (ed.), *The Labyrinth: Further studies in the relation between myth and ritual in the ancient world* (S.P.C.K., 1935)

JAMES, William, *The Varieties of Religious Experience* (Longmans, 1952)

KITTEL, Rudolph, *Bible Keywords from Kittel Series: Sin* (A. & C. Black, 1951)

KNOX, Ronald, *Enthusiasm* (Oxford, 1950)

LAMPE, G. W. H. (ed.), *The Doctrine of Justification by Faith* (Mowbrays, 1954)

LAW, William, *Selected Mystical Writings* (ed. Stephen Hobhouse: Daniel, 1938)

MACKINTOSH, H. R., *The Christian Experience of Forgiveness* (Nisbet, 1927)

MENZIES, Lucy (trans.), *The Revelations of Mechthild of Magdeburg* (Longmans, 1953)

NEWMAN, J. H., *Lectures on the Doctrine of Justification* (3rd edn., 1874)

NIEBUHR, Reinhold, *The Nature and Destiny of Man*, Vol. I (Scribner, 1945)

NYGREN, Anders, *Commentary on Romans* (trans. C. C. Rasmussen: S.C.M., 1952)

ST JOHN OF THE CROSS, *Ascent of Mount Carmel* (trans. E. Allison Peers: Burns Oates, 1943)

ST AUGUSTINE, *Confessions* (Everyman edition)

SANDAY, W. and HEADLAM, A C, *A Critical and Exegetical Commentary on the Epistle to the Romans* (1895)

SCOTT, Charles Anderson, *Christianity according to St Paul* (Cambridge, 1939)

TAYLOR, Vincent, *Forgiveness and Reconciliation* (Macmillan, 1946)
WATTS, Alan, *Myth and Ritual in Christianity* (Thames & Hudson, 1954)
WILLIAMS, Charles, *The Descent of the Dove* (Longmans, 1939)
WILLIAMS, Charles, *Witchcraft* (Faber, 1941)

(2) *Jung*
    1. From the Collected edition (Routledge & Kegan Paul):
        (a) *Two Essays on Analytical Psychology*
        (b) *The Practice of Psychotherapy*
        (c) *Psychology and Alchemy*
        (d) *The Development of Personality*
        (e) *Psychology and Religion   West and East*
    2. *Psychological Types* (trans. H. G. Baynes: Routledge & Kegan Paul, 1923)
    3. *The Psychology of the Unconscious* (trans. B. M. Hinckle: Routledge & Kegan Paul, 1944)
    4. *The Secret of the Golden Flower* (trans. C. F. Baynes: 1931)
    5. *The Interpretation of Nature and the Psyche* (trans. R. F. C. Hull: Routledge & Kegan Paul, 1955).

(3) *Psychological* (other than Jung)
ALLPORT, G. W., *The Individual and his Religion* (Constable, 1951)
BERG, Charles, *Deep Analysis* (Allen & Unwin, 1946)
HORNEY, Karen, *Our Inner Conflicts* (Kegan Paul, Trench, Trubner & Co., 1946)
SILBERER, Herbert, *Problems of Mysticism and its Symbolism* (New York, 1917)

(4) *General*
ARISTOTLE, *Nicomachean Ethics* (Bohn edition)
KANT, *Critique of Pure Reason* (Everyman edition)
LOTZE, R. H., *Outlines of the Philosophy of Religion* (Dickinsons, 1887)
PLATO, *Five Dialogues* (Everyman edition)
RYLE, Gilbert, *The Concept of Mind* (Hutchinson's University Library, 1949)

GENERAL INDEX

unconscious, the, 31, 37, 100, 116, 125f, 143–147, 184, 188, 201, 204, 206, 223, 236, 340. *See also* accepting the unconscious, antagonism, collective unconscious, personal unconscious
unconscious complexes, 189
unconscious elements, 37–40, analysis of the idea, 48–78; becoming conscious, 64f, 122; construction of, 50–52; detached from consciousness, 38f; like conscious elements, 37f, 49, 187; links in causal chain, 54f; not 'things', 48–50; value of concept, 27, 52f, 56; and *passim*, in chapters 4, 6, 8, 10

vanity, 161
visions, 226

Wesley, John, 237, 240
whole man, 229f
wholeness, 306
witchcraft, 235
works of the law, 86f, 173
works, way of, 86, 178f
world, this, and God, 10f, 297, 316f, 319f
wrath (of God), 176f, 182f, 292, 323, 334
wrong-doing, 153

INDEX OF QUOTATIONS

(for abbreviations see pp. xiii–xiv)

Milton Keynes UK
Ingram Content Group UK Ltd.
UKHW020628161123
432684UK00008B/377